James William Massie

America

The Origin of her Present Conflict; her Prospect for the Slave, and...

James William Massie

America
The Origin of her Present Conflict; her Prospect for the Slave, and...

ISBN/EAN: 9783744729055

Printed in Europe, USA, Canada, Australia, Japan

Cover: Foto ©ninafisch / pixelio.de

More available books at **www.hansebooks.com**

AMERICA:

THE ORIGIN OF HER PRESENT CONFLICT;

HER PROSPECT FOR THE SLAVE,

AND

HER CLAIM FOR ANTI-SLAVERY SYMPATHY;

ILLUSTRATED BY

INCIDENTS OF TRAVEL, DURING A TOUR IN THE SUMMER OF 1863,
THROUGHOUT THE UNITED STATES, FROM THE EASTERN
BOUNDARIES OF MAINE TO THE MISSISSIPPI.

BY

JAMES WILLIAM MASSIE, D.D., LL.D.,

LONDON,

One of the Deputation appointed to convey to Ministers in America the Address adopted at the
Ministerial Anti-slavery Conference, held in the Free Trade Hall, Manchester, 3rd June, 1863.

LONDON:
JOHN SNOW, 35, PATERNOSTER ROW.
MDCCCLXIV.

TO

THOMAS BAYLEY POTTER, ESQ.,

BUILE HILL, MANCHESTER.

———◆———

Sir,

My Mission to the United States of America was prompted and sustained by your liberal philanthropy; and, in this memorial of my service, I gratefully acknowledge your constancy in supporting the cause of the Union, and the emancipation of the enslaved and oppressed. To be able to identify your name and generous sympathy for the working-classes as of a follower in the footsteps of your much-honoured and venerated father, adds intensity to my gratification in adopting this mode of rendering a tribute of sincere personal esteem to yourself.

I am, Sir,

Your faithful and obliged,

JAMES WILLIAM MASSIE.

Lonsdale Square, London.
January 23, 1864.

CONTENTS.

⁎ Errors and oversights in the press I hope will be found only few ;
but one has occurred at page 86, which I will thank the reader to
correct. On the line ninth from the bottom, insert "not" before the
words "in a slave state." Connecticut was the State. The Church
assembling in the Tabernacle, Jersey City, N.J., adhered, by resolution, to the response from New York.

AMERICA:

THE ORIGIN OF HER PRESENT CONFLICT,

ETC., ETC.

———✦———

INTRODUCTORY EXPLANATION.

ORIGIN AND OBJECT OF THE MISSION.

A LETTER, expressing generous and enlightened sympathy with the descendants of Puritan and Nonconformist ancestors, was received and read at a meeting of the Committee of the Congregational Union of England and Wales, in the summer of 1862. The occasion of the letter was the proposed celebration of the Bicentenary of St. Bartholomew, 1662, when two thousand clergymen submitted to ejection from their livings and prospect of preferment in the Church of England, rather than constrain or wound their conscience by obedience to the dictates of royal or prelatic policy in things belonging to God. The letter was written by the Rev. J. P. Thompson, D.D., Minister of Broadway Tabernacle, New York, under the appointment of an assembly of Congregational ministers in the United States. The expediency and form of a reply were considered at a meeting of the Committee, and the care of preparing a draft for adoption, at a more public

B

assembly, was devolved on the writer of these pages. The condition of America, the past intercourse sustained between Congregationalists in England and the United States, and a desire to advance the cause of American bondmen, suggested the line of thought which it was too confidently anticipated the assembly would unanimously approve. The discussion then produced led to action in another form, which renders worthy of a record what had been proposed. It was affirmed "that the Congregational Union has ever regarded their brethren of the Congregational churches in America as their lineal and collateral kindred, representing the same fathers and teachers, of early Puritanic and Nonconformist lineage, who testified and suffered as witnesses to the sovereign and revealed will of their Lord and Redeemer, and the inviolate and sacred rights of conscience, and who, by their sacrifices, virtues, and labours, on both sides of the Atlantic, for the truth and sufficiency of God's word, have maintained and extended the life and purity of evangelical churches; and in remembrance of such prolonged ecclesiastical affinity, the assurances of cordial sympathy and congratulation, conveyed by the letter of the Rev. Dr. Thompson, were hailed with grateful satisfaction; and it was proposed to approve of the replies returned by the Committee, and remit to that body all *further correspondence* arising from this communication.

"The cordial assurance was avowed, that Congregational brethren in America have preserved their churches from the polluting and contaminating fellowship of the slavedealer and the slaveholder; in the belief that slavery is the summing and concentration of all social evils, and the stronghold in which the principle of tyrannical power reigns triumphant: with this assurance the assemblies of this Union had repeatedly addressed, in the freedom of Christian confidence, their American brethren in behalf of brethren in bondage, pleading that they should employ their influence in their own country for the entire abolition of slavery, in resistance to the aggressive policy of rulers and representatives, chosen and imposed by the influence of a slaveholding oligarchy, and the gains of commercial intercourse. It was hoped the assembly would adhere to their former importunities, and again emphatically renew them for the speedy and effectual liberation of all who are held in slavery throughout America.

" It was sought to pledge the assembly, without entering into the occasion or question of the war now raging, to express its unfeigned compassion for the people who suffer, and its sympathy with the Christian brethren who long for the immediate cessation of this fratricidal conflict; to commend in fervent prayer to God, as Ruler among the nations, the cause of the poor and oppressed, and entreat Him to bring to a speedy termination the unnatural hostilities by which the principle of popular government is covered with reproach, the work of righteousness and peace is resisted, and our common Christianity is dishonoured and impeded."

About the time when the Congregational Union held its autumnal meeting, the British organization of the Evangelical Alliance was convened under the presidency of the late Sir Culling Eardley, Bart. When this association was first inaugurated, the question of American slave-holding, as affecting membership, was warmly discussed; leading to the exclusion of all who held slaves. The committee of the Paris branch now interposed a plea against sympathy with any organization in the slave-holding States which should approve of slavery. The action taken in the Alliance in September, 1862, did not satisfy the French correspondents, and led to private remonstrances. Disappointment, in some quarters, induced a movement for the formation of a " Committee of Correspondence on American Affairs," consisting of earnest friends of emancipation among Christians of all evangelical denominations. Some information was thus diffused, and the sympathies of many were ascertained. Friends of America and of the slave were stimulated to action, who did not wish to confine their co-operation to religious designations; and hence arose " the Emancipation Society" of London, willing to work with "the Anti-Slavery Society," or any other kindred organization, and "the Union and Emancipation Society of Manchester." These societies proceeded in right earnest to raise funds, and with efficiency to pursue their benevolent object. They prepared and published lectures, tracts, and documents, fitted to impart knowledge. They convened meetings in large halls, in chapels, school and lecture rooms, in the metropolis and in the provinces; and invited some of the most distinguished and well qualified advocates of freedom to lend their assistance by writing and by lectures in all parts of the country. One of the members, holding relation to both societies, having occasion to visit Paris, and enjoying the friendship of highly honoured Protestant pastors in that city, availed himself of repeated intercourse with the enlightened and earnest friends of universal liberty in that metropolis, to suggest a reconsideration of the claims of the champions of emancipation in the United States. He was most cordially sustained by Frederick Monod, G. Monod, George Fisch, Grandpierre, Eug. Bersier, De Pressensc, Pulsford, and Rognon, all of them pastors and honoured Christians. Ultimately they issued a letter for the signature of ministerial brethren throughout France, which was signed by more than seven hundred and fifty Protestant pastors; and, through the hands of their correspondent, it was laid before the committees of the two "Emancipation" societies and published in several newspapers. The document deserves a place in the records of anti-slavery agitation. It was entitled—

"TO THE MINISTERS AND PASTORS OF ALL EVANGELICAL
DENOMINATIONS IN GREAT BRITAIN.

"Paris, February 12, 1863.

"Honoured and beloved Brethren in the Lord,—It is the glory of England to have given to the world the example of abolishing first the slave trade, and then slavery.

It is her glory to have continued for the last sixty years the work of suppressing universally the slave trade and slavery, at a cost, it is asserted, of fifty millions of pounds sterling. And it is, under God, chiefly to her religious men, to her Clarksons, her Wilberforces, her Buxtons, to her missionary societies, that England owes this glory. Will not the sons and successors of these great Christians complete their work, by urging their country to declare itself openly for the holy cause of the liberation of the slave in the terrible struggle which is at present convulsing the United States of America?

" No more revolting spectacle has ever been set before the civilized world than a confederacy, consisting mainly of Protestants, forming itself, and demanding independence in the nineteenth century of the Christian era, with a professed design of maintaining and propagating slavery; a confederacy which lays down, as the cornerstone of its constitution, the system of slavery as it exists at present in the Southern States—a system which may be defined briefly as the right to treat men like cattle, and to commit adultery and murder with impunity. Setting aside all political considerations, can any Christian heart fail to be stirred to indignation at hearing the chief of that confederacy answering a decree of emancipation by an implied threat of extermination?

" The triumph of such a cause would put back the progress of Christian civilization and of humanity a whole century. It would make angels weep in heaven, and demons rejoice in hell. It would enable the friends of the slave trade and of slavery in all lands to hold up their heads, ever ready as they are to reappear at the first signal, in Asia, in Africa, and even in the great cities of Europe. It would give a fatal blow to the work of evangelical missions. And what frightful responsibility would rest on the church which should remain a silent spectator of such a triumph!

" If there is a peaceable means of hastening the end of the war, and of rendering its issue such as is desired by all the friends of humanity, is it not that the sincere Christians of Europe should give to the cause of emancipation a powerful testimony which would leave to those who fight for the right of oppressing the slaves no hope of ever seeing those Christians give them the hand of fellowship.

"Ministers and pastors of all the Evangelical denominations of England, Scotland, and Ireland,—it is here we need your assistance. Take the lead, and let us call forth a great and peaceful manifestation of sympathy for the coloured race, so long oppressed and debased by Christian nations. Let us thus discourage the partisans of slavery. Let us strengthen and encourage those who wish to abolish it, at the same time disposing them to listen to our suggestions. It is in free England that such manifestations can be powerful. What may we not hope for if, throughout Great Britain, the voice of all the ministers of the crucified Saviour—and in France, our voice echoing theirs —pray and plead that soon there may no longer be in the United States a coloured man that is not free and equal with the whites!

"May God grant it, and may his blessing rest alike on Great Britain and the United States, in Christ, the true Liberator!

"Attested by Grandpierre, Pasteur ; G. Monod, Pasteur Suffrageant, Paris ; Louis Rognon, Pasteur ; Louis Pulsford ; Fred. Monod, Pasteur ; Eug. Bersier.

"Paris, March 13, 1863."

The Committee of the London Emancipation Society resolved that funds should be appropriated to secure a suitable response to the French appeal. A conference of ministers, being Members of the Society, was convened at their offices ; and it was by them resolved, that a reply should be sent forth for signature throughout the United Kingdom. The draft of the document was prepared by the chairman, the Hon. and Rev. Baptist W. Noel, M.A., and, with some modifications, unanimously adopted in the terms following :—

"Dear Brethren,—We, whose names are undersigned, share in your views, we rejoice in your zeal, and we are thankful for your exhortations. It is honourable to France and to French Protestantism, that you so heartily wish the destruction of the Slave system, which makes Four Millions of negroes wretched, debases their masters, has been a vast calamity to a great Protestant nation, and dishonours Christ, by whose professed servants it is upheld.

"Like yourselves, we feel a deep compassion for the slaves, who are a part of the human family; we wish by all means in our power to discourage those who are seeking to found an empire on their degradation; and we wish success to all just and humane measures for their deliverance.

"With these sentiments, we beg to assure you, that, following where you have so nobly taken the lead, we shall do what we can to accomplish those benevolent objects to which you invite our attention.

"Accept our fraternal wishes that you may enjoy the favour and blessing of God, through Jesus Christ our Lord."

Sub-Committees of the London and Manchester Emancipation Societies now devoted the needful energies and time to circulate this response, and solicit the approving signature of ministers in all Britain. By publication in newspapers, and by private letters, addressed probably to thirteen thousand ministers, the application was widely made; and finally, more than four thousand attested names were appended as subscribers to the letter replying to the French pastors. The names of French and British adherents, and the documents to which they were attached, were inserted in the "Manchester Times and Examiner" as an advertisement.

In London and in Manchester, simultaneously but independently, the question was anxiously considered, what further measures should be taken with relation to these national tokens of fraternal sympathy and intercourse. Facilities were provided in the latter place with promptitude; and, as the conference at London had resolved that it should continue in permanence, ready to be called together again, the convener, then appointed, agreed to issue the circular requisite to give effect to this resolution. The summons was sent to all such as were associated in name or co-operation with the two Societies, and others whom it was hoped to enlist. A conference assembled in the Free Trade Hall, Manchester, on the 3rd of June, and the Rev. Richard Slate of Preston, as the senior Congregational minister in the county of Lancaster, was voted to the chair. After deliberation by the whole assembled ministers and by a sub-committee, carefully selected, the "Address to Ministers and Pastors of all Christian Denominations throughout the States of America," was unanimously adopted :—

"ADDRESS TO MINISTERS AND PASTORS OF ALL CHRISTIAN DENOMINATIONS THROUGHOUT THE STATES OF AMERICA.

"Dear Brethren,—The letter which emanated from the French Protestant pastors, and was signed by 750 from all parts of France, was addressed to ministers and pastors of all evangelical denominations of England, Scotland, and Ireland, and designed to urge them to take the lead in 'a great and peaceful manifestation of sympathy for the coloured race, so long oppressed and debased by Christian nations.' They desired by this means to 'discourage the partizans of slavery,' and 'strengthen and encourage those who wish to abolish it, at the same time persuading them to listen to friendly suggestions.' No such combination of names and objects ever previously occurred in the intercourse of Europe; and surely a letter, so universally approved, deserves the most respectful and considerate attention. It is the utterance of pure Christian philanthropy, and breathes the spirit of divine benevolence—not alone for the negro, but also for all who may be involved in his doom.

"It was brought under consideration of a conference, convened of such ministers as had adhered to the London Emancipation Society, all of whom were invited who were in London. The Hon. and Rev. Baptist W. Noel, M.A., presided, and the unanimous decision was that a brief reply, then submitted, should be adopted and issued, to accompany the letter from the French clergy to all Protestant ministers of every denomination in Great Britain and Ireland.

" The aim of the reply was to avow a deep compassion for the slaves, as part of the human family; to discourage, by all means in the power of the subscribers, those who are seeking to found an empire on their degradation; and to express the desire for success to all just and humane measures for their deliverance. The letter and the reply have been widely circulated, and the adhesion of ministerial names has been solicited among all Protestant ministers. Many may have overlooked the application as a common printed circular, but already about four thousand attested names have been subscribed.

" Both documents concur in representing slavery as a calamity to the nation in which it exists, and as dishonouring Christ when upheld by any of his servants; while they denounce the system because it gives to man the opportunity to treat his fellow-men as cattle, and often to commit adultery and murder with impunity. The census of the United States, taken in 1860, gives the number of slaves as 3,953,760 men, women, and children, reputed, as we understand, the property of 350,000 slaveholders. These millions are all liable to be sold and bought at an auction mart, in lots or severally, at the pleasure of the traffickers, every feeling of delicacy, every endearment of parental and filial tenderness and dependence being crushed, violated, and set at nought; doomed to toil, suffer, and die for the gain and at the caprice of another. These poor victims are not our immediate kindred, but they are our fellow-men, whom their Creator hath made of the same blood with ourselves; and by the laws of Providence they are marked as our neighbours, whom God (who is over all) hath commanded us to love as ourselves; while the standard is inflexible for them as it is imperative for all—'as ye would that men should do to you, do ye even so to them.' We have not been left to abstract reasonings or conjecture to form our opinion of the wrongs inflicted by slavery on these millions, but are warranted to accept the description given by President Jefferson, in his prophetic augury of what awaited his country when he exclaimed, 'What an incomprehensible machine is man! who can endure toil, famine, stripes, imprisonment, and death itself in vindication of his own liberty, and the next moment be deaf to all those motives whose power supported him through his trial, and inflict on his fellow-men a bondage, one hour of which is fraught with more misery than ages of that which he rose in rebellion to oppose. But we must wait with patience the workings of an overruling Providence, and hope that He is preparing the deliverance of these our suffering brethren. When the measure of their tears shall be full, when their groans shall have involved Heaven itself in darkness, doubtless a God of justice will awaken to their distress, and diffusing light and liberality among their oppressors, or at length by his exterminating thunders, manifest his attention to the things of this world, and that they are not left to the guidance of a blind fatality.'

" The friends of America in France and Britain looked anxiously to her statesmen and patriots, hoping that they might soon inaugurate the era when slavery should be doomed, as it had been denounced by her philanthropists; and that its abettors, enlightened and warned, would seek a peaceful solution of their great national problem. The United States had already contended with and overcome greater difficulties than might be found in the enfranchisement of the negro population. Their national independence had been secured amidst many dangers and sacrifices. They had opened paths in the primeval forest, reared cities in the wilderness, and found ports in every part of the world for their produce and commerce. They had risen from being a colony of outcast pilgrim fathers to occupy an equality with the greatest nations, and be welcomed as an ally with the most renowned empires on the earth. Their sails were unfurled, and their standard floated in every region, on every sea, and before every wind. They had become a great nation, and might legitimately contemplate the noblest and most philanthropic achievements. Yet the foul blot of slavery remained upon their banner.

" Strangers should not presumptuously intermeddle in political debate as to the power, prerogatives, or relative obligations of the several states in Federal union. The language and declarations of official men, however, and the ordinances of seceding States, are published. South Carolina leading, Alabama, Texas, and Virginia following, avow slavery as the origin of the strife ; and the intention of the war was declared by Mr. Alexander H. Stephens, vice-pre-

sident of this Confederacy, when he exulted in the 'fact
that the new government is founded upon exactly the opposite idea to the old constitution; its foundations are laid,
its corner-stone rests upon the great truth that the negro
is not equal to the white man, that slavery—subordination
to the superior race—is his natural and normal condition.'
Our solemn conviction is that no darker nor more dreary
calamity could threaten any nation or people on earth than
the successful establishment of a republic whose corner-
stone is the slavery of the working man.   The curse thus
entailed would extend its poisonous influence far beyond
the utmost range of the black population, and involve in
moral degradation, corruption, and bondage, not only all
the white people, rich and poor, but the government ruling
them, the States holding friendly relation with them, and
the merchants made rich by their merchandise and depending on their favour.

"But we cordially congratulate the statesmen and
Christians of America that already the shadows begin to
disperse, and the cloud is edged with the radiance of a
brighter day.   Slavery has been abolished by the wisdom
of the ruler and legislature in the district of Columbia, the
representative centre of the Republic.   In the year 1860
the census numbered 3185 slaves as resident there; but
they are all free now, as are the negroes working in
national arsenals and fortresses, the price of liberty being
compensated from the exchequer of the Union to the former
owner, while we rejoice to learn that the liberated men
show themselves able to appreciate their freedom.   We
congratulate the people of England and America that slave-
trading vessels are now subjected to the right of search by
reciprocal treaty between the two governments, in such
latitudes on the high seas as were formerly scoured with
impunity under the American flag.   The sea pirate knows,
too, that already has capital punishment overtaken one ad-
venturer who thus violates the law.   We look now to the
territories of the republic as lands sacred to freedom, destined to become the homes of industry, commerce, and
Christian fellowship, since the American legislature and the
President have guarded them by laws which henceforward
will bar from them the intrusion and pollution of slavery.
It is well that thus recently have the Christian Indians

been taught to exclude from their communities those who would practise slaveholding and traffic, which they had learned from the slavedealing white. Emancipation, too, is already a state provision in Western Virginia, embodied as an organic law in her constitution, when admitted by the signature of Mr. Lincoln to the Union two months ago.

" We read with deep and prayerful interest the proclamation of emancipation by the President, and rejoice that, notwithstanding the fears entertained by some good men, the results have been so beneficial. It has already brought liberty to myriads, who were held in bondage. The first day of 1863 will be identified with the name of Abraham Lincoln in the history of many future citizens of the United States. If the opinion of Mr. Attorney-General Bates be established as law, that any man born within the recognized territory of the United States is a citizen, then we must anticipate henceforth even that the negro, who is a man and a brother, will be also able to say, 'I am an American,' in the hour of threatened danger. May the day soon come, as longed for, when the President's counsel will be accepted, and the measure he recommends be made law, that all loyal states may emancipate their bondsmen, and the whole Union be willing to share the responsibility and expense ! Even now, hundreds of thousands of negroes, slaves when Mr. Lincoln first occupied the presidential chair, are not only freed men but also servants of the state, and actively co-operating for the redemption of their native country. They are Americans, though coloured men, and ready to make every sacrifice for the restoration of peace, the establishment of liberty, and the triumph of equitable government. Men they are, whom the diplomatic representatives of Hayti and Liberia, now admitted to the brotherhood of American nations, when associated with ambassadors of imperial sovereigns, need not fear to recognize as kindred people at the capital of the American republic. Let the rulers and statesmen of the North persevere in such policy, pursue the course of equity, freedom, and universal liberty ; and especially endeavour to requite the African people by a God-like benevolence for the ten thousand wrongs which have been inflicted on them, and they will find it both more pleasant and more safe and easy to do justice, to love mercy, to undo the heavy

burdens, and let the oppressed go free, than it is to do evil
with both hands. With what renovated energy, with what
moral power, with what hallowed consistency and honourable courage will the whole nation then be able to rise to
their highest destiny! Then will the work of righteousness be peace, and the effect of righteousness quietness and
assurance for ever; and the people shall dwell in a peaceable habitation, in sure dwellings, and in quiet resting-
places. The greatness of the country will be then identified
with goodness, and its name will be as ointment poured
forth. It will have wiped from its banner every stain inconsistent with liberty, to which heretofore the finger of
derision has been pointed, and will have established for its
leaders a claim to the admiration of all enlightened men,
as the benefactors of a long oppressed and injured people.
It is the duty of American statesmen and Christian ministers (which all these considerations emphatically enforce)
to guard against any reaction in the policy of emancipation,
when arrangements, consequent on the termination of the
present war, may come under discussion. A retrograde
course would assuredly give a triumph to the adversaries
of freedom, and put to shame all who have sympathized in
the progress of the cause of the slave.

"RICHARD SLATE, Chairman."

The large hall was crowded in the evening by more
than six thousand persons, Thomas Bayley Potter, Esq., in
the chair; and to them the proceedings of the conference
and the address were reported. The approval of the latter
was signified by three rounds of cheering. There was,
however, a noisy opposition, conducted by Mr. J. Barker.
The sub-committee, who had conducted the preliminaries
to this conference, took into consideration the manner in
which the address should be most effectually conveyed to
America; and the result of their deliberations was a request that Dr. Massie, London, and the Rev. J. H. Rylance,
St. Paul's, Lambeth, should be the bearers of the message
of fraternal counsel to the friends of freedom in the midst
f their present conflict. The principles of their mission,

and the manner in which they should conduct it, were indicated in the letter of instructions which was put into the
hands of Dr. Massie. The Emancipation Society of London
expressed their concurrence in the appointment which had
been made, and sent after Dr. Massie a resolution expressing their approval, which is added to the following letter
of instructions.

"To the Reverend James W. Massie, D.D., LL.D. and
to the Reverend J. H. Rylance.

"Dear Sirs,—I have the pleasure to hand you a copy
of a Resolution unanimously adopted by the sub-Committee
charged with the arrangements for the Anti-Slavery Conference,* by which you will see that you are appointed a

* Resolved—"That the Rev. Dr. Massie and the Rev.
J. H. Rylance be requested kindly to take charge of the
Address to the 'Ministers and Pastors of all Christian
Denominations throughout the States of America,' unanimously adopted by the Ministerial Conference, and acting
as a deputation to the United States for that purpose, to
take such steps as may appear to them desirable to place
the Address in the hands of such leading ministers as, from
their recognized social and public position, may be able to
secure the co-operation of ministers of all denominations
and of all political parties, and that a letter of instructions
be drawn up, guarding the deputation most carefully against
anything like the appearance of dictation to the United
States on the question of Slavery, or of interference with
any party differences on the mode of its extinction, and
pointing out the propriety of limiting themselves to the
formal presentation of the Address to such ministers as
they may agree upon, and of leaving all public proceedings
to be initiated and directed by the United States' ministers
themselves, and either taking part in these proceedings or
otherwise, as may be advised by such ministers.
"That Mr. Potter, as Chairman of the public Anti-
Slavery meeting on the 3rd instant, be requested to forward
a copy of the Proceedings of the Ministerial Conference
and a Report of the Public Meeting to the President of the
United States."

deputation to convey the address adopted by the conference to such ministers in the United States as, after due consideration, you may consider best suited to further the end in view, namely, to bring the proceedings of the conference and its address before ministers of all Christian denominations throughout the States, without regard to any party distinctions.

" I apprehend your first object will be to place yourselves in communication with three or four clergymen and ministers of high standing, who may be regarded as representative men, great care being taken to select such as, by their reputation for moderation, will secure the co-operation of all sects and political parties.

" You will then, of course, place all the documents in their hands; and, after frank and friendly conference, leave the initiation of all ulterior proceedings to them.

" Should they advise any public demonstration, I apprehend you will be prepared to acquiesce in such arrangements as they may make; but I would strongly urge that you should make it manifest in all your proceedings, and in all public announcements, that on American ground you are acting a subordinate part, and should let Americans themselves occupy the foreground.

" The American public would be justly sensitive of anything like an attempt to school them into Abolitionism, and great care will be needful to prevent any misconstruction of your object in this respect. You are embarked on a mission of good-will and Christian friendship; and, whilst you will faithfully represent the nature and object of the various addresses you bear, you will see the propriety of carefully abstaining from even appearing to dictate to America the mode in which they are ultimately to free themselves from the curse of slavery. That is a question purely for themselves, and not for foreigners. No doubt public opinion in America is ripening fast on the subject of Slavery, and is fast approaching that state when no political party can be said to favour Slavery. There are, however, two great political parties, representing different degrees of hostility towards the system, and it would be most unwise to give the more moderate party the opportunity of connecting the distrust of England, which has been fostered in the United States by the misrepresentations of our own press on the questions at issue between North and South, with the Abolitionist party, and thereby retard the consummation devoutly wished for by all sincere friends of negro emancipation.

" The earnest desire of all true philanthropists is to bridge over the differences between these two great parties, and thus to secure the end in view ; and, as a means to this end, you would, of course, dwell on that part of our Address which recognizes the substantial progress which has been made towards abolition.

" One great object of your mission will be, whilst maintaining a due regard to the dignity of our own country, and a position of perfect neutrality as regards direct interference in the war, to calm down this feeling of distrust by an assurance that, notwithstanding these misrepresentations, the heart of England is still true on the question of slavery, and whatever causes of irritation may float on the surface, any real rupture between the two countries would be regarded with unmitigated sorrow.

" I would just suggest, in conclusion, as indirectly connected with your mission, that much good would arise to ourselves, and great benefit to future generations, if materials for history could be collected and arranged in a calm, unbiassed, and philanthropic spirit, representing the true state of public feeling on the great questions now seeking solution in America by the fierce arbitrament of the sword, and the precise stand-point which has been reached both socially and politically during this great crisis in the history of the Republic. The previous experience of one of your number, and his intimate knowledge of American society before the rebellion, leads me to hope that something of this kind may be attempted.—I am, dear sirs, yours truly, " THOMAS BAYLEY POTTER.

" *Manchester*, June 13th, 1863."

"THE EMANCIPATION SOCIETY.

" At a Meeting of the Committee of the Emancipation Society held at the Offices, 65, Fleet-street, London, on Monday, June 16th, 1863, it was resolved—

" That this committee, entertaining the highest appreciation of the eminent services which the Rev. Dr. Massie has by his zeal and ability rendered to all the objects it has in view, and recognizing in him one of the oldest living advocates of the great cause of negro emancipation in this country, gladly avails itself of the opportunity presented by his mission to the United States on behalf of the conferences of ministers at London and Manchester, to commend him to the warmest sympathies and cordial co-operation of the friends of freedom in America.

" (Signed by direction and on behalf of the Committee,)

" WILLIAM EVANS, *Chairman.*
" F. W. CHESSON, *Hon. Secretary.*"

WELCOME TO SYMPATHY.

AND the tears are in my eyes,
When I think you sympathize
With my country, rent and torn
By dissension's cruel thorn :
    Bleeding fast.
God alone can tell how fast,
Possibly her best and last
Patriot blood.   O God ! I bless,
In this hour of our distress,
Our confusion, loss, and strain,
Shuddering hopes and throbbing pain,
Thee I bless that o'er the main,
Comes one honest human tone,
Freedom's, Truth's, Religion's own,
    Us to cheer !
Thus across the troubled water,
I, America's sad daughter,
From our fields of death and slaughter,
Stretch my hand
Gratefully to you————.
        PAMELA S. VINING.

c

CHAPTER I.

FACTS TO BE KNOWN AND CONSIDERED.

THERE are in the United States constitutional questions and political denominations which rise to the surface of society : for a right comprehension of which, a familiar knowledge of facts and opinions is requisite. But without this knowledge much confusion will prevail where the authority of declamatory partisans is accepted. Political antagonists, aiming at ascendancy, have been prominent there, as Whigs and Democrats, Know Nothings and Free Soilers, Americans and Republicans ; and even among philanthropists, seeking freedom for the slave, Abolitionists and Emancipationists have been discriminated as occupying different claims in the anti-slavery conflict. The peace Democrat is reputed of a different school from the war Democrat, in more recent classifications ; and the Republican is more favourable to the present administration than even the latter, since he is the champion of the constitution as settled by Madison, Jefferson, and Washington, which claims the people in all the states as its constituents ; while the Democrat is supposed to maintain the doctrine of *State rights*, and that states are paramount to the Federal Government. Great authorities may be cited in support of the republican interpretation. Mr. Madison held, that after a state had consented to the form of constitution agreed to by the Convention of 1787, it was bound by it. " Should all the states adopt it," he said, " it will then be a government established by the thirteen states of America ; not through the intervention of the legislatures, but by the people at large." Mr. Washington had given this version his solemn sanction when he affirmed—

"*To the efficacy and permanency of your Union a government for the whole is indispensable. No alliance*, however strict, between the parts can be an adequate substitute; they must inevitably experience the infractions and interruptions which all alliances in all times have experienced. Sensible of this momentous truth, you have improved upon your first essay, by the adoption of a constitution of government, better calculated than your former, for an intimate Union and for the efficacious management of your common concerns. . . . The basis of our political system is the right of the people to make and alter their constitution of government; but the constitution which at any time exists, till changed by an explicit and authentic act of the whole people, is sacredly obligatory upon all. The very idea of the right and the power of the people to establish government presupposes the duty of every individual to obey the established government."

Elsewhere Washington reminded the people that their constitution contains a provision for its own amendment, so that the "established government," of which he speaks, must for ever be the actual expression of the will of the whole people or of a majority of the whole. That provision is found in Art. v.

"The Congress, whenever two-thirds of both houses shall deem it necessary, shall propose amendments to this Constitution, or, on the application of the legislatures of two-thirds of the several states, shall call a convention for proposing amendments, which, in either case, shall be valid to all intents and purposes as part of this constitution, when ratified by the legislatures of three-fourths of the several states, or by conventions in three-fourths thereof, as the one or the other mode of ratification may be proposed by the Congress."

It was unnecessary to resort to rebellion, or secession, or war, that changes might be effected, according to the wishes of the people, or the exigencies of the times. Misconduct in the rulers could be exposed and unqualified officials had but a short time to exercise their power. These were, however, not the causes of Southern revolt, for Mr. Alexander H. Stephens frankly admitted that the South had always possessed the control of the Government; had a majority of the presidents chosen from among themselves, and the management of most of those chosen from the North; had sixty years of presidents, while the North had only twenty-four; had eighteen judges of the Supreme Court and only eleven sprung from the North, and this they had required to guard against any interpretation of the Constitution unfavourable to Southern interests. Presidents of the Senate had been twenty-four for the South, against eleven for the North; and speakers of the house twenty-three to twelve; attorney-generals fourteen for the South, against five for the North; and foreign ministers eighty-six to fifty-four; though three-fourths of the business requiring diplomatic agencies abroad were from the free states. The higher officers of army and navy were, by a vast majority, men of the South, while the soldiers and sailors were Northerns. More than two-thirds of clerks, auditors, comptrollers filling the executive departments, two thousand out of three, for the last fifty years, have been nominees of the South, though only one-third of the white population of the entire country belonged to the South, and more than three-fourths of the revenue collected for the support of the Government have uniformly been raised from the North. These are admissions made by Mr. Stephens, after Mr. Lincoln had been elected, and in answer to himself at the time when Mr. Stephens inquired—

"What right has the North assailed? What interest of the South has been invaded? What justice has been denied? And what claim founded in justice and right has been withheld? Can either of you to-day name one governmental act of wrong deliberately and purposely done by the Government of Washington, of which the South has a right to complain? I challenge the answer."

It is strange, that a man proclaiming such views and facts, should yet so soon after accept the vice-presidency of the rebellious confederacy? Some other potent cause, adequate to the occasion must have influenced him and the other leaders to this final and fatal secession. For a brief season Anglican sympathizers with them, imported into the representation of their motives the Morrill tariff, and the protectionist policy of Northern manufacturers.

The itinerant orators of the South have great faith in the powers of perversion, when remembering the admissions of Mr. H. A. Stephens already recited, they stand up in public assemblies, and affirm that taxation had been imposed upon the Southern States by the North; that thus heavy duties have been laid (by the North) upon every article made in Great Britain and Europe, and a line of policy has been adopted to make the South buy the commodities manufactured in the North at the prices fixed by them; and gradually the tariff has been fixed so high as to render it difficult in the extreme for Southerns to obtain articles of European manufacture!

At the close of the year 1859 there was much nervous excitement in Congress about the state of the country apprehending civil war. Mr. Buchanan was still president. A select committee of thirty-three—one member of Congress from each of the states—was appointed to ascertain if possible how the differences could be removed, and what the South demanded. The deliberations and inquiries of this committee were embodied in a report; they had continued in session from 11th December, 1859, till 14th January, 1860. The Slave States had been asked what they wanted. Their grievances from first to last all referred to the maintenance of slavery, demanding from the North powers to increase slavery, to extend it and make treaties with foreign powers requiring the surrender of escaped slaves—slavery throughout, and not one syllable about the tariff or taxation, but slavery was only the burden of complaint from the Southern States and by their representatives. The champions of their cause in England are wiser.

The bait was probably designed for the free trade portion of the British people; but it was not warranted by the allegations of the Southerns themselves. Mr. Jefferson Davis, Mr. Cushing, Mr. Crittenden and Mr. Stephens, being witnesses, we have a uniform testimony that the interests of slave-holding and slave-dealing proprietors were the dominating motive in their proceedings; and *that* not only to maintain slavery as it had been, but to extend the area of its operations, and to render all the lands and states of the Republic subordinate to its maintenance, and all the functionaries and operations of law, and all the people and revenues of the United States, subject to its ministration, enforcement, and promotion: such must be the end and design of the American Union. Mr. Jefferson Davis had in 1858, at Jackson, warned the slave-holders of his state in words of plain and direct significance :—

"If an *abolitionist* be chosen president of the United States, you will have presented to you the question of whether you will permit the government to pass into the hands of your avowed and implacable enemies. Without pausing for an answer, I will state my own position to be that such a result would be a species of revolution by which the purposes of government would be destroyed, and the mere forms entitled to no respect. In that event, in such a manner as should be most expedient, I should deem it your duty to provide for your safety *outside the Union*."

He again offered on the 22nd December, 1860, in the Congress of the United States, before he retired to effect and perfect his rebellion, his *ultimatum :*—

"That it shall be declared by *amendment* of the constitution *that property in slaves*, recognized as such by the *local law* of any of the states of the Union, shall stand on the same footing in all *constitutional* and *federal* relations as any other *species of property* so recognized ; and, *like other pro-*

perty, shall *not* be subject to be divested or impaired by the *local law* of *any other* State, either in escape thereto or by the *transit* or *sojourn* of the owner therein. And in no case whatever shall such property be subject to be divested or impaired by *any legislative act* of the *United States*, or any of the *territories thereof*."

Mr. John Crittenden, a Senator from Kentucky, interposed as mediator from a slave state, with a design to meet difficulties by a compromise, and proposed—

"1. That by amendment of the constitution, *slavery* should be allowed and recognized in *all* the territory south of latitude 36 degrees 30 minutes.

"2. That Congress should have no power to abolish *slavery* in the States permitting it.

"3. That Congress should have no power to abolish *slavery* in the district of Columbia, while it exists in Virginia and Maryland; nor to prohibit the officers of the government and members of Congress from bringing slaves therein, and holding *them* as such.

"4. That Congress should have *no* power to hinder the transportation of *slaves* from one State to another, by land, or navigable rivers, or sea.

"5. That Congress should have full power to pay to the owner of any fugitive *slave* the full value thereof, when the national officer is prevented arresting such fugitive.

"6. That Congress should *never* have power to interfere with *slavery* in the states where it is now *permitted*.

"7. That the *right* to have property in *men* should be legal, not only in the territory *then* in possession, but also in *all territory* to be *thereafter* acquired."

Mr. Cushing had been Attorney-General of the United States; and was, at the beginning of the present struggle, a leading member of Legislature in South Carolina. In his own name he had declared, "The Union is in danger, not by reason of invasion from abroad, but from revolution at home, produced by a conflict of opinion and action between the Northern and Southern states as to slave labour, which exists in Southern states alone;" and on the 20th of December, 1860, when South Carolina seceded and issued her Address, he joined in language which leaves no doubt what caused the conflict.

"Agitation on the subject of slavery in the South is the natural result of a consolidation of government. Experience has proved that slave-holding states cannot be safe in subjection to non-slave-holding states. The people of the North have not left us in doubt as to their designs and policy. In the late presidential election they have elected as an exponent of their policy one who has openly declared that all the states of the United States must be free states;" not one word about tariffs, commercial grievances, or different interests. "Citizens of the slave-holding states of the United States, Providence has cast our lot together by extending over us an identity of pursuits, interests, and institutions. South Carolina desires no destiny separated from yours. *To be one of a great Slave-holding Confederacy, stretching its arms over a territory larger than any power in Europe possesses,* with productions which make our existence more important to the world than that of any other people inhabiting it, with common institutions to defend, and common dangers to encounter, we ask your sympathy and federation. United together, and we must be the most independent, as we are the most important, amongst the nations of the world: united together, and we require no other instrument to conquer peace than our beneficent productions. We ask you to join us in forming a *Confederacy of Slave-holding States.*"

New converts are often more explicit and frank than their masters, and Mr. A. H. Stephens inaugurated his adhesion to the new doctrine, when he had accepted the vice-presidency of the Confederacy, in language which cannot be misunderstood. With vaunting triumph he proclaimed:—

"Our new government is founded on the great truth that the negro is not equal to the white man, that slavery is his natural and normal condition. Our new government is the first in the history of the world based on this great physical, philosophical, and moral truth. This stone, which the first builders rejected, is become the chief stone of the corner in our new edifice. Negro slavery is but in its infancy. We ought to increase and expand our institutions. All nations when they cease to grow begin to die. We should, then, endeavour to expand and grow. Central America, Mexico, are all open to us."

Dr. Palmer, New Orleans, confirmed the doctrine of Mr. Stephens:—

" The providential trust of the South is to perpetuate the institution of domestic slavery as now existing, with freest scope for its natural development. We should at once lift ourselves intelligently to the highest moral ground, and proclaim to all the world that we hold this trust from God, and in its occupancy are prepared to stand or fall. These slaves form part of our households, even as our children. It is a duty we owe to ourselves, to our slaves, to the world, to Almighty God, to preserve and transmit our existing system of domestic servitude, with the right, unchallenged by man, to go and root itself wherever Providence and nature may carry it."

Further demonstration of the *Southern* cause of the present conflict cannot be required by the candid inquirer. Slavery—its perpetuation and undisputed sovereignty in the whole United States—is the huge and disfigured idol of allegiance which the leaders of secession required all America to worship.

The response given to this demand by the constituted authorities of the Union, is clearly, tersely, and emphatically expressed in the almost unanimous vote of both houses of Congress by a resolution, which has since been endorsed by majorities in the suffrages of every loyal state :—

" Resolved, That the present deplorable civil war has been forced upon the country by the disunionists of the Southern States, now in arms against the constitutional government, and in arms around the capital; that in this national emergency, Congress, banishing all feelings of mere passion or resentment, will recollect only its duty to the whole country ; that this war is not waged on their part in any spirit of oppression, or for any purpose of conquest, or subjugation, or purpose of overthrowing or interfering with the rights or established institutions of those states, but to defend and maintain the supremacy of the Constitution, and to preserve the Union with all the dignity, equality, and rights of the several states, unimpaired ; and that as soon as these objects are accomplished, the war ought to cease."

Some writers, and others who claim to speak in the

interests of peace and humanity, who dwell with much pathos on the horrors of *American* war, and profess to deplore the multitudes who have been slain on both sides, have urged that the seceding states should be allowed to depart, and have enforced this project by the incongeniality of character and temperament between the North and South, ascribing a *chivalrous* lineage and bearing to the latter, and a diversity of habit in their several pursuits; alleging also the vastness of American territory as affording scope for both, and anticipating that two competing Republics would be a check on each other for the welfare of other countries; and that the South would be compelled to abolish slavery. There may be other occult or latent reasons instigating the advocates of such a policy from among the admirers of aristocratic and hereditary distinctions, and of established religions, and conservative politics. But the answer to the proposal must come from the Americans themselves. Observant and impartial philanthropists, as well as the avowed advocates of negro emancipation and friends of Africa, might have suggestions to make, not impertinent or captious, in such a discussion. There are states which have remained in or have returned to the Union, which have been called slave states, and have interests involved in the settlement of the present strife. A large part of Virginia, Florida, and Louisiana, all Maryland, Kentucky, Missouri, East Tennessee, and the lands which give the undisputed control of the Mississippi, belong to Federal government, and the people, white and coloured, dwelling there, are its subjects, to whom an equitable administration of all the advantages of a good government are due. In the states involved in rebellion there are said to be many thousands groaning under oppression, faithful in heart and purpose to the Federal authority, and waiting for its restoration where they dwell. Can a paternal government surrender those

who have never broken their allegiance? or can it leave
the feeble and helpless victims of oppression, brought into
bondage by its former abuse of power, to continue sufferers
of a brutal thraldom which threatens their utter destruction?
Mr. Moreheart, an emissary from the South, affirmed that
he had been one of a deputation to negotiate terms of peace
with Mr. Lincoln, the President. His testimony must be
left for what it is worth ; but he tells us—

"We appealed to him [Mr. Lincoln] to give the guarantees which were demanded by the Southern men in this
peace conference. He said that he was willing to give a
constitutional guarantee that slavery should not be molested
in any way, directly or indirectly, in the states; that he
was willing to go further, and give a guarantee that it
should not be molested in the district of Columbia; that
he would go still further, and say that it should not be
disturbed in the docks, arsenals, forts, and other places
within the slaveholding states; but as for slavery in the
territories, that his whole life was dedicated in opposition
to its extension there ; that he was elected by a party which
had made that a portion of its platform, and he should
consider that he was betraying that party if he ever agreed,
under any state of the case, to allow slavery to be extended
in the territories."

Whatever truth may be in this representation, it cannot be questioned that the President had duties towards
the loyal people in the slave and free states, toward negroes
who confided in the platform which he avowed, and their
coloured kindred and uncoloured guardians, who had obtained their confidence. The free and loyal citizens of the
United States had then, and have still, a voice in the deliberations which are occasioned by the war of slavery.

Moreover, before those who claim the reputation of
friends of the negro, and consistent advocates of the emancipation of the slave, and the abolition of slavery and the
slave trade in all lands, can wisely urge a recognition of
this Confederate slave power by any government, especially

the American, they must determine what are the boundaries demanded, and how they can be secured from the prey of the robber and man-stealer, and what shall be the security against the revival of the African slave trade and the extension of the curse into other lands.

How few Englishmen know the extent and geographical relation of the states for which secession is demanded, or the position of the territories yet unorganized into states; the relation of the arterial rivers and coast harbours which may be included in the coveted boundaries; and the extent to which the commerce of the principal cities might be affected by the inter-relations of the states stretching along these confines. By what process could we ascertain the proportion of white adherents to the Northern union shut up in the rebel states, or the negro population who have been transported from the land of their birth by slave traffic. If this birth made them citizens of the Republic, surely liberty to enjoy their rights should be guaranteed by the supreme authority. The principle involved in the right of secession is of essential moment to the integrity of the American Republic and the duty of resistance by constituted authorities; as also the responsibility of a representative government to the citizens by whom its members have been appointed, for the territory entrusted to their care, however its inhabitants may be located, and cannot be determined by a newspaper paragraph. Where mercenaries have been exhibited in the struggle by royal belligerents, it may be a small matter what their claims are internationally; but where citizens are arrayed in the battlefield, and the best blood of the nation has been consecrated to the issue, the question of compromise cannot be arbitrarily determined. Since the Parliamentary wars of England, between 1641 and 1656, there has not been so unquestionably a national appeal to the arbitrament of war. It is a figment of partizanship to represent the army of the North as a band of mercenaries; prior to the conscription, the President's call for 75,000, and subsequently for volunteers for three years, or during the war, was responded to by the choicest flower of national loyalty and personal bravery. The United States' army, in its rank and file, as also in its noncommissioned and commissioned officers, was truly a representative of the national mind; and the young men who still consecrate their bravery and endurance to the service of the Union, testify what the electors of the Republic feel and think of the objects and end of the war. The President and his cabinet cannot ignore the opinions and services of these generous patriots. It may be true that the Southern armies have followed their officers—men trained in the schools and at the expense of the North or rather the Republic, and who, guilty of treason to their oath and honour, fight the more earnestly as they are renegades and traitors. It may also be indisputable that many officers of the North have received commissions by the patronage of state functionaries; yet the ten thousands that have fallen from the ranks, and the sons and kindred of the most distinguished and faithful citizens who have risked their all in the issue, demonstrate how universal is the purpose of the nation to subdue the rebellion. The army does not, it is true, consist only of soldiers moved by patriotism; others have joined in tens of thousands, and their number daily increases; but they, too, are the representatives of millions, whose claims cannot be justly set aside, and whose destiny is identified with the crushing of the rebellion and destruction of its cause. The coloured troops cannot be regarded as mercenaries or mere accessories to the strength of the army. When two hundred thousand of this class have been trained to arms and made to realize their position as principals in the conflict, the future constituency of the United States' army will have assumed an importance in the measures of politicians which will secure consideration. The coloured regiments already occupy a place in the statesman's estimate of probabilities, and must have weight in any determination of the controversy between the rebels and the rulers.

It is not reasonable to anticipate that the loyal states will give up the old Federal Constitution, pull down the old flag, and run up the Confederate banner and adopt its constitution. Will they ever surrender the principle which accounts secession in a state, at its own discretion, impossible without treason; or will they yield up the right of the people to elect a president by a constitutional majority, and consent to nationalize slavery; and add to this the further sacrifice of the liberty of the press, and suppress the right of private opinion? Were all this possible would peace follow? Assuredly not; it would only excite a perpetual storm of agitation. "Abolitionism" would be roused like a giant refreshed with new wine. Dr. Bacon affirms, that—

"Though the martyrdoms for prohibition against slavery should be more numerous than the martyrdoms for Protestantism in the reign of Mary, or the martyrdoms for Christianity in the reign of Domitian, a host of living witnesses would spring from the ashes of every martyr; and 'fanaticism,' as you call it, would become ten times more fanatical and tenfold more contagious under the heat of persecution."

The passage which follows defies abridgment, and can only be expressed in the author's own words; but it is presented as the calm response of an American sage and divine, who is worthy of all honour, to the demand to *consent* to the attempted separation of the revolted states from the *Union*. At first sight it seems a hopeful method, and we are told "that after a few years of peace the dissevered Union may begin to be restored."

" This method proposes that there shall be, henceforth, two nations in what is now one country. Think how those two nations will be related to each other. No natural barrier will hold them apart. Here an invisible parallel of latitude, there a river, there the height of land between two streams, will constitute the boundary. On the two sides of such a boundary, there will be two nations of kindred blood, with one language, with similar forms of government, at least for the present, but with systems of policy, at home and abroad, irreconcilably opposite. On one side of the line everything is subordinated to the institution of slavery; and the chief end of the national policy at home and abroad is to guard, to strengthen, and to propagate that barbarous institution. On the other side all are free ; and society is jealous and sensitive for the liberty of the humblest individual. On one side is the slave-market, where men, women, and children are purchased of all comers, and no impertinent questions asked about where the merchandise came from. On the other side are free negroes—in all a quarter of a million, and perhaps three times as many—men, women, and little children, whose price, in a not distant market, will pay for the risk of stealing them. What will be the result? Is there anybody here too ignorant to answer ? Can we live with a nation of kidnappers, separated from us only by that boundary line ?

" And where shall that boundary line be drawn ?—and how ? Look on the map and see. Shall it cross the Mississippi, and sever the upper waters of that ' father of waters' from the lower ? Think you that the people of the great north-western states, whose streams, descending from the Rocky Mountains on the west, and from the Alleghanies on the east, discharge themselves through that great continental artery into the gulf of Mexico, will ever permit a flag not theirs to wave over the fortresses that guard its entrance into the sea ? That majestic river is the natural highway on which the wealth of their prairies, their forests, and their mines goes forth to mingle with the commerce of the world : and never will they consent that any other sovereignty than that of the United States shall hold the key that can shut the gate of their access to the ocean ? By the force of a geographical necessity impressed upon the continent by its Creator, the Mississippi, from its head-springs in the region of perpetual snows to its estuary in the climate of perpetual flowers, is an indissoluble bond of union to all the states along its course. Where then, and how shall the boundary line be drawn between the United States of liberty, and the proposed Confederate States of slavery? Look on the map again. Trace the long mountain ranges that break the surface of the states now held by this rebellion. This side of the Mississippi, those ranges proceeding from the north, stretch through the conterminous regions of Virginia and Kentucky, and of North Carolina and Tennessee, and only in Georgia and Alabama do they slope down toward the Southern gulf. On their rugged flanks are the homes of a hardy race of whom thousands are now in arms for the Union, and thousands more wait only for the opportunity and the summons. Such regions, in whatever land, are the natural retreats and fastnesses of liberty; and shall the dwellers in these mountains be given over to be ruled in the interest of slavery? How shall a boundary line be drawn across, or through, the Alleghanies, populous on all their slopes, and in all their valleys, with a free and laborious yeomanry, one in speech and lineage? A congress of sovereign monarchs may revise and reconstruct the map of Europe at their discretion—may separate provinces that have grown together for ages—may partition nationalities, giving one part to this jurisdiction, and another to that; but who shall do that sort of thing in America?

"But, supposing this difficulty to be surmounted, how shall the commerce and intercourse between two such nations be adjusted? All along that boundary, wherever it may be marked upon the map, there must be, on either side, a cordon of inland custom-houses and of military posts. On every highway from one country into the other, there must stand at that line an inspector and collector of customs. Along that line there must be large standing armies, confronting each other, and always ready for collision. What will be the result? How long will such a peace continue?

"There is yet a greater difficulty attendant on this method of conciliating the rebellion. No separation of the rebel states from the loyal, or of the slave states from the free—no separation of the South from the North by whatever boundary, can be agreed upon without a compact for the surrender of fugitive slaves. Then we must have, as we have now, a fugitive slave law. Do you say it is impossible to have such a law or such a compact? So I think; but till there is such a compact there can be no peace. Without such a compact, the great interest for which the rebellion was made, and which is to be the corner-stone of the new confederacy, will have gained nothing by the dissolution of the Union, and will have lost all its old security. Do you say that even if such a compact should be made, no fugitive slave law can be executed? I will not deny that I am of the same opinion; but let me ask you to think what the result will be if there is such a compact, and the government cannot or will not carry it into effect. Doubtless there are those who think not only that such a compact would be quite reasonable in a treaty with the revolted states, but also that every fugitive black man ought to be surrendered, without question or delay, to any white man that may take the trouble to pursue him. But who is there among us, so destitute of common sense as not to know that henceforward a compact with a foreign power for the extradition of fugitives from oppression, even if by any possibility it could be made, can never be carried into effect among the people of those states, otherwise than by mere force, suppressing and crushing the sense of justice in thoughtful and generous souls?

" Surely, then, the thought of conciliating those revolted states, and living in friendship with them by consenting to a separation, must be given up. We cannot live with such neighbours as they would be in that case.

" There remains one other method, and only one. The rebellion must be subdued. The constitution of the United States must be established as the supreme law of the land, the constitutional laws and government of the United States must be established (I was going to say re-established, but the word is inappropriate) wherever the rebellion is now dominant. God calls us to this duty and we must do it, or be recreant to Him. It is an arduous duty—no nation was ever called to a work more arduous, but we cannot escape from it. Every day is showing to us more and more how great the work is, and how much it will cost us; but there is no escaping from it, God has

D

shut us up to it, and we must do or die. We have already had some experience of the sacrifices which it involves, and our experience of sacrifice and of sorrow must be yet greater ere the work is finished.

"When will it be finished? When shall there be from the Aroostook to the Rio Grande, and from the Rock of the Pilgrims to the Golden Gate, one imperial nation, with one Federal constitution, and one destiny? I will tell you when.

"Our work of conflict will be finished when God's purpose shall have been wrought out. He who cannot see God in the calamities which have come upon us is an atheist. He who is not compelled to recognize in the conflict now pending God's providence over the world, may read all history and find no God in it. If there is in this world's history a plan and providence of God—if there is any progress of events toward a universal reign of justice —if the world, under God's government, is to grow better as it grows older—then this great crisis in our national history has not come but in the development of God's plan, nor will it pass till He shall have wrought out his own design.

"Our work of conflict will be finished, when God shall have sufficiently purified us in the furnace of this great calamity. He is cleansing us with his own baptism of fire, and till the cleansing is accomplished how can this conflict end? He is teaching us great lessons of public spirit, of self-sacrifice, of loyalty to principle and to the powers ordained of God, of contempt for the mean trade which knaves call politics, and of impartial reverence for the rights with which the Creator has invested every human soul. Not till we shall have learned those lessons of true manliness, will God's purpose be wrought out in its bearing on our welfare.

"Our work of conflict will be finished when God shall have wrought the destruction of slavery. I do not say that an act of Congress, or a proclamation from the President, can abolish slavery throughout the regions occupied by the rebellion. There is no need of raising any doubtful disputation on that question. In the providence of God it has come to pass that we are waging war, desperate war, for our Constitution, for our Union, for the principle of popular self-government by free election, for our national existence. And whatever may be the purpose of our government in regard to slavery, whatever the purpose of this or that commanding general, whatever the purpose of one party or another among the people, however unwavering our determination to prosecute the war for no other purpose than that which was announced in our national manifesto, it is becoming every day more palpably manifest that in this war God has a purpose in regard to slavery, and that his purpose is marching to its consummation. The President may have his scruples about the Constitution—Congress may doubt how far the legislative power of the nation may be extended at this crisis—the people may dispute and be divided in opinion between theories of indefeasible state-rights and theories of state-suicide. But God is not compelled to work under our Federal Constitution. He is above our Constitution; and while we hesitate and know not what to do, the historic forces that are working out his purposes will not be hindered by our scruples. The work to which we are shut up, the awful duty from which we cannot escape, is war and nothing less. We are at war with a desperate and powerful enemy. Every hour the conflict grows more desperate. Just in proportion as the people, and the government, and the military commanders, awake to comprehend the fact that what we have on hand is not a riot to be quelled, but war in its direst reality—the strange delusion that we are nevertheless, and at all hazards, to be the faithful allies of our deadly and desperate enemies against their slaves, will lose its power. When that delusion is gone from us our enemies will know it, and their slaves will know it. I do not say that there will be a servile insurrection in our favour. I do not say that Congress will enact, or the President proclaim an 'abolishment' of slavery. It is enough that civil war will have its natural course. The millions of slaves now an inert machinery employed against us by our enemies will become a power, will choose for themselves which side to serve; and that choice, whether it be to serve the rebellion or to serve the Union, will be in effect the assertion of their liberty. Already thousands of slaves, in spite of all our scruples, have been emancipated by our armies; and as the war works out the natural results of a protracted civil war, each party putting forth its utmost strength, tens of thousands more will gain their freedom on one side or the other. How is it possible for slavery to outlive such a war? The rebellion itself, in the rage and despair of its utmost agony, will be compelled to emancipate its slaves, and to proclaim the end of slavery."

The passage from Dr. Bacon illustrates the state of opinion, its rapid progress, and absorbing power, not merely in the ministerial mind but also in the most intelligent classes of the laity, mercantile and intellectual, in America. Few pastors sustain so high a reputation for maturity and sobriety of judgment, and for moderation and authoritative decision, as does Dr. Bacon; and his counsels and opinions have a weight among ministerial brethren, richly merited by a long course of ministerial activity and consistency. But the large congregation who sit under his ministry numbers among its members men of the highest mercantile position and influence in the United States. The recent development of sentiment with reference to slavery and its action in American society, is surprising to even those who are natives of the country; and cannot be imagined by casual and distant observers, far less by prejudiced and hostile aliens. Three years ago, or even two years since, the same truths could not safely have been stated in public assemblies, which are now not only accepted but welcomed by tokens of most cordial approval in some of the largest cities in the Union.

The political elements which operated in the election of Mr. Abraham Lincoln are but partially understood by *cis-Atlantic* critics; but they must be correctly apprehended before the political action of his administration can be properly appreciated. His difficulties in entering upon his office, and the perplexities which give an appearance of hesitation and dilatoriness in his decision and action, could be most reasonably explained by events and combinations, which were preliminary to his presidential appointment.

The canvass and near approach to success of Colonel Fremont indicated to him who was the successful candidate, and his sympathizers what might occur in 1860; and consequently they employed every means within their reach as government officials, first to prevent the triumph of the Republican party, and then to thwart the Executive under a new president. The alienation of finances and government stores of military munitions, and the scattering of ships and other naval and arsenal resources, were part of the plan. The antagonism cherished and strengthened among Democratic electors was legitimate opposition; but it was intensified by government influences : while honourable ambition stimulated other candidates and their adherents. Mr. William H. Seward was at first the favourite candidate of his own state, and had a fair prospect in others, but although he withdrew, four other competitors remained in the field. The English reader may be reminded that the term of a president's tenure of office is limited to four years. This was designed by the founders of the Republic to bring the policy of the government to the ordeal of the national suffrage : and, therefore, at such a season the political parties reduce the principles they desire to have grafted into the policy of the government, for the ensuing quadrennial term, to a series of resolutions known as a "platform." These various platforms are submitted to the solemn arbitration of the people of the United States, and from their decision there is no appeal. This was the course pursued in 1860 ; one portion of the Democratic party proclaimed the dogma that slavery was to be tolerated and protected in the territories; another wing of that party desired full national recognition, and protection of slavery *wherever* the constitutional authority might extend ; and the Republican party proclaimed its intention, while refraining from interference with slavery in the states where it legally existed, of restricting it within those limits, and of recognizing it not as a national institution, but as a creature of the *lex loci*. All parties profess to appeal to the arbitration, to whose adverse decisions the North had repeatedly bowed; and when the voice of a constitutional majority of the people proclaimed its selection of the Republican ideas, all parties deferred to it except the Breckenridge Democrats: who, having proclaimed their platform, nominated their candidate, canvassed the country, and gone through all the usual forms of the contest, when the verdict was awarded, refused to abide by it, took up arms, fired the first shot at Fort Sumter, drew the first blood at Baltimore, and precipitated the country into a civil war which, for the magnitude of its operations, the extent of its disasters to human life and property, and the vastness of suffering entailed upon the innocent, not only of America, but of other countries, is unequalled in history.

The suffrages were so divided as to leave a constitutional majority to none of the candidates, though 1,857,610 electors united upon Mr. Lincoln; and therefore the question devolved for decision on the electoral college, not to scrutinize the votes, but to elect by their own suffrage.

Of the four candidates for the presidency in 1860, it must be borne in mind that only Mr. Breckenridge represented the revolutionary party, who required the legalizing of slavery in every free state, territory, or wherever the arms of the United States can protect its flag, as the price of remaining in the Union. The will of the people, therefore, as to the question of secession or slavery, is evidenced by the aggregate vote for Mr. Breckenridge as compared with that of his three competitors; that comparison is found in the following figures:—

Total popular vote	4,662,170
Breckenridge	847,953
Lincoln, Douglas, Bell	3,814,217
Majority against secession	2,966,264

Even in the slave states, the united vote for Douglas and Bell, both Union candidates, and opposed to secession, was 679,498, as against 540,871 for Breckenridge. Making a majority against secession in the slave states of 138,627.

It is presumed none of the Whigs who had survived the dissolution of their party voted for the Republican candidate, as it is presumed they were included in the 590,631 who gave their support to Mr. Bell of Tennessee. The transition which has befallen the Whigs, no longer a party, which numbered nearly 1,400,000 in the year 1852, has left the dissidents from it to be distributed as Southern pro-slavery partizans, as Democrats and nondescripts. Many Democrats have passed to the Republican platform, and more are yielding themselves to the conviction that freedom more than party deserves their support. Such men are Vice-President Hamlin, Hon. C. F. Adams, the Ambassador to England, and in 1848 President of the Buffalo Democratic Convention; N. P. Banks, ex-Governor of Massachusetts, and Major-General in the Federal army; Henry Wilson, Senator from Massachusetts; John P. Hale, Senator from New Hampshire; Charles Sumner, Senator from Massachusetts; Galusha A. Grow, ex-Speaker of the House of Representatives, and for ten years the champion of the Homestead Bill.

The opprobrium of recent times to which the section of anti-slaverymen, distinguished as Abolitionists, have been exposed is a phenomenon of strange import in the intercourse of American philanthropists. Extreme opinions on the terms and provisions of the Constitution do not sufficiently explain it; though, perchance, they were mingled with a cynical acerbity towards others who differed in judgment. It became a sect everywhere spoken against, partly because some of its most zealous champions were also earnest sectaries in religious opinions. The Emancipation party were less calumniated or shunned, because they were deemed less revolutionary, and might, perhaps, accept improvement in the condition of the slave in "bit-by-bit" reforms.

The earnest and most intense Abolitionists had their stronghold in Massachusetts, and cordial supporters in Pennsylvania and New York. The experience of these zealous and persistent advocates of freedom led them to the conclusion that the Constitution of the Union must be changed to give scope to abolition. They saw three clauses of that document, which seemed not only to acknowledge the existence of slavery, but also required by the oath which was taken, that every one who subscribed it should uphold that Institution in its integrity. The provision introduced to regulate taxation, which reckoned five slaves held by any one as equal to three votes in the election of candidates to Federal offices; the power given to any one holding persons to service to pursue his fugitive servant into other states, to claim his rendition, and permission to continue the slave trade for twenty years from 1787, were adduced in proof that the Constitution could not be worked for the abolition of slavery, while the doctrine of *State sovereignty* was a bar to any interference by Congress or President in the slave laws of slaveholding states. The conviction thus cherished constrained a growing number of Abolitionists to abstain from holding office themselves, or giving their suffrage to others. They therefore proceeded to assail the Federal Constitution—an object so dear to myriads that it had become a popular doctrine that there was "no higher law as a rule for political action than the Constitution of the United States." Argument and controversy ran high —multitudes being ready almost to say of their Union, "He that toucheth thee, toucheth the apple of my eye."

The Abolitionists were charged, even by patriotic and discerning men, as holding "not the simple doctrine of abolition—viz., that slavery ought to be abolished, but a peculiar and distinctive doctrine of their own, the doctrine of *immediate abolition;* or, in other words, that instead of some process of gradual abolition, which shall guard the slaves, and the masters, and society against the perils incident to so great a change, slavery ought to be abolished instantaneously and without regard to consequences." To this the reply was given, "look at slavery and its barbarism;" look at its cardinal *principle,* the undoubted law in all the slave states, "that the slave is not to be ranked among *sentient* beings, but among *things*—is an article of property, a chattel personal." They singled out the assumptions of United States' senators, sent by the slave states; from Mr. Calhoun, who pronounced "*Slavery the most safe and stable basis for free institutions in the world,*" and Mr. M'Duffie, who accounted it *the corner-stone of the Republican edifice,* to Mr. Hammond, who admired its *forms of society as the best in the world;* Mr. Jefferson Davis had represented it as but *a form of civil government for those who are not fit to govern themselves;* and his colleague, Mr. Brown, vaunted it as *a great moral, social, and political blessing—a blessing to the slave, and a blessing to the master;* Mr. Hunter advanced in his panegyric of what he called *the Social System of the slaveholding states,* exalting *slavery as the normal condition of human society, beneficial to the non-slaveowner as it is to the slaveowner, but for the happiness of both races;* and glorified that as *the very key-stone of the mighty arch, which, by its concentrated strength, is able to sustain our social superstructure, which consists in the black marble block of African slavery;* knock that out, he says, *and the mighty fabric, with all that it upholds, topples and tumbles to its fall.* M'Duffie crowned the eulogy by exclaiming, "*Slavery supersedes the necessity of an order of nobility.*" In response to these encomiums the Abolitionists hunted their victims as "the Barbary of the Union" from its African home, through its practical results, in its own States, comparing them with other parts of the Union, on the character of the oppressors, whom the system barbarizes, and on the oppressed, whom it consigns to degradation.

The Abolitionists had disfranchised themselves, and were constrained to accept ostracism by their fellow-citizens. They believed principle was at work in their country ; men who then thought their doctrine mischievous in its effects on their own minds and hearts, and mischievous in the re-action it produced, branded them as led by infidels and zealous mistaken fanatics under erroneous pleas of philanthropy, and speaking evil of the Word of God, to denounce the Federal Constitution and Union as fraught with guilt sufficient to provoke the judgments of heaven; that therefore these extremists demanded immediate and unqualified emancipation, or, as an alternative, denounced the Constitution, and sought to hasten the dissolution of the Union by whatever might increase its difficulties. The heat of debate and the use of free speech among such belligerents, for a time opened a wide gulf between these friends of the slave, and occasioned misapprehensions among distant observers. But their own divisions and misconceptions have been gradually subsiding, and their tendency to union and influence is daily augmenting. What argument and the Congress and the Constitution had not previously accomplished, the seceding and rebellious slaveholders have effected under the providence of God for the slave's emancipation. There is some lingering antagonism on constitutional questions between the Democratic and Republican politicians, as to the power of the President and his administration : but the members arrayed under the banner of State sovereignty, as paramount to the Republican Federation are gradually and even rapidly diminishing. Englishmen may be excused if they do not quite comprehend how far the *imperium in imperio* can be recognized, and the right to secede be denied to the several states whose chosen representatives may determine to assert their independence. It is, however, asserted that State sovereignty was surrendered after the experiment from 1777 to 1787; and the convention, chosen to act in the latter year, prepared and submitted the present Constitution, whereby the Federal Congress, Senate, and President, became sovereign, which was accepted by eleven of the states on the 17th of September, 1788, when Congress resolved that it should go into operation on the 4th day of March, 1789. The other states afterwards adhered.

The acts of sovereignty as between America and other nations, declaration of war, treaties of amity, or commercial intercourse for all the states, the raising and supreme command of the army and navy, coining money, and the sovereignty of the territories, were all transferred from the several states, and are vested in the President or his subordinate administration in responsibility to the Federal Congress. Traitors, rebels, and their property, in whatever state, are amenable to presidential control.

But the presidential prerogatives have either been exaggerated or misapprehended in Britain, especially by such as have objected to the policy of Mr. Lincoln during the past two years. He has been charged with doing too much, and failing to do what ought to have been done. Why have he and the Congress failed to abolish slavery, since not only did he avow himself opposed to it before his election, but it has manifestly been the cause of all the recent conflict? Why did he proclaim freedom to the slave in the rebel states, where he had no power, and leave it untouched in the loyal states, where his power was dominant? Why did he tell the Chicago deputation that he must maintain slavery, if to do so would strengthen the Union, and would abolish slavery if not doing so would weaken the Union? Why has he not allowed the slave states to retire and form a separate Republic, but has issued conscriptions, forcing on an unwilling people warfare and bloodshed, involving the United States in irretrievable debt and ruin? Why does he remove generals in the army from commands where they are popular, and sustain generals and others in authority who fail in their duty? Why does he employ coloured slaves to fight against their masters, and refuse to hear their masters' remonstrances from the lips of Mr. H. A. Stephens when sent with a flag of truce? Why does he not accept terms of peace, though they have not been offered, except as they were spoken of by such peace democrats as Mr. Wood and other tools of faction for divisive purposes?

The President is not a lawgiver; but in times of peace and loyalty is simply an administrator of duties prescribed by the Constitution. He may send messages to Congress; but he has not a vote or seat in that assembly, nor any one to represent him in its deliberations. He can veto measures proposed and carried by the two houses of legislature, and whatever has been carried by majorities is not a law till it has received the President's signature. He has no vote, place, or control in, or over the legislature of the several states, and no power to set aside their legislation, or the action of their governors, as far as they relate to the internal economy of their own state. He can interdict their coinage of money, raising of an army for war, or treaties with other states of the Union, or other governments, but he cannot send a message or propose to the legislature of any one state the enactment of a law, or the abrogation of a statute, or interfere with the internal administration of any institution, or inflict a punishment for any violation of any state ordinance. His private opinions, or the platform of his party, could not become the rule of his presidential action, which is regulated by the Constitution. His propositions, whatever they are, must be enacted by the two houses of legislature before he could carry them out; and had the senators and members of Congress from the South continued in their place, they might have frustrated every item of his policy, or at least embarrassed its action. His two proclamations respecting the slaves of masters in disloyal states, the one giving warning of the other by a period of two months, were issued in his character of commander-in-chief, an office with which the Constitution invested him, and which he could only discharge towards a foreign enemy, or rebellious citizens; and they enforced only the *confiscation act of Congress* against rebels in arms. The measure was demanded by the pressure of the war and the urgent importunities of many virtuous citizens in private and public.

Had not such a measure been adopted, not alone would the rebellion have been strengthened by disappointment among able-bodied slaves, but the sympathies and convictions of millions of friends of the slave would have been turned from the government of the Union. The commander-in-chief had no right to interfere in the administration of loyal states, or to confiscate their nominal property. The President therefore did not extend to them the action of his proclamation. But in the proper season he addressed a message to their representatives, urging that a measure of emancipation should be considered by them. Mr. Lincoln explained to the Chicago deputation 'coming from his own state, not that his private opinions had changed, but that as a faithful man who had taken the oath of President he must employ his prerogatives only in a constitutional manner for maintaining the Union; and that the abolition of slavery must proceed from the proper quarter before it could become an act of his administration. In like manner, his oath and the demand of the people constrains the President to seek to preserve the territories of the Union unbroken and undiminished, as he had received them to keep and not only to punish rebels but protect many a loyal citizen yet remaining in the States, where a conspiracy of traitors had fomented and forced rebellion. The conscription was enacted by Congress as a law at the urgent call of men, some of whom subsequently sought to employ it to the discredit of Government, and the men who resisted it by violence were doubtless the dupes of knavish and unprincipled demagogues. The debts which have been occasioned by the war, are assumed by a loyal people who prefer that the bonds for it shall be paid by themselves. The conduct of Mr. Lincoln to the generals is not only gracefully accepted by the men themselves most personally concerned, but is so far approved by the whole people as that it may be safely said never was a President so popular in the United States.

The power over the slave and to maintain slavery in the South had never been touched by congressional legislation or presidential authority; nothing was proposed to be done by Mr. Lincoln as successful candidate, or by his supporters. The oppressed and crushed slave remained exposed to the brutality of his tyrant; though such men as Senators Preston and Hammond had declared from their places in Congress, that if an abolitionist should come within the borders of their state, or if chance should throw him in their way, he might expect a felon's death; "notwithstanding all the interference of all the governments on earth, including the Federal Government, we will hang him." Thus it was resolved by the leaders of rebellion that the liberty of speech and of the press would be abolished, and a felon's death would await him who dared to print or utter any denial that slavery is just or moral; and in the declaration of causes for secession by Carolina, the chief one set forth was "the election of a man to the high office of President of the United States whose opinions and purposes are hostile to slavery;" by this it was asserted, the Federal government will have become their enemy. The prerogative of a free election was therefore denied to the

North; and further it was declared, that as the North did not act efficiently in catching fugitive slaves and returning them to slavery, the constitutional compact had been deliberately broken, and South Carolina was released from her obligations.

"Thus, then, it stands. The South, stimulated by self-interest, saw that an experiment which never had succeeded in the world before, was about to fail here also: the experiment of maintaining in perpetuity, side by side, under the same government, two conflicting labour systems. She saw that her 'philosophical truth' must be accepted as the corner-stone, or else altogether rejected by the builders. She saw that the North would *not* accept it. She saw that public opinion at the North would continue to condemn it as sinful and unchristian. She saw that the North would never consent to have freedom of speech and of the press suspended throughout half the republic. She saw that the pride of the North would never submit to the passage of a constitutional amendment, making Anti-Slavery opinions a disqualification for the Presidency. She saw that under any plan of reconstruction short of assimilation of labour systems, fugitive-slave law difficulties would increase, in number and bitterness, year after year.

"Between Slavery and National Unity was her only choice. She selected and emblazoned Slavery; drew the sword, and severed the political bonds which connected her with the Free States.

"The men of the North say, 'Shall we tempt her again into fellowship by an offer to restore to her her constitutional rights, and a promise to maintain intact her system of slave-labour?' Vanquished, exhausted. but with her convictions unchanged, she might agree to such an armistice. Permanent she knows well it could never be; but she knows also the vast advantage, in her present prostrate condition, of two or three years' breathing time. Shall we offer her an opportunity so excellent to recruit her strength and replenish her resources?

"The ninth section of an Act of Congress, commonly called the 'Confiscation Act,' approved July 17, 1862, reads thus :—

" ' That all slaves of persons who shall hereafter be engaged in rebellion against the Government of the United States, or who shall give aid or comfort thereto, escaping from such persons and taking refuge within the lines of the army; and all slaves captured from such persons or deserted by them and coming under the control of the Government of the United States ; and *all slaves of such persons found or being within any place occupied by Rebel forces and afterwards occupied. by forces of the United States*, shall be deemed captives of war, and shall be for ever free of their servitude, and not again held as slaves.'

" By the decision of the Supreme Court already cited, *all* the inhabitants of the insurrectionary states are, in law, persons 'engaged in rebellion.' Therefore, all refugee slaves from insurrectionary states are, by this statute, declared free.

" Further : as all the insurrectionary states have been 'occupied by Rebel forces,' and as we may reasonably conclude that, if we prevail against the South, all these states not already ' occupied by forces of the United States' will hereafter be so occupied, it follows that, by the operation of this law, all the slaves in the insurrectionary states, even if no Emancipation Proclamation had ever been issued, would, before the end of the war, have probably been entitled to freedom.

" Strictly in the spirit of the above statute, and going only so far beyond it as to declare slaves in portions of the insurrectionary states not yet ' occupied by forces of the United States,' to be free in advance of such occupation, has been the President's action in the premises. Let us glance at that action.

" On the 25th of July, 1862, the President, in pursuance of the Act just quoted, issued a Proclamation warning all insurgents to return to their allegiance within sixty days, on pain of certain forfeitures and seizures.

" This warning proving ineffectual, the President, when the sixty days' notice had expired, issued a second Proclamation, declaring that the slaves held within any state, which on the 1st of January then succeeding should still be in rebellion against the United States, ' shall be then, thenceforth, and for ever free.'

" On the 1st of January, 1863, ' by virtue of the power in him vested as Commander-in-Chief of the Army and

Navy of the United States,' he declared certain states, namely Arkansas, Texas, Louisiana, Mississippi, Alabama, Florida, Georgia, South Carolina, North Carolina, Virginia—certain parishes in Louisiana and certain counties in Virginia excepted—to be then in rebellion against the United States: and he further declared that all slaves in the said ten states, with the exceptions aforesaid, ' are, and henceforward shall be, free.'

" Were these proclamations legal? Had the Commander-in-Chief of the Army and Navy of the United States the right to issue them?

" Our Supreme Court, in the decision already alluded to, thus endorses a well-known law of war :—' The right of one belligerent not only to coerce the other by direct force, but also to cripple his resources by the seizure or destruction of his property, is a necessary result of a state of war.' Or, as Vattel has it :—' We have a right to deprive our enemy of his possessions, of everything which may augment his strength, and enable him to make war.'

" Humanity bids us respect the private property of non-combatants. It is barbarous to burn or pillage dwellings, to lay waste farms, to destroy public edifices, not military. But if property of an enemy be of a dangerous character, so that its existence imperils the success of the war, or if it be such as has been, or may be used with effect against us to prolong the war, we violate the clearest dictates of prudence if we neglect any opportunity to deprive the enemy of it. Thus of ammunition, of quartermaster's, and commissary stores. Thus, also, of forts, entrenchments, and the like. Let us apply these principles in the present case.

" Certain of our public enemies with the same rights (and no other) as alien enemies have, held on the first day of January last, within the above-named insurrectionary states, claims to the service or labour for life of some three millions of persons.

" This class of claims is, beyond all else, such property as imperils military success, such as ' augments the enemy's strength,' such as ' enables him to make war,' nay, gives him aid on a scale so vast, that without it the war would already, in all reasonable probability, have been brought to a close. It is not, indeed, quartermaster's and

E

commissary stores, but it is that which supplies both. It is not forts or entrenchments, but it serves to build the one, and throw up the other. We cannot more effectually 'cripple the resources' of the enemy, than by destroying it.

"Nor is this all. The dangerous character of this property is attested by the enemy himself. He acknowledges that Jefferson prophesied truly, when he predicted that this was the rock upon which the old Union would split. The owners of these claims themselves declare them to have been the immediate cause of the war. What chance have we of domestic tranquillity while they exist? There is—in the nature of things there can be—no security for peace or loyalty from a slave state.

"Does international law exempt such claims from seizure? Are they not to be reckoned as part of an enemy's property? Vattel expressly tells us:—'Among the things belonging to the enemy are likewise incorporeal things— all his rights, claims, and debts.'

"Therefore, the Confiscation Act, including its ninth section, already quoted, is in strict accordance with the laws of war.

"Therefore, too, our Commander-in-Chief was in his right when he took and cancelled the claims to service and labour in the insurrectionary states. The law of nations sanctions the Emancipation Proclamation. By that instrument three millions of slaves were legally set free. The deed is done—righteously, lawfully done. It is true that many of these people are working as slaves still; but in the eye of the law, they are freedmen. Our own right to freedom is not better than theirs.

"This deed, demanded alike by prudence and justice, forms an era in our national history. It severed the past from the future. It substantially changed, of necessity, the policy of the government. In the early stage of the war, Congress proposed, and the majority of the nation expected, as the issue of this contest, a mere rehabilitation, with Southern laws and Southern institutions re-acknowledged in their pristine form. Again and again warning was given, and the return of the insurgents to their loyal duty on these conditions was urged upon them. But their hearts were hardened, and they would not. By their obstinate perversity they closed the door against themselves. They persevered in their conspiracy against public law until Emancipation became an imperative measure of self-defence. Let us not take credit to ourselves for generous philanthropy. The South, reckless and blind, was the unwitting agent of human liberty. And thus, in the providence of God, the very effort, by armed treason, to perpetuate an abuse has been the means of effecting its eradication.

"That which might have been can no longer be. When politicians talk now of reconstruction, with the 'peculiar institution' of the South left intact, the words are nothing else but a mischievous mystification. If the South conquer, she may, by superior force, hold as slaves the negroes who shall remain to her, though by our laws they are free. But for us there *is* no longer a peculiar institution in any of the insurrectionary states to be left intact. We can build up anew that peculiar institution; not legally, it is very true, for neither the President, nor Congress, nor any judicial tribunal in the land, has any more authority to consign a freeman to slavery than they have to hang him without crime or trial; but we may build it up, if we have power enough, or connive at it if we are shameless enough; just as a highwayman may seize a purse, or a burglar carry off a basket of silver-ware."

CHAPTER II.

THE Census Tables in "The National Almanac and Annual
Record" of the United States for 1863, supplies an analysis
of the nationality and occupation of immigrants arriving
in that country from 1820 to 1860. Among the *curiosities*
are the facts that the class containing 872,317, the greatest
number, is designated "labourers;" while the class of
"farmers" numbers 764,837. "Mechanics" are reckoned
407,524, besides shoemakers, tailors, weavers, spinners,
engineers, printers, painters, masons, hatters, millers, and
butchers, altogether 26,175. There are 29,484 mariners;
30,967 miners; 5246 seamstresses and milliners; actors
are 588; clerks, 3882; lawyers and physicians, 9875; manufacturers, 3120; teachers, 1528; artists, 2490; musicians,
720, and clergymen, 4326. It might be an interesting
question which collegiate institutions supplied the greatest
proportion of these emigrant clergymen. Bakers are computed, 1272; servants, 49,494; other occupations, 26,206;
and 2,978,599, have no specific occupation.

During the period from 1820 till 1860 the total number
of aliens who entered the United States was 5,062,414;
while others of American descent, returned to their birth-
place, were 397,007. Great Britain, including England,
Ireland, Scotland, and Wales, and British America, contributed as their quota 2,866,016 of this vast mass. Germany
and Prussia sent 1,546,476; France, 208,063; China, 41,443,

and the West Indies, 40,487; Norway and Sweden, 36,129; Spain, Belgium, Holland, Denmark, Portugal, altogether contributed 55,853. But Poland has sent only 1659, and Russia, 1374; while Switzerland swelled her numbers to 37,733, and Italy, Sicily, Sardinia, etc., added 13,920. South and Central America gave 24,935; besides other fractional items; 180,854 are reported as having arrived without stating from what country they had departed; many of them, no doubt, were wives and children. One of the ingenious defenders of the South assumes, with more plausibility than truth, that these races commingled give as their product "two peoples, originating from ancestors so different and with such differences of opinions, habits, institutions, laws, and feelings, and occupying for CENTURIES (!) regions so distinct they could hardly be expected to live together peaceably for ever." Surely the premise does not warrant so curt a conclusion.

An American commentator, in the most dispassionate manner, criticises the alleged phenomena and their physical antagonism:—

"Nothing can be more absurd than the drawing of this imaginary line of races between the Northern and Southern states; it is very true, indeed, that Virginia was first settled by the younger sons of English gentlemen, persons who, cut off by the laws of primogeniture from inheriting their paternal estates, sought to found others for themselves in the New World, and, regarding manual labour as disgraceful to gentle blood, gladly welcomed the Dutch captain who, in August, 1620, introduced the first cargo of Africans, in whom the colonists thought they discerned a better substitute for the English peasantry than the comparatively few and discontented whites they had been able to "spirit" away from the mother country. It is equally true that Massachusetts was first settled by the Puritans, men in whose souls the spirit of Hampden and Cromwell was reflected,—men of a stern theology, who had small love for kings and aristocrats, and who regarded all toil as honourable,—men who had none of the advantages of the settlers

of South Carolina, who enjoyed the partnership and patronage of Shaftesbury, Monk, Clarendon, Ashley Cooper, and
other.favourite courtiers whose rapacity obtained from the
debauched Charles II. the grant of all lands lying between
twenty-nine degrees and thirty-six degrees thirty minutes
north latitude, and from the Atlantic to the Pacific Oceans.
But to contend that the two Anglican classes—for they can
scarcely be described as races—which thus first settled the
English possessions in America have ever since maintained
their distinction, and now divide the country between North
and South, is simple folly. Ten other and mainly distinct
peoples have been mingling their blood and ideas with the
two antagonistic English stocks. The waves of Dutch,
German, Irish, Scotch, French, and Sclavonic races have
flowed over the South as well as over the North. Before
the close of the seventeenth century the French Huguenots
had settled in both sections of the country. Massachusetts
owes to a Huguenot the far-famed Fanuil Hall, in Boston,
fondly termed 'the cradle of liberty;' while in South
Carolina, in the revolution, it was a Huguenot, Judith
Manigault, who gave his entire fortune for the service of
the country which had given his mother a shelter from the
religious fury of Louis XIV. America presents the spectacle, not 'of two peoples' 'occupying for centuries'
distinct regions, but of twelve or fifteen peoples who, constantly intermingling for less than two centuries, have
formed a peculiar race, observing no geographical boundaries, and divided in opinion now only upon one question,
i.e., the dignity or the disgracefulness of labour.''

The connection between English Puritans and Nonconformists, the earliest settlers in the Massachusetts Bay, and
the present population, not alone of New England, but of a
large portion of the Western states, deserves more than a
passing allusion. As old England inspired her children,
who peopled Connecticut, New Hampshire, Vermont,
Rhode Island and Massachusetts, with their endurance and
love of liberty, so has her descendant animated the vigorous
and enterprising colonists in Western lands. It may be
true that Illinois and Indiana received their *early* settlers
from among the poor whites of Kentucky; and that, having

a full knowledge of the slave-master's inclination to rid himself of the burden of supporting aged negroes, they expected an emigration of coloured paupers along the frontier of their states; and therefore enacted in their state constitution, as slavery was excluded from their territories by the Missouri compromise, that no person of colour, though free, should be admitted to citizenship within their limits. But during the last fifteen years a very different class of settlers have resorted to their prairies and forest-lands, and have rendered the exclusive law almost an obsolete statute, and the 110,000 of inhabitants in Chicago can too well appreciate the value of free labour to exclude any man able and willing to work. In Kansas, Minnesota, Wisconsin, and Iowa the men of New England lineage and sympathies abound, as in Milwaukie, Dubuque, and every other rising town. 'The Border Ruffians' of Missouri found many men, like Captain John Brown, ready to contest the introduction of slavery into that debateable land; while Detroit, which has increased during ten years by more than 117 per cent.—giving about 50,000 where only 21,000 were previously—witnesses the enterprise of Old Englanders and New Englanders, too, in her pathway upon the mighty lakes, gathering their waters from other regions and lakes which border her own state, Michigan. A striking fact is deduced from the census of the decade ending 1850; 609,371 were found in the Free states, who had been born in the Slave states, and 206,638 born in the Free states were found in the Slave states; and, since the white population of the Free states is double that of the Slave states, it is concluded that the proportion of whites moving from slavery is six times greater than that of whites moving into slavery.

In this simple fact is disclosed something of the aversion to the domestic institution which is aroused even in the Slave states. But another humiliating feature occurs in what has been affirmed, that the New England men, who

migrate into Slave states, become the greatest oppressors of
the slave, and are the bitterest opponents to the abolition of
slavery, or to the claims of the Federal union.

The older states, however, retain their original and
distinctive characteristics, while manifesting adventitious
peculiarities, derived from fresh immigrations.   Dutch
names and associations linger in New York, amidst the
cosmopolitan lineaments which are derived from her universal commerce and facilities for navigation.   Gentile and
Jew, Protestant and Catholic, Presbyterian in multiplied
phases, Irish, English, Scotch, French, Dutch, German,
Negro and Caucasian, Greek and Chinese, Asiatic and
South American people her crowded streets, and mingle in
the turmoil of her commerce, or in her scenes of amusement and religion.   New Jersey is more like a rural
province of the states attached to New York than like a
separate state.   She was settled in 1627, and contains
672,035 of a population ; while the population of New York
numbers 3,851,563, and was settled in 1609.   Delaware
was settled in Charles I.'s time, by a grant to Lord Delaware, 1627, and contains only 112,216, of whom 19,829 are
coloured and free.   There are also 1798 slaves, three-fifths
of them residing in one county.   It is believed, however,
they are rapidly making themselves scarce.   In area and
population this state ranks thirty-second of the whole, and
does not increase the improvement of her lands in proportion to the neighbouring states.   Maryland received her
name before she was recognized as a governing body.
Among her 687,000 of a population are 80,000 free coloured
persons and 87,190 slaves; but the latter are escaping
without the pursuit of a fugitive slave law, in thousands
apparently, to the relief of their former owners.   Baltimore
is the crown of Maryland's fame and influence, and its
commerce has rapidly increased in recent times ; while her
population has risen, in ten years, from 169,054 to 212,418.

Secession proclivities have, however, marred her reputation. Her neighbour state, Pennsylvania, settled under the auspices of William Penn, as a friend of the Stuarts, in 1682, contains a population of 2,906,115. She has the same area as New York, 46,000 square miles. Philadelphia contains 562,529, an increase, during ten years, of 222,484; while Pittsburg·and its suburbs contain 100,000, all rejoicing in their power to labour, and in the reward of their work.

Philadelphia strikes a stranger as possessing the capacity for increase and the well-being of its inhabitants equal to what any other city in the Union enjoys, and the *élite* of the residents there manifest the manners of a people who live in their birth-place and among their kindred. They are Americans, and occupy themselves in matters which claim their sympathies, yet are they observant of the rites of hospitality. The educational statistics of the city are reported as, 347 schools : denominated as, high schools 2, grammar schools 57, *unclassified* schools 48, secondary 59, and primary 181. Institutions for deaf and dumb, for the blind, for idiotic and feeble-minded children, and insane hospitals, all evince a philanthropic provision for the inhabitants of the city. They have also a supply of correctional institutions for all criminal classes, white and coloured. Their prisons are conducted on benevolent principles, and are intended to reclaim even more than to punish. There was in the census reported of the state, an excess of white males in the whole population of 6626, while there was an excess of coloured females of 4103 ; probably the war has altered the proportions in the sexes.

Massachusetts was the home of the Pilgrim Fathers, and though her area hardly reaches a sixth part of New York or Pennsylvania, her population is 1,231,066, approaching to nearly the half of Pennsylvania, and more than a third of New York. Her first settlement was in 1620. The population is not so nearly balanced in the sexes as was

Pennsylvania, the females exceeding the males by 37,640. The coloured population numbers 9602. The state ranks first in density and in absolute increase of the inhabitants in the square mile of all American states, and takes rank after New York and Pennsylvania in manufacturing production. The number of newspapers and periodicals published in the state was 232, and their aggregate circulation was 102,000,760 copies. Its criminal and educational statistics exceed in detail and abundance every other state in the Union. The joint-stock companies, fire and life assurance, railroad companies, represent an amount of capital which can hardly be credited, and is, perhaps, unequalled not only in the Union, but in any equal extent of population anywhere. Taking along with Massachusetts, Connecticut, Vermont, New Hampshire, and Rhode Island, we have the homes and the race of New England. The area of these four latter states extends to 24,235 square miles, together with Massachusetts, embracing 32,000 square miles; their gross population amounts to 1,275,956, to which, if we add the inhabitants of Massachusetts, the number will be 2,507,022. The excess of female population in these four states was 17,645, which, added to the excess in Massachusetts, would make 55,285 more women than men in these five states prior to the war. Probably this feature of New England statistics arises from the adventurous colonizing spirit of the people, which leads to the fact that New England men are found in every state of the Union. There is less proportionate accession to the native born inhabitants in these states from emigration than in other parts of America, and the coloured population, though generally in better condition of life, seems to be not so numerous as in states more toward the South. There are more towns in these states, and the population is more disposed to draw together, than in the Western states. The residences of the people are all superior to the towns of the old country, and the streets and suburbs are more tastefully laid out and have more of the appearance of independence and comfort than do the country towns of England. Hartford, New Haven, Cambridge, Worcester, Salem, Springfield, Norwich, Laurence, and Lowell, with many other thriving and increasingly populous towns, appear the homes of a wealthy and almost aristocratic yeomanry; while Boston sits as queen in the midst of all, with her suburbs containing probably 250,000 inhabitants, and presenting streets, and squares, and drives, and contrasts of town and country, of water and land, interspersed with public buildings, monuments, and philanthropic institutions; she has more the air of a new edition of a quaint old prosperous city than any other place in America. Her citizens impress the stranger with the idea that they are all homogeneous, that they have been born there, and have known and assimilated with each other from boyhood, and retain a living interest in each other's welfare and prosperity. Female society exercises a most benignant influence in all her associations, and give heart and attractions to the homes of husbands, sons, and brothers.

The state of Maine skirts the seaboard as far east as the boundary of British possessions in New Brunswick, was originally a portion of Massachusetts, but now, as a separate state, extends over 31,766 square miles, and contains 628,276 inhabitants, a people brave and loyal. They are truly by descent and association entitled to be classed as the sons of New England, and the kindred of the Puritan fathers. Many of the present families have joined the original emigrants, and have contributed to refresh and strengthen the tide of English feelings.

The genial sympathy between Old and New Englanders, notwithstanding revolutionary feuds and a brief war fever in 1812 and 1813, runs deep, and evinces its strength even in complaints of seeming alienation in the present struggle.

The emotion which approaches irritation, and breaks out in language of displeasure, is the consequence of disappointment and sorrow. The people are *vexed* to think that those whom they had regarded as their own kindred, and loved as an elder though absent brother, should misapprehend or suspect their conduct toward the slave and the suffering. They had expected that England would remember how Massachusetts had borne reproach and calumny for the sake of the oppressed negro. Connecticut contains 8627 free coloured inhabitants, and Vermont and Massachusetts have not had a slave in all their territories since the year 1800, though the people of these states have helped many thousands who were slaves to the land of freedom by their underground railway.

Their English ancestry were men who loved their country, though they sought to love and serve their God with a more fervent zeal. In their temporary exile, to which persecuting prelates and benighted rulers had driven them, when they sought a European home, they witnessed with regret the amalgamation of their offspring with the blood of other nations, and the lisping speech of their children in foreign languages. *They* thought in and responded to the utterances of their mother tongue. Their English accent had for them a thrill of tenderness, and a power of expression belonging to no other dialect. They had a sacred preference for the English Sabbath and its solemnities, the hours and assemblies of English worship, and the fellowship of English hearts in the house of God; and, therefore, since they could not return to England to renew these sacred pleasures they separated themselves for a farther exile, and sought to find a land which should be their own, and a community with whom they could worship under their own vine and under their own fig-tree. They embarked for Plymouth Rock that they might plant a New England, and carried their own language, and its literature, and its stores of hallowed devotion, its treasures of theology, and its priceless gem the English Bible.

The noble principles which sustained their Puritan ancestry, separated themselves as a peculiar people. These stalwart sons of liberty were moral giants, fitted to mould the destinies of the world; they took precedence of their times, and antedated the history of freedom by centuries. They broadcast among other nations the seeds of liberty, civil and religious, and hedged round the plantations of an exotic race, by the principles of mutual right, popular suffrage, administrative responsibility, and the sovereignty of the people, as claiming for religion superiority to civil control, and bringing it within the prescriptive rights of Him alone who is King of kings, and whose right it is thus to reign. The wild woods of America heard and welcomed the heralds of such principles; and opening their bosoms to the exiles who sought their shores for refuge, gave them a home and ultimately a dominion which extends from the Atlantic to the Pacific, and travels in the greatness of its strength from the shores of Newfoundland to the utmost bounds of California.*

---

* "It is a mistake to say 'they were not men of letters;' that they could not defend themselves, or that they ever evinced any 'contempt for human learning.' We cannot admit the reproach against an Owen, a Howe, a Baxter, a Milton, or a Marvell. They might, indeed, have failed to cultivate the lofty and pompous eloquence which distinguished the hollow hypocrisy of Charles the First, and they might loathe and deprecate the easy good breeding in which the harlot court of Charles the Second paraded its vices. But their treasure was not concealed in a leaden chest — as witness Mrs. Lucy Hutchinson's 'Memoirs,' Andrew Marvell's 'Rehearsal Transposed,' and Milton's prose writings, or his 'Paradise Lost.' The men who roused England to resistance, who directed their measures through a long series of eventful years, who formed, out

The theology, books of devotion, psalmody, and experimental religion, the sacred literature, which flowed from Puritanic sources and in Nonconformist channels, were an heir-loom and a valued inheritance to these children of

---

of the most unpromising materials, the most martial army Europe had ever seen; who trampled down church, king, and aristocracy, because they resisted or waged a war of extermination; who, in the short intervals of domestic sedition and rebellion, formed and plotted by the monarchies of Europe, made the name of England terrible to every nation on the face of the earth, were no vulgar fanatics. To civil and military affairs they brought a coolness of judgment and an immutability of purpose which were the effects rather than the pretensions of religious zeal. The intensity of this feeling made them tranquil on every other matter. This one overpowering sentiment subjected to itself pity and revenge, ambition and fear. Religion was all; for it, death had lost its terrors and pleasure its charms. Their smiles, their tears, their raptures, and their sorrows were not in relation to the things of this world. Their minds, cleared from every vulgar passion and prejudice, had been raised by their generous enthusiasm above the influence of danger and corruption.

"The compound character of the Puritan has been exaggerated, though with a colour of truth, when, by an eloquent antithesis, it is said, he dared to set his foot on the scaffold of his king, yet prostrated himself before his Maker in the dust. Amid his self-abasement, his penitence, and grateful fervour, he sustained a lofty bearing—calm, inflexible, and sagacious. In his devotional retirement his prayers were mingled with groans and tears; in his meditations, if he heard not, yet had he communion with the songs of seraphs and the lyres of angels; and by the eye of faith he caught a vision of the land which was very far off, and beheld the eternal King in his beauty. It was no reproach to Fleetwood that he should cry in the bitterness of his soul because he thought, for a season, that God had hid his face from him. But it is a distortion to represent the generous Vane as thinking himself entrusted with the sceptre of the millennial year.

England. The reproductions from the pens of the Stoddarts, Mathers, Edwards, Hopkins, and Bellamys, proved the richness of the original seed and the carefulness of the culture, and served to endear the exiled race to their

---

" If ever a dominant party arose among men who, uninspired, might be presumed qualified, these were the men to consolidate religious empire, to determine a national religion, and establish a church with creed and formularies for the people. It is not wonderful that among them were millenarians contending for the recognition of a fifth monarchy, for the secular establishment of the kingdom of Messiah, or for banding together all the nations in solemn league and covenant as the sworn subjects of the Lord Jesus Christ. They had been nursed in the thoughts of doing battle for their religion, for their altars, and 'their hearths set free;' they had gone forth to war carrying their Bible in one hand and their broadsword in the other. Their camp was a sanctuary, their battalions companies of the saints, and their officers thought it no disparagement to be the pastors of their troop, the spiritual advisers and comforters of their armed subordinates, whom they accounted their brethren in the Lord, and admitted as fellow-heirs to the communion of believers. Their watchword was, 'For God and his church;' their war shout, 'The sword of the Lord and of Gideon;' and their song of victory, *Non nobis, Domine.* When the spoil was divided it was consecrated to the service of religion, and the power acquired was deemed a sacred trust deposited, for which the possessor was responsible to the King of kings. Fairfax and Manchester fought and prayed for Presbytery and the Covenant; Lockhart and Whitelock, ambassadors, carried with them into other lands the *insignia* of the conventicle and the *formulæ* of Puritan worship; Blake ploughed the main, carrying the flag of England in triumph over every sea, as the admiral of Cromwell, and the guardian of England; Sir Matthew Hale searched for precedents, took the engagements, and presided at the Common Pleas for the administration of justice; the Lord-lieutenant of Ireland, and the Governor of Dublin, severally communed as private members of an Independent and Baptist church, while

fatherland ; while Owen, Baxter, Watts, Doddridge, Erskine, Gillies, Whitfield, and Wesley maintained the intercourse. Religion consecrated the filial and parental bonds, but philosophy, history, science, law, and works of genius flowed in refreshing streams between the nascent states and the old country. And still the language is one, and serves to extend the influence of the Anglo-Saxon race, wherever its accents are understood. The spirit of British law has been infused, so far as it is good, into American jurisprudence, and the administration of it in both countries still bespeaks its lineage. The separation of the junior race into an Independent Republic has only stimulated both branches of the family to aspire to greater things. The younger government may have vaunted itself a little, but the older regimen has learned to relax its disposition to exact and overbear among its own subjects. The commerce which has grown between the two lands has served to increase the personal intercourse of the two families, and a mutual dependence for produce and supply tends to enrich the merchants on both sides of the Atlantic and make all feel their brotherhood and obligation.

England and America united, can contribute essentially to each other's welfare, and make each other an influence among all the nations of the earth. Speaking one language they render it a paramount vehicle of thought, not alone in their own territories or colonies, but also among all civilized peoples. Their evangelical missions, in co-operation or harmony, may extend a common Protestantism, and diffuse scriptural truth in every land to which their heralds are sent. The sister churches of both lands demonstrate the

a Baxter and a Peters, an Owen and a Howe, performed the duties of chaplains to the forces, preachers to the Houses of Parliament, and were numbered among the virtuous and the wise with whom Cromwell surrounded himself."—*Liberty of Conscience.* By Dr. MASSIE.

general unity of the faith; and the Catholic communion of Christians of various name, illustrates the cardinal unity and power of the truth. American missions in Greece, Turkey, Armenia, Persia, Burmah, China, India, and Polynesia; and Bible and tract societies sustained by American Christians, serve the same Lord with like organizations from Britain, and hasten the glorious advent of his kingdom. All this is appreciated and understood by the men of New England; and they would honestly deplore any circumstance which would threaten a severance of the ties of consanguinity and the fellowship of Christian peoples.

The Irish emigration is animated and moved by other influences and considerations; though there be many who have gone from Ireland in her earlier troubles, who have become true and loyal Americans, and would sustain a friendly intercourse with Britain for the good of all. They emigrated before O'Connell's time and found a home and field for profitable enterprise, in which they have established for their descendants wealth and associations, as well as religious fellowship, which identify them with the most respectable circles of society. There are others and later emigrants from the Green Isle who, though educated and qualified to move in literary circles, or in sacerdotal offices, can influence, through the press and among the humbler classes of their countrymen, the popular mind. They have a grudge against the nation which, as they believe, robbed their church, oppressed their people, persecuted their clergy, and enforced for them a servile and subordinate Union with England. They hate the Church and the Government as by law established in their old country; yet these are not the masses of Hibernio-Americans. From the year 1846, when the potatoe famine first threatened, there has been a tide of emigration, which increasingly flowed from Ireland till 1858; and has continued, though with abated force, yet in a powerful current, till the year 1863. For ten years, more

F

than 300,000 every year left Ireland, and for seven years
since more than 200,000 have followed yearly in their wake.
Many paused in their route on the shores of England, but
they did not count that their home.

The authorities at the Census Office in America may be
able to approximate to the actual number of Irish residents,
or the resident descendants of Irish people in the United
States; but it is hazardous for a casual observer to conjecture how many they are. It is not alone on the piers or
wharfs of New York, or Boston, or Baltimore, or wherever
labour is required in every transatlantic city, that they may
be found. The Roman Catholic Church of the United
States reckons 3,000,000, one million more than she computed twelve years ago; and her communion is chiefly
nourished by the Irish immigration. They are found in
Ohio, on the Mississippi, in Baltimore, and Boston, in the
lumber regions and in the quarries, driving cars and bearing
burdens everywhere. They habitually dread thé freedom of
the negro, lest he should become a competitor in the labour
market. There cannot be less than 5,000,000 of Irish,
or the descendants of Irish, resident in the United States,
though the former do not fill the ranks of its army. The
females are servants in families of all classes; and in hotels
and boarding-houses, from Eastport in Maine to St. Louis
on the Mississippi, they are the chamber-maids, nurses,
charwomen, and menials. And they are not a subordinate
power in these circles, since they often dictate terms, especially in their attendance upon priestly operations, or their
absence from family worship. Their only competitors in
families appear to be young German women. The Irish
vote has an influence in many of the elections, especially in
such municipalities as New York.

The old Spaniard of Florida, the Frenchmen of Louisiana
and in the higher Mississippi, the mixture of all classes in
California, and the Mormonites in Utah, a territory, the

German and Irish in Ohio, the British and Canadian in Michigan, the hereditary Kentuckian and Virginian, with their pretensions as the aristocratic slaveholders of former times, but now scattered in Illinois, Indiana, and Missouri, mingled as they all are by modern immigration from Britain, Germany, and New England, present the elements of society in the Western states, which it devolves on the educational system of America and the Home Mission apparatus of all evangelical churches in that land, to mould and elevate, and direct as loyal citizens.

There remain, besides all these, the slaves still in bondage, the coloured people who are free, and the recently freedmen. Fully to present the interests here involved, a few words are required as to the states still in loyal union with the north—Maryland, Delaware, Kentucky, and Missouri. The number of slaves reported in them at last census were 429,401. In the last-named state, a law was adopted at a convention, whose legality is disputed, fixing the emancipation of the slaves at several periods, beginning from 1870. A large number of the citizens in the state demand that an act of immediate emancipation shall be passed by the legislature. In the mean time, the 114,931 of slaves have been greatly reduced by a process which the fugitive slave law has not been able to check. The same tendency is manifest in Maryland, and the owners of such *property*, find its tenure uncertain and insecure. It would be hazardous to pursue the fugitives, and they are silent. Delaware held only 1798 slaves, the remnant of a decaying and hateful system. Kentucky talks little about her 225,483 slaves, and probably experiences influences from without holding her in constraint as to the treatment of her bondmen. There were, in 1860, free people of colour in these four states numbering 118,027. Their increase is a contemplation of the future. There are states, or portions of states, which have been practically reclaimed to the Union, where free people of colour reside, Tennessee, Western Virginia, Louisiana, Florida, and parts of Georgia. In the first four, with all abatements demanded of the census of 1860, we may reckon 56,879. The bondmen in Tennessee, Louisiana, and Florida were 669,190, and we may add 150,000 for Western Virginia, making a total of 819,190. The free people of colour in these two classes of states numbered 174,906, and the same class in the free states of the Union were reported 237,618, giving as objects of administrative care, 412,524, many of them retaining an affectionate solicitude for kindred and relatives still in bonds. The recently freedmen who have during the war or in virtue of the president's proclamation largely added to the number of free people of colour, perhaps 600,000 more, increase the multitude for whose right and liberties the North is bound to care.

The states still associated in rebellion, besides the nominal representations of Florida, Louisiana, Tennessee, and Virginia West, are Eastern Virginia, Texas, Alabama, Georgia, Mississippi, South Carolina, North Carolina, and Arkansas, by whom 2,501,920 human beings are held as chattels, and numbered as the herds of their flock. Arkansas is now, however, reclaimed. Besides these, 75,372, who were free people of colour, are held subject now to the caprice and martial law of Confederate rebels; who affirm that the normal condition of all people of colour is that of slavery, and that they have no rights which a white man is bound to respect. These states cover an area of 512,422 miles. From the breaking out of the insurrection, till August, 1863, the United States Government resumed its sway over and through a region of 302,000 square miles, which had been claimed by the South as secession territory. But since that month Generals Rosecranz and Grant have delivered all Tennessee, and entered the higher parts of Georgia. General Banks has led an army into Texas, cutting off French sympathizers from Southern co-operation, which is consolidating again the power of the Union in that vast state. The extent of territory in Tennessee and Texas alone is 282,021 square miles added to the territory previously reclaimed. The coasts and sounds of North Carolina, half of Mississippi, part of Alabama, the whole sea coast of Georgia, and South Carolina, and a large portion of the coast of Florida, are also held by the ships and army of the Federal Government. It has been said of South territory that "in happiness of climate, adapted to productions of special value, in exhaustless motive power distributed throughout its space, in natural highways by more than fifty navigable rivers never closed by the rigours of winter, and in a stretch of coast along ocean and gulf, indented by hospitable harbours, the whole presenting incomparable advantages for that true civilization where agriculture, manufactures, and commerce, both domestic and foreign, blend—in all these respects, the Slave states excel the Free states, whose climate is often churlish, whose motive powers are less various, whose navigable rivers are fewer, and often sealed by ice, and whose coast, while less in extent and with fewer harbours, is often perilous from storm and cold." Mr. Charles Sumner, from whom this extract is taken, after completing a comparison between the slave and free states, by the testimony of witnesses which he designates as "unerring and passionless *figures*," concludes a summary in the following sentence :—

" Thus, at every point, is the character of slavery more and more manifest, rising and dilating into an overshadowing barbarism, darkening the whole land. Through its influence, population, values of all kinds, manufactures, commerce, railroads, canals, charities, the post-office, colleges, professional schools, academies, public schools, newspapers, periodicals, books, authorship, inventions, are all stunted, and, under a government which professes to be founded on the intelligence of the people, one in twelve of the white adults in the region of slavery is officially reported as unable to read and write. Never was the saying of Montesquieu more triumphantly verified, that countries are not cultivated by reason of their fertility, but by reason of their liberty. To this truth, the slave states constantly testify by every voice. Liberty is the powerful agent which drives the plough, the spindle, and the keel; which opens avenues of all kinds, which inspires charity, which awakens a love of knowledge, and supplies the means of gratifying it. Liberty is the first of schoolmasters."

The white population reported in the census for 1860 resident in the Confederate states, omitting Tennessee, Florida, Louisiana, and Western Virginia, are represented as 4,065,052. There may be among them some who were citizens of the excepted states, and there may be volunteers from other lands who are usually called mercenaries; but the casualties of war have diminished the total number probably by 200,000, while the 2,500,000 slaves in their plantations must give occupation to their guardians and taskmasters. They are called to contend in martial array against more than 22,000,000 of a Northern population, which is every day gaining accessions from other lands. The cause for which they contend is the perpetuation and extension of slavery, and it may serve a good purpose to listen to the testimony of some who well know, as they saw and experienced the system before the rebellion commenced. One who has only skimmed the border of the region, or passed through the luxurious dwellings of those who wallowed in the indulgences contributed by the field-slave, need not pretend to describe what slavery is. "The denial of all rights in the slave can be sustained only by a disregard of other rights common to the whole community, whether of the person, of the press, or of speech. Where this exists there can be but one supreme law, to which all other laws, legislative or social, are subordinate, and this is the pretended law of slavery. All these things must be manifest in slave-masters; and yet, unconscious of their true condition, they make boasts which reveal still further the unhappy influence. Barbarous standards of conduct are unblushingly avowed; the swagger of a bully is called chivalry, a swiftness to quarrel is called courage, the bludgeon is adopted as the substitute for argument, and assassination is lifted to be one of the fine arts. Long ago it was fixed certain that the day which made man a slave 'took half his worth away'—words from the ancient harp of Homer, resounding through long generations. Yet nothing here is said of the human being at the other end of the chain. To aver that on this same day all *his* worth is taken away might seem inconsistent with exceptions which we gladly recognize; but, alas! it is too clear, both from reason and from evidence, that, bad as slavery is for the slave, it is worse for the master." Such is the testimony of Mr. C. Sumner, whom the "bludgeon" of a planter felled to the ground, and rendered an unconscious victim, because he dared to utter such sentiments on the floor of the Congress Hall. Colonel Mason, a slave-master from Virginia, gave his evidence in debate on the adoption of the national constitution, when he asserted, "Slavery discourages arts and manufactures. The poor despise labour when performed by slaves; they prevent the emigration of whites, who really enrich and strengthen a country. They produce the most pernicious effect on manners; every master of slaves is born a petty tyrant; they bring the judgment of Heaven upon a country." Mr. Jefferson spoke out in terms which have strong significance what he *felt*. "There must be an unhappy influence on the manners of our people, produced by the existence of slavery among us. The whole commerce between master and slave is a perpetual exercise of the most boisterous passions; the most unremitting despotism on the one part, and degrading submissions on the other. Our children see this, and learn to imitate it. The man must be a prodigy who can retain his manners and morals undepraved by such circumstances; and with what execration should the statesman be loaded who, permitting one half of the citizens thus to trample on the rights of the others, transforms those into despots and these into enemies, destroys the morals of the one part and the *amor patriæ* of the other. With the morals of the people their industry also is destroyed." Opinions, however, may require to some the corroboration of facts, and the "Georgia Messenger" presented one which spoke volumes; though it be but one of thousands. "Run away—my man Fountain; has holes in his ears, a scar on the right side of his forehead, has been shot in the hind part of his legs, is marked on his back with the whip. Apply to Robert Beasley." Another advertisement, and how full of insinuated licentiousness to the infamous libertine! "For sale— An accomplished and handsome lady's maid. She is just sixteen years of age; was raised in a genteel family in Maryland, and is now proposed to be sold, not for any fault, but simply because the owner has no further use for her. A note directed to C. D., Gadsby's Hotel, will receive prompt attention." The sated voluptuary wishes to sell his victim!

In further illustration, a slave master's recipe to cure run-away slaves will suffice to satisfy—to horrify the mind of the reader:

"I can tell you how you can break a nigger of running away. There was an old fellow I used to know in Georgia that always cured his so. If a nigger ran away, when he caught him he would bind his knee over a log and fasten him so that he could not stir; then he would take a pair of pincers and pull one of his toe-nails out by the roots, and tell him that if he ever run away again he would pull out two of them, and if he run away again after that he told him he would pull out four of them, and so on, doubling each time. He never had to do it more than twice; it always cured them."

The intermediate agents of slavery, or its master, are

the overseer, the trader, and hunter. The first, with his bloody lash, himself belonging to the class, which is "last and lowest, most abject, degraded, unprincipled." The second, who knows no distinction between a "brood mare" and female slave, and who, to produce his crop of human flesh, promptly converts the plantation into a *grand mena-gerie*, where men are reared for the market as oxen are for the shambles; while the slave-hunter is not ashamed to advertise his brutal *bloodhound*.

"I have two of the finest dogs for catching negroes in the south-west. They can take the trail twelve hours after the negro has passed, and catch him with ease. I live four miles south-west of Bolivar, on the road leading from Bolivar to Whitesville. I am ready at all times to catch run-away negroes.—DAVID TURNER."

Thus, since slavery became a political passion and slave-masters began to throw aside all disguise, the bloodhound has become the representative of their barbarism in one of its worst forms, while in pursuit of a fellow-man asserting his inborn title to himself.

A single sentence will serve to introduce another aspect of the influence which the system asserts. Through the bludgeon, the revolver, and the bowie-knife the slave-master governs his plantation, and secretly armed with these, he enters the world: they are his congenial companions; to wear them is his pride; to use them becomes a passion, almost a necessity: they regulate his sense of dependence and morals. A duel is not dishonourable; a contest known as a "street fight" is not shameful to slave-masters, and modern imitators of Cain have a mark set upon them, not for condemnation, but for compliment and approval. Violence is so much the practice, if not the rule, that even the governors of slave-states have found it expedient to denounce the consequences. "We long to see the day," said the Governor of Kentucky in 1837, "when the law will assert its majesty and stop the wanton destruction of life which almost daily occurs within the jurisdiction of the commonwealth. Men slaughter each other with almost perfect impunity. A species of common-law has grown up in Kentucky, which, were it written down, would in all civilized countries cause it to be re-christened in derision, the *land of blood*." The Governor of Alabama confesses in the same year: "We hear of homicides in different parts of the state continually, and yet have few convictions, and still fewer executions. Why do we hear of stabbings and shootings almost daily in some part or other of our state?" The mode of such conflicts is described by Mr. Sumner: "Two or more men, armed to the teeth, meet in the streets, at a court-house, or a tavern, shoot at each other with revolvers, then gash each other with knives, close, and roll upon the ground, covered with dirt and blood, struggling and stabbing till death, prostration, or surrender puts an end to the conflict." Such is a truthful feature of the chivalry of the South! and such are the effects and manifestations of that system, upon which as a corner-stone the present rebellious confederacy have resolved to erect their new republic.

The strife that now rages in America was not the result of any quarrel between states, or between the coloured people and slave masters, but rather it arose from the disposition of Southern planters to resist the Federal Government, which they anticipated would exercise a favourable influence on the emancipation of the slave. Hence the wise policy of bringing in the sympathies and military subserviency of the coloured people to aid in deciding the conflict. The freedom which has been conferred on thousands of slaves, and the enrolment of tens of thousands of freed-men in the ranks of the United States army, were judicious and beneficent measures, not merely as a penalty on the rebels, but as creating an element of strength for the cause of freedom in the North. It is not probable that the farmers, mechanics, and tradesmen in the United States will prefer to continue a soldier's life, even when war has ceased. The drill and subserviency of military life would be irksome to the citizen free man. It is, however, a step higher to the coloured man, who has been a slave, and is not uncongenial to his past habits of servitude. He is imitative, and amenable to authority, and the idea of his liberty will be identified with the success of the army; but as a trained soldier he cannot be returned to slavery with impunity. It has been urged by men having influence, that at least 200,000 coloured troops be enrolled, not merely to fight present battles, but also to garrison Southern forts and fulfil such duties as are likely to arise from the lingering animosity of subdued rebels. But such a number of men can only be expected from a population four or five times as many more. Their wives and families rising into manhood will claim the considerate provision of governing authorities in their future policy for the whole country. Already is the honour of the State pledged to coloured freed-men, as well as to all slaves affected by the President's proclamation, as far as it can or may reach them. No course could bring more enduring infamy upon statesmen than any desertion of the cause of oppressed and confiding millions, in departing from the pledge solemnly given, after protracted consultation and warning; and the only measure of deeper disgrace would be the portion of a nation of free-men who would either tempt or countenance their rulers in belying their solemn promise of emancipation. Mr. Abraham Lincoln will not be a party to such abandonment of the negro's cause. The North may not have been so prompt or unequivocal in accepting his measures or means of emancipation; but the Republican party and the honourable Democrats have endorsed it as a *fait accompli.* There may seem points which rival jealousy

may detect, of short-coming in the anti-slavery action of
the North ; but it is a poor demonstration of anti-slavery
zeal in men professing friendship for the slave, to expend
their wit and influence in captious suspicions and ungener-
ous insinuations, that North Americans have not always or
spontaneously sought the abolition of slavery. Rather
would the honest philanthropist and Christian emancipationist be forward to help on the faltering or repentant
coadjutor in the cause of freedom, and to remove difficulties
out of his way. The English anti-slavery champions in
1832, and the anti-corn law league in 1846, accepted the
co-operation of former antagonists, and strengthened the
hands of Sir Robert Peel and his small band of converts
to the principles of Free Trade. So will the honest friend
of the American negro hail the co-operation, and gratefully
acknowledge the late but avowed convictions of hundreds
of thousands of citizens in America, who now rally round
the banner of immediate and unconditional emancipation.

The religious element pervading the American mind
cannot be overlooked in the present crisis of the country.
Some of the largest denominations were agitated by the
question of slavery years before the issues now contemplated came up before the most thoughtful. The Methodist
Episcopal Church was divided south and north, and that
division was attended with accusations of spoliation and
the threatening of protracted litigation. The Presbyterian
Church was rent in twain, and the old and new school
appreciated with much discordant controversy and diversity
the claims of the slave. The commotion gave to Congregationalists in the newer states an extended influence,
and modified the interchange of ministerial services.
Among Baptist churches the subject was keenly agitated,
and part held with the slave, and part held with his oppressor. The reformed and united Presbyterians generally
preserved their communion unpolluted by the contagion.

Episcopalian clergy and bishops were variously influenced and divided. This subject will come up again more at length. An opinion has been expressed that the revival which visited Protestant religionists of all denominations during 1858 prepared many devout minds for a more tender consideration of the claims of the slave, and a more steadfast determination to make sacrifices in the path of recognized duty. Even in the Fulton-street prayer meeting, in New York, a prayerful and earnest feeling was cherished and expressed on the subject. It is affirmed by well-informed episcopal Methodists, that a greater number of members of their body than of any other are enrolled in the United States army. It is well known that ministers of the old school Presbyterians have recently identified themselves with anti-slavery agitation, and opened their churches for public assemblies when the subject would be discussed. Religious communities, though no longer ranking as state churches, exercise great influence among the people from their wealth as corporate bodies. So is it with the Dutch Protestant Reformed Church, with some episcopalian incorporations, and such bodies as the Roman Catholic Jesuits and the Trappists. In their measure they can all affect local, and even more general movements, to which representative candidates cannot be indifferent.

It is an article in the creed of some Northern politicians that the Southern confederacy owes much of its powers and consolidation to the clergy and ladies of the South, because they so strongly sympathize in favour of slavery. The impression has led to searchings of heart among friends of the Northern Union and the abolition of slavery, that if the church were sound in principle on this subject the government would be strong. Albert Barnes, in the time when he more prominently agitated this subject than he has done lately, affirmed "that there was no power *out* of the church which could sustain slavery an hour, if it was not sustained *in* it." There were frequent and animated discussions in the A. B. C. F. for missions in the Bible Society and Tract Society, owing to pro-slavery action or non-resistance. Other societies were organized to counteract their procedure. But the change which has pervaded all religious associations is so marked and favourable to emancipation, that it is fondly predicted the clergy and the ladies in the North will unite not only in supporting the Federal government, but also in washing out the disgrace of slavery from the national reputation, and in establishing the claims of the coloured classes to equal benefits from law and government, and the full enjoyment of all the advantages of the American constitution for men and citizens.

CHAPTER III.

THE extended influence of anti-slavery sentiment in the
United States, in the year 1863, is a *phenomenon* which
suggests further inquiry. Nations do not leap into revolutions, or become the theatre of great events, without preliminary and adequate influences. Causes, however latent,
and processes of preparation, however unobserved, operate
in the minds of the people. Thus has Italy become the
arena for the march of freedom, and thus are the present
struggles in Prussia and the hopeful though bloody strife
in Poland schooling these nations for a higher position in
Europe. The time of Austria or Russia is not yet. France
had a tedious course, beginning with the Edict of Nantes,
the events of its revocation, the butcheries of St. Bartholomew, the luxury, licentiousness, and despotism of the
Grand Monarque, the hollow hypocrisies and fawning
flatteries of the fifteenth Louis; the feeble, vacillating and
gaudy extravagances of Louis the Sixteenth and his queen;
while a corrupt priesthood and pretentious hierarchy left
the people a prey to infidel philosophy and aspiring demagogues; until the revolutions, conventions, and exasperated
victims of oppression overturned the altars and the throne,
and opened the path for Napoleon, his code of laws, and
imperial ascendancy. The seat of liberty has not yet been
there established in righteousness; but there is progress.
England passed through the times and tyranny of the

Tudors, and arbitrary efforts for despotism of the Stuarts ;
before the Puritanic, Parliamentary, and Nonconformist
contests, sufferings, and virtues gave hope of the maturity
of a constitutional government. Both these great nations
had a baptism of blood to inaugurate freedom.

America is no exception to the same law, however Republican her Constitution. The occasion of the struggle
is identical in her and them ; the liberty of all usurped by
a privileged class. The Dutch captain who, in 1620,
introduced to Virginia the first cargo of negroes, did not
settle the question of slavery. The submission of Americans to the element of slavery as a power in the state was
gradual and in the midst of much opposition from enlightened patriots and statesmen ; and the process of her partial delivery from its ascendancy has been and must be
through much tribulation. The path of a nation's repentance does not lie through the vales of paradise, though
leading to a better state ; and where repentance comes not,
there is judicial compensation. The ten plagues of Egypt
opened the way for Israel's escape from thraldom, but were
the precursors to the annihilation of Pharaoh's host in the
Red Sea. The sunny side of Southern slavery has been
painted by weak, wicked, or interested visitors who have
brought back reports of the happy and contented condition
of the slave population, which the writer witnessed. He
had been in the parlour, not in the kitchen ; in the con-
servatory, not in the cane or cotton-tree field. He had
not followed the gang under the driver or overseer ; it
would have been a poor pastime, uncomfortable or intolerable in a cold or hot day. He had not been invited, and
he had not been so intrusive as to go unasked to the negro
quarters or inquired of the wearers what clothes were worn
in the fields, what food provided, how and when it was
allowed to be eaten, when, how, and where were the indo-
lent, perverse, and refractory punished. But the emissaries

and spies of abolitionism were becoming too inquisitive and prying, and the impression was apprehended as likely to prevail that fancy pictures, presented by apologists for the South, were a violation of truth and a caricature of facts. Therefore it was, numerous instances occurred of arbitrary and pro-slavery pretension to the administration of justice. John L. Brown was seen walking with a young coloured woman in South Carolina; he was accused of having attempted to aid her escape, was tried and sentenced to death by the governor of the state. Tidings of the sentence reached England. Lord Brougham brought the fact forward in the House of Lords; indignation at the atrocious sentence was expressed at public meetings in Edinburgh and elsewhere. British public opinion aided other influences. The Carolina governor's sentence was commuted to fifty lashes, and afterwards the lashes were remitted on condition the innocent man should leave the state. This was in 1844. Two years before this date the Rev. C. T. Torrey had been imprisoned at Annapolis, Maryland, for taking part with the coloured people; but during his incarceration he found time to reduce to a system what has since been called " the Underground Railway ;" whereby the fugitive was entrusted to one accredited agent after another, till he was conveyed from the slave states to Canada. By his own direct instrumentality he knew he had liberated four hundred human beings from a state many times worse than death. On the 25th of June, 1844, he was arrested at Baltimore on the charge of helping slaves to escape. After much delay, and three days' trial, on the testimony of witnesses whose perjury was manifest, he was declared guilty, sentenced to six years' imprisonment in the penitentiary. After protracted suffering, he died, on the 9th May, 1846, a martyr to the cause of the slave. About the same time, for the same offence, Messrs. Thompson, Work, and Burr were sentenced to three years' imprisonment, while their families were exposed to poverty and their own health was greatly injured. Captain Walker had permitted seven slaves to sail in his vessel from Pensacola in Florida: his vessel was captured—the slaves returned to their bondage—Captain Walker imprisoned till his life was endangered, was tried, convicted, and placed in the pillory, when the letters S. S. (slave-stealer) were *branded* on his hand with a red-hot iron. His was "the Branded Hand" for freedom's sake.

The election of a republican President who had been free to utter the sentiment that a nation could not prosper or be at peace which was "half slave and half free," brought to a culmination causes which were previously in operation. It is a perversion, which only a dishonest abettor of slavery could deliberately commit, to represent the election of President Lincoln a fraud upon the South, on the ground that he had previous to his candidature expressed himself violently opposed to anything which would disturb the peace of the Southern people, and had not only declared his intention not to interfere with their domestic institution, but had commenced his administration with that determination. The public speaker who can argue thus, and the fact notoriously before him, that Carolina had seceded, and the convention at Montgomery had inaugurated the Confederacy, prior to Mr. Lincoln's occupation of the Presidential chair, will dare to say anything. But we must look elsewhere, and search for causes further back and deeper, into the ramifications of American society to ascertain the springs of conduct which ultimately developed the reasons of the conflict. The constant pressure of the slave power in the legislature and upon the policy of their creatures, the presidents, was intensely directed to the increase of slave states in the Union.

The annexation of Texas in 1846, and the war with Mexico in 1847, were Southern measures, and added greatly to the slave power, as they were both designed to do. Cuba has been coveted, conspired for, and sought to be secured by purchase in the same interest; and the filibustering expeditions which exposed Americans to destruction and disgrace, were promoted for the same object. The state procedure in the South had in view their "institution" when they laboured for the suppression of free speech, free schools, and a free press. Nothing should be said or made known about operations and offences of slavery. Legal offences it was not acknowledged to have. The influence was secured of unscrupulous advocates and abettors of the system in churches and church courts, in religious organizations, in courts of law and in Congress. The vigilance of espionage was exercised, and the terrors of lynch law were invoked. The party were disappointed by the political attitude of California, which they had hoped to have brought into the Union as a slave state; but this only stimulated them to more vigorous and unscrupulous means. The Missouri Compromise had been accepted by the slave power, though it did not afterward work to their satisfaction. In the year 1820, the eastern portion of territory belonging to Massachusetts was yielded to the disposal of the general government to be organized as a free state; the slave power opposed it, unless a new slave state should be also constituted on the banks of the Missouri and Mississippi. This was opposed by the North with a threat to dissolve the Union unless it should be allowed as a condition annexed that no slave state should be organized within the parallel of 36° 30′ north latitude, and west of the Missouri; the northern side of the line being held sacred to freedom. The vote on this occasion did not however bind a future Congress. The act was passed in March 1820; but further negotiation was rendered necessary by a provision in the state constitution presented to the next meeting of Congress. The Missourians complied with the conditions thence required, and they were admitted to the Union, August, 1821, by the President's proclamation. Furtive attempts to extend the area of slavery were made, and with success. In 1836 a fertile addition to the *west* of the line was obtained by a violation of treaties with the Indians. Smuggled through Congress as the bill was, the North was not timely enough apprised of it so as to prevent the sanction of law. But hence originated much of the strife in Kansas. In 1853 and 1854, an attempt was made to create two new slave states out of lands solemnly consecrated to liberty by the " Compromise ;" the Kansas Nebraska bill was passed, nullifying the enactment designing to facilitate the organization of states bearing these names and appropriated to slavery, in the Senate on the 4th of March, 1854, and in the House of Representatives on the 15th of May. Mr. W. H. Seward and Mr. C. Sumner vigorously, but unsuccessfully, opposed the measure of enactment ; but the Northern, chiefly New England people, frustrated the device by occupying territory in Kansas, and fighting against the Missouri border ruffians. Nebraska remains a territory and Kansas is a free state. The compromise was repudiated by the South, yet the guilty parties were not strengthened by their scheme.

Emigration flowed rapidly into Kansas both from North and South. In the North, societies were formed to promote the migration of anti-slavery settlers, that they might uphold the cause of freedom. But for a time the majority was favourable to slavery. Missouri bordered Kansas, and her population was pro-slavery, and jealously guarded the interests of Southern conspirators. Every obstacle was thrown in the way of Northern emigrants. They were driven back ; they were tarred and feathered ; their claims and allotments of land were seized ; their cabins were burned down ; they were often ordered by committees of

Southern emigrants, or the interlopers from Missouri, to leave the territory at once under penalty of death. A paragraph of a speech from one of the latter class will illustrate their mode of procedure. He had assumed the title and authority of a general :—

"I tell you to mark every scoundrel among you, who is the least tainted with abolitionism, or free-soil-ism, and exterminate him. Neither give nor take quarter from the —— rascals. . . . . I advise you one and all, to enter every election district in Kansas in defiance of Ruder (the acting governor) and his myrmidons, and vote at the point of the bowie-knife and revolver. . . . . It is enough that the slave-holding interest wills it—from which there is no appeal."

For months was this conflict maintained, and President Pierce knew it and winked at the barbarities perpetrated in the behalf of slavery. Atrocious murders were allowed to pass unnoticed. The polls for election purposes were kept closed at various place; never once did the Federal authorities interfere to preserve the purity of the ballot-box, or the right of free speech. A clergyman had said in private conversation, that he was a *Free State* man : he was tarred, feathered, and sent down the river on a raft— Federal office-holders leading and encouraging the rioters. Yet the Northern emigrants persevered in the struggle, suffered, and prayed, stood by each other until their minority triumphed; and Kansas was admitted a Free State into the Union by Mr. Lincoln, January 29, 1861.

Nebraska, with an increasing population, already more than 30,000, remains a territory of the United States, but a law has passed the legislature, and received the President's signature, that the Territories shall be for ever free of slavery.

A mode of benevolent and philanthropic interference in behalf of the bondmen, which has not only illustrated the system prevalent in slave states, but has awakened increasing sympathy with their lot, and abhorrence of the power under which they are held, is the attempt to impart the knowledge of letters, and an acquaintance with the Word of God for their salvation. Kentucky and Maryland are the only slave states in which it is lawful to give the bondman any instruction in letters. But, in 1834, the Synod of Kentucky gave this testimony : " *Throughout the whole land,* so far as we can learn, there is but one school in which, during the week, slaves can be taught." A delegate of Virginia expressed his judgment in the following words : " If we could extinguish the capacity (in slaves) to see the light, our work would be completed. They would then be on a level with the beasts of the field, and we should be safe ! I am not certain that we would not do so, if we could find out the process, and that on the plea of necessity." In the same spirit is the legislation of Alabama, Louisiana, Georgia, North and South Carolina. Virginia alone does not interdict the *owner* from teaching his slaves to read. South Carolina discriminates the several persons whose guilt shall be punished, each in their respective degrees— a free *white* person, a free person of *colour*, a slave, severally as follows : a fine and imprisonment ; fifty lashes and fine ; and fifty lashes. But farther, if any slave or free person of colour shall keep a school for teaching a slave or *free person of colour*, the same punishments shall be inflicted. In an atmosphere so darkened, Miss Prudence Crandall, whose home was in the village of Canterbury, in a slave state, advertised, March 1833, that she would receive into her female boarding school, "young ladies and little *misses of colour.*" The parents of some of her pupils had already objected to their children being associated with children of colour, if more than one little girl of very light colour, already in the school, were admitted. A town meeting was called on the appearance of the advertisement, and the school was denounced. The state passed a law making it a penal offence to establish any school for the instruction of coloured persons not inhabitants of the state, etc. Miss Crandall persevered with her school, was imprisoned, bailed out, tried, but escaped by a disagreement of the jury; was again prosecuted and convicted, appealed to a higher court, bore up against a long prosecution. Her fences were pulled down, her wells filled up, local traders refused to supply her with goods, her pupils were refused admission to the churches, her windows repeatedly broken at night, the parents of her pupils menaced, and she was at last compelled to retire from the place.

Mrs. Beecher Stowe has described the case of Miss Miner, which further illustrates the virtues of a heroine and the baseness of the slaveholder. "Miss Miner has been for many years a heroic and most indefatigable labourer for the coloured people of Washington. She has been gifted by nature with singular talents for this work, and endowed by God's grace with a courage, zeal, and devotion, such as are given to but few. When her school was yet in its infancy it excited bitter opposition. A man one day called upon her, and told her that a mob was organized to destroy her school-room, as they were determined that her school should no longer exist. 'What good will it do to destroy my school-room?' was her reply; 'I shall only get another and go right on.' 'But,' said he, 'we will frighten your scholars, so that they will not dare to come to you.' 'No, you will not,' said she; 'wherever I dare to go to teach they will dare to come to learn.' Then, fixing her eyes very decidedly on the man, she added, 'You may tell your associates that destroying any number of school-houses will not stop my school; you cannot stop it unless you take my life.' The man retired, and the school-room remained unmolested. This school has exerted a great influence on the minds of many slaveholders, who on visiting it have been struck with the capabilities, under education, of the very

people whom they hold in slavery." Amidst trials and difficulties this school continued for many years; Mrs. Stowe
appropriated to its support 1000 dollars of the "Penny
Offering" fund. Mrs. M. Douglas, of Norfolk, Virginia, was
a respectable widow lady, who, with her daughter had settled there from South Carolina. They were quietly and
honourably maintaining themselves, and doing deeds of
charity. About the end of the year 1851 Mrs. Douglas had
met with some intelligent little coloured children, who
were earnestly desirous of learning to read. She offered
the services of her daughter to help them; and, after a time,
finding they made great progress, it was decided to open a
regular school for little coloured children. This was an
entirely satisfactory undertaking, and for nearly a year the
little ones came with great pleasure to learn to read and
write, and evinced great aptitude. On the 9th of May,
1853, under the authority of the Mayor, constables were
sent to arrest Mrs. Douglas, her daughter, and their
eighteen or twenty coloured pupils. The latter were dispersed, and Mrs. Douglas and her daughter were remanded
for examination. Mrs. Douglas was quite ignorant of the
laws of the state, which prohibited the teaching of coloured
children; nevertheless, when summoned for trial, she
pleaded her own defence with a dignity most unexpected
by the prosecuting party. She was sentenced to a month's
imprisonment, and her sufferings and privations connected
therewith were not bounded by the length of her sentence.

The story of Lane Seminary gives collateral illustration,
and is worthy a place among conspiring *causes*. Dr. Lyman
Beecher was president; forty theological students attended
the lectures, most of them about the age of twenty-one
years, and many of them sons and brothers of slaveholders.
They felt the institution must exercise an influence not
alone in Cincinnati, where it was situated, but over the
Western states, and even on the condition of the two slave

states which bordered Ohio. They aimed, therefore, to
sustain Lane Seminary, as occupying high moral ground.
They recognized as a principle "that *free* discussion with
corresponding effort is a DUTY, and, of course, a *right*," and
applied it to the lectures they received—to Missions,
Sunday-schools, Temperance, and *Slavery*. They decided,
after discussion, that slavery is a sin, and ought immediately to be renounced; and on this conclusion they *acted*.
Here, however, they met obstacles which became insuperable in their relation to the seminary. Slavery was *forbidden*
as a theme of farther consideration by the faculty, and the
power of expulsion was conferred on the Executive Committee of the College for any violation of the interdict.
The proximity to slave states and the dependence of the
institution for at least part of its resources upon the good-
will of slaveholders were regarded as prudential motives.
Two of the forty theological, and five of the sixty classical
students succumbed to authority, and remained. The president and faculty testified to the respectful and orderly
conduct of the dissidents who, with sad and unmurmuring
resolution, renounced their place in the seminary, where
they had enjoyed facilities for acquiring useful instruction;
but a solemn conviction of duty prompted, and a calm survey of the difficulties in their path did not appal them.
The lives of some might have been imperilled had they returned home, and the resources of many were cut off, but
they took up their cross. Forty students of the number
sought to found another institution, where freedom of
thought and speech might be secure, and where students of
all conditions and colour might be educated. In the north-
east of Ohio they repaired to the forest, cleared a tract of
land, and raised for shelter a building made of pieces of
rough wood laid one upon the other. Without endowment,
and with little pecuniary help, they toiled through the
winter of 1834 and 1835, and commenced the college of

Oberlin. Their difficulties, though great, were overcome, but they established a reputation which attracted men, learned, noble, and of disinterested minds, who offered to become teachers of such pupils. The tutors laid aside their upper garments, toiled in the forest for one part, and gave lectures in another part of each day. Applicants, men and women, sought admission, to be qualified as teachers of coloured people, and their answer when told there were no funds was, " We will provide for ourselves if you will let us stay." A brick house was erected containing ninety-two rooms; a practical farmer superintended the industry of the young men, and the young women cared for the dairy, the household, and the clothes, while time was given to all to acquire learning fitting them to act as teachers of others; simple fare sufficed such aspirants for usefulness, and few were sick. When the clothing of one was worn bare and he had to go abroad, another lent his garment. One student laid down his all for the institution· A farmer drove over a cow from a distance—the only gift he had to bestow; another living eleven miles off accommodated the new candidates who could not be received into the establishment—for a year and a half he boarded and lodged *seventy.* Another of like spirit welcomed thirty students and their professor for the same length of time. A noble woman, subdued by her toil and care, died with generous resignation, yielding to the cause heart and hand in co-operation with her husband. Thus Oberlin rose, situated within about thirty miles of Cleveland, and survives as an ornament to Ohio. In 1858 its liberal principles were tested. A poor fugitive slave was decoyed in the adjoining fields, and almost carried off, by kidnappers, to slavery; the students, joined with others, rushed to the rescue, delivered the victim of oppression by sending him to Canada. A professor, ministers, students, teachers, and other citizens were imprisoned and severely fined; but the spirit which

Oberlin inspires, and God who sustains the right and the cause of the needy, upheld the martyrs, and the prison gave forth testimonies to freedom, and the cause of the slave, which brought honour upon Oberlin and prayers for its prosperity.

The students who worked while they pursued their academic course were not unwilling to work for the same cause when they had finished. Amos Dresser, one of their number, acting as a colporteur, and thus circulating the Bible and other congenial books, proceeded from Cincinnati southward to Tennessee. At Nashville he was arrested on the suspicion of being an Abolitionist. He was guiltless in action, as he had not spoken to a slave nor distributed books among free people of colour. Sixty-two of the inhabitants, among whom were seven *elders* of a Presbyterian church, sat as a *vigilance* committee to examine him, and his trunk. Three anti-slavery volumes for his own reading, and some newspapers of abolition character, put in to preserve the volumes from chafing each other, and his private journal and letters, were found; the chairman could not decipher these last, but he affirmed they were " evidently very hostile to slavery." The committee agreed he had broken no law, but resolved to make *law for the occasion* to protect slavery against attacks from opinion. The traveller was found guilty on three points : belonging to an Abolition society in another state, possessing books of anti-slavery tendency, and being presumed to have circulated some of these in his journey. The judges had debated whether the offender should be sentenced to thirty-nine or a hundred lashes, or death by hanging. He was, however, condemned to receive twenty lashes in the market-place, and just as the chimes were ushering in the Sabbath morning, by torch-light the brutal sentence was inflicted. Mr. Dresser bore the suffering without fear, and with thanksgiving, the utterance of which was drowned in oaths, and cries of "stop his praying." A considerate inhabitant stealthily received him to his house, washed and dressed his wounds, and sent him on his way disguised.

Another of the forty students at Lane Seminary was Theodore Weld, who continues the firm and unflinching advocate of the slave by his pen, his social position, and by his *voice* when he is able to use it. His wife, Angelina Grimke, with a grace and eloquence peculiar to women when wont to address public audiences, pleads the same cause, though the daughter of a Southern judge, and sister of a Southern slaveholder. Her well-weighed testimony is that "no one who has not been *an integral part of a slave-holding community* can have any idea of its abominations. It is a whited sepulchre full of dead men's bones, and all uncleanness." At their brother's death, she and her sister became heirs to his estates. They strove by all means to ameliorate the condition of the slaves conveyed by inheritance. They attempted, in defiance of law, to educate them. But finding that the benefits of freedom cannot be imparted to slavery, they surrendered all prospects of gain at the dictate of conscience. They freed their slaves, enabled them to provide for themselves in a free state, and themselves retired to live on the remnant of their former opulence. From such retirement, the devout spirit of self-sacrifice comes forth in a "hope" which "gleams across my mind that *our* blood will be spilt instead of the slaveholder's; our lives will be taken, and theirs spared. I say a hope, for of all things, I desire to be spared the anguish of seeing our beloved country desolated with the horrors of a servile war."

Reubin Crandall, Esq., M.D., of Westchester county, a gentleman of high literary and scientific acquirements, manners and deportment alike honourable to the scholar, and a devoted Christian, was reputed one of the purest, most disinterested, and amiable of men. But, like his sister, his sympathies were favourable to freedom for the coloured people. He had settled in Washington as a teacher of botany, and was arrested, and thrown into prison, August 11, 1835, charged with circulating incendiary publications, intending to excite the slaves to insurrection. Kept in jail for eight months, he was brought to trial before Judge Cranch. It was proved that he had in his trunk some anti-slavery pamphlets and papers, but that the latter were used for wrapping his botanical specimens in, and that, on request, he had lent to a white citizen one of the pamphlets. The " incendiary " matter read in court from these papers were articles against slavery, and in favour of the right of the free coloured people to reside in America. The effort to prove more, or even that he was a member of the Anti-slavery Society failed. Yet was it urged by the district attorney that the jury should find him guilty, with a view to capital punishment. The verdict returned was "not guilty," but the prosecutors had done their cruel work. Eight months' close confinement in a damp dungeon, un-tried, unguilty, and with spotless integrity struck the arrow of a lingering consumption in his system, of which he died while trying to recover by change of climate. Though ad-judged innocent, himself a free citizen of the great Re-public, yet was he effectually murdered on the national hearth-stone in the Federal districts, under exclusive "juris-diction of Congress," because *suspected* of having dissemi-nated publications hostile to slavery.

Elijah P. Lovejoy was a citizen of Maine, and prac-tised law at St. Louis. Afterward desiring to enter the ministry, though a graduate of Westerville College, he finished his preparations at Princeton, N. J. The Sunday-school Union employed him as their agent, but he was sub-sequently appointed editor of a religious paper at St. Louis. In this position he advocated the right of free discussion. When a free coloured man was burnt to death near the city he denounced the outrage, for which he was compelled to leave Missouri, when he settled at Alton, Illinois, 1837. Here he avowed his sentiments as an Abolitionist, publishing a full statement of his views in the "Alton Observer." In consequence, his press and office were three times destroyed, and as often replaced by the friends of liberty and law. Early in November in the same year, at a public meeting convened ostensibly to allay excitement, but really to intimidate him and crush the liberty of the press, Mr. Lovejoy appeared, and in a speech of great power, defended his cause and rights. A new press was procured, and lodged in a stone warehouse, where Mr. Lovejoy and other friends stationed themselves, in the apprehension that it would be attacked. The fear was realized, both parties were armed, several volleys were fired, and an attempt made to set fire to the building. Mr. Lovejoy went out to prevent its success, and fell pierced by three buckshots. His wife had previously, at St. Charles, stood by him when he was brutally assaulted. When his mother heard of his death, she said, "It is well. I had rather he should fall a martyr to his cause than prove recreant to his principles." He left a widow and children to Divine providence. His companions effected their escape.

General William L. Chaplain, a lawyer by profession, though a native of Massachusetts, a citizen of the state of New York, a lecturer, an editor, a reporter of proceedings in Congress, a political leader and candidate for office in the liberal party, was arrested irregularly by the Washington police, within the borders of Maryland, in the night season. His carriage wheels were blocked, he was knocked from his seat, conveyed back into the city, and thrown into prison, charged with carrying away slaves. The Governor of Maryland made requisition of the Federal Executive for the delivery of Chaplain to be tried for an offence committed in that state. Bail in 6000 dollars from the district prison placed him at the disposal of the Maryland authorities, and he was conveyed to Rockville, Maryland, where he was held for three months, when he was released on the extravagant bail of 10,000 dollars, raised by his friends in the free states, all because he had ranked as an advocate of the coloured race, and had done something for their liberty.

William Shreve Bailey started in Newport, Kentucky, as a machine-maker, about 1849; his sympathies were aroused for the slaves, and though in a slave state he ventured to plead their cause in a newly-started paper. The wrath of the neighbouring slaveholders was excited, and they extracted from the publisher the name of the writer. He was visited in his machine-shop, and, but for his workmen, the assault might have ended in his death. To meet the demands of the proprietor, he purchased the press and printing materials, and the "Newport News" henceforth issued from the machine-shop. The paper succeeded for some time amidst violent opposition from slaveholders, who at last resorted to their ultimate expedient, and on the 6th October, 1851, set fire to the premises, burning down machine-shop and press. Mr. Bailey's loss amounted to 16,000 dollars. His operatives aided him to set up another press in his private house. A fresh set of types was produced, and the "Free South," a new name, was given to the journal. The scheme was now adopted to tamper with his workmen, who refused to work with him; he then had his own family taught to print. By degrees his wife and ten children learned to work as well and expeditiously as the other printers in the town. In 1857, a friend described the establishment: "Father, mother, and children, and even the little ones, toiling amid obloquy, reproach, and savage foes to redeem their state from the dreadful curse and sin of slavery. Mortgaging the homestead, working till midnight, practising rigid economy, making their house a citadel, where the weapons of truth must be defended by the weapons of death, and that not for the sake of praise, but to honour 'God, to save slaves and slaveholders, and wipe from Kentucky its foulest blot and shame,"—the wife and mother, the children and the brave man, husband and father, all nobler than any Spartan patriot. Death invaded the toilworn circle, and one of the little Abolitionists was carried to the grave by father, mother, brothers, and sisters, who returned again to labour for freedom and the slave amid reproaches and assaults. On the 29th of October, 1859, the last outrage of violence was perpetrated. The pro-slavery mob, having the night before forcibly entered the office, carried the types and scattered them along the streets, returned to assault the house; laying a plank, they battered down the door, entered the house and took off everything within reach, including Mr. Bailey's pocket-book containing nearly all his money. On this occasion the damage sustained was estimated at 3000 dollars. However, he again repaired the press, gathered the types from the streets, and once more the "Free South" was issued. But the resolute manager of this forlorn enterprise was seized and committed to prison on a charge of issuing incendiary publications. He was bailed and liberated for a time, when he sought in America and England to raise means which would enable him to renew the conflict. Mr. Lincoln's election brought matters to a different issue.

America was agitated from south to north and far west toward the close of 1859, and the earnest friends of the negro throughout Europe had all their sympathies awakened by events which had occurred at Harper's Ferry, and by *quasi* judicial proceedings at Richmond, and which terminated in the execution of Captain John Brown on a field about half a mile from the jail of the capital of Virginia, to which he had been conveyed in a furniture waggon. The sufferer was escorted from his prison to the place where he should yield up his life, by "Captain Scott's company of cavalry; one company of Major Loring's battalion of Defensibles; Captain William's Montpelier guard; Captain Scott's Petersburg Greys, company D; Captain Miller of the Virginia volunteers; and the young guard, Captain Rady; the whole under the command of Colonel T. P. August, assisted by Major Loring—the cavalry at the head and rear of the column." On the road to the scaffold he thus replied to an inquiry: "It has been a characteristic of me from infancy not to suffer from physical fear. I have suffered a thousand times more from bashfulness than from fear." As he drew nearer he looked up earnestly at the sun and sky, and all about, and then remarked, "This is a beautiful country. I have not cast my eyes over it before, that is, while passing through the field." As the procession entered the field he remarked, "I see no citizens here; where are they?" "The citizens are not allowed to be present; none but the troops," was the reply. "That ought not to be," said the old man; "citizens should be allowed to be present as well as others." When he descended from the waggon and passed through opened ranks towards the scaffold, with firm step and erect form he calmly walked past jailers, sheriff, and officers: "Gentlemen, good-bye," said the hero, and mounted the steps—the hour had come—the officer approached him. To Captain Avis, his jailer, he said, "I have no words to thank you for all your kindness to me." His elbows and ankles were pinioned, the white cap drawn over his eyes, and the hangman's rope (a present from Kentucky) adjusted round his neck. John Brown waits to be ushered into the Divine presence. "Captain Brown," said the sheriff, "you are not standing on the drop; will you come forward?" "I can't see," was his answer, unfalteringly spoken; "you must lead me." He was led to the centre of the drop. "Shall I give you a handkerchief," asked the sheriff, "and

H

let you drop it as a signal?" "No: I am ready at any
time; but do not keep me needlessly waiting." For ten
minutes, in answer to the shout of an officer, "Not ready
yet," and a military display hither and thither followed.
At last the trap fell; its hinges gave a wailing sort of creak
that could be heard at every part of the field.

With his sword and voice John Brown had demonstrated the unutterable villany of slavery. His corpse was
destined to continue the lesson. The surgeons pronounced
the victim dead; they declared that his spinal column had
been ruptured. They said that the countenance was now
purple and distorted. They knew that the cord had cut a
finger's depth into the neck of the strangled corpse. The
body was delivered to his widow at Harper's Ferry, and by
her it was carried to North Elba, where it now lies at rest
on the bosom of the majestic mountain regions that he
loved when living. There was no vast assemblage of the
so-called great at the interment; no pompous parade, no
gorgeous procession, but loyal worth and noble genius
stood at the grave of departed heroism. His friends and
his family wept as the eloquent Wendell Phillips, chief of
American living orators, pronounced the eulogium of John
Brown, the latest and bravest martyr of the cause and
claims of the long-injured negro.

Wherefore this execution, and why this parade of
military power? the uninformed reader may inquire; and
the headings of the first American telegrams announcing
what many thought was the guilty occasion, read thus :—
" HARPER'S FERRY.—Fearful and exciting intelligence!
Negro insurrection at Harper's Ferry! Extensive negro
conspiracy in Virginia and Maryland! Seizure of the
United States arsenal by the insurrectionists! Arms taken
and sent into the interior! The bridge fortified and defended by cannon! Trains fired into and stopped! Several
persons killed! Telegraph wires cut! Contributions levied

on the citizens! Troops despatched against the insurgents
from Washington and Baltimore!" Harper's Ferry is
situated in Jefferson County, Virginia, at the confluence of
the Potomac and Shenandoah rivers, and is 173 miles distant from Richmond. The alarm given by the telegraph
showed that the slave masters expected a universal revolt,
in all the State, of the slave population. The explanation
given by some who took part in the movement, which
spread such alarm, was that "the original intention of John
Brown was to seize the arsenal at Harper's Ferry on the
night of the 24th of October, 1859, and take the arms
there deposited to the neighbouring mountains, with a
number of the wealthier citizens of the vicinity as hos-
tages, until they should redeem themselves by liberating
an equal number of slaves. But it was suspected there
was a traitor in the company, and therefore the premature
attempt to strike the blow on the 17th. The precipitation
of the movement caused its defeat, as negro parties, not
being warned, were not ready. One of his confederates
reports Captain Brown as closing an address to his followers, on the preceding Sunday, in this language:—
" And now, gentlemen, let me press this one thing on
your minds. You all know how dear life is to you, and
how dear your lives are to your friends; and in remembering that, consider that the lives of others are as dear to
them as yours are to you. Do not therefore take the life
of any one, if you can avoid it; but if it is necessary to
take life in order to save your own, then make sure work
of it." In proof of his own readiness and self-possession,
the description given by Colonel Washington, contending
against him, will suffice:—" He was the coolest man he
ever saw in defying death and danger. With one son dead
by his side, and another shot through, he felt the pulse of
his dying son with one hand and held his rifle with the
other, and commanded his men with the utmost com-

posure, encouraging them to be firm, and to sell their lives as dearly as possible."

The captain himself spoke freely with Colonel Washington, and referred to his sons. He said he had lost one in Kansas, and two here. He had not pressed them to join him in the expedition, but did not regret their loss. They had died in a good cause. Wise, Governor of Virginia, spoke the result of his conference with Captain Brown in a few sentences. "They are themselves mistaken who take him to be a madman. He is a bundle of the best nerves I ever saw; cut and thrust, and bleeding, and in bonds. He is a man of clear head, of courage, fortitude, and simple ingenuousness. He is cool, collected, and indomitable; and it is but just to him to say that he was humane to his prisoners, as attested to me by Colonel Washington and Mr. Mills, and he inspired me with great trust in his integrity as a man of truth." His defenders could not ask more to accredit his own account of what he intended by his invasion of Virginia, and his occupation of Harper's Ferry. His last words, before he was pronounced guilty and doomed to death, were his version as before the bar of the Supreme Judge, and in it the knell of slavery was sounded :—

" I have, may it please the court, a few words to say. In the first place I deny everything but what I have all along admitted, the design on my part to free the slaves. I intended certainly to have made a clear thing of that matter, as I did last winter when I went into Missouri and there took slaves without the snapping of a gun on either side, moved them through the country, and finally left them in Canada. I designed to have done the same thing again, on a larger scale. That was all I intended. I never did intend murder or treason, or the destruction of property, or to excite or incite slaves to rebellion, or to make insurrection. I have another objection, and that is, it is unjust that I should suffer such a penalty. Had I interfered in the manner which I admit, and which I admit has been fairly proved—(for I admire the truthfulness and candour of the greater portion of witnesses who have testified in this case)—had I so interfered in behalf of the rich, the powerful, the intelligent, the so-called great, or in behalf of any of their friends, either father, mother, brother, sister, wife, or children, or any of that class, and suffered, and sacrificed what I have in this interference, it would have been all right, and every man in this court would have deemed it an act worthy of reward rather than punishment. This court acknowledges, as I suppose, the validity of the law of God. I see a book kissed here which I suppose to be the Bible, or, at least, the New Testament. That teaches me that all things, 'whatsoever I would that men should do unto me, I should do even so to them.' It teaches me further to 'remember them that are in bonds as bound with them.' I endeavoured to act up to that instruction. I say, I am yet too young to understand that God is any respecter of persons. I believe that to have interfered as I have done, as I have always freely admitted I have done, in behalf of His despised poor, was not wrong but right. Now, if it is deemed necessary that I should forfeit my life for the furtherance of the ends of justice and mingle my blood further with the blood of my children and with the blood of millions in this slave country, whose rights are disregarded by wicked, cruel, and unjust enactments, I submit. So let it be done.

"Let me say one word further.—I feel entirely satisfied with the treatment I have received on my trial. Considering all the circumstances, it has been more generous than I expected. But I feel no consciousness of guilt. I have stated from the first what was my intention and what was not. I never had any design against the life of any person, nor any disposition to commit treason, or excite slaves to rebel, or make any general insurrection. I never encouraged any man to do so, but always discouraged any idea of that kind.

"Let me say, also, a word in regard to the statements made by some of those connected with me. I hear it has been stated by some of them that I have induced them to join me. But the contrary is true. I do not say this to injure them, but as regretting their weakness. There is not one of them but joined me of his own accord and the greater part at their own expense. A number of them I never saw, and never had a word of conversation with them till the day they came to me, and that was for the purpose I have stated.

"Now I have done."

Probably no event ever excited so much attention or stimulated so much sympathy in America, even among those who could not defend Captain Brown's mode of proceeding. The alarm, however, of the slaveholders, of what they evidently thought was possible, the outbreak of a servile war in the slave states, not only lifted the veil from the dark omens of the system, but also demonstrated how unprepared they were to have resisted such a rebellion. Brown's personal virtues, his services and sufferings in Kansas, his stern antagonism to slavery, and his submission to Divine authority, taught many thoughtful Americans to abhor slavery more heartily, and seek its overthrow.

The tone of America was intensified by the Echoes from Harper's Ferry, and the funeral solemnities at Elba in the mountains—preparatory for the last Presidential election; and when the tocsin sounded for the civil war from Fort Sumter and the army of the Potomac, many rallied the more readily round the Stars and Stripes because John Brown had been doomed to death by a Virginia sentence and slaveholding functionaries. The "Life of Captain John Brown," and the "Echoes of Harper's Ferry," by Redpath, present proofs, and strikingly illustrate the power, of anti-slavery sentiment among the people of New England. They also furnish evidence of the nervous apprehensions of the slave-masters, how critical and insecure was their tenure of power, both as states and as slaveholders. The heroic old man, John Brown, did not live or die in vain, and his death did more for the ripening of the public mind for the abolition of slavery than has been accomplished by the lives of many much-lauded patriots and champions of liberty.

It would not be a task to fill pages of narrative and personal delineation of men who have laboured with the tongue and the pen, and have endured reproach and persecution in the cause of the coloured people of America. James G. Birney was one of these; a man of rank and high in office and wealth, and political influence in his state, who unexpectedly declared himself an abolitionist. True to his convictions, he removed from Alabama, emancipated and settled all his slaves, started a newspaper in Cincinnati, where he stood his ground and established freedom of speech and of the press, notwithstanding threatening attempts on his life and liberty. Mr. Lewis Tappan, who has sustained a long and blameless life as the sympathizing friend of the negro, had his house sacked in New York, and his furniture burned in the street by a pro-slavery mob. William Lloyd Garrison, who still lives as the Liberator of the negro, was assailed with the cry, " Lynch him, Lynch him," was threatened to be thrown out of a window, and with a rope round his body was dragged by a furious crowd that they might tar and feather him. His hat was knocked from his head, while brick-bats were flying in all directions. He was lodged for safety in a prison, and thought it his honour to suffer for the cause of freedom. Wendell Phillips, the most effective orator of the United States, has consecrated his powers to the same service, and welcomed the opprobrium of abolitionism and exclusion from the highest offices which a more worldly use of his talents might have secured. Gerrit Smith, possessing influence and opportunities for aiming at the Presidency, with boundless wealth and extensive possessions in land, has yet contented himself to be the friend in need and patron of the coloured man and those who suffer for his sake. Dr. Channing, by a life-long devotion of his personal influence

his voice, his pen, and his pulpit, advocated the cause of the
negro, and promoted the emancipation of the slave. Lyman
Beecher and his honoured sons, receiving honour from their
parentage, and returning honour to a venerable father, and
not less honoured by the pen and talent of their sister,
have served the cause of the oppressed by personal sacrifices and life-long toils. Henry Ward Beecher has sustained untarnished the reputation acquired in America by
his gigantic labours in Europe as the unpaid advocate and
ambassador of his people. Dr. Cheever may have been
misunderstood, and his idiosyncracies may have tempted
him to magnify special points in the anti-slavery controversy. Yet no more honest, persistent, self-denying advocate of the cause has, for long and trying years, sacrificed
himself and consecrated his literary services to advance
the liberty of the coloured man, and the honour of his
country.

Men there are, though not much mentioned in English
circles, who have yet laboured efficiently, and written well
on slavery and anti-slavery. Some of them are now patri-
archs, and might reckon on the reward of the retired
warrior. The Revs. Messrs. William Goodell, Geo. Whipple,
and S. S. Jocelyn, will have their place in the honoured
throng, to whom it shall be said, "Inasmuch as ye have
done it unto the least of these my brethren, ye have done
it unto me." There are in New York three venerated
names, always received elsewhere with honour, and used as
a power by all who know their worth : the Revs. Dr. Tyng,
rector of St. George's; Dr. Asa D. Smith, president of
Dartmouth College ; and Dr. J. P. Thompson, of Broadway
Tabernacle. The unfeigned adherence of these distinguished clergymen, in circles of vast social and religious
influence, to the cause of the coloured people, slave or free,
guarantees the progress of the cause, and attract to it the
co-operation of multitudes throughout the land. Their

meetings, lectures, and epistolary communications, command deferential attention and confirm the wavering.

The statesmen who identified themselves with the cause of freedom from the days of Washington, including Thomas Jefferson, John Randolph, John Quincy Adams, till the present times, when W. H. Seward, S. P. Chase, Charles Sumner, Senator Wilson, and Mr. J. P. Hale, are united with others, would afford materials of great and various interest, to mark the progress and approaching triumph of the anti-slavery cause. The first President continued an indulgent slave-master ; but in apprehension of eternity, manumitted his slaves in his last will and testament. Thomas Jefferson left his slaves in slavery ; but surely it was because he anticipated the change which he said was "already perceptible" since the origin of the present (first) revolution. "The spirit of the master is abating, that of the slave is rising from the dust, his condition mollifying, *the way I hope preparing, under the auspices of heaven, for a total emancipation.*" He had often dreaded the time "When the measure of their tears should be full, when their groans should have involved heaven itself in darkness, when doubtless a God of justice would awaken to their distress, and by his exterminating thunders, would manifest his attention to the things of this world, and that they are not left to the guidance of a blind fatality." "I tremble for my country," he said, "when I reflect that God is just ; that his justice cannot sleep for ever. The Almighty has no attributes that could take sides with us in such a contest as between slaves and their masters."

John Randolph had in 1816 moved in the House of Representatives for a committee to inquire into "the inhuman and illegal traffic" for buying and selling slaves, and in 1820 he rebuked the recreants to liberty, in the matter of the Missouri Compromise, by the designation which he coined on the occasion, to describe them as the "doe" which startles at her own shadow in the water when she comes to drink; "they saw," said he, "their own doe faces and were frightened." John Quincy Adams had opposed the annexation of Texas and the Mexican war, which were designed to promote slavery. He maintained that in time of war the government possessed a discretionary power to emancipate slaves. He proposed in Congress a plan for the prospective abolition of slavery through an amendment of the Constitution, in which he received only feeble support; and, finally, the crowning act of his laborious public life, and which rendered him the benefactor of his country, was the restoration to the people of the right of petition, which slaveholders had denied in Congress. He was therefore threatened with assassination, with an indictment by the grand jury of the district, and with expulsion from the house; and finally an ineffectual effort was made to pass a formal censure upon him for his persistency in pleading the cause of liberty. Messrs. Seward and Chase have attained their present position as the advocates of freedom and opponents of slavery. In 1847 the liberty party proposed, or nominated as candidate for the Presidency and Vice-presidency, Gerrit Smith and John P. Hale, an independent democrat, who had refused to do homage to the slave power, and was a party to the convention, which "Resolved, that it is the duty of the Federal Government to relieve itself of all responsibility for the existence or continuance of slavery, wherever that government possesses constitutional authority to legislate on that subject, and is thus responsible for its existence."

Mr. Charles Sumner is a younger man than those with whom he has now been classed, and he was elected in 1851, a senator, in succession to Mr. Daniel Webster. He denounced, as with a tongue of fire, the Fugitive Slave Bill, and fulfilled his intention during a speech on Kansas, May 19 and 20, 1855, "to pronounce the most thorough philippic against slavery ever uttered in a legislative body;" and in 1860 he dissected and exposed with the knife of a skilful anatomist, "the barbarism of slavery." His personal services to the Republic as a senator have been unremitting ever since his election. But neither he nor any other man ever did so much for the overthrow of the hideous and brutal system of slavery, as he effected when he fell on the floor of Congress. in the sight of senators and representatives, under the bludgeon of Preston Brooks, on the 22nd of May, 1855. Brooks was a representative of South Carolina, and his colleague was Keitt. They both drew toward Mr. Sumner while he was busily engaged writing at his desk, stooping over his paper, and unprepared for resistance. Brooks struck him several severe blows on the head with a cane chosen for the deed ; the blows were repeated till Mr. Sumner fell, bleeding and senseless, on the senate chamber floor. The assailant avowed afterwards, that had any attempt been made to resist, his intention was to have killed Mr. Sumner. Other Southern senators, Messrs. Douglas, Slidell, and Tombs were spectators and approvers. Messrs. Murray and Morgan of the state of New York interposed and rescued the helpless victim, upon whom the assailant continued to repeat his blows. Ladies and distinguished personages in the South, in public meetings and by letters and presents, expressed their admiration of the deed, and showered their applause on the perpetrator of the crime. Mr. Sumner suffered long, and apprehensions were entertained he never would be able to *think* again. After a long interval of travel in Europe, intercourse with great and distinguished statesmen and patriots, and a recess from protracted thought, he again resumed his place and services. Europe and the world had been scandalized by the brutality and publicity of the crime. Never was any more fitting illustration of the system. It was not done, as Charles the First attempted to seize the free speaking members of the English Commons, but as fiends would destroy their victims. The Northern states were roused hereby to bolder action in the Presidential election, when Colonel Fremont was the candidate; and a new era was inaugurated for anti-slavery action. Civilization, liberty for white as well as coloured people, freedom of speech in the legislative halls and everywhere, freedom everywhere, Christianity in its noblest enterprises, demanded a new order of things.

It is well known and felt that the most potent buttress of slavery in the South is female influence, and hence the special fitness of things that the women of the free states should co-operate with other agencies for its overthrow. The women of the anti-slavery cause are numerous, and their services are felt by their foes and appreciated by their allies. Mobs and villanous violence have been employed to put down their organizations. Incendiary and murderous conspiracies in Boston and Philadelphia were developed amidst tumultuous assemblies, to intimidate and overawe, but only with momentary success. Mrs. Chapman, Lydia M. Child, Mrs. Beecher Stowe, Fanny Kemble, added to the daughters of Mr. Grimke, may serve as the representative women to tell who have worked for their coloured sisterhood still under the brand of slavery. Mrs. Chapman, from her social position, possessing influence in society and talents to sustain any measure of responsibility in the work of a committee, was called to an important position, and by epistolary communications and wisdom in counsel, she served the cause at home and abroad. Lydia M. Child, as an authoress of popular reputation, wielded her pen and attached her name in the "Appeal on behalf of that class of Americans called Africans," and produced "The Right Way, the Safe Way, proved by Emancipation in the British West Indies and elsewhere." The sale of her publications as household volumes declined; and thus she suffered in estate and reputation because she pleaded for the oppressed. But it did not abate her zeal or diminish her efforts in behalf of the slave. She is still a willing and efficient helper with her pen. Fanny Kemble's volume, the narrative of her own experiences and observations in the plantation and among the family and progeny of planters, has done more to disclose the abominations, cruelties, and miserable degradation of the slave charnel-house than was ever expected from eye-witness testimony. Her facts are stronger and worse than fiction, and corroborating " Uncle Tom" in the darkest touches of the moral picture. Mrs. Beecher Stowe by the magic of her pen, and the *vraisimilitude* of her narrative, effectively mingling a religious sympathy and evangelical truth with the soft and affectionate tenderness of the negro character, gave attractiveness and power to her work which could not be resisted.

The hundreds of thousands of copies, in every variety of publication, which were sold of " Uncle Tom's Cabin," and the many thousands which followed of " The Key," and of " Dred Scott" served to leaven the Anglo-Saxon mind in both countries, and inspire an abhorrence of the system which the planters deplored, and by which a strong impulse was given to the Anti-Slavery cause everywhere. The work was a preparation for the political events which have followed in the North and South. Beautifully does the authoress express herself: " I wrote what I did because, as a woman, as a mother, I was oppressed and heartbroken with the sorrows and injustice I saw; because, as a Christian, I felt the dishonour of Christianity; because, as a lover of my country, I trembled at the coming day of wrath. It is no merit in the sorrowing that they weep, nor to the oppressed that they gasp and struggle, nor to me that I must speak for those who cannot speak for themselves."

Happily, coloured men are coming forward to contend, as well as speak for their own cause in America. But already there have been many instances of talent and energy among the freed and the free-born men of colour. Mr. Frederick Douglas, Mr. Charles Remond, Mr. William Craft, the Rev. H. H. Garnett, the Rev. J. Sella Martin, and a host of other coloured gentlemen, who have occupied prominent and ministerial positions in the northern parts of the United States, are witnesses of the patriotism and loyalty of their kindred. They pray for the permanent "peace of their country, based upon liberty and the enjoyment of man's inalienable rights, for the preservation of the American Union, and for the reign of that righteousness in the hearts of the people that saves from reproach and exalteth a nation." They have also laboured and suffered for this end, in proof that their prayers have been sincere. The coloured clergy of all denominations, who faithfully discharge ministerial and pastoral duties among a despised and suffering people, give proof that talent, piety, and diligence may be found among the ransomed people, who have heard the joyful sound. The necessary improvement in their condition, following the present changes, will afford yet wider scope for the energies and zeal of these servants of God and their country.

The ecclesiastical influences, from 1800 till 1850, which pervaded America on the slave question, have been analyzed by the Rev. William Goodell, in his "Slavery and Anti-Slavery;" and having passed in review the proceedings of each sect—the Methodist Episcopal Church, the Presbyterian, new and old school, the Congregationalists, Baptists, the Protestant Episcopal Church, and other sects—he condemns each for complicity, either for selling or holding slaves, or for *supporting* candidates for Congress or office who supported the system, and having quoted, endorses the truth of the representation : " If slavery be a sin, and advertizing and apprehending slaves with a view to restore them to their masters is a direct violation of the Divine law, and if the *buying*, *selling*, and *holding* a slave FOR THE SAKE OF GAIN is a heinous sin and scandal, then verily three-fourths of all the Episcopalians, Methodists, Baptists, and Presbyterians in eleven states of the Union are of the devil. They hold, if they do not buy and sell slaves (with few exceptions), they hesitate not to apprehend and restore runaway slaves, when in their power"—the words of the Rev. James Smylie, M.A. He further quotes the editor of a periodical of the Methodist Episcopal Church, as corroborating the statement: " If, however, the holding of men, women, and children in bondage, under the *ordinary cir-cumstances* that connect themselves with *slavery in the Southern states*, constitutes us (the Methodist Episcopal Church) a pro-slavery church, then we are a pro-slavery church in this restricted or privately-understood interpretation, for we do not regard slaveholding as sinful as it *exists in the Southern states*, provided the master feeds, instructs, and governs his slaves, according to the directions laid down in God's word." Mr. Goodell affirms the fact is established by credible testimony, that slaveholding church members, in general, did not give their slaves any more religious instruction than did other slaveholders, which in most cases was none at all; so that the slaves, to use their own language, were in the condition of heathenism. In 1801 the general conference of the Methodist Episcopal Church uttered this sentiment: " We are more than ever convinced of the great evil of African slavery, which still exists in these United States." Dr. Hedding, one of its bishops, declared, 1838, " the right to hold a slave is founded on this rule—' Therefore, all things whatsoever ye would that men should do to you, do ye even so to them, for this is the law and the prophets' !!" The conference of this body was divided into antagonist bodies in 1840; the action which led to separation was "simply against slaveholding by the episcopacy, upon the ground of expediency. It is computed that there were, in 1850, not less than four thousand slaveholders in the Methodist Episcopal Church, North, and twenty-seven thousand slaves."—*True Wesleyan.* The Presbyterian Church, in 1794, recorded its testimony, "that it is *man stealing* to keep, sell, or buy slaves, or retain men in slavery." In 1836 a report was accepted by their synod, affirming that slavery is connected with the laws of the states, with which it is by no means proper for an ecclesiastical body to interfere. In 1837 their General Assembly excinded four presbyteries on the alleged account of theological differences; but these presbyteries contained the most vigorous anti-slavery members. The new and old school Presbyterians separated in 1838, probably for the reason for which the four presbyteries were cut off; however, three slaveholding presbyteries were represented in the New School, and nearly forty such presbyteries adhered to the Old School, which firmly held the dogma, "that slaveholding in itself is a crime, is not only an error, but it is an error fraught with serious consequences." This was a view inculcated by Professor *Hodge* of Princeton. In 1843 the General Assembly of the New School "censured the action of those anti-slavery presbyteries which had excluded slaveholding from their pulpits and communion tables, and requested them to rescind their acts;" and in 1850 it unanimously adopted the proposal to commune, or at least expressed a readiness to do so, with the Old School, at the time when a great portion of that body, at the South, were zealous for the extension of slavery, were slave sellers and propagandists. The Congregationalists, from the independency of their ecclesiastical action, cannot be so closely scrutinized. The Congregational ministers in convention, in 1848, affirmed that it well became them, as of the ancient commonwealth of Massachusetts, solemnly to declare to the world their deep conviction of the injustice and inhumanity of the system of slavery, and of its absolute repugnance to all the principles of the Word of God. The Congregational ministers of Maine are reputed to have been a little more earnest in their condemnation of slavery than those of Massachusetts and Connecticut. The Baptists are even more miscellaneous in their ecclesiastical relations than are the Congregationalists; but among them, as among the Protestant Episcopal Church, there was less resistance to the slave system than in the other denominations. These summaries are here presented to demonstrate what was the atmosphere in which anti-slavery organizations were called to move, and amidst what discouragements the friends of the slave had to proceed when they sought to contend against the prejudice to colour, or to seek to elevate the freed negro or the refugees from slavery.

The Fugitive Slave Law was enacted in 1850, and was indebted to Daniel Webster and Henry Clay for its acceptance, as the project of thirteen members; constituting a committee to counteract the admission of California and New Mexico as free states, for which the people of those countries had applied. The conspirators had all the aid of Mr. Mason, recently an envoy from the Confederates in England. The proposal excited alarm and opposition in all free states, especially New England. But ultimately the measure was carried, and received the signature of Millard Filmore in the *greatest haste*. General Taylor, President, had died. The substance of the law is summarized by Mr. Goodell: "It is supplementary to an act in 1793, for facilitating the recapture of fugitive slaves. It effectually breaks down all the remaining defences of personal liberty in the non-slaveholding states; and every man, black or white, it makes no difference, holds his exemption

I

from chattelhood, so far as legal protection is concerned, at the mercy of any Southern man who may choose to claim him as his slave, in connection with any one of a horde of government officials to be appointed for the special purpose, who is authorized to surrender him without jury trial, with no testimony but that of the claimant or his agent, while the testimony of the person claimed is not to be received. All citizens are commanded to assist in seizing and surrendering fugitives, and all persons are forbidden to harbour them or aid their escape, under penalty of one thousand dollars; with imprisonment not exceeding six months, besides one thousand dollars to be recovered in a civil suit for damages, for each slave so aided or harboured."

So soon as the enactment was effected, slave catchers and thieves were on the alert; no coloured man or woman was safe in all the United States, even of those who by state laws were born free; many such were kidnapped and enslaved. Miss Wigham, in her interesting little work on America, says, "Terror reigned, and whole families, and the larger portion of coloured churches, set out under cover of night, in the cold winter of 1850-1, to seek the protection of Queen Victoria in Canada, where their sufferings from the climate and inadequate provision were very great. The Abolitionists had work enough now on their hands— to warn the fugitives of danger, to aid them to escape, to defend them in court if brought to trial, to stand by them in every circumstance, and to share their trials by sympathy and fellow-suffering." The cases in which public commotion followed the seizure of the victims of this law, were numerous and monstrous. In one case nearly fifty coloured men rallied to the rescue of the alleged fugitive; the slaveholder claiming his slave was killed, and his son wounded, and an exciting trial was conducted under a Judge Grier, when, strange to say, the accused were acquitted. Another case occurred at Syracuse, when the fugitive escaped. A third case may be mentioned, where a free woman was seized; she and her sister were released, but the kind man who had befriended them and borne witness to their freedom, was found suspended from a tree, after he had left the court to return home. A Mr. Kauffman was prosecuted for concealing a fugitive, because a night's lodging and food had been supplied in his barn; he was assessed with 2800 dollars as damages, though it had not been *proved* that he knew the coloured people were slaves. The case of Anthony Burns, arrested on the 24th May, 1854, in Boston, and carried to slavery on the 2nd June, excited much attention. This case drew forth from their retirement 4000 leading merchants as petitioners to Congress for the repeal of the law. They had never intermeddled in anti-slavery matters before. One of the police authorities resigned his office rather than have such work to perform; and an influential meeting of gentlemen convened to do honour to him, presented a testimonial of their admiration. The Fugitive Slave Law helped to mature the public mind for the present crisis. One other stage, in the national theatre, was enacted in the Supreme Court of the United States—a court to which appeals from *all* the states may be carried in civil cases, regulated by Federal laws.

The number of judges is nine; and, as appeared, four were from the slave states, and three others sympathized with slavery. One, named Judge Taney, argued so strongly as to express an opinion on what was not before the court, and affirmed that " *black* men have no rights which white men are bound to respect." In vain might the black man plead that not his sin but his God had made him black; that more than half of the human family have dark complexion, and that many men of colour have a mixture of white men's blood in their veins, by descent from their masters; but that inspiration had taught that " God hath made of one blood all nations of men to dwell on all the face of the earth." Dred Scott was claimed as a slave by a Missouri planter. The master had taken him into Illinois, and to a territory where slavery had been prohibited by Congress. He claimed his freedom on his return to Missouri, because his master had voluntarily taken him into a free state; and since the laws of that state held him free he could not be again enslaved, though now living in a slave state. The court to which his case was submitted upheld the validity of his claim for freedom, and his master appealed to the Supreme Court. Here two judges, M'Lean and Curtis, sustained the decision of the lower court; but Judge Taney and a majority reversed the judgment, and restored Scott to bondage. The decision aroused a spirit of antagonism in several Northern states. New York, Maine, and Ohio passed laws securing freedom to all coloured persons brought by their masters within their borders. Other kindred enactments for coloured persons were passed, indicating a desire to show righteous and liberal legislation. Personal liberty bills were prepared to prevent the seizure of persons entitled to their freedom. Such measures could not nullify the Fugitive Slave Law of the Union, but they withstood the removal of the person claimed as a slave from the state under process of law, until time was given to establish his legal freedom or till the slaveholder's representative could prove the property which was alleged in the slave. Maine provided that legal defence should be furnished at the cost of the state, for any person claimed on its borders as a fugitive slave. Ohio prohibited the incarceration of any fugitive slave in her prisons. Wisconsin forbade that any penalties should be enforced against persons condemned under the law within the state. The moral effect of these proceedings was felt in the mind of the citizens in free states; and thus a preparation was made to accept God's dealings, when He should arise to defend the poor and needy. He has taken to Himself the prerogative of righteousness and justice, as the Judge of the whole earth; and He has promised to defend the oppressed from the oppressor. When his judgments are abroad upon the earth, the inhabitants thereof learn righteousness.

The candidature of Colonel Fremont was a token of Northern earnestness, in meeting the emergency forced upon their Republic by the aggressions of the slave power. He was put forward on the free-soil platform, and consented to the stipulation that no more territory should be conceded to the slave power. He did not then avow so strongly, as he has since, his anti-slavery sympathies and preparedness to provide liberty to the slave, as far as the Constitution of the Republic would warrant the procedure. The twelve hundred thousand suffrages which were gladly cast into the ballot-box, showed then the rapid progress of opinion among the people. The Abolitionists saw that the cause of the slave was advancing; the slaveholding party apprehended it with fear and rage. Even the slaves in Tennessee were anticipating their jubilee, and had too confidently reckoned on its near approach, when tidings came of the triumph of the tyrant party. Vigilance committees, patrols, and spies were the weapons by which they were met. Arrests, torture, Lynch law, scourging, and hanging were the measures meted out in Dover and Cumberland. Nineteen negroes at one of these towns, and nine at the other, were hung; while others, free coloured and slave, were killed by lashing and the rope; men of Northern sympathies living in the South were expelled from their home for the simplest words in conversation which seemed to favour the cause of Fremont. Trial or jury was not granted to the supposed offender, but prompt banishment or worse was threatened to the loss of trade and property. Thus did the South hug the possession of arbitrary power, which seemed to threaten an early departure.

The ministration of the Southern candidate was imbecile and pusillanimous, sustained by chicanery and subserviency to the party which had placed him in power. Buchanan's conduct as President was traitorous and hostile to the North, servile and full of sycophancy to the slave party. His cabinet was composed of men who conspired against the Constitution, and employed their offices as affording facilities to plunder the Treasury of their country, spoil its arsenals and fortresses, enfeeble its army, bribe its trained officials, and scatter its navy beyond the immediate call of the Executive. The Floyds, the Toombs, the Masons, the Slidells, and Jefferson Davises were his instruments of perfidy, or he winked at the knavery and treason, while they prepared for a sanguinary and fratricidal rebellion. And even so late as December, 1860, after his successor had been chosen, and he knew the hostile courses upon which the conspirators had entered, and their determination to dissolve the Union for the sake of slavery,—a union which he had solemnly sworn to uphold—he feigned to cast upon men who were ready to sacrifice their all for its maintenance in righteousness, the onus of the strife, and imputed to them the dangers which impended. His message on the 3rd December, 1860, affirmed that the peril mainly arose from "the fact that the incessant and violent agitation of the slavery question, throughout the North, for the last quarter of a century, has at length produced its malign influence on the slaves, and inspired them with vague notions of freedom. Hence a sense of security no longer exists around the family altar." Thus did he pander to the interests of the slave power, and labour to weaken the hands of his lawfully appointed successor.

Some well-meaning, but not well-informed critics of the Lincoln Government have charged the earlier acts of the administration with vacillation, and the utterances of the President as temporizing and indicative of a willingness to prolong slavery, and sacrifice the slave for the Union. An anti-slavery policy subsequently adopted, it has been affirmed, was only an after-thought, and adhered to only as a war measure; while Mr. Lincoln in his replies to the Chicago Deputation, and to Mr. Horace Greely, put the Union before freedom, and the unity of the Federation before the righteous claims of its long-oppressed and degraded African subjects. The platform on which Mr. Lincoln became candidate was not for emancipation. He was not chosen to abolish slavery whatever was the object he was to resist. He was an avowed advocate of anti-slavery policy; he had spoken at meetings for emancipation, but he had not proposed to dissolve the Union for it, or to bring the Federal power to work in violation of state laws. Two points were emphatically prescribed in the Chicago platform, and to them Mr. Lincoln faithfully adhered. They are expressed in the following clauses :—

"That the new dogma that the Constitution, of its own force, carries slavery into any or all of the territories of the United States, is a dangerous political heresy, at variance with explicit provisions of that instrument itself, with contemporaneous exposition, and with legislative and judicial precedent, is revolutionary in its tendency, and subversive of the peace and harmony of the country. That the normal condition of all territory of the United States is that of freedom; that as our Republican fathers, when they had abolished slavery in all our national territory, ordained that 'no person should be deprived of life, liberty, or property, without due process of law,' it becomes our duty by legislation, whenever such legislation is necessary, to maintain this provision of the Constitution against all attempts to violate it; and we deny the authority of Congress, of a territorial legislature, or of any individuals, to give legal existence to slavery on any territory of the United States."

The import of this avowal was manifestly, that the Federal

power should not be employed to extend slavery, and that the Territories should not be opened for its extension. Mr. Lincoln was elected as President of the United States, and took an oath to defend and maintain the Union. The action of the Confederate conspiracy forced emancipation into the conflict, and rendered the war an anti-slavery struggle. The President constitutionally could only administer the government in concert with Congress and the Senate, and by the legitimate action of subordinate authorities; but all the principal supporters he could look to must themselves be chosen by the popular suffrage. There were members of legislature who, in both Houses, could impede or prostrate the action or proposals of the administration, which must first obtain their approval. The peculiar circumstances attending the election of Mr. Lincoln constituted further matters of deliberate consideration. Four candidates had been started for the Presidency, Mr. Douglas, Mr. Breckenridge, Mr. Bell, and Mr. Lincoln; each of them had numerous adherents. Messrs. Bell and Douglas stood as Union candidates, and for them 1,956,607 of the electors voted, a clear majority over Mr. Lincoln of nearly 100,000. The incoming President had to bear in mind, in all his sayings and doings, the voice of this majority in every annual election throughout the states. The purely Southern element in his antagonism was represented by 847,953 who voted for Breckenridge. Another phase of the national mind was presented in the Electoral College, to whom the decision reverted by the law of the Union, since neither of the candidates had a nett majority of the total popular vote, 4,662,170. Some of the College voted for Mr. Lincoln for one reason, and some for other reasons, all which deserved his respectful consideration. He had learned that the wisdom of the prudent is to understand his way, and he that handleth a matter wisely shall find good, and while a prudent man foreseeth the evil, yet the poor wise man may by his wisdom deliver the city; it became the President of the United States, in 1861, not only to be faithful in judging the poor, that he might establish his authority, but also watchful in his communications to guard himself against any false oath or rash procedure.

Mr. Wendell Phillips comprehended the philosophy of the position, when, at the beginning of 1863, he declared, "Never until we welcome the negro, the foreigner, all races as equals and metted together in a common nationality, hurl them all at despotism, will the North deserve triumph, or earn it at the hands of a just God. But the North will triumph. I hear it. Do you remember in that disastrous siege in India, when the Scotch girl raised her head from the pallet of the hospital, and said to the sickening hearts of the English, 'I hear the bagpipes; the Campbells are coming,' and they said, 'Jessie, it is delirium.' 'No, I know it; I heard it far off.' And in an hour the pibroch burst upon their glad hearts, and the banner of England floated in triumph over their heads. . So I hear in the dim distance the first notes of the jubilee rising from the hearts of the millions. Soon, very soon, you shall hear it at the gates of the citadel, and the stars and stripes shall guarantee liberty for ever, from the lakes to the gulf."

CHAPTER IV.

A VISIT TO NEW YORK, WASHINGTON, THE WHITE HOUSE, AND PHILADELPHIA.

THE address by the Manchester Anti-Slavery Conference was entrusted, by the sub-Committee, to the Rev. J. H. Rylance, of St. Paul's, Westminster Road, Lambeth, and to myself. As Mr. Rylance was under arrangements to proceed to America on private affairs, he accepted the Mission, agreeing to perform its duties as far as he could, consistently with other engagements. He had arrived in America a week before me: domestic and clerical duties prevented him from rendering the services he was well qualified to discharge, except by a brief attendance at the New York committee, and two meetings at Philadelphia. His correspondence with England was more extended, and deemed valuable. It devolved on each member of the deputation to arrange for our own special duties, and to proceed on our journey according to our several routes. I will report my own proceedings without circumlocution or farther reference to my colleague; except to observe that I believe, Mr. Rylance is a true and earnest friend and sympathizer with the citizens of America, among whom he has become a resident clergyman. He is a genuine lover of freedom and a true friend of the slave.

I sailed from England in the steam-ship "City of Baltimore," and returned in the "City of Washington." I left Liverpool on the 17th of June, and sailed from New York on the 3rd of October. Variety of character and national relations marked my fellow-passengers on both going out and coming home. Roman Catholic priests, American clergymen, Presbyterian and Episcopalian, and Baptist missionaries mingled in the company; Irishmen who had lived in America, and now had more sympathy with the South than the North; Englishmen who had become American in their associations, and sympathized strongly with the North; American sea-captains, who were peace democrats, and hated the slave; a Virginian slaveholder, who acknowledged owning thirty slaves; a Secessionist and a Southern emissary; men who had become rich, and others who had become poor; American ladies of intelligent and patriotic zeal for their country and religion, and some who hated the forms of religion except in a storm; Jews, Frenchmen, and men born in India; educated and ignorant persons; card players and a professional singer; some that were very pleasant, and others who were destitute of all conversational attraction, formed the motley company. I preached in the cabin, on the poop, and on the forecastle. The cabin and the steerage passengers, besides the crew, supplied the congregation which then assembled. On the voyage out there were 750 who ranked as the latter; but many of them were of the Romish church, and among them the *priest* was welcome. We went out in thirteen days, and came home in about twelve. There was a sneering tone in the would-be critics toward the American army. The "Times" was a principal authority, and the wonderfully eloquent letters of some of "our correspondents" were greatly admired. The "Alabama" and "Florida" were often discussed as we went, and on our way back the Rams were the principal objects of apprehension. The sympathies of the majority on our return voyage were with the North. It is usual that those who have been *in* America are more cordial as her friends than those who have heard of her in other lands.

The scene witnessed at Queenstown, where we took on

board a large increase to our steerage company, was characteristic of the people and the land. The mourning and lamentation of aged relatives seemed intense and overwhelming; wringing their hands, clasping in their bosom, wailing with weeping and distracting cries when parting from young men who were reeling under the influence of drink; nothing more vehement could have been displayed if the travellers were going to execution. Aged women rushed to the verge of the pier, and even on board of the tender, till the observer feared they would precipitate themselves into the sea, as if they could not sever themselves; while other members of the same family were indulging in free and easy conference, or would turn aside for a moment to soothe the agitation of their aged kindred. It was discovered after we had sailed from Queenstown that five men had stowed themselves on board, without paying, and affirming they had no money to pay their passage. They were marked on the back with numbers, to distinguish them, and then made to occupy themselves in menial services on the deck. An unsuccessful attempt was made to move the cabin passengers to subscribe to aid one of these schemers by the begging box being carried round. I suppose the authorities managed to secure payment in America.

Besides the vessels we passed at sea, two occasions occurred to arouse general attention; the first was an iceberg, and the other was the Associated Press boat at Cape Race. The iceberg was a mass of snow and ice, which probably rose 200 feet out of the sea, and, as we were assured, was, doubtless, twice the depth under the surface. A sort of haven or harbour on one side appeared as if it had been excavated to shelter the seals or sea monsters. The thermometer was sensibly lower in the vicinity; whether from the influence of such a mass of ice, or that the region was colder. The same kind of object was visible on our return, and not very far from the same latitude and longitude. The weather was foggy as we came toward Newfoundland, and we feared we should have to bear off from its shores without the opportunity of providing a telegraph to be sent before us. But the atmosphere suddenly cleared up, and our captain was able to communicate with the shore, so that a message was sent to New York forty-eight hours before we arrived in the harbour. As we proceeded we saw 'the lighthouses on the coast of Maine and Massachusetts. Nantucket stood out conspicuously, and soon after we passed Sandy Hook and came within sight of New Jersey heights, and then entered the estuary which receives the waters of the Hudson. It was pleasing to witness the kindly welcome which Americans gave to the headlands of their native country. All passengers were cheerful and on the alert to mark the conspicuous objects on the banks of the majestic estuary, forts and towers, pleasant villas and watering places, which had each a name and a history, and which indicated the approach of our vessel to New York, and the termination of our voyage.

In the times of Dutch power, 1614, this city was designated *New Amsterdam*. I have not come to sketch the harbour, or describe the city, and yet I must say a word on what was so attractive, as we sailed past the "Narrows." The circumference of the harbour from Sandy Hook light to the Narrows is twenty-five miles; and within its outer circle the effect of land and water, ships and vessels, large and small, cities, villages, and villas, from the water's edge to the hill tops, gave variety and attraction to the scenery. The inner harbour, which embraces a basin of water eight miles in length, within the Narrows, is a beautiful bay fringed with picturesque fortifications and defences, which the friend of peaceful commerce would rather look on for ornament than use. Governor's, Bedlow's, and Ellis's islands are occupied by such towers of defence as Fort Columbus, Castle William, and a battery commanding "Buttermilk Channel," which stands as a sentinel for the city of Brooklyn. Forts Hamilton and Lafayette defend Long Island shore; and, on Staten Island, Forts Tomkins and Richmond protect the passage of the Narrows, which is here about two-thirds of a mile in width. Staten Island is six miles below, to the south of the city of New York, stretches fourteen miles in length, and varies in width from four to eight miles. On the north extremity of the island Richmond hill commands the view of all around at an elevation of 300 feet above the sea; and, as the path ascends, elegant private residences give life and charm to the scenery. The forest of masts and the flying *insignia* of all nations, which spread out, line the shores, and throng the piers and recesses of the bay, give a *coup d'œil* which, I think, is not seen either in London or Liverpool. I will not say there are more vessels at New York, but more are visible at one view. The immense, castellated, white-painted, snorting ferry boats, which traverse the bay from and to Brooklyn, Jersey City, Hoboken, and Weehawken, Staten and Coney Islands, add much to the stir and apparent concourse of the navigation. The multitudes passing and repassing every five minutes, give to all the appearance of one gigantic metropolis. The aspect of the custom-house, at least that part of it where our luggage was examined, pleased me. It was insignificant and temporary in its structure, as if the authorities anticipated the time as near when all such barriers to the freest international commerce would be swept away. The examining official showed me every courtesy. There was no passport to be examined, and no personal inspection to be submitted to. This, in one instance, I almost regretted, as thus the *Secession* emissary escaped detection, though, I believe, he carried with him materials or despatches intended for the Confederates. His haste in *disappearing* evinced no small amount of discretion and zeal in his mission.

I went, as had been advised, to the house where my colleague had fixed as the rendezvous for us both. But my arrival was sooner than he had expected, and in his absence no such arrangements for my accommodation as I had proposed was made. By the suggestion of the gentleman at whose house I called I promptly engaged apartments in a boarding-house, whose inmates I soon found were sympathizers with the Southern party. Though I remained all the time I was in New York in my first lodging I found in it no social intercourse, and had not time to cultivate it beyond the breakfast-table. In the afternoon of the day on which I landed I searched out Mr. Oliver Johnson, editor of the "Anti-Slavery Standard;" we were known to each other by name, not personally. I had reason to confide in his discretion, and found him worthy of all the trust I placed in him. His paper is the organ of what is reputed an extreme party, but he exercised toward me the wisdom of a most moderate counsellor. He saw that my safe course was to avoid identification with any ultra section of the people, but to take counsel with men of determinate and unwavering policy—men that had taken their stand on principle, but were discreet in action. I frankly disclosed my mission, objects, and manner in which I should seek to proceed, my knowledge of some Americans, and most limited intercourse with others, and then solicited his advice. The two first men on whom he relied for my ends were Drs. Tyng and J. P. Thompson; and we forthwith proceeded to Dr. Tyng, whom we met pacing in front of his own parsonage. After mutual introduction we all resorted to the doctor's study, and here, in explicit and frank communication, my statements and "instructions" were again submitted. Mr. Johnson had fulfilled his spontaneous duty; but every hour of my stay in America he was a ready, judicious, and able adviser, and an efficient coadjutor, though his name was never prominently given.

The cause which my mission was intended to promote owed much to the Rev. Dr. Tyng for his clear, enlarged, and generous counsel and co-operation. He had unlimited confidence in the faithfulness and zealous co-operation of Dr. J. P. Thompson and Dr. Asa D. Smith, and undertook to invite them to act with himself in further consideration of the nature and ends of my mission. I left my documents with him, and engaged to meet him and the other gentlemen in his study next day. Happily in the interval I met my colleague, explained to him my procedure, and invited him to join the three in conference. He cordially promised to be present, and attended somewhat late in the interview. Drs. Tyng, Thompson, and Smith, an Episcopalian, Congregationalist, and Presbyterian, agreed to act as a provisional committee on our behalf, and cordially undertook each in his own sphere to solicit the presence of ministerial gentlemen in the city and suburbs at a meeting to be held in the following week. They also held themselves responsible to secure a central and respectable place where the conference might be conducted. I had hurried from England, that our address might be made public in America prior to the "4th of July." But that day was now so near, while other appointments interposed to prevent clergymen from assembling, that it was determined to convene the men selected on the 8th of July. The large and commodious buildings of the Bible House were selected, and rooms of the A. B. C. F. Missions were opened to receive the gentlemen who might accept the invitation. British friends of the American slave will not overlook the indication thus afforded of progress in anti-slavery sympathy amongst American organizations. I found the highest and most honoured officials of these institutions not only cordially polite, but warmly expressing their sympathy in my mission. Time works changes, but Divine Providence has marvellously over-ruled events for the progress of opinion, and the cause of the long oppressed slave. Dr. Asa D. Smith effected the arrangements for the conference being held in the Bible House.

The interval, between these preliminaries and the meeting, afforded me opportunity for exploring New York under the guidance of a friend, whom I had met in Paris. The Rev. H. D. Ward earnestly sympathized in the proceedings of French and English clergymen, and desired a cordial reception in America to the anti-slavery address. Toward myself, he and his family manifested all the friendship and reciprocation of international hospitality. The Rev. B. N. Martin, Professor in New York University, evinced the most generous attention, and was ready in all ways to minister to my success and comfort. By the mediation of these gentlemen, other friends materially promoted my work.

On the Fourth of July I attended a morning prayer-meeting in Dr. Tyng's lecture room. I was not observed by the officiating minister till after the service, and heard the pastor in his usual style among his people. The attendance was not crowded, but good and respectable. The sentiments of the address were Christian, faithful, and loyal. The battle of Gettysburg, and the surrender of Vicksburg were imminent, or had occurred, but were not yet known. I heartily enjoyed the service. I attended the Democratic assembly, for partisan orations, in the Music Hall, and heard the *three* distinguished speakers, Horatio Seymour being the most prominent. He is Governor of New York, the supreme magistrate in the state, and hopes to become the successful Democratic candidate for the Presidency, when Lincoln's time expires. The hall was densely filled, and well arranged throughout, for the party

K

fuglemen to lead on the applause. There was much and systematic cheering, as the orators proceeded. Many of the auditors were going in and out, rather as observers than as belonging to the party. I thought Seymour's speech was a well-ordered, heartless, voluble, and insidious piece of claptrap. He had no word of censure for the malignant men who had distracted the people by the fire and carnage of civil war; no word of sympathy for the families and parents whose supports and ornaments had fallen for their country; no sign or hint of admiration for the bravery and self-sacrifice of those who had rushed to the forefront of the battle to rescue their government and nation from disgrace. He magnified the alleged despotic action of the Federal Government in its measures to repress treachery, treason, and rebellion, whereby the Democratic party were repressed, and popular liberty was endangered; he laid the odium and blame of all upon the Republicans, and called on them, for the *peace* of the Republic, to yield themselves and the country to the irresponsible management of himself and his party. The expectation of the New York Democrats that day was, that Lee would overrun Pennsylvania, press on to Washington: and some of them are suspected to have been in the secret of the prospective riots in New York. I learned something by this demonstration of the stump orator, the mass meeting, and the policy of Democratic demagogues.

I surveyed New York as a city in its Broadway and Bowery; its avenues, cross, and parallel streets, squares, public buildings, and environs; sometimes alone and sometimes under the guidance of my friend, who has lived in it more than thirty years, and who could point out as transitional places isolated buildings, familiar to him as his own times. The east river on the one side, and the Hudson on the other, the limits of Manhattan, insulate the city and seemed to prevent its expansion; any great divergence from

the central streets brings into view the watery barrier.
But from "the Battery," situated at the extreme south end
of the city, and which contains eleven acres, planted with
trees and laid out in gravel walks, and its adjacent "Bowl.
ing Green;" passing on to the park, in which stands the
City Hall; and still onward.to Canal Street, the former
boundaries of New York, beyond which lanes, fields, and
rural excursions then invited the pleasure-seeking citizens,
and where are now situated the principal marts of commerce, Wall Street, the Merchants' Exchange, built of
Quincy granite and fire-proof, the Custom House, the Post
Office, and the "Tombs," or Hall of Justice ; the publishing
offices of the "New York Times," "New York Herald,"
"The Tribune," "Independent," the "Evening Post," "The
World," and Barnum's Museum. Still higher up are trading rather than residential parts of New York. But
Broadway, beginning at the Bowling Green, No. 1, ascends
to Haarlem, lined on either side with magnificent buildings,
brick, stone, marble, and iron-framed structures, some of
them reared six and eight stories, close by others which are
not more than two. This vast thoroughfare, thronged with
omnibuses and every other description of vehicle, wide
enough for six or eight carriages to pass each other, and
shooting out its ramified branches, along which pour incessant tides of population and conveyances, prolongs its
course more than a mile before it crosses *First Street*. The
wondrous *tale* is then continued till One Hundred and Tenth
Street becomes the furthest boundary of the *Central Park*,
which lies between the Fifth and Eighth Avenues east and
west. This park occupies eight hundred and forty-three
acres—two miles and a-half in length, and half a mile broad.
The receiving reservoir of the Croton aqueduct enriches
this park, as being the source of water supply to New
York, after having flowed from Croton Lake, a distance of
forty miles :—the cost of the water-works was 13,000,000 of

dollars. But millions more have been expended, and are yet required to be expended on the magnificent park. The work of improvement rapidly proceeds; 3000 labourers are the staff of its progress; the avenues, drives, and walks, hills and dales, lawns and lakes, shrubberies and gardens, attract multitudes for recreation. In the winter time its frozen ponds are covered with thousands, male and female, whose diversion is in skating, or in looking on upon the merry throng.

New York has three hundred churches of all persuasions, and for architectural display the Baptist and Unitarian rival the Episcopal edifices—the Unitarian churches are named, Church of the Messiah, and Church of All Souls. The Hebrew synagogue, "Shaarai Tephita," gates of prayer; the passer by understands the force of the one title as well as the other, but may be perplexed by the title assumed by the Universalists in their "Church of the Divine Unity;" "Church of the Holy Communion" is assumed by an Episcopal church on the Sixth Avenue, Twentieth Street; and "Church of the Puritans" is the name ascribed to a building in Union Square. Many of these structures have been reared at great expense, and have lecture rooms, parsonages, and other accessories connected with them, showing the liberality of their congregations, or the munificence of individual members; all of them were built and are sustained from funds voluntarily contributed; while the salary provided for the clergyman is handsome and freely given. Public institutions, which are in sympathy with liberty and religion, are numerous. Such are the New Bible House, one of the largest structures of brick, covering the area between two streets, and providing in its back parts for printing, binding, and other subordinate purposes. The Board of Commissioners for Foreign Missions has its offices here also. Columbia College, chartered by George II., under the title of King's

College, has now removed from Park Place, where its green lawns and venerable pile have been supplanted by buildings constructed for the purposes of commerce. A more eligible site has been found elsewhere. The New York University, its competitor, occupies a gothic edifice of white marble in Washington Square. Its accommodation appears more extensive than its present requirements. The whole range of building is one hundred and eighty feet long. The Free Academy, Lexington Avenue, is an academy of the highest rank. Its students are chosen from the pupils of the public schools only; it will accommodate one thousand. The Cooper Union was founded by the generous munificence of Peter Cooper, Esq., and the building was erected at the cost of 600,000 dollars. It is devoted, by the design of the benefactor, still living, to the free education of the people, in the practical arts and sciences. It was opened November 1859, with 2000 pupils; one department is a school of design for women. There are also in it a spacious free reading-room, and a magnificent hall for public lectures. The General Theological Seminary of the Prot. Ep. Ch., and the St. Francis Xavier Union Theological Seminary, occupy prominent positions. I might specify the New York Historical Society, the Lyceum of Natural History, American Geographical Society, New York Law Institute, American Institute, Mechanics' Institute, New York Society Library, Astor Library, and the Mercantile Library, the Deaf and Dumb Asylum and Institution for the Blind, as giving proof of the public taste for knowledge, and the means for its diffusion in this flourishing city.

I spent my first Sunday in America at Broadway Tabernacle, and was gratified to hear announced in the morning, for the exercise of devotional thanksgiving, a telegram from the President at Washington, relative to the battle at Gettysburg. Dr. Thompson preached, and intimated that I had consented to occupy his pulpit in the evening, and

deliver the message I had conveyed from ministers in Great
Britain to ministers and pastors in America. The sermon
which he delivered was characterized by much beauty and
sweetness, full in evangelical unction, and affording instruction in divine truth to the thoughtful and studious in
sacred Scripture. The church was large, and the congregation corresponded in numbers and outward respectability.
Here, as in many other churches, besides library-room and
private vestry, the minister had a convenient study furnished for continual resort, and supplied with all things
necessary for comfort, books, paper, etc. Here he could be
retired from domestic visitation during the whole day, and
yet receive visitors, with whom his appointment might be
made. In the evening the assembly was large; Dr. Thompson introduced me by kind and generous mention of my
previous efforts in behalf of the slave, and an assurance that
my sympathies were warmly enlisted with America in her
present conflict.

I prefaced the address by a statement of what had been
done in France to elicit the opinion of her Protestant pastors, and what had been the measures adopted in England
to evoke a response to their appeal. The motives which
prompted 4000 ministers to sign the reply, and the reasons
which probably prevented as many more from attaching
their signatures to the document, were explained as a
principal cause. I mentioned the doubt that many in
England had, as I thought, without sufficient ground
for this suspicion, that the Northern ministers were not
generally in favour of emancipation. I ventured, however,
to give the assurance, that the intelligent working classes
and Nonconformists generally would not consent to the
recognition of a republic based upon the slavery of the
working classes; and that the sympathy between the New
England descendants of the Puritans and their kindred in
the mother country was so strong as to render a state of

hostile alienation distasteful to both peoples. I spoke from personal knowledge, and assured my auditory that the cotton workers in Lancashire had, while enduring want and poverty, from the war policy of the contending parties, persistently withstood all Southern stratagems to draw from them any expression in favour of Confederates; because they were attempting to enforce and extend unrequited labour, to crush the labourers and render secure the power of slave-holders. The address of the Conference was then read, and a few words added detailing the proceedings attending its adoption. The response of the audience was repeatedly uttered in tokens of approval; and when Dr. Thompson followed in expressions of generous commendation, the whole assembly concurred in testimony of cordial concurrence. It was reckoned there were two thousand people in the congregation; and I believe the report which went forth into other parts of America, tended to secure for the mission a favourable reception. Friends came forward to give assurance of their approval, and cheer me on in the service I had come to perform for the welfare of two nations and the liberation of the long-oppressed coloured people of America.

My mission was now ostensibly inaugurated, and I felt bound to avail myself of introductions to conductors and contributors in the press. I saw Mr. Ward Beecher's *locum tenens* in the " Independent," the editors of the " Principia," the editors of the " Examiner," the " Tribune," and the " Evening Post," and others connected with the press. I also came into contact with some who represented the more extreme opinions on the subject of Abolition, and frankly explained my position, both from the " Instructions" I had received and my own judgment, on the course I should pursue. I avowed I was prepared to present the address to all ministers and pastors throughout the United States; and to receive any response which any of them thought it

wise to present. I undertook to preach on the following
Sunday in Brooklyn, in Madison Square Presbyterian
Church, and in the church of the Puritans, in compliance
with the personal request of Dr. Budington, Dr. Adams,
and Dr. Cheever.

I had conferred with Dr. Tyng and his two coadjutors
about the approaching conference; and one of their number,
with the design that something pertinent should be placed
before the assembled clergy, kindly prepared a draft of a
reply which, however, was only to be produced when proceedings reached so far. This document was read to me in
the courteous consideration of the writer. I felt therefore
assured that the deliberations would be conducted to some
issue. The day and hour of appointment arrived, and
promptly assembled twenty-five ministers—Episcopalian,
Presbyterian, Congregationalist, Reformed Presbyterian,
Dutch Protestant Reformed Church, Baptist and Methodist
Episcopalian Church, being represented ; others had been
invited, which would have added Unitarian and Old School
Presbyterian to the divers bodies. One of these was chairman of the Sanatory Commission ; but the sanguinary field
of Gettysburg called him away from New York, while he
signified his concurrence in the conference, and twice
requested me to preach in his pulpit. The meeting was
called to order, and the Rev. Dr. Vinton, Rector of Trinity
Church, was unanimously invited to fill the chair, and the
Rev. J. T. Duryea was appointed clerk. Before I proceeded,
in answer to the call of the chair, to explain the object of
my mission or the terms of my appointment, one of the
reverend brethren, highly esteemed among the clergy, de-
murred to any proceedings which would sanction or open
the way for the interference of British ministers, or of any
anti-slavery deputations in the present agitations in America. He had been in England and had not received what
he thought was courteous treatment from intemperate or

over-zealous advocates of abolition ; and if it was my intention to provoke agitation or interfere by any organized
action in the United States, he was disposed to object. He
would act toward the delegate with all the propriety which
was due to a gentleman: and he believed Dr. M. was worthy
of all deference and consideration in his private intercourse.
But he would resist all public recognition of any official
and organized intermeddling in American affairs. It became
me to be silent at such a time: my friends in the sub-
committee were quite able to disabuse the mind of Dr. V.
They had read my instructions, and had confidence in my
adherence to the course prescribed. While the greatest
consideration was paid to the position and feelings of the
objector, he was convinced that my mission did not trench
upon the lines which he had drawn. So entirely was he,
afterwards, satisfied with my intentions and objects that he
seconded the motion of welcome and commendation to the
deputation, and before the whole conference invited and
importuned me to preach in one of his pulpits. I was at
first requested to offer any explanations I deemed suitable ;
and when I had done so and sat down, I was again requested
to present the address of which I was the bearer.

The discussions which followed were fraternal and deli-
berative, none were taken by surprise, nor did any one concur only to please another. It was concluded that an
answer should be returned to the address, and that a representative committee should be nominated to agree upon a
draft of address to be submitted to the conference. Seven
gentlemen were appointed, and retired to determine the
course of action. Dr. Tyng was placed in the chair, and the
Rev. R. W. Sloane was requested to act as secretary, both
intense and consistent advocates of emancipation. After
deliberation for nearly half an hour, the chairman reported
that the sub-committee advised an adjournment of the conference to meet again in the same place in two days, when

time would have been allowed for a suitable preparation as required by the response of the conference. In accordance with this recommendation, it was resolved to adjourn till Friday, the 10th of July. At the hour appointed, nearly all the clergymen present at the first meeting, and five or six others, assembled. The committee brought up a report, to which all had agreed. The utmost freedom of discussion followed; amendments were made, accepted, rejected, and replaced by others. The whole draft was again read, and each clause, *seriatim*, put to the vote; and all was adopted without a division or dissentient. It was not so long, nor did it so enter into details as the draft primarily prepared, but it spoke the sentiments of all the conference, who agreed to sign it. Resolutions commending the mission to ministers in other parts of America, and inviting the signatures of other ministers in the state of New York, were passed, and the Rev. J. T. Duryea, was authorized to incur necessary expenses in making public the arrangements and action of the conference, and in procuring signatures to the response. Such signatures were requested to be forwarded, addressed to him at the Bible House; and after some delay, caused by the riots at New York, a report of the proceedings appeared in every denominational journal in the state of New York.

The address has been engrossed and signed by the members of the conference, and is as follows :—

REPLY TO AN "ADDRESS TO MINISTERS AND PASTORS OF ALL CHRISTIAN DENOMINATIONS THROUGHOUT THE STATES OF AMERICA," FROM MINISTERS IN FRANCE AND GREAT BRITAIN.

REVEREND AND DEAR BRETHREN,—We have received with much pleasure the " Address to Ministers and Pastors of all Christian Denominations throughout the States of America," adopted by the " Anti-Slavery Conference of Ministers of Religion," held in the city of Manchester on the 3rd of June, 1863, and presented to us by the Rev. James W. Massie, D.D., LL.D., of London, and the Rev.

J. H. Rylance, M.A., of Westminster, who were appointed a deputation for that purpose.

The personal character of the gentlemen composing this deputation, and the honourable and dignified assemblage which they represent, bespeak for the Address our most respectful attention. And its importance is enhanced by the consideration that it represents not only the immediate Conference at Manchester, but also 1000 ministers of Great Britain, and 750 ministers of France, who had agreed in protesting against the recognition of " a Confederacy which lays down as the corner-stone of its constitution the system of slavery as it exists at present in the Southern states." That so many intelligent and thoughtful men in the ministry of the Gospel should have united in such a protest, is equally honourable to them and gratifying and encouraging to us.

Perhaps we ought not to wonder, and certainly we will not now complain, that the severe struggle in which we are engaged, is looked upon by our transatlantic brethren so exclusively in its relations to the 4,000,000 of Africans held in bondage upon our soil. As Christian men, we also are fully awake to the sin and shame of American slavery, and are instant in prayer to God, that the time may be at hand when this hateful institution which has inspired the present gigantic Rebellion shall be utterly destroyed.

But we are Americans, contending in arms for the preservation of our national life, and for all the great interests of Constitutional liberty and order, which are at stake upon the issue of this conflict. The dismemberment of our Republic would be, not merely the loss of territory and power to the Federal Union, not merely the ruin of existing forms and institutions of Government, but the downfall of Constitutional liberty itself upon the North American Continent. Nor can there be any well-founded hope of ultimate deliverance for the enslaved among us, but in the triumph of our arms between antagonistic civilizations—the one asserting and vindicating the dignity of labour, the other scorning labour, and trampling it under foot.

That we are to succeed in this struggle, and by the blessing of God come out of it an unbroken nation, we do not doubt. It appears to us also to be the purpose of Providence, that the Rebellion and its guilty cause shall be buried in the same grave. In this, as Christian men, we do greatly rejoice. It sweetens the bitterness of our present lot, to believe that in vindicating, against an inexcusable conspiracy, the just and beneficent authority of the nation, at so great a cost of treasure and of blood, we are at the same time serving the cause of universal liberty.

We thank you, dear brethren, for your words of cheer. We rejoice in the fellowship of the saints. And most heartily do we unite our prayers with yours, that the powerful Christian nations to which we respectively belong may never be arrayed against each other in deadly strife, but may stand up together for the maintenance of righteousness, of peace, and of freedom. And to this end, may the Christian people of these nations cultivate a mutual respect and regard, and be ready to co-operate in any good work for the welfare of mankind, and the advancement of Christ's Kingdom in the world.

Francis Vinton, D.D., Assistant Minister, Trinity Church, New York; Stephen H. Tyng, D.D., Rector of St. George's Church, New York; Rosswell D. Hitchcock; Asa D. Smith, Pastor of the Fourteenth Street Presbyterian Church, New York; Theo. Lidyard Cuyler; Talbot W. Chambers; Milton Rodger, Secretary Assistant, Home Missionary Society, New York City; Jos. P. Thomson, Pastor of the Broadway Tabernacle Church, New York; Henry Dana Ward; Henry G. Weston, Pastor Madison Avenue Baptist Church; George Whipple, Secretary of the American Missionary Association; Joseph Duryea, Min. Col. Ref. D. Church, Secretary; Thos. Armitage, Pastor of the Fifth Avenue Baptist Church; Alfred Cookman, Pastor of Trinity M. E. Church; Benjamin N. Martin, Professor New York University; Thos. E. Vermilye, Minister of the Collegiate Church, New York; Henry B. Smith, Professor in Union Theo. Seminary, New York; Howard Crosby, Pastor of the Fourth Avenue Presbyterian Church, New York; W. D. Gause, Pastor of the North West Reformed Presbyterian Church, New York; I. R. W. Sloane, Pastor of the Third Reformed Presbyterian Church. Two hundred and twenty more names were added in an authenticated list.*

---

* 26, West, 36th Street, New York City,

Rev. Dr. Massie,　　　　　　　*October 7th*, 1863.

My dear Brother,—I am exceedingly sorry that I was

These proceedings sufficed to accredit the mission to other parts of the United States, and gave access to leading citizens in New York and in Washington. I found some willing to

---

misinformed in reference to the time of your departure for England. I would have had our response in your hands promptly the day before the sailing of the steamer. I trust it will now arrive in season for all practical purposes by express. With reference to the matter, I desire to make a little explanation.

When you arrived, our clergymen were just departing for their summer recreation. It was, therefore, difficult to get your address before them for any concordant action. Our body, by which you were received, was not as extensively representative as it might have been under other circumstances. We could not, therefore, expect as many to send us their names to be appended to our response as if we had been a great national society, such as the Anti-Slavery Society of the country. Again, the names received have been sent us without the slightest solicitation on our part, except the general invitation through the public press.

In one or two cases, a clergyman has constituted himself our agent, circulating the address himself in person, in his vicinity, gathering a score of names. From which fact, we believe, could we have sent out agents to solicit signatures, we might have received from five to ten thousand names. Some one was needed in hundreds of cases to call attention, awaken interest, make explanation, in order to secure the end. It will, however, be remembered that this response is but one of many which you bear to your brethren. It is a single expression among scores you have received in your most useful fraternal visit among us.

Now that you have departed let me say, the result of your efforts is beginning to appear. You will be long remembered with gratitude and affection, and your name and mission will remain a part of the history of this eventful period of our national existence. We are, as a nation, fast becoming Abolitionists. Conservative men are slowly be-co-operate and solicitous that I should extend my mission much further than had been contemplated when first undertaken. To my hesitation on the score of finances a prompt answer was made to free me from any anxiety. I was introduced by Professor Martin to Mr. Opdyke, Mayor of New York, who entered most minutely and calmly into the object of the mission; and, in the midst of pressing and important duties, arranged for my having a free pass by rail to and from Washington, through Philadelphia and Baltimore; so that 1 could pause at each place, and though in the midst of much military and popular excitement, I was introduced to men in authority, at times most convenient to myself. Thus I was permitted to witness some results of the New York riots, which I could not otherwise have known. I had letters also to the highest functionaries of the state, and personal introductions, which seemed all I could desire. My intercourse with Dr. Budington of Brooklyn, and his congregation, though only to preach a gospel sermon, was most useful and pleasant. I saw the Harpers, Carters, and Putnams, New York publishers; the law advisers of the local and general government; merchants who had their correspondents in almost every city of the West, to whom I received letters of introduction. My clerical friends drew out my chart of progress, and furnished me with minute directions how and where to proceed, and whom first to see. Thus facilities and a position of authority were derived in New York which guaranteed final success. I was requested to

---

coming radical. God is delaying our final triumph over rebellion until we do justice and love mercy.

God bless you, and make you the heir of the Saviour's promise and benediction—"Blessed are the peacemakers, for they shall be called the children of God."—Yours in the best of bonds,

JOSEPH T. DURYEA.

deliver the address in the church of the Puritans, in which Dr. Cheever was pastor. Till Saturday I had not anticipated any other than a sermon and its usual accompaniments; but in the newspapers of that morning I saw an announcement that the English address and a reply would be presented. The assembly was large, and some prominent men, as Mr. Horace Greeley, were present. I endeavoured to discharge my duty without compromise or offence to other parties. After I had delivered my explanatory statement and read the address from the Antislavery Conference, Dr. Cheever presented a reply much longer than the one adopted by the Conference, and expounding the peculiar views which he has elsewhere advanced. When he had closed, and I was expected to finish the evening's engagements, I observed that I presumed it was not expected I should make any comments on the address of Dr. Cheever, which was in the name of a committee and signed by three gentlemen. I do not here make any comments on the positions, arguments, and aim of the address, but judge it worthy of thoughtful consideration, whether for reproof, correction, or instruction. I feel it due to the eminent men who sign it, and the cause to which they have consecrated their talents, lives, and reputation, to give their address a place, *as a note*. It would be too long for incorporation here. I do not suppose that had I appeared in New York under Dr. Cheever's auspices alone, I should have generally found so cordial a welcome, or had such assurances of approbation. Truth does not always however bear a gilded banner, nor is popularity always an infallible criterion, and its champion must sometimes consent to be numbered in a minority.

I had another engagement in New York, which deserves a special notice; but as it was among brethren of colour, and in whose behalf I was willing to labour and, if need be, to suffer, I will defer any account of it till I come to speak of the New York riots. I left this city on the second day of their occurrence, and not anticipating the serious and threatening character they afterward assumed. Happily for me, I met at the Jersey City Railway Station Mr. Montgomery Gibbs, connected with one of the departments, whom I had but casually been introduced to, in the parlour of Mr. Barney, collector of New York Customs. I am indebted to him for a hundred comforts and conveniences derived through his considerate attentions during that week, on the road and at Washington.

The route of that day's journey commenced at Jersey City Ferry. But an incident occurred, owing to the rioting then in progress, which served to show the occupation of the public; no one could be found at the boarding-house who could convey my portmanteau to a street car; no coach could be procured. I started, carrying it myself rather than lose my train; hoping I might meet man or boy who would consent to bear the burden for a reward. But my hope was vain. Finally and laboriously I reached the Broadway; but though hundreds of conveyances passed in half an hour, they were all filled—omnibuses, carriages, etc. In my despair I caught the eye of a porter driving his empty cart. He stopped; I asked could he convey the portmanteau to the railway station? He could. What would be his charge? He would leave it to myself. No, but I wished to know what would satisfy him, he would still leave it to myself. The portmanteau was placed on the cart; but now what was to be done with myself? I had not time to walk; I could not leave my luggage with a stranger, over whom I had no check. The only alternative was for me to mount, and sit or stand on the shaking cart, moving as fast as the horse could proceed down Broadway, a mile and a half toward the river, and through the dense mass of the agitated population. I thought if some old friend from England, or some new acquaintance in America should discover my position, I should be deemed a fit subject for ridicule or wonder. I therefore sat down on the open cart, making a seat of my portmanteau for twenty minutes; took my spectacles off, resolved *I should see no one*, whoever might perceive me. I reached my destination; after having discovered my mistake in going to the wrong pier. I asked the porter his charge again, but he would not specify any amount. I offered him a quarter of a dollar, which he accepted with many hearty thanks. And now I was on my route for Washington, *via* Philadelphia. The clerk at the station entered my luggage and gave me a check for the latter place, the error of which I did not apprehend till I was at this intermediate stage of the journey. We passed by Jersey City, Newark, Elizabeth, New Brunswick, Princeton, Trenton, Camden, and Philadelphia, travelling over a distance of ninety miles. It is an immense thoroughfare, and, in some parts, passes over a flat, uninteresting country; but as it tracks its way by Trenton, some of Washington's achievements are recalled to the glory of the American and the reproach of English soldiers.

The route proceeds through Delaware, a state only ninety-six miles in length and thirty-seven in breadth. The earliest settlers here in 1627 were Swedes and Finns. The Dutch in 1655 acquired the territory, and the British extended their rule over it in 1664. Wilmington and Havre-de-Grace are the only towns on this part of the road passed by the railway. In the former the population rapidly increases, and its manufactures give employment to an industrious community. The latter is at the head of the Chesapeake Bay, on the Susquehanna river in Maryland, which the railway cars cross by a steam ferry. I passed through Philadelphia by street cars and too late to remedy the mistake discovered that my portmanteau would be left here by the conductor of the luggage van. Means

L

however were found to have it forwarded by a succeeding train. From this city to Baltimore the distance is ninety-seven miles, and as 'there was doubt of being able to proceed all the way to Washington, sweeping floods having injured bridges on the road, I consented to sleep at the Eutaw house under the auspices of my fellow-traveller. Next day after breakfast a train started for our destination, but the passengers were detained for hours under a broiling sun, and unsheltered, at the Thomas viaduct, which crosses the Patuxent. Here we saw large bodies of troops hastening on to New York to quell the Irish rioters; they had two hundred miles to travel, but would probably arrive before dawn next morning. In our dreary delay, at a distance from any place of refreshment, some of the passengers wandered around gathering blackberries, some occupied themselves discussing politics. I found two or three who had recently returned to America from Europe, and had the latest news from England. Among the crowd waiting at the station-house were two Secession prisoners; taken, I suppose, under circumstances of special aggravation. Their appearance had all the significance of the wretchedness of warfare. One was without shoe, stocking, or covering for his head, and lay upon the ground sleeping as a dog would lie, a seeming mass of misery; the other moved about like a culprit in chains, braving the looks of all around him; but yet proving the alienation produced by a war for slavery. They had not the air of either patriots or of martyrs in their manners.

All the passengers were glad to find occupation to mind or body, and after half the day was spent we were enabled to proceed, passing Bladensburg and entering the District of Columbia, which extends over sixty square miles. Washington the capital and Georgetown are the towns situated within its bounds. I arrived and was guided at once to Willard's Hotel, where I was provided with a private room, giving me many conveniences which were a special favour, without extra charge.

I had proceeded to the capital furnished, I believed, with such testimonials as would assure me of admission to any of the distingushed men holding office. Mr. Charles Sumner gave me a private letter to the President, in consequence of a protracted interview we had. Messrs. Cobden and Bright had written to him, mentioning my mission and their personal knowledge of me. To illustrate the estimate in which the latter is held in America, he mentioned having received a letter from Mr. Bright, soliciting the forbearance of Government toward a young man from Birmingham, who had been detected as a ringleader in conspiring against the Union in the far west. He only requested that if consistent with policy and justice, leniency might be exercised. Mr. Sumner on receipt of the letter went in to the President and laid the communication before him. It was unknown at Washington to what department at California the case might belong. Mr. Lincoln authorized Mr. Sumner to telegraph to the chief authorities and request that no action should be taken, or any sentence of punishment, till he had considered the matter and seen the proceedings. A telegram was instantly forwarded and an answer received the same day in time for the post, which Mr. Sumner dispatched to Mr. Bright in London by the return mail. Mercy was subsequently exercised to the offender. I had letters to the Secretaries of State for the Treasury, the Foreign and the War departments; I had also the personal services of Dr. Budington from Brooklyn, Mr. M. Gibbs, and Mr. Aspinwall. I was promptly received by Mr. W. H. Seward, and had opportunity to lay before him the design and origin of my mission. He gave a patient and considerate hearing to all I thought right to state. He advised I should see Lord Lyons before any official and formal communication with

the President, and promised to apprise the ambassador of
the object of my visit; and accompanied me to the *White
House*, where he introduced me to Mr. Lincoln. This
interview lasted about a quarter of an hour. Both were
affable and courteous, and conversed without restraint on
matters of general interest; kindly accepting my apology
for not appearing in ministerial garb, as my baggage was
still delayed on the road. On the same day I was introduced to Mr. Salmon P. Chase, and to General Heintzelman, adjutant-general. I dined with Mr. Seward, and met
at his house Mr. Senator Wilson, and two gentlemen who
had been in England on a private mission from the American Government. I waited on Lord Lyons at the
embassy, and was immediately received by his lordship. I
gave him a copy of our address and of the proceedings of
the Conference at Manchester, and explained to him the
aim of my mission generally, what my instructions were,
and in what mode I intended to proceed. I submitted for
his perusal if he desired, but he declined, the letter intended for the President of the United States. He gave
the fullest and most patient consideration to the whole
matter; spoke as a sincere friend of America and as re-
posing entire confidence in Mr. Lincoln and his administration, so far as England was concerned; signified his
general approval of the object and appointment of my
mission, and wished and hoped for me full success. Lord
Lyons does not need any good word from me; but I believe
him eminently qualified for his office, and worthy of the
confidence of the American Government.

As soon as I had obtained my audience of the ambassador I felt at liberty to forward my documents, and
request an interview with the President. I made this
application through the Secretary for Foreign Affairs. Mr.
Seward had given a satisfactory reason for the precaution
he had commended. He said their government were

anxious to retain the entire confidence of their English
allies, and to do nothing but was known to them. On this
principle, when addresses sent from public meetings in
London, in Manchester, and other towns in Britain had
come to the President, they were shown to the British representative ; and before an answer was officially made it was
shown to Lord Lyons and sent to the American Ambassador in London, that he might submit it to the perusal of
Lord Russell, before it should be forwarded to the parties
for whom it was ultimately intended. I received an
acknowledgment from the Secretary of State, intimating
that the President would admit me to an audience next
day (Saturday), at twelve o'clock. I found Mr. Lincoln in
the midst of a revision of the sentences of court martials,
which seemed to him a matter of serious and conscientious
responsibility. He referred to the feeling which this produced, and also to a case which occurred immediately after
he entered on his office as President, and expressed the
emotion produced in his mind in the fact that he was the
last on whose *fiat* a man's life depended. There was here
no trifling with death, or indifference to the issues of warfare. Mr. Lincoln read aloud to me, he had already
perused, as he assured me, the letter I conveyed, and
entered freely into a review of its contents, showing me
that he fully apprehended the subject, and was prepared
to maintain the position assumed in his proclamation of
the 1st of January, 1863. I remained with him about half
an hour, and left him when I considered my mission was
discharged. There was no witness to our interview, and I
will not publish any report of it. I will only add that I
believe he is an honest anti-slavery friend of the negro,
wishes the emancipation of every slave within the limits
of the Republic, and will faithfully stand by every word of
the proclamation, not receding one step. I think him a
true but unassuming Christian, in his integrity resolved to

prove himself an American patriot, and eminently fitted for the place and time to which by Divine Providence he has been raised. He may be slow in his purposes, but when formed, sure in their execution.

To His Excellency ABRAHAM LINCOLN,
President of the United States.

Sir,—As Chairman of a large Public Meeting recently held in the Free Trade Hall, I have the honour to forward you the enclosed documents—

(1) Report of a Conference of Ministers of religion, held in this city on the 3rd instant, convened by circular inviting the attendance of ministers to receive the report of the committee having charge of the reply to the French Pastors' address to Ministers in Great Britain on American Slavery, and the revolting spectacle of a Confederacy forming itself with a professed design of maintaining and propagating slavery.

(2) Address of the French Pastors.

(3) Reply—Address signed by nearly four thousand British Ministers of Religion.

(4) The Conference—Address to Ministers and Pastors of all Christian Denominations throughout the States of America.

(5) Report of the Public Meeting in the Free Trade Hall.

You will not fail to observe that whilst all these documents scrupulously avoid any reference to differences of opinion which may be supposed to exist in the United States respecting the extinction of slavery, they one and all condemn those who are seeking to found an Empire upon it as the "chief corner-stone."

The French Pastors remark that "No more revolting " spectacle has ever been set before the civilized world than " a Confederacy consisting mainly of Protestants forming " itself and demanding independence in the nineteenth " century of the Christian era, with professed design of " maintaining and propagating slavery—a Confederacy " which lays down as the corner-stone of its constitution " the system of slavery, as it exists at present in the

" Southern states, a system which may be defined briefly
" as the right to treat men like cattle, and to commit
" adultery and murder with impunity."

To this the British Ministers reply :—

" Like yourselves, we feel a deep compassion for slaves,
" who are a part of the human family. We wish by all
" means in our power to discourage those who are seeking
" to found an empire on their degradation, and we wish
" success to all just and humane measures for their deliver-
" ance."

And the address, adopted by the Ministerial Conference,
after giving an able summary of both these documents,
observes—

" Our solemn conviction is, that no darker nor more
" dreary calamity could threaten any nation or people on
" earth than the successful establishment of a Republic
" whose corner-stone is the slavery of working men. The
" curse thus entailed would extend its poisonous influence
" far beyond the utmost range of the black population, and
" involve in moral degradation, corruption, and bondage,
" not only all the white people, rich and poor, but the
" Government ruling them, the states holding friendly
" relation with them, and the merchants made rich by their
" merchandize and depending on their favour."

On the other hand, the address just referred to cordially recognizes the great progress which has been made
towards complete emancipation by the Government of the
United States in the abolition of slavery in the District of
Columbia. The reciprocal treaty between England and
America on the slave trade, the abolition of slavery in the
Territories, the offer of compensation to such loyal states as
are willing, voluntarily, to emancipate their slaves, the
recognition of the Republics of Hayti and Liberia, and the
emancipation proclamation of the first of January last,
respecting which it remarks—

" We read with deep and prayerful interest the pro-
" clamation of emancipation by the President, and rejoice
" that notwithstanding the fears entertained by some good
" men, the results have been so beneficial."

The whole of these proceedings were reported to a
meeting of at least 6000 citizens of Manchester, assembled
in our Free Trade Hall, and as chairman of that meeting

I have much pleasure in bearing testimony that notwithstanding the pre-arranged and systematic efforts of a small section of people to create disturbance, the sentiments expressed in the address and reiterated by the various speakers, were cordially responded to by an overwhelming majority, certainly not less than nine-tenths of the meeting.

I have also the honour to inform you that the Reverend Dr. Massie, of London, and the Reverend J. H. Rylance, of St. Paul's, Westminster, have been appointed a deputation to convey these various documents to their ministerial brethren in the United States, and to express to them our goodwill and sympathy with your country in the case of human freedom.

I have the honour to remain, Sir,
Your obedient servant,
(Signed)   THOS. BAYLEY POTTER.
Manchester, *June 12th*, 1863.

Legation of the United States, London,
22nd August, 1863.

Sir,—The President of the United States having received, at the hands of the Rev. Drs. Massie and Rylance, the address of the meeting recently held in the Free Trade Hall, Manchester, I have now the honour, under instructions from Washington, to forward to you the accompanying letter in reply, from the Secretary of State.

I have the honour to be, Sir,
Your obedient servant.
CHARLES FRANCIS ADAMS.

THOMAS BAYLEY POTTER, Esq.

Department of State, Washington,
25th July, 1863.

Sir,—I have had the honour to receive from the Rev. Dr. Massie and the Rev. Dr. Rylance your address, in the name of a large public meeting which was recently held at the Free Trade Hall, Manchester, to the President of the United States, together with papers which constitute the accompaniments of that communication. These papers have been submitted to the President of the United States, and I am charged by him to inform you that he has read them with the most lively satisfaction, and with a profound sense of the obligation which the reverend religious pastors in France and the reverend religious pastors in Great Britain have laid upon the world by their correspondence with each other, and their common address to the Christian ministers and pastors throughout the United States.

The proceedings of the meeting at the Free Trade Hall, and its address to the President, touchingly and admirably harmonize with the sentiments which pervade the correspondence before mentioned.

The parties in these proceedings will readily understand that the attempted revolution in the United States sensibly affects this Government and American society itself in many ways, which it has not fallen within the province of those parties to examine. While the interests thus naturally, and not improperly, overlooked in Europe furnish the strongest possible motives to the people of the United States for suppressing the insurrection and maintaining the Constitutional Government received at the hands of their fathers, the President readily accepts and avows, as an additional and irresistible motive, the suggestion made by the friends of our country in Europe, that the success of the insurrection would result in the establishment, for the first time in the history of the human race, of a State based upon the exclusive foundations of African slavery.

I have the honour to be, Sir,
Your very obedient servant,
WILLIAM H. SEWARD.
THOMAS B. POTTER, Esq., Manchester, England.

Till I had brought my mission to the President to a conclusion, I did not involve myself in other engagements; but on the morning of Saturday, I waited on two prominent clergymen of the capital. One of them seemed ready to counsel, and take part in arrangements proposed by another resident pastor; from this position, however, he subsequently receded, for reasons which I need not suggest. The second clergyman at first hesitated, and then positively declined taking part in any anti-slavery procedure. He gave as his reason the offence and opprobrium heretofore attached to such agitation, and added that he believed

" if Jesus Christ had inaugurated his gospel with the prefix *anti-slavery*, there were thousands, even now, who would refuse to be called Christians." This gentleman and his *wife* were from the South. I replied, " It is the fact, sir, Jesus Christ did introduce his gospel with a pre-face of equal import. When He stood up in the synagogue in Nazareth for his first service of ministration, the place of the Scripture which He read was where it is written, ' The spirit of the Lord is upon me, because He hath anointed me to preach the gospel to the poor. He hath sent me to heal the broken hearted, to preach deliverance to the captives, and recovering of sight to the blind, to set at liberty them that are bruised, to preach the accept-able year of the Lord. And He closed the book, and He gave it again to the minister and sat down. And the eyes of all them that were in the synagogue were fastened on Him. And He began to say unto them, This day is the Scripture fulfilled in your ears.' "

I did not mention this man's name to the President, but recited to him the substance of my reply and the con-clusion I would adduce, that to be *anti-slavery* was Christ-like. It was arranged that I should preach in the First Presbyterian Church in Washington on Sunday morning, and that in the same church I should deliver my message to " ministers and pastors" in the evening. In the morn-ing I delighted myself in the great truths of a divine redemption, and found acceptance among many hearers. The Rev. Dr. Sunderland, pastor of the church, arranged for the evening, and prepared a response to be read at the close of the English address. The evening audience was immense, filling to overflow the large church. I was informed gentlemen of distinguished position and office were among the congregation. The prefatory address was in the same strain as I have represented that delivered at the Broadway Tabernacle, though a little amplified, and

with a reference to the President and his reception.
Throughout the evening the congregation repeatedly
applauded the speaker, and at the close many gentlemen
waited to assure me of their earnest sympathy and entire
concurrence. The reply read by Dr. Sunderland was submitted to the revision of Mr. Lincoln, and having his
approval, was put into my hands. Under such circumstances, the Washington address comes with an emphasis
deserving general attention. But there were other men
present whose concurrence would speak for numerous influential portions of society. I was assured that had a
similar service been conducted in that city eighteen months
or two years before, and such sentiments been uttered, the
speakers would have been mobbed, and probably the building endangered. No doubt, it would have been a different
audience. Slave-holders and their rough and ruthless
myrmidons were then pursuing their unrighteous trade,
now the inhabitants of Washington, black and white, are
all free.

THE MISSION OF REV. DR. MASSIE.

A large concourse of citizens assembled in the First
Presbyterian church, Four-and-a-half Street, last Sabbath
evening, to witness the presentation of addresses from
French and British clergymen to the Christian ministers of
this country, and the reply of some of the ministers of
Washington to those addresses. The large church was
early filled to its utmost capacity, and for two hours the
audience remained as though riveted to the spot, exhibiting every sign of the most intense and unwearied
interest.

Without the formality of an organization, as by common
consent the pastor of the church presided, and conducted
the services of prayer, reading the Scriptures, and singing,
assisted by the Revs. Messrs. Gray, Mitchell, Noble, Howlett, and Morris.

The Rev. Dr. Massie was introduced to the audience as

the senior member of the deputation from the Conference
of Ministers lately held in Manchester, England. For an
hour and a half he held the great assembly enchained by his
clear statement of the varieties of sentiment in Great
Britain, and by his words of burning eloquence, touching
the vast and solemn issues of the American struggle. In
the midst of his address he read the formal and published
documents of the French and British ministers, and explained the circumstances of their origin and of his own
connection with the mission which brought him to our
shores.

The reply of the Washington clergymen was read by
the Rev. Dr. Sunderland, and is as follows :—

Dr. Massie.

REVEREND BROTHER,—We address you as the senior
member of the deputation charged by the conference lately
held in Manchester, to present to Christian ministers in
America the addresses of the ministers of France and
Great Britain, and convey to them such responses as you
may receive in the United States ; and we respectfully request you to report to our brethren across the waters this
answer in our behalf.

The undersigned are but few out of the many pastors
and resident clergymen in the capital of the nation. The
reason of this is, that some who have been approached de-
cline all connection with the proceeding, while the most
part have not been consulted for want of time, and we cannot say what they might do in the premises. You have
come a long distance to bring to us the greeting of a great
company of the servants of Jesus in Britain and in France.
Your mission to this country is a remarkable moral phenomenon, the full providential significance of which neither
yourselves nor we can at present comprehend. You find
us in one of the most terrific struggles of human history,
and you have perceived, as we do, that it involves the
condition of the enslaved negro, as well as that of our own
free race, and that upon this issue evasion is no longer
possible.

Under these circumstances, the grateful sense we feel of
your former kindness and the assured sympathy of so many

of your fellow-countrymen is deepened by the fact that the subjects of a Government so connected with the origin of slavery in this land are now willing to encourage us in the removal of the stupendous evil. We do not receive you as ambassadors of civil government, but as the servants only of that gracious Kingdom of our Lord, "which is righteousness, and peace, and joy in the Holy Ghost;" and therefore on this occasion we cannot speak of the course of any European government, as it may be thought to affect our own in this momentous period.

We have listened with attention to the appropriate addresses which you have so earnestly presented. We recognize your Christian interest in the bondman of America and your urgent desire for his liberation and enfranchisement. We discover also your abhorrence of an empire sought to be founded on the corner-stone of human slavery, and of the frightful consequences which must follow its successful establishment in every part of the world. We appreciate the vision of our country's security and greatness which you describe in such fervent eloquence, when once the dark problem that now confronts us shall have been solved in the certain course of Providence.

In all these expressions of your views we cannot doubt the sincerity either of your philanthropy or of your friendship for our country, or of your profession of the sublime faith of our common Christianity. We, therefore, truly respect your motives, and heartily reciprocate your wishes in every way that is compatible with Christian candour, or that Christian courtesy would dictate.

While we acknowledge before God and in the hearing of mankind that our nation is deeply involved in the crime and the curse of slavery, we yet feel bound to declare that this institution stands not alone in the infatuation of the people of the States where it exists to-day, but likewise in the baleful prejudice against the black race which so widely prevails in all our borders. With this frank confession we do not, however, for a single moment admit that American slavery is the only evil which provokes the anger of the Supreme Ruler of the world. On the contrary, we do know that such is the complicity of all the leading nations of the earth with violence, injustice, and irreligion, that none of them can assume a station of superiority above another, and say, "Stand aside, for I am holier than thou."

We are historically a youthful nation, and whatever may be our faults or our vices at home, we know comparatively little of the intrigue of diplomacy in which the older governments have become adept. We wish "to avoid all entangling alliances." We would most importunately deprecate the woes of a general and internecine war, and most sedulously study the things that make for a righteous and universal peace. But the issues of both peace and war are in the hands of Him who "doeth according to his will in the army of heaven, and among the inhabitants of the earth." When He "rises up" who "can stay his hand?" When He "creates evil" who shall hinder it?

And now, reverend brother, receive for yourself and the thousands you represent our most heartfelt and Christian salutations. May the good providence of God go with you! May you speed well in your mission, and have an open door in America! May you find warm hearts and cordial greetings everywhere. May you be successful in "strengthening the things that remain" beyond your most sanguine hopes, and when it shall please God to have fulfilled his work by you in our country, and to have brought you again in safety to your own land, may you have a wonderful story of experience to tell them, and the abundance of Divine grace to cheer the countenance of your brethren and ours in the Lord. Bear to them our Christian love; confirm our fellowship in the labours of the Cross, and constantly relate our prayers, that when we leave this world we may come together to "the General Assembly and Church of the firstborn" in a heavenly and a better country.—B. Sunderland, Pastor of First Presbyterian Church; T. R. Howlett, Pastor of Calvary Baptist Church; B. F. Morris, Minister of Sixth Presbyterian Church; E. H. Gray, Pastor of E Street Baptist Church; James Mitchell, Commissioner of Emigration, and Minister of Methodist Episcopal Church; Mason Noble, Chaplain of United States Navy; hobert McMurdy, Presbyter of Protestant Episcopal Church; E. Goodrich Smith, Minister of Presbyterian Church (Fourth Presbytery, New York); J. D. Turner Cote, Chaplain of United States Volunteers; H.

W. Read, Minister of Baptist Church; J. W. Monfort, Minister of Presbyterian Church; W. B. Matchett, Chaplain of United States Volunteers; Robert Kellen, Chaplain of United States Volunteers; W. M. D. Ryan, Pastor of Foundry Methodist Episcopal Church; J. G. Butler, Pastor of St. Paul's Lutheran Church; T. B. McFalls, Pastor of Assembly's Presbyterian Church; W. Y. Brown, Chaplain of United States Hospital; J. J. Ferre, Chaplain of United States Army; J. M. Driver, Chaplain of United States Hospital; N. B. Northrop, Chaplain United States Hospital: G. G. Gass, Chaplain of United States Army; J. W. Alvord, Secretary of American Boston Tract Society; J. J. Marks, District Secretary of American Tract Society; C. P. Russel, Congregational Minister; Isaac Cross, Missionary American Missionary Association; A. P. Pitcher, Missionary of Young Men's Christian Association.

I had much pleasure in a survey of the Smithsonian Institution, in penetrating all the apartments, library, and halls of the Congress, and tracing the plan on which Washington has been built. The public buildings, on a scale of magnificence more correspondent to their national purposes than the parts of the city by which they are surrounded, are worthy of admiration by the visitor. The incipient national monument to the first President, the White House, and Treasury buildings have a substantial and imposing appearance; the General Post Office, the Patent Office, the National Observatory, where the rebel, Maury, reached his celebrity; the Navy Yard, the City Hall, etc.; the National Cemetery and the New Park would claim distinction in a descriptive work. But I had one thing to do; I found a series of wards of a hospital for the soldiers, who had returned, wounded or diseased, from the field, and enjoyed a quiet interview with a good man in charge of the religious department. Twice I passed the bridge of the Potomac, through George Town into Virginia; once escorted by General Heintzelman's staff, to survey Arlington Heights and the forts erected in that part of Virginia for the protection of Washington. The house was shown to me where the Confederate general, Lee, resided, as the heir of Mr. Custis, and thus related to George Washington. The bed on which the President died stands there—a frail couch for a great man. The pictures in rooms and hall are miserable pretences; the apartments are in a state of dilapidation, which must have been in progress before the war. I conversed with one of Mr. Custis's slaves, who had fallen into the hands of General Lee, and who gave an unvarnished and veritable account of the woman-flogging performed by the chivalrous general. He claimed *legacy duty* on the slaves whose freedom had been bequeathed by their old master, and charged it as high as five years' servitude. They claimed immediate freedom as by will of the testator, and left the premises; whereupon Mr. Lee sent after and seized them, ordered them to be flogged by the overseer. The obedient scourge did his bidding for the males; but he was not spaniel enough to whip the women; and the brave general himself took the whip, and extracted their legacy duty in tears and blood; and, it is said, poured not oil, but brine into their open wounds. Thus I saw the slaves and hearthstone of that military captain whom the "Times" delights to honour. We went farther, beyond the contraband and to convalescent camps, where were 8500 sick men and paroled prisoners. Properly it was a threefold camp, viz., Straggler's Camp, Parole Camp, and Camp Convalescent. The second name belongs to that part where men taken prisoners by the Southerns, but paroled, were placed under medical and military care. The site of the whole is contiguous to Alexandria. In the earlier and less matured arrangements of Government after the rebellion, as many as twenty-two thousand were collected here; when, though tents and rations were provided by their authority, the soubriquet of "Camp Misery" was its popular name, from the condition of the men. The suffering was unparalleled and appalling; despondency and despair, aided by cold, hunger, filth, vermin, and disease, pressed heavily upon thousands of hearts, and attracted the special attention and action of Congress. The Christian commission listened to appeals, urgent, earnest, terrible. Their delegates, day and night, for a season occupied two tents, abundantly supplied stores, and adopted every feasible measure for the relief of suffering humanity. They distributed waggon-loads of clothing, delicacies, and comforts for wounded and sick men; wrote hundreds of letters for the helpless and the dying; *buried* many dead; obtained hundreds of discharges for the disabled; distributed 20,000 Testaments, hymn-books, and papers, a million pages of tracts; held daily prayer-meetings and preaching services; secured a chapel tent—the first one, temporary and of small dimensions, which was afterward substituted by a boarded chapel, and the appointment of a minister, known as " Chaplain of the camp," and other earnest men were "located" in the camp. Such had been the efforts before my visit.

I closely examined the wards, the food, and dispensary, and am happy to say the provision and care were as comfortable as would be an ordinary infirmary in England. They had a chapel and service every evening, and during the day, when any of them chose to associate together. I was interested by the ministrations provided for sick and dying. Some of the poor men I saw in the moments of dissolution. War is a fearful and appalling calamity. I was invited by General Casey to accompany him into Virginia, where he was going to review a regiment of coloured troops, the first of the United States army. I went; and, together with him, reached the parade-ground. His *cortege* was formed in view of the regiment; the men, in obedience to command, formed, marched, and filed off in companies so close to me that I

M

could count their ranks and calculate their numbers. They
were equal in physical form and strength to any ordinary
regiment of white soldiers, and pleased the general by
their attainments, and appearance, and manœuvres. The
officers were all whites, and, excepting only a few, were
young and newly commissioned. It is a novel life to them
all; there can be no doubt that coloured troops will
occupy a prominent position in the future of the American
Union when slavery is abolished, and Southern fortresses
and arsenals require to be garrisoned. Their adaptation
to the climate, their habits of submission, obedience, and
imitation, and their personal interest in the good government of the country where they were formerly oppressed,
will conspire to strengthen the policy already in favour
among men of influence in the United States. 200,000
coloured troops will change the order of things. I was introduced to the Union Loyal League Club of Washington,
and spent a pleasant evening in company with men who
were officers of the higher grades, with professors and
medical men, whose conversation was more upon literature
and philosophy than the politics of the day in their own
country; yet I fancy I was invited because of the mission
on which I had visited their capital. They were more concerned to hear from England than to occupy me with the
affairs of America. There is not, while Congress is not
assembled, any great number of the ·mercantile classes in
Washington, yet the population of 1860 was more than
61,000. The outline of the city appears as if provision
were intended for three times this number, and there is no
reason why mercantile pursuits should not occupy the inhabitants of a city which, by the Potomac, has such easy
access to the sea.

From Washington to Baltimore the distance is forty
miles, and in ordinary times communication by railway is
frequent. I spent two nights in this city, but did not an-

ticipate any welcome from its pastors, who had resolved to
conduct their ministrations without any evidence, whether
they were or not anti-slavery, or in favour of Union or
Secession. I therefore did not try to find time for personal visitation. I paid my respects to the memory of
Washington, by the usual fee at his monument, and as-
cending to the top of that structure, lamp in hand. The
total elevation is more than three hundred and twelve feet;
and the loftiest part is the colossal statue of the old general,
sixteen feet in height. Around the top of the Doric shaft,
on which it stands, there is space for the visitor to walk,
and survey all the city, suburbs, and country. The range
of view is extensive and picturesque; a building near to
it, just finished, is the Peabody Institute; the Romish
cathedral is contiguous. I entered it; a large, bare and
unattractive edifice, though outside it is surrounded by
ornamental pretensions. The "Battle monument" com-
memorates those who fell defending the city in 1814; in-
scriptions on four Egyptian doors, which give a square base
for a column to rest on, relate [some incidents in the conflict, sculptured letters record the names of the local heroes.
The Armistead monument recounts the achievements of
Col. G. Armistead, who repulsed a British fleet in the same
year. There are public buildings for lectures and exhibi-
tions; the Rotunda, Carroll Hall, and the Exchange; the
University of Maryland, the College of Loyola, and the
Athenæum, with other structures, evince a love for display
in the monumental city. It received its name in 1745, in
honour of Lord Baltimore. The first pavements were laid
in 1782, and at the same time a coach began to run to
Philadelphia regularly. The city was incorporated in 1797,
when only a few thousand inhabitants resided in it. In the
year 1860, the population was 212,608. Built on hill slopes
and terraces, it gradually ascends from the water of the
Patapsco river, which flows into the Chesapeake Bay, and

forms an imposing object, when looked on from beneath, or is surveyed from Washington's monument. It was in this city, when Mr. Lincoln was proceeding to Washington to enter on his presidential duties, that the Secession conspirators were said to have laid an ambush for his life. The men who made such an attempt are able to contemplate any villany. They were defeated, and Mr. Lincoln lives to fulfil a higher destiny under wiser auspices.

From Baltimore the road to Philadelphia by rail is ninety-seven miles. Many historical scenes would invite the attention of the pleasure-seeking tourist throughout Pennsylvania, and even, in recent days, the war which now occupies many minds, has created memories of deep interest. The Schuylkill, the Wissahickon, Harrisburg, the Susquehanna, the Juniata, the Katawissa, the Valley of Wyoming and Wilkesbarre, and other scenes, are familiar to the traveller. My path, however, was limited to a single purpose, and hence I obeyed local arrangements, which were proposed on my account. The Rev. Dr. Brainerd had consented to make preliminary and contingent plans for a public meeting. His church was selected for a week-evening assembly; and on my arrival, it was recommended I should seek personal intercourse with such clergymen or others who had not retired for the hot season to watering-places. I had interviews with some members of the Society of Friends, whom I greatly admired for their piety and sympathy in the negroes' cause. I spent a morning in finding Albert Barnes, and discussing with him the duties of the crisis. Something had occurred which restrained him from any active participation in present efforts. He had written to me pleading growing years and weakness of vision as his reason for not actively preparing to receive me, and added that the distance of his home from the centre of resort would prevent his attendance at any public meeting. In private interview I expostulated, urged his

own past testimony to the duty of the Church—the importance that in his later years he should not recede; asked
him to respond to our address by speech, or letter, and to
countenance the movement among his neighbours. I left
him, convinced that some personal matter was the stum-
bling block, and regretting to see his name withdrawn,
when it might have seasonably aided the slave and influenced many English admirers. I was introduced to the
loyal Union League of Philadelphia, at their club house,
and an *impromptu* conversazione was organized. Perhaps
fifty members gathered in, and I was urged to deliver some
account of our English anti-slavery sentiments and sympathy with Americans in their present conflict. The presence of Mr. Rylance was useful, and we were welcomed
and assured of their co-operation in gathering an audience
for the following evening. One of their number unequivo-
cally affirmed that slavery was the cause of the struggle,
and that peace could not be anticipated but by the abolition
of the evil. He appealed to the other members if any of
them held another opinion—all assented.

The assembly convened to hear the English address was
numerous, and composed of many most respectable citizens,
some of them occupying offices of great responsibility as I
was told. They gave a cordial reception to the sentiments,
and welcomed the assurance that the British nation had
not abandoned the cause of emancipation; though some of
the aristocracy and the journals, which represented hereditary antipathies to the Democratic Republic, would wish to
sympathize with a slave-holding oligarchy. They evinced
their grateful pleasure when informed how the Emancipation and Union and Emancipation Societies of London and
Manchester had been organized, to cherish a sympathy and
extend widely a correct knowledge of the aspects of the
question and struggle now distracting America. The
movement in France, from which had emanated the first

address, and the measures taken to elicit a suitable response from England, and the consequent conference in Manchester, were severally explained; and the assurance given that the working classes in Britain strongly resisted the appeal for recognition from the South, and cordially encouraged the North in anti-slavery policy, and in giving freedom to the millions heretofore held in bondage. The race from which Americans have descended are represented by the Nonconformist and Evangelical churches, from which, in England, still comes forth the plea for oppressed and enslaved Africans. When the address had been presented, the presiding minister requested as many present as were clergymen to stand up, and thus signify their reception of what had been delivered to "ministers and pastors in the United States of America." Nearly fifty venerable and accredited clergymen answered to the call before the assembly: Episcopalians, Episcopal Methodists, Presbyterians, Baptists, and others, were included, and a large number came forward to salute the deputation at the conclusion. Resolutions were moved and seconded by Baptist, Episcopalian, and Presbyterian ministers, which were expressive of entire harmony with the address, and of thanks to the bearers of the message, who had travelled so far in their mission. It was announced that a subsequent meeting would be held, of clergymen alone, to determine whether a response, specially for Philadelphia, should be adopted, and in what terms. I left, however, by the same night's midnight train for New York; and if a reply has been forwarded, it has not yet reached its destination.

The language of patriotism, from the pen of Dr. Brainerd, and published by his sympathizing friends at Philadelphia, may be accepted as a response, though not formally so intended:—

"Our Southern brethren had a right to manage their own affairs in their own way, within the limits of the

Constitution; to take their own time and mode to regulate their relations to the coloured race, leaving the press of the land free. This right was awarded to them, not alone by the Constitution, but by the solemn declaration of the President and a resolution of Congress. It was endorsed by the sentiments of ninety-nine hundredths of the North, who, claiming liberty to speak and write their honest opinions of slavery, as did Washington, Jefferson, and Franklin, would still have abhorred any and every attempt to enforce by violence their views upon the South. The whole North, almost before a blow was struck, protested its respect for every Southern right. But all would not avail; something more was wanting.

"If we could have consented to stultify the conscientious suffrages of the great majority, as to planting slavery, with its fetters and manacles, on the free soil of our territories; if we could cheerfully have agreed to stand as sentinels through all time, to drive the escaping slave back to his bondage; if we could conscientiously have commended a system which shuts out four millions of our fellow-men, in our own land, from reading God's Word, from lawful marriage, from family integrity and purity, and from the right to fair wages for their toil; if we could have cherished at the capital the shambles where men and women are bought and sold, and could have heard the slave-dealer's lash on bleeding flesh without pity; if we could have disgraced labour by contempt, and flattered the pride of those who grow rich on the uncompensated industry of other men; if we could meekly have allowed the slave lords of the South, accustomed to rule over menials, whom they had by force degraded to their feet, to rule through all time over us, there would have been *no war.*

"If we could have allowed our fellow-citizens at the South to be tarred and feathered, because they were true to their country; if we could have permitted our mints, arsenals, forts, and vessels to be seized, our generals to be bribed to treason, and our soldiers on the frontiers surrendered as prisoners to those whom they had gone to protect; if we could have allowed our country's flag to be trampled in the dust by traitors, and our garrisons to be hailed out of our own burning forts by bursting shells; had we borne this submissively, there would have been *no war.*

" But would peace in these circumstances have marked our virtue or our corruption? our glory or our infamy? Our war is the proper protest of justice and humanity, against injustice, cruelty, and perfidy. It is the struggle of right and philanthropy, against outrage, oppression, and bloody treason.

" We have received from ages gone by the fruits of man's long struggles for civil and religious liberty, and the right of self-government; we have received a broad, beautiful, and healthful country, to every foot of whose soil we have an equal claim as citizens; we have received a civil constitution, which embraces the concentrated wisdom of the sages of the Revolution; and we have taken up arms to declare that no traitor hand shall cut the telegraphic wire on which these blessings are passing down to other generations. The cry of humanity, from ages to come, has called us to this bloody strife. It is simply a defence of our own institutions."

The testimony borne by all classes with whom I conversed, of the worth, loyalty, and integrity of the coloured people, in the midst of whom Dr. Brainerd lives, as securely for his property as he could in any circle of society, gave assurance that they are worthy of all equal privileges in the eye of law with their fellow-citizens.

During my stay in Philadelphia, the Rev. B. F. Morris, son of a late Senator of the United States, accompanied me to an hospital camp, about fifteen miles from the city. His mission was to inquire for and visit wounded or sick men from his own state, inquire into their wants and minister to their comfort and instruction as the delegate from the Christian Commission. My desire was to examine the entire establishment, and see the condition of the men. I was most courteously received by the authorities, was shown into every department, from the kitchens and stores to the dispensary and operating hall. One of the assistants deputed to conduct me had been manager in a Virginian plantation, whose converse revealed to me facts and phases of slavery which cannot be written. I was much surprised at the conveniences, I might call them luxuries, of the whole establishment, though but a wooden fabric and a temporary hospital.

I was truly gratified with my visit to this vast and yet growing city, and thankful for the generous hospitality with which I was entertained. I arrived in New York early next morning, and prepared for other work, grateful to a merciful Providence for the abundant goodness which had attended all my intercourse and journeyings, as a stranger from a far land, but a messenger of peace and liberty.

I arrived at the Astor House, Broadway, and secured my room for the time I should be here engaged. I found, however, my old tormentors ready to give me every token of attention. As there were no mosquito curtains to guard the bed from their attacks, I was thankful to have been seasonably and warmly invited into a suburban villa, ten miles up the Hudson.

CHAPTER V.

THE friends of the mission in New York were ready to welcome and speed me on in the further progress of it. The
acceptance and success which have followed the efforts in
Washington and Philadelphia, of which they had heard,
encouraged the expectation that the people of New England would be not less cordial. To Drs. Budington and
Thompson I owed many kind introductions by the way,
while the conductors of the provincial press heralded my
progress. The younger and active sons of Mr. W. E.
Dodge (Messrs. Phelps and Dodge of New York), acted as
if I had been committed specially to their care. Under
the personal guidance of the Rev. G. S. Dodge, I started
from New York for New Haven, *via* Stamford, Norwalk,
and Bridgeport. Norwalk is a summer retreat for ramblers
in Connecticut. Bridgeport is at the mouth of the Pequan-
nock river, on the Long Island Sound, and is a port for New
York steamers. I was much pleased with New Haven.
Its umbrageous paths, and streets, and numerous villas
embedded among trees and shrubbery, fully entitle it to be
called a city of Elms in Elmsland. These trees are cared
for by municipal regulations, many of them being en-
circled ten or twelve feet up the stem by a preparation intended to prevent insects which would consume the foliage
from creeping up from the soil. The squares are adorned
by lines of these trees, some of them as old as the earliest
plantation. It was arranged that I should reach New

Haven in time for the "commencement" at Yale College, which is famed for having sent out more graduates than any other institution in America. The buildings of this college and three churches, which are conspicuously placed in front, and stand apart, distant from each other, in grounds ornamented with old trees, give special attraction to the site. Besides college halls, apartments devoted to the fine arts and libraries, chapel and chambers for commons, etc., there are other edifices, which the munificence of patrons have erected and endowed. New Haven contained a population of 20,345 in 1850, which had increased in 1860 to 39,267, and was still expanding at the time of my visit. I had been invited to be the guest of two friends whose society I equally coveted. I therefore pleaded permission to divide my time with them. Dr. Bacon accepted me for the first few days, and Mr. Pelatiah Perit, long an honoured merchant at New York, entertained me for the residue of my stay.

I reached my destination on Saturday, the 25th July, and found all arrangements for my services complete. On Sunday morning I preached for Dr. Bacon. On Monday evening it was my privilege to embody in a lecture the subject and objects of my mission, and on Tuesday I met from eighty to one hundred ministerial brethren, who conferred in free discussion on the response which should be adopted. The assembly was large on Monday evening, and the resolutions passed on the succeeding day were evidence of the favour with which my mission was regarded. Dr. Nadal, Mr. Eustise, Professor Fisher, Mr. Wood, Dr. Patton, Dr. Bacon, and others took part in the discussion. Subjoined are the minutes forwarded afterwards.

MINUTES OF A CONFERENCE OF CHRISTIAN MINISTERS HELD AT NEW HAVEN, CONNECTICUT.

July 27th and 28th, 1863.—At a public assembly including many Christian ministers resident in New Haven and in other parts of Connecticut, with some from other states, convened in the church edifice of the First Church of Christ in New Haven, Monday evening, July 27th, 1863,

The Reverend Dr. Massie, as delegate from a conference of ministers held at Manchester, in England, presented the address of the conference " to ministers and pastors of all Christian Denominations throughout the United States of America."

Whereupon the ministers present, the Reverend Joel Hawes, D.D., Pastor of the First Church of Christ, in Hartford, acting as chairman, resolved to meet in friendly conference with Dr. Massie, on the morrow, at two o'clock, p.m., in the lecture-room of the North Church, and appointed the Reverend Leonard Bacon, D.D., Pastor of the First Church in New Haven, Edward A. Lawrence, D.D., Professor in the Theological Institute at East Windsor Hill, and B. H. Nadal, D.D., Pastor of the First Methodist Episcopal Church in New Haven, to prepare a suitable response.

Tuesday, July 28th.—The Conference of Ministers met according to appointment. The Rev. Samuel W. S. Dutton, D.D., of New Haven, was appointed chairman, and the Reverend Leonard Woolsey Bacon, of Stamford, secretary.

The committee appointed to prepare a suitable response to the address presented by the Reverend Dr. Massie, reported through their chairman, submitting a series of resolutions to be adopted by the conference. The report was accepted, and after a free discussion, in which the Reverend Professor Fisher, William Patton, D.D., William T. Eustise, and Bernard H. Nadal, D.D., of New Haven, C. W. Clapp of Rockville, Professor Lawrence of East Windsor Hill, George J. Wood of Guildford, Edward Beecher, D.D., of Galesbury, Illinois, and William Ives Budington, D.D., of Brooklyn, New York, with others, took part, the resolutions were unanimously adopted as follows :—

Resolved.—1. That we receive with grateful sensibility the fraternal "Address" of the conference at Manchester, with the exposition of it by their delegate, setting forth the sympathy with which thousands of Christian ministers in Great Britain regard our country in its conflict with a great rebellion that has for its avowed purpose the perpetuation and indefinite extension of an atrocious slave trade, and the establishment of an empire founded on slavery.

2. That for ourselves, and for evangelical ministers generally in this country, we gratefully acknowledge the efforts of those Christian ministers and laymen in Great Britain who have manfully, and in the face of opposition, asserted the righteousness of our cause as a nation in this conflict.

3. That while we rejoice in the signatures of more than four thousand ministers in Great Britain to a letter responding to the fraternal appeal of Protestant pastors and ministers in France, and expressive of sympathy with our nation at this crisis of our destiny and the world's, our joy would be greatly enlarged if we had more and clearer evidence of sympathy from the more than six thousand non-subscribers in the ministry of the voluntary churches, and the more than sixteen thousand non-subscribers among the clergy of the English and Scotch established churches.

4. That, as a nation at war with rebellion, we are contending in the Armageddon of the world for the conservative principle of established order and peaceful reformation against revolutionary violence, and have, therefore, a right to cordial sympathy from all the intelligent and honest friends of established governments.

We are contending for the principle of constitutional government by constitutional majorities in lawful elections, against the principle of government by the will and arbitrary force of armed minorities, and, therefore, have a right to cordial sympathy from all the honest and intelligent friends of constitutional liberty and popular self-government in every nation.

And we are contending for the freedom and dignity of labour against the tyrannical usurpations and demands of a system that identifies labour with the lowest human degradation, and have, therefore, a right to the most outspoken sympathy from all philanthropists throughout the civilized world.

5. That, with rare exceptions, the evangelical ministers of New England, and generally throughout the Free States of the Union, have the credentials of their fidelity to God and to the gospel against slavery, in the hatred and execration which are poured on them as a class by the defenders of slavery, and the sympathizers with rebellion.

6. That we entreat our British brethren not to believe the accusations which have been or may be preferred against us by men who find it for their interest to be regarded as the only American opponents of slavery, and not to hold us responsible for the strange things which exceptional and erratic men may say in apology for slavery, as if they were our representatives.

7. That our confidence for the abolition of slavery in this land is in the providence of a righteous God, who cannot permit a system so stupendous in its wickedness to be permanent under his government of the world, and that we devoutly accept as a pledge of the restoration and perpetuity of our union, the necessity which God has laid upon us of conquering or being conquered, and, therefore, of exterminating slavery or becoming ourselves enslaved.

The Conference then adjourned without day.

SAMUEL W. S. DUTTON, *Chairman.*
LEONARD WOOLSEY BACON, *Secretary.*

The services connected with the "Commencement" at Yale College were to me novel and interesting, though I could only be present at some of them. The *concio ad clerum* was delivered on "the Christian Sabbath" by Rev. J. N. Burton of Hartford, Dr. G. Beecher led the devotion. Gentlemen of all professions and positions attended and took part in the proceedings as *alumni.* The governor of the state, Mr. Buckingham, Major-General Anderson (who commanded at FORT SUMTER when the rebellion began), Professor Lieber, Mr. Perit, late President of the Chamber of Commerce, New York; Dr. Dwight, son of the distinguished theologian who had been President of this College; Professors Silliman, Dr. Patton, and Dr. Woolsey; missionaries returned from Palestine and other Eastern lands, and professors from colleges in the far West—all mingled in celebration and in commemoration of the deceased and distinguished alumni; an orator being selected from the graduates of several periods, some as far back as 1813 being among the speakers.* I spent part of two days in company with General Anderson, now so much an invalid from his exciting services at Fort Sumter, as to require absolute retirement from the army. I was much benefited and informed by intercourse with Mr. Perit, and enjoyed at his table the intercourse of the senior Professor Silliman, and was introduced to President Woolsey and other magnates. I was honoured by an invitation to address the

---

* HYMN INTENDED TO BE SUNG AT THE MEETING OF THE ALUMNI OF YALE COLLEGE, 1863.

TUNE—*Lenox.*

Beneath these sacred shades,
　　Long-severed hearts unite :
The tempting Future fades,
　　The Past alone seems bright.
　　　　O'er sultry clime
　　　　　　And stormy zone
　　　　　　Rings clear the tone
　　　　Of Mem'ry's chime.

We come to tread once more
　　The paths of earlier days,
To count our blessings o'er,
　　And mingle prayer and praise ;
　　　　For Mercy's hand,
　　　　　　From skies of blue,
　　　　　　Hath linked anew
　　　　Each broken band.

We come, ere Life departs,
　　Ere winging Death appears,
To throng our joyous hearts,
　　With dreams of sunnier years :
　　　　To meet once more
　　　　　　Where Pleasure sprang,
　　　　　　And arches rang
　　　　With songs of yore.

alumni; and though not one of them, I could gratefully acknowledge having drank of the streams which had rendered verdant the groves of that academy, when the profound Edwards was a student, and the eloquent Dwight, his descendant, was afterwards an instructor. The writings of these and other men had consecrated in my memory the name of Yale College. I referred to my mission as one of peace, designed to maintain the concord of former times and the fellowship of enduring kindred. My address was received kindly; and when, afterwards, a younger and rather belligerent professor, in a bellicose style, adverted to the "Alabamas" and "Floridas," and the certainty that they would hereafter be remembered, and perhaps revenged, a resolution was proposed, seconded, and enthusiastically carried, thanking me for my mission of conciliation and my services to cherish brotherhood. I am bound to record that any irritation evinced on the "Sea Pirate Question" was excited by younger orators, and the peaceful influences proceeded from the seniors. The capture of mercantile vessels by the "Alabama," just at this time, was, however, frequent and peculiarly provoking to men who lived by commerce.

I had consented to attend a week-evening meeting in Hartford and at Springfield during this week: they were both accessible by rail; and on Wednesday and Thursday I was favoured by the attendance of numerous congrega-

---

Not all, not *all* are here :
  Some sleep 'neath funeral flowers,
Where falls the mourner's tear,
  And weep the evening showers.
    Yet, thankfully,
      Let every heart
      Its love impart
    To Him on high.

tions. Hartford is seated on the right bank of the Connecticut River, 50 miles from the Long Island Sound; the stream is navigable all the way. The city is one of the twin capitals of the state, and contains nearly 30,000 inhabitants: more than double the number recorded for 1850. It is 112 miles from New York, and 124 from Boston. The citizens are not ashamed of their literary and educational institutions—the Wadsworth Athenæum, Trinity College, and the Connecticut Historical Society. Among antiquities were shown to me a relic of the Charter Oak, recently prostrated by a violent storm, and divers memorials which have survived since the landing of the Pilgrim Fathers upon these shores. A retreat for the insane and an asylum for deaf and dumb, betoken their philanthropy, and the fact that Mrs. L. H. Sigourney made this city her residence, and that Mrs. Beecher Stowe is building an "Uncle Tom's Cabin," where she hopes to spend her later years, is no less a gratification to the attached citizens. An indulgent friend drove round the suburbs and showed me the colony or gigantic establishment which Colt had founded by the profits and for the manufacture of his revolvers. That man had sprung from small beginnings, made rapidly an immense fortune, and prematurely ended his life. The vicinity, the rides and scenes of Hartford have a peaceful, prosperous, and comfortable aspect, inviting to all who would prefer the sunny shade. My brief sojourn was chiefly occupied in my mission. A large assembly convened in Dr. Hawes's church to receive the address. In private, I conferred with Judge Ellsworth, Mr. Ward, and Mr. Cone, wealthy and active citizens, and received a response to my appeal:—

"SYMPATHY OF BRITISH CLERGYMEN.

" A large and deeply-interested audience was addressed in the Centre Church on Wednesday evening last, by the

Rev. J. W. Massie, of London, who visits this country, in company with another gentleman, to present to our loyal people the assurance of the fraternal sympathy of 4758 Protestant clergymen of England and France in our great national struggle.

"It is impossible to do justice to the address of Dr. Massie—whether we consider its matter, its manner, or the tone and spirit which pervaded it. So unlike, in these, was it to what we are accustomed to read in many of the English prints and reviews, that the audience could not restrain their feelings of surprise and delight when the reverend gentlemen, with emphasis, assured us that such papers did not represent 'the bone, blood, and muscle' of that country, but rather the sentiments of the aristocracy, who, he said, did not approve or believe in our theory of government. This enunciation was indeed doubly consoling, since we have so long suffered from the misrepresentations of the privileged classes of England, as well as from not a few of her time-serving, if not subsidized writers and unscrupulous traffickers and ship-builders. We hail such messengers and messages with delight. Let them be repeated and multiplied, and let them come swiftly and heartily unto us from her who was our parent, though of late she has seemed to play a step-mother's part. They will be received and responded to with an unreluctant approval and delight.

"The voice of these pastors and ministers is, we may assume, the voice of their parishioners and associates, and such a voice in that country must greatly influence the views and policy of her politicians and statesmen. Indeed, the speaker assured us that so clearly are the *people* of England with us, that no cabinet of ministers could survive a recognition of a Southern Confederacy founded on slavery, or any open committal of the government to its support.

"At the close of the address, as during its progress, the audience heartily applauded the speaker, and with entire unanimity proceeded to vote a suitable response to such noble, generous, and Christian sentiments."

RESPONSE FROM HARTFORD, CONNECTICUT, TO THE MISSION OF REV. DR. MASSIE, ETC.

Subsequent to a large and enthusiastic meeting held in the Centre Church, Hartford, Connecticut, July, 1863, to hear the Rev. Dr. Massie of London, and receive certain communications addressed through him to the ministers of Christ in this country, the following Resolutions were adopted by the ministers present on that occasion. *Resolved*,

1. That we have received with unusual satisfaction the Appeal of seven hundred and fifty French Protestant pastors and the Reply of four thousand English clergymen, accompanied by the Address of the Anti-Slavery Conference, held at Manchester, June 3, with explanations and appeals by the Rev. Dr. Massie, expressing their sympathy with us in the great civil conflict through which we are passing, their earnest desire that it should terminate in the destruction of slavery throughout the United States, and their solemn protest against any recognition of a Confederacy based on human bondage.

2. That we cordially reciprocate the fraternal spirit of our brethren, and assure them of our unabated attachment not merely to the great Christian brotherhood, but also to the principles of order, freedom, and progress, to which both they and we are pledged.

3. That the fate of the coloured man and that of the white, and, by consequence, that of free institutions in this country, are indissolubly blended, so that the present war cannot be waged successfully for any single end, like that of emancipation, but must embrace the maintenance of constitutional order and the unity of the national life.

4. That the great majority of evangelical ministers in New England and in the United States generally, are, heart and soul, devoted to the cause of human freedom, regarding slavery as a great moral, social, and political evil, for the speedy removal of which they constantly labour and pray, and we entreat our French and British brethren to use their best endeavours to correct the false reports upon this subject constantly propagated in Europe by the enemies of freedom and progress. We can assure them that we look upon slavery—the cause of all our present troubles and the source of untold evils besides—with an

intensity of aversion and horror which those only can feel who are grappling with the monster in a struggle for good order, Constitutional liberty, and national existence.

5. That we feel ourselves entitled to the sympathy and prayers of all Christians in this momentous conflict, inasmuch as the success of the slaveholders' rebellion in this country would be a deathblow to the hopes of the universal church with reference to human freedom.

6. That we are gratified to learn from Dr. Massie that he represents largely the working men of England in his friendly mission, and that their sufferings in consequence of this war have changed neither their principles nor their affections ; and we entreat him to assure them, in return, of our unchanging confidence and sympathy.

ROBERT TURNBULL, D.D., *Chairman.*
WOLCOTT CAULKINS, *Secretary.*

Further up the Connecticut, twenty-six miles, is situated the town of Springfield, with a population of from 15,000 to 20,000, a large number of whom are employed in the United States arsenal. Here thousands of persons *live* by the manufacture of implements of destruction, and rejoice in the yearly production of hundreds of thousands of arms, that thereby the enemies of their country may be resisted, and the homes of liberty be kept secure. A lady of Christian benevolence and patriotic energy, with great vivacity and intelligence, conducted me through the several departments, and introduced me to an earnest and devout Christian, who holds a high office in the management of the establishment. There are in the town, also, other manufactories for smaller fire-arms, sustained and conducted by private enterprise. I did not undertake to judge for them, or make my conscience their standard. But I felt it was an essential part of the calamity which the rebellion had brought on the Christians of America, that they should feel constrained so to depart from the halcyon times of millennial wisdom, when men shall learn the art of war no more. The view from the arsenal hill is far more to my mind, looking down upon the verdant vales, the beautiful town and the flowing river. This is the starting point, the Springfield of the Connecticut valley routes, to the White Mountains and the quiet homes of Vermont and New Hampshire. The Rev. Mr. Buckingham, brother of the Governor, though in the midst of much domestic affliction and anxiety, showed me fraternal attention, and made all needful arrangement for my comfort and success. · A large audience assembled in the South Congregational Church to receive the message I had been sent to deliver. At the close of the service a committee was appointed to make a suitable response, and some days afterwards I received from Judge Chapman the following communication, which will sufficiently indicate my reception :—

"SPRINGFIELD, MASSACHUSETTS,
"*August* 6, 1861.

" Sir,—You will recollect that a committee was appointed by the congregation which was addressed by you at the South Congregational Church in this city last week, to make a suitable response to your address. As chairman of the committee I desire to express the thanks of the congregation to you, and to those excellent ministers of France and Great Britain who are represented by you. We feel that, as you have come to us in a friendly, candid, and Christian spirit, it should be our duty as it is our pleasure to receive you and your suggestions in the same spirit.

" The importance of your mission cannot be overestimated. This is peculiarly true in respect to this country and Great Britain, for it is quite probable that if peace is long preserved between us, it must be mainly through the influence of the Protestant Christians of the two countries.

" There is, indeed, in this country a high appreciation of the character of the British Queen, and a confidence in her friendly disposition towards us. And the whole public mind of the country was deeply affected by the noble conduct of the English working men, who in their deep distress, refused to be seduced by our enemies into the expression of sentiments hostile to us. Our people would

feel reluctant to engage in a war against a nation having
such a Queen and such working-men.   But we believe
that your mission will be still more powerful for the preservation of peace.

"We were gratified at your remark that you had assured the working-men of your country, that the *labour
question* lay at the foundation of a civil war.   We knew
this to be true, and wish it were more fully understood in
Europe.   The actual contest relates to slavery, but it presents a much broader question than slavery; and there is
really an 'irrepressible conflict' going on in Europe in
respect to it, which interests the labouring people there as
deeply as it does ourselves.   You are aware that the rebels
hate the Puritans with peculiar bitterness.   It is principally because of our position in respect to labour.   Our
policy has been, as you will see for yourself, to give to
operative labour the benefit of knowledge and skill, and a
voice in the decision of all questions that concern it.   We
have therefore established a system of universal education, by means of unsectarian common schools.   The
system succeeds perfectly.   Labour is efficient, skilful, and
well paid, and accumulates capital.   To preserve good
order and peace, we rely on the Bible.   Its influence is
sufficient to secure the labouring population in favour of
good government.   Our rioters and disturbers of the peace,
and most of our paupers and the tenants of our prisons,
are foreigners, who were brought up in ignorance, and
especially without the Bible.

"The rebels maintain the extreme of the opposite
system.   Their policy is to keep labour in extreme ignorance and degradation.   They do not favour common
schools, and they keep the Bible from their slaves.   But
they go so far as to outrage all decency and humanity.
Virginia has long been engaged in the despicable business
of raising coloured children to sell as slaves, and many of
them have the blood of their masters running in their
veins.   The laws of most of the slave states withhold all
legal protection to the chastity of female slaves, and
authorize masters to sell husbands and wives, parents and
children from each other; and when a husband or a wife
is sold, a second marriage may take place while the parties
are all living.   Even their church members and clergymen

have become so corrupt, as to contend stoutly that all this is sanctioned by the Christian religion.

"And though many of the slaveholders are of low origin they set up pretensions to aristocracy, based on the fact that they are maintained by slave labour. They affect to regard labour as degrading to the blood, and they despise the white labourer quite as much as they despise a slave, and allow him no influence, and would keep him in a degraded social position.

"Yet by being loud-mouthed in their pretensions to democracy the slaveholders have been able to obtain the votes of a large majority of our working-men who were born in Europe, and have kept political power mainly by the votes of this class of people. Our recent riots and threats of riots, have come almost exclusively from foreign emigrants. It is but just to say they are persons who do not read the Bible, and are not Protestants; and it should be added that multitudes of Irish Catholics understand the matter aright, and are true and loyal citizens.

"We do not ask any foreign aid in our contest, and we do not feel that we stand in need of sympathy; but the expression of friendly, candid, and Christian sentiments is extremely grateful to all our people, and we especially desire that Christians, and indeed all people who are interested to maintain the comfort and welfare of the working-classes, shall understand our true position, and shall not aid or encourage the rebels.

"Permit me to add, that so far as I have heard your mission spoken of, it is universally considered that those whose messenger you are have been extremely happy, not only in the expression of their sentiments, but in the selection of their agent.

"With great respect,
"I am your obedient servant,
"R. A. CHAPMAN,
"Chairman of the Committee.
"Rev. J. W. Massie, D.D."

I was earnestly importuned to visit Worcester. I could only set apart for a service here a week evening, which I regretted, as it is one of the old cities of New England, which have with me a fragrant memory, and is distin-

guished for its schools and manufactures. Its population
was in 1850 only 17,000, but had risen in 1860 to 25,000.
It lies in the centre of a most productive agricultural
region, and is the heart of intercourse with many surrounding districts; the Boston and Albany lines meeting here,
and the road to the St. Lawrence river and the city of
Providence issuing thence. I was delighted with the
extended and beautiful suburban drives, passing many
sequestered villas, mingled with old farmsteads. Track-
ways for cars, however, are not only permitted, they are
almost necessary luxuries; the soil is so loose and the roads
are not macadamized, while the habitations are situated at
remote distances from each other. I was indebted to the
Rev. M. Walker, recently a chaplain in the army, and now
settled as pastor in the oldest Congregational church, still
a wooden fabric. He had not yet become a housekeeper,
though lately married, but had rooms at the hotel where
he hospitably entertained me as guest. I found this a
mode of living not infrequent among settled pastors in the
western states, conforming to Archbishop Leighton's preference, who wished to die at an inn. I went, under Mr.
Walker's instructions, to the place where the assembly
gathered to receive my message. I found afterwards in
the Worcester "Daily Spy" the following account of what
passed :—

"The meeting at the Old South church last evening
was one of marked interest. For more than two hours,
despite the great heat, the Rev. Dr. Massie held the undivided attention of every hearer while he spoke of the friends
and enemies of the American cause in England as one
thoroughly informed in all that relates thereto. His statements in regard to the London 'Times' were perhaps new
to many of his hearers; but his charges that it was the
enemy of the abolition of slavery in the West Indies, that
it was the advocate of the Corn Laws until the league had
won its great victory over them, and that it has always
shown the most mercenary spirit on all the great issues of

our generation, were easily substantiated. The evidence he presented of a deep and powerful religious sentiment in England warmly interested in our success, was most gratifying to every lover of liberty present, and will do much to awaken grateful feelings toward these true men. The Doctor came as the representative of more than four thousand British and seven hundred French ministers, whose addresses he has brought to us. He also declared his purpose to be twofold.

" First, to beseech Americans to be true to the principles of universal liberty in all the trials before them, never forgetting those in bonds ; and secondly, to do what they can to preserve friendly relations between the two great nations which have so much in common, and who, unitedly, are to mould the future of so many nations. He spoke with great plainness as compared with the manner of our own countrymen. At the close the Rev. Mr. Richardson was chosen chairman of the meeting, when Rev. M. Walker offered the reply of the New York city clergymen for adoption, which, after remarks by Rev. R. A. Miller and Deacon Harris, was carried unanimously by a rising vote."

I arrived in Boston on the last day of July, and avoided all intercourse with local friends till the evening of the 1st of August. I had promised to join in the celebration of the twenty-ninth anniversary of Emancipation in the British West Indies, by the Massachusetts Anti-Slavery Society at the Island Grove in Abington, distant about seventeen miles from the city. It was a novelty to me, as I had not yet witnessed any of the popular demonstrations in America. I took my quarters at the United States Hotel, where I continued till my departure for Providence. Early on Saturday express trains were on the move for and beyond Abington ; return fares, etc., and a mixed company, white and coloured, young and old, leaders and followers—some carrying pic-nic provisions, and others expecting, as I did, to share what the forethought of others had made ready. I was unknown by face, and unmarked by costume, and therefore had opportunity to look on and learn. However,

just as the train started, a question I put led to my discovery. The train was delayed on the way, waiting for
branch contributions from other towns, and during the
interval free and social converse made strangers feel at
home. The Island Grove was reached, and multitudes who
had come for other pleasures than negro sympathies, were
scattered in groups among the trees. I should have been
pleased had my space permitted a full report of this most
unique meeting, and any approach to justice in avowing
my estimate of the character, heroic course, and transcendent labours, achievements, and worth of the chairman of
the day. It was to me a cause of inexpressible regret that
the indisposition of Mr. Wendell Phillips prevented his
attendance and eloquence on that day. The proceedings
were reported in the "Boston Liberator," from which the
following extract is taken as the comment of the editor :—

"THE FIRST OF AUGUST AT ABINGTON.—The commemoration of the anniversary of West India Emancipation
never fails to bring together at the beautiful Island Grove
in Abington, a large assemblage of the earliest, most reliable and intelligent friends of the Anti-slavery cause, who,
through the long and desperate struggle of years with
popular prejudice and all-abounding pro-slavery hostility,
have kept their course steadily onward and upward. Not
less than two thousand people were present on Saturday.
The proceedings were, as usual, of a very interesting character. The songs of our Hutchinson friends (Asa B. and
family) added much to the inspiration of the occasion.
The absence of Mr. Phillips (bodily debility, in this instance,
being the cause) always leaves a large vacancy to be filled ;
but, happily, the presence and speeches of Rev. Dr. Massie,
of England, and Hon. Henry Wilson, helped largely to
mitigate the general disappointment. A good deal of zest
was added to the proceedings by a very racy and telling
speech made by Mrs. Van Benthuysen, a native of Middle-
borough in this state, but a relative of Jefferson Davis by
marriage. It was an instructive revelation of the plottings
of that arch traitor and his accomplices to dismember the

Republic for many years past. Especially gratifying was it to many present to see and hear those early and beloved coadjutors Theodore D. and Angelina Grimke Weld."

The conspicuous persons who took part in the discussion, besides those already named, were Mr. Samuel May, William Wells Brown, Mr. Edwin Thompson, Thomas Sims, who had been carried off and rescued as a fugitive slave, and had recently stood among the coloured troops at Vicksburg. Theodore D. Weld and his wife Angelina Grimke Weld were patriarchal memories of the past to me. Senator Wilson's speech was thorough and yet judicious, while sustaining Mr. Abraham Lincoln's policy.

It is not my purpose to occupy these pages with reports of what I said; and yet I may be permitted to give a brief extract of what I ventured to say, as a representative of an old Anti-slavery organization, at an American commemoration of what we in England accomplished thirty years ago :

"Mr. Garrison, on taking the chair, spoke of the almost literal fulfilment of the prophecies made by Abolitionists of the good working of emancipation in the British West Indies; and of the storm of reproach through which the British Abolitionists passed during the debate which preceded that event. In our own country slavery, like a rope of sand, is fast wearing away, and we hope soon to rejoice in its utter extinction. Mr. Garrison read, as eminently appropriate to the occasion, the fifty-eighth chapter of Isaiah, and pointed out how the predictions of the prophet have been fulfilled to the letter, wherever a loosening of the bonds of oppression has been practised.

"Mr. Garrison informed the meeting that, among others present, was the Rev. Dr. Massie of London, who had come to this country as a representative of various English religious denominations, and as bearer of an Anti-slavery Address from British Christians; and he hoped we should hear his voice among us. He was also glad to see Hon. Henry Wilson present, one who never lost an opportunity to attend an anti-slavery meeting, and from him also we should hope to hear. As Mr. Wilson came to the platform,

he was warmly cheered.   Mr. Garrison then read a portion
of a recent statement of Mr. Edward S. Philbrick—formerly
of this state, and son of our late treasurer, Samuel Philbrick
—now manager and proprietor of numerous estates on the
Port Royal islands, showing by numerous facts and statistics 'how favourably freedom is working for the emancipated people there."

Rev. Dr. Massie, of London, was then introduced; he
was received with applause, and spoke somewhat as
follows :—

"I have unspeakable pleasure in being present here to-
day, and in meeting the men, and the women too, who
have so long stood together in behalf of the Anti-slavery
cause in America.   I have a deep respect for these friends,
and it was long my domestic pleasure to act, from year to
year, in behalf of the annual bazaar held in Boston, to aid
in the cause of the total abolition of slavery.   I was then
associated with one who was as truly a member of the
Massachusetts Anti-slavery Society as if she had lived
within the bounds of your state.   [This allusion of Dr. M.
to his wife (since deceased) whose warm heart and active
mind had greatly endeared her to many in this country,
was received with sincere emotion.]   I was one of the
workers in behalf of that emancipation which we to-day
are met to celebrate.   I do not say I was a great part of
that work, but rather that I was one of the least of those
workers; but whatever aid I could give, travelling, speaking, using my political and personal influence in its behalf,
that I did give.   We then had amongst us a class, fully
equal in temper and conduct to any 'copperheads' or 'rat-
tlesnakes' which you know anything about in this country.
I am sorry to feel obliged to tell you that the English
nation never has been wholly Anti-slavery.   At the time
spoken of, the lordlings and aristocracy of England put
every possible obstacle in the way of the great measure of
emancipation, and Wilberforce (himself more than a whole
bench of Lords and Bishops) was glad, in a Parliament of
six hundred, to find forty-five men to stand by him.   But
the subject was agitated, and an agency society was instituted.   Then it was that my friend George Thompson
(applause) and many others went forth to labour, and soon

tho petitions to Parliament began to roll in. At this time there was not more than one bishop of the Church who would vote for Emancipation! Hardly a dozen clergymen throughout the kingdom were ready to be identified with the measure! But Mr. Stanley (now Lord Derby) and others saw that it had become an absolute necessity, as a measure of peace at home, to take up this question of Emancipation in earnest, and the great measure at length triumphed.

"Recently a large body of Protestant ministers of France—seven hundred and fifty—addressed the clergy of England, desiring them to make a public expression of their interest in the contest now going on in America, as a contest against slavery and in behalf of liberty and justice. To that address four thousand and eight ministers of Great Britain signed a strong and sympathetic reply. On the 3rd of June last, a meeting of clergy at Manchester joined in an address to the churches and people of America, and they have now sent it hither by the hands of deputies. That address I have with me to-day. I had the pleasure to read it to an audience of six thousand persons in the Free Trade Hall in Manchester. I have read it to large assemblies in Philadelphia, New Haven, and elsewhere in this country. I had also the honour to present it to President Lincoln at Washington, whom I am happy to believe firmly and heartily opposed to slavery. He thought Mr. May had not done full justice to the spirit of many of the English aristocracy. Many of them are widely different from their class. Lord Carlisle, Lord Lyons, the Duke of Argyle and others are noble and excellent persons, whose influence is just what we could desire. The Government is not opposed to the abolition of slavery; and a vast preponderance of the people are strongly in favour of it. I wish not to sever the friendly ties between this country and England, but to bind them more closely. Let nothing be done, let nothing be even said, by any friend of freedom in America or England, to provoke hostility between the two countries.

"Mr. Garrison most cordially responded to the sentiments expressed by Dr. Massie against hostility between this country and England. He hoped he should never live to see a war between these two countries. But the aim of

the Copperhead press and population here is to excite
enmity against England. He believed the great mass of
the English people were in feeling with the North."

I found on my return to my hotel that friends had been
inquiring for me, and soon I learned that I was expected
to preach in the morning at Roxbury, and deliver my message at Park Street Church, one of the largest sanctuaries
in Boston, in the evening. It was always a pleasure to me to
have the privilege of preaching and mingling my sympathies in the devotions of American congregations. Therefore, besides fulfilling the duties assigned in the morning, I
attended the celebration of the Lord's Supper in the church
under the ministry of Mr. Means. The suburb of Roxbury
is quiet and retired, and the residences of the Bostonians
here are seated as the homes of comfort, removed altogether
from civic turmoil. I never experienced heat more oppressive than it was on that day, in both places of meeting.
Even Americans acknowledged it had been the warmest in
the season. The people seemed to me to loiter at the church
doors, afraid to encounter the heat within. Park Street
Church, however, was filled, and, much to my astonishment, the Rev. Dr. Kirke was seated in the pulpit before I
entered. He had come to take a decided part in promoting
my mission, which he previously had welcomed by letter.
At the close of my address he was pleased to say the paper
he had prepared was not cordial enough to respond to one,
introduced by an address so much more to his mind than
he had anticipated. I will transcribe what was said in the
local journals on the occasion :—

"Dr. Massie is one of the earliest and most untiring of
English Abolitionists, and has long evinced a most friendly
interest in the welfare and prosperity of this country. He
is very highly esteemed for his moral worth, his amiable
character, and his unbounded benevolence. Lately Secretary of the Board of British Missions, he has been wisely
delegated to bring to this country, in behalf of 4000 of

the evangelical ministers of England, a message of sympathy with the cause of the United States, and also to present the views of English Christians on the subject of the American war, as embodied in an address very happily conceived and expressed. This address, in connection with a similar one signed by 750 of the Protestant ministers of France, Dr. Massie laid before a public meeting at Park Street Church, in this city, on Sunday evening last—accompanying it with a very lucid and eloquent exposition of its origin and object.

" Dr. Massie condemned the Southern rebellion in the strongest terms, as being an attempt to disorganize and demoralize human affairs, and thwart the law of God ; and gave a history of what was done in the great meetings, in different parts of the kingdom last autumn.

" He remarked that the class in England who have not entered into sympathy with America are, to a great extent, those who delight in appellations of nobility, but who are not the religious men of the nation, nor men whose knowledge of the geography of America, or its local politics, is accurate or extensive. He assured the audience that the *people* of Great Britain are on their side, and will continue to be so. He deplored a prospective war between the two countries as likely to bring disaster upon themselves and disgrace upon the civilized world.

" The amount of labour performed by the gentlemen who had the control of the sympathetic movement in Great Britain and France, as well as the extent of the sympathy shown to exist in these countries towards the United States, took the audience by surprise. As was observed by Deacon Hoyt, had such a feeling been known to exist, Music Hall would not begin to contain the crowds who would have flocked to receive Dr. Massie.

" At the conclusion of Rev. Dr. Massie's remarks, there was a discussion as to the best method of presenting a suitable reply on behalf of the Christians of Boston, the speakers being Rev. Dr. Kirke, Rev. T. N. Haskell, Rev. Professor Seeley of Amherst College, and Henry Hoyt, Esq. It was voted at ten o'clock to appoint a committee of nine to prepare such a reply. The remarks of several of the speakers during the evening, notwithstanding the sanctity of the place, drew out marked applause. Henry Hill, Esq.,

presided, and the introductory religious services were performed by Rev. John O. Means of Roxbury. The committee
referred to was to be appointed by the chairman, and was
to represent the various religious denominations of the
city."

I promised to return and comply with the request to
give a second lecture in Tremont Temple, when the response
to be made should be ready for publication, and in the
meantime I could visit Andover, Providence, and Portland,
so as to extend the knowledge of the message as far east as
I could carry it.

One of the trustees of Andover Seminary, Judge Chapman, urgently advised I should attend the "Commencement" at Andover, which was announced for Tuesday the
4th of August, and would have extended to the evening of
the 6th, but for the Fast which the President had proclaimed. I had so much enjoyed the services at Yale, that
I needed little persuasion for this occasion. I was assured
of hospitable entertainment, and the judge promised to
write on my behalf. The town of Andover is twenty-
three miles from Boston, and accessible by trains. Having,
however, arranged my procedure by a wrong line, I was
detained several hours at the station, and thus was later in
arriving at the seminary than I had intended. Soon after
I was received into conference with the Board of Council,
and assured by them of cordial interest and a desire to
arrange for an opportunity to make a statement of my
mission and objects. In the evening Bishop Clark, of Providence, was expected to deliver an address to the members
and friends of the Institution; and it was determined that
I should follow him, to present the address from England.
I had much pleasure in listening to his discourse, which
was marked by wide and comprehensive range of thought,
clearness of perception, and liberality of opinion, without
any lordliness of assumption on *authority in religious belief.*

I believe he was Congregationalist when passing through college, and he showed now none of the usual alienation of a dissident from the faith of his fathers. I feared there might be felt some incongruity in the juxtaposition of our two subjects, before the same audience. But probably the sense of this was more with myself than with my hearers. The attention of the congregation continued unflagging till near ten o'clock, and it was resolved that the subject should be resumed again next day at dinner. In fulfilment of this purpose, after dinner, but before the removal of the cloth, I was requested to read the address. It was then moved by Professor Stowe, and seconded by another clergyman, and carried, the Rev. Dr. Dwight in the chair, that the company then assembled should adhere to the response which had been adopted at New York.

I attended throughout one of the Sessions of the "Commencement." The students, professors, and visitors walked as a body from the Mansion House to the church, about a third of a mile. As a stranger I was ranked with one of the Faculty, and seated in the part of the church assigned to them. Besides music and prayer, there was an official report of certain proceedings of the Board, and a new professor was installed. The graduates who had passed their degree were named in a printed list. There were five from *States* out of New England, ten were from Connecticut, seven were from Vermont, three from New Hampshire, eight were from Massachusetts. Their themes were diversified: Kingsley and his Theology; the Writings of F. D. Maurice; the French Philosophy of the last century; the Nature of Divine Inspiration; Theology a Progressive Science; Adaptation of the Bible to Man's Religious Wants; Christianity in conflict with the Roman State; Common Sense in Religious Theories; Sacrifices of the Mosaic Law; Patriotism a Christian duty; Birthday of the Christian Church; Divine Character of the Theme of the

o

Theologian; and other subjects of cognate character had been assigned one to each of the graduates. A professor presided; the president, Dr. Parke, had sailed for Europe. Each graduate stood on the pulpit platform as he recited his composition. I thought they all evinced talent and the characteristics of their training, intellectual rather than evangelical; yet none were unevangelical or frivolous. The culture of the mind was manifest as well as its exercise. Every man seemed to have *thought* independently and spoke for himself, and yet all harmonized in theological bias and utterance. They recited from memory; one or two with restraint; but of the thirteen who answered to their names, with the two exceptions, a casual observer would not have discerned the exercise as an effort of memory. I was invited to close the Session with prayer, and had much pleasure in commending the institution and graduates to the Divine benediction.

Besides the Seminary, there is, at Andover, a large public grammar-school, which has, for many years, attracted multitudes of young pupils, and led to the temporary residence of families in the vicinity. Professor Stowe is about to leave Andover, disposed, I fancy, to enjoy the *otium cum* —for which he may have been the more easily tempted, by his wife's success as an authoress. Mrs. Beecher Stowe was kind enough to commission her husband to invite me to visit her in "Uncle Tom's Cabin." It was to me a pleasure to comply, and thus was I introduced to her sister Catherine, hardly less famed at home for *her* writings in another direction. I also was introduced to young Mr. Stowe, an officer on the staff of one of the generals in the war; I believe in the artillery. This son of Mrs. B. Stowe had received a wound in the head, by which a part of the skull had been removed, and there had been great danger of concussion on the brain. I thought the invalid was still in a critical state. Our conversation turned principally on

the public feeling in Britain, and the responses her letter
had drawn forth. Mrs. B. Stowe recalled some of her
"Sunny Memories," with some abatement in the silence of
those who had fluttered round her in the *gala* day of
"Uncle Tom." I liked her manner more at home than
when she was obliged to be "the observed of all observers,"
and thought she had more the air of a mother and wife
than I expected. I was tempted to visit the circle again
of my own accord, and found no less hearty a welcome,
while I fancied her mind was more at ease, and conversation more social. The appearance of *this* Andover—
there are two places so named—was rural, and the houses
were scattered across roads and over fields rather than in
streets or terraces, giving the whole the air of a new
settlement in a country district. But the college buildings
and churches recalled the assurance that the place was the
same of which I had read forty years ago.

A minister and a missionary from Lawrance attending
the Andover meetings, had solicited me to accompany them
on their return home, and take part in their services next
day. On deliberation I consented; but in two hours afterward, the clergyman of the second church, in Andover,
applied to me to undertake the conduct of the Thanksgiving
services in his church. This was deemed a manifestation of
a great change, as he was reputed to have been more a
sympathizer with the South. I adhered to my promise for
Lawrance, and travelled in company with my new friends
over three or four miles, into the forest, as it appeared. We
came to the banks of a flowing river, the Merrimac, the
attractive secret of the origin and prosperity of the town.

Twenty-five years ago there were not six houses in the
region. There are now between 20,000 and 25,000 inha-
tants, all busied in manufactures, chiefly cotton, but some
others also. The district had been surveyed, a company
was formed, and directed and regulated the water power,

and then sold the land to those who would erect mills, etc.
Houses of a comfortable description rose in connection
with the mills, manufactures began and prospered, though
one of the public works, after it had been employed as a
mill, fell and mingled in its ruins two or three hundred
working people. Means were being employed to rescue
the victims still living, though buried among fallen beams,
machinery, and the crumbling walls. Some one incau-
tiously introduced, where their living friends were still
immured, a light, either to guide in rescuing their friends,
or to comfort the prisoners. The materials caught fire,
and thus many who were still alive were roasted to death.
About two hundred persons died in this calamity; but a
substantial mill stands, and is worked where the disaster
occurred. The town is laid out in green squares, broad
shaded streets, self-contained houses adorned with shrubbery, and ten or a dozen churches; schools and public institutions are sustained; newspapers and literary associations prosper; Englishmen, Scotchmen, Irishmen, and New
Englanders, masters and workmen, mingle together; and
their solemn assembly gathers hundreds of well-dressed and
orderly worshippers. I was twice in the town, and addressed assemblies each time; and on the second occasion a
company, which had volunteered for nine months' service
to the war, had that day returned, and were entertained to
a late dinner by the authorities, to welcome home again
those who had served their country. I was requested on
my first visit to officiate, instead of the minister who was
to have delivered the Thanksgiving address on the 6th of
August. I therefore directed my remarks to the state of
affairs in America more than to English sympathies,
though I tried to combine both subjects in the service. The
ministers and leading friends united in thanking me for
this service, but they pleaded that I should return and give
fully the glishEn address. To this I consented, and met

on the second time about a thousand, chiefly the factory workmen and their wives. The renewed visit gave me a further opportunity for marking the superior comforts and advantages of the American mechanic over those of his brethren in the old country. I subjoin the official report, which was given in the "Lawrance American," of the visits and their accompanying services :—

REPLY TO DR. MASSIE.

"At a meeting held in Central Church, on occasion of the National Thanksgiving, Dr. Massie, of London, delivered an exceedingly interesting address; and a Committee was appointed, consisting of the pastors of the several Protestant churches of the city, to prepare a reply and report at a subsequent meeting. The second meeting was held in City Hall on Monday evening last, and a full house was again addressed by Dr. Massie, who read also the two letters which he brings, one from France, the other from England. The Committee then reported, and the meeting adopted the following reply :—

"The Committee recommend for adoption by this meeting the response given to Dr. Massie by the ministers and pastors of New York city; but we cannot forbear expressing, in stronger language than is there used, our deep interest in the visit of Dr. Massie, as admirably calculated to allay the irritation everywhere existing among us against England, and which has been produced by the conduct of so large and influential a part of the British Press. We can conceive of no measures more likely than his addresses, and the facts which he brings to our notice, to convince the people of this country that such Edomitish conduct is not an expression of the views and sympathies of the people of Great Britain, but of certain classes and parties only, who for certain reasons are interested against us; while the people—the religious people generally, we hope—but especially the working men, understand our position and their own interests, and are of one mind with us, both as respects that which must on our part be the first aim—to save the nation, and preserve the foundations of good government and of social order—as well as in the desire that rebellion and slavery may perish together.

"In this benign and truly Christian effort we wish Dr. Massie most abundant success, and pray that, by the blessing of God, his labours may be the means of preventing strife between our two countries; strife than which there can scarcely be conceived a greater calamity.

"C. E. FISHER, *Chairman.*
C. M. CORDLEY, *Secretary.*"

"The importance of Dr. Massie's addresses, to say nothing of their eloquence, consists in the facts which he presents, and in the misconceptions which he corrects. While admitting that we have enemies, and that powerful parties and interests are working against us in Great Britain, as, for instance, the London "Times," and other wayward and selfish adversaries of liberty; the aristocracy, with some honourable exceptions; and certain shipbuilders like Mr. Laird; he declares as what he knows to be true, that the mass of the people of England and Scotland, in the manufacturing districts especially, are very strongly on the side of our loyal states, and of the policy of President Lincoln. The significance of the French letter lies in this, that it is an appeal signed by 750 pastors of Protestant churches in France, to Christian ministers of every denomination in Great Britain, expressing alarm at the very thought of the recognition of a confederacy founded on the enslavement of the negro, and entreating that every means may be used by Christians especially, in Great Britain and Europe, to prevent such a calamity. When it is remembered that France has but about 1100 Protestant ministers of religion, and when the strong language of the letter is considered, it certainly should encourage us to know that 750 of those 1100 were willing to sign such an appeal. We may be sure that the Protestant churches of the Old World will not permit a slave power to establish itself among the nations, if any remonstrance of theirs will avail against it. It must have been gratifying to Dr. Massie to notice that, although greeted with frequent applause while speaking of this country and of its President, nothing he said was received with more evident satisfaction than his tribute of respect and of admiration for England's noble Queen."

On the afternoon of the Thanksgiving Day I passed through Boston to Providence, Rhode Island. This city

had peculiar and personal attractions, from its early historical associations; the name, opinions, persecutions, and
triumphs of Roger Williams. He was, perhaps, the first
truly to understand the principle of religious liberty,
though his apprehension of its legitimate exercise may
have been derived from his own mistakes, as well as the
blunders of the ecclesiastical authorities, from whom he
differed. To him America owed the foundation of the first
Republic, which recognized simply the rights of conscience,
and frankly adopted them in intercourse with all who
differed from them. The tale of his outcast life, wanderings
among the Indians, his negotiations with them for the land
which they conceded and he accepted as a white man's
settlement, might interest many a youthful student of
history. But I had here residing a brother whom I had
not seen for thirty-four years, and from whom the circumstances of separation had often been a subject of thought.
When I passed into the platform at Providence, the sup-
position occurred, "*Perhaps he may be here.*" I had not
been able to fix the precise day; he did not, therefore, expect me, yet I imagined it possible he *might* be on the
platform. I looked out and saw a man who, I thought,
might be he; I looked again and fancied it was, hurried
out, leaving an over-coat which I never saw again, went
straight up to him, looked him in the face, asked if his
name was *Massie*. He answered feebly. I asked again.
He answered, "Yes." "My name is Massie too," I said.
He looked intensely, the tear started, and trickled down
his cheek. "You're not he," he said. I could stand it no
longer, and we both rejoiced together in a mutual recognition and silent thanksgiving. At Providence I saw Dr.
Swaine, and was invited to his hospitality. His wife was,
indeed, his crown and honour. Her consideration and
ministrations made me feel at home, and only regret that
my wife was not there to share her kindness. Arrange-

ments were made for a meeting in the First Baptist or William's Church on the evening of August 9th. I preached at Pautucket in the morning for Dr. Bludgett, and enjoyed with him and his people the fellowship of saints. A public intimation had appeared the previous day:—

" The Rev. Dr. Massie, of England, is in town. Our readers are aware that he and the Rev. Mr. Rylauce came to this country to bring a memorial signed by a very large number of ministers, clergy, and pastors of various Protestant denominations in England and France, and expressing sympathy with us in our struggle, and especially in our opposition to African slavery. Dr. Massie has addressed crowded assemblies in New York, Boston, and other cities, and has been received with the favour which the nature of his errand and his distinguished abilities deserve. He will speak to-morrow evening at half-past seven o'clock in the First Baptist Meeting House."

The report, which has been since transmitted to myself, is from Dr. Swaine, who is pleased to say, " I regret that I could not have seen you again, and greatly rejoice at the success of your visit to this country. I am sure it must result in great good."

" In accordance with previous notice a public meeting was held in the First Baptist Church, in the city of Providence, on Sabbath evening, August 9, 1863, to listen to a discourse by the Rev. James W. Massie, D.D., of London, the reading of the address of the ministers of France and Great Britain, to ministers and pastors of all Christian denominations throughout the States of America.

" At the close of the meeting, during which the spacious church was filled to overflowing, the Rev. Dr. Caswell, of Brown University, being in the chair, the following ministers of Providence were chosen as a committee to prepare and send a reply in behalf of the meeting:—From the Congregational Church, the Rev. L. Swaine; from the Episcopal Church, the Rev. Bishop Clark; from the Baptist Church, the Rev. J. L. Caldwell; from the Free-will Baptist Church, the Rev. G. T. Day; from the Methodist

Church, the Rev. S. B. Gould; from the Unitarian Church, the Rev. A. Woodbury.

"After due conference the committee agreed to adopt the New York reply to the address, as in their view expressing the sense of the meeting and of the religious community in the midst of which it was held. A copy of the reply is enclosed herewith.

"L. SWAIN, THOMAS M. CLARK, S. L. CALDWELL, GEO. T. DAY, AUGUSTUS WOODBURY.

"The Rev. J. B. Gould, of the Methodist Church, was absent from the city when these signatures were taken."

I must not leave this really beautiful city without a word upon its features or history. I feel as if Roger Williams calls from the rock on the banks of the Seekoak, "What cheer," as the Indians saluted him when he landed from the Massachusetts side to make his first settlement. Situated on the shore of the bay called Narraganset, and connected with distant places by rail and water conveyance, it ministers the pleasures of city and country life, and by natural scenery presents a diversity which charms the tourist. It dates back to 1635, but looks young and vigorous, though the home of refinements and amenities in its social character, which have been matured by ages of culture. Providence, R. I., is the seat of Brown University, over which some most distinguished scholars have presided, and where many more have been nurtured; it is reported one of the best educational establishments in America. Founded originally at Warren, 1764, it was removed to Providence in 1770. Its structure is in the style of a literary institution, its library is extensive and valuable, and is rich in rare and costly works. Dr. Wayland has recently retired from its presidency, but has left a savour of his learning and good name. The population of Providence in 1850 was 41,513, and had increased in 1860 to 50,666; they are well employed as manufacturers of jewellery, in steam machinery, in tools, and implements of all sorts ; and Providence furnishes the greater part of all 'the screws used in the United States. Years ago the annual product of cotton-mills and print-works in this city was valued at more than 4,000,000 of dollars. In its suburbs was erected the first cotton-mill built in the whole of America. Formerly its rich ships, crossing all seas, rendered it an important commercial depôt, and still the city is distinguished for its enterprise and wealth. The appearance of Providence as approached by the waters which flow into its bay, presents a beautiful panorama, and its quiet and well shaded streets are orna-mented with gay cottages and handsome residences. Pau-tucket, with its water power and manufacturing enterprise, has long ministered to the well-being of Providence ; and the quiet affluence which prevails in the retired habitations of its residents, shows how the hand of the diligent maketh rich. Newport has become a source of growing luxury and a temptation to pleasure among the people of Pro-vidence. It is not only now a summer watering-place and resort for invalids, but the school of the United States navy ; and the vessels of war which cruise near the harbour, added to the natural and picturesque beauties around, give attraction, for amusement or gain, to the inhabitants of Providence and its vicinity. I wished to visit this, as " the most elegant and fashionable of all American watering-places ;" but found that the magnificent boat by which I must have sailed, carried on her deck and in her saloons one thousand passengers daily. I sought pleasure where there was less concourse.

I was at Tremont House, Boston, early on Monday morning, and had my arrangements complete to sail by the steam-boat for St. John, New Brunswick, at eight o'clock. A finer day could not be desired, as we passed down Massachusetts Bay. The route was new to me, and, for some time, towns on the shore were discoverable

which only from the map could I distinguish as to their
name and precise locality; but there was every temptation
to linger on the prospect, from the fineness of the day and
the smoothness of the sailing. Lynn on the north-east
shore of the bay, nine miles from Boston, and accounted a
famous place for the manufacture of ladies' shoes—as many
as 4,500,000 pairs are made in a year, giving work to
10,000 hands: Nahant and its boundless sea-coast view,
with its grotto called the *Swallow's Cave*: Nantucket
Beach, celebrated for its fine shell-fish, sea-fowl, and good
bathing: Salem and its historical associations and re-
miniscences, of commerce, literary institutions, and burnt
witches: Beverly and its long bridge: Wenham and its
lake for ice in winter and fish in summer: Newbury port,
considered one of the most beautiful towns in New England, and hallowed as the burying ground of George
Whitfield: Hampton and its fine views of the ocean, and
its invigorating air for invalids: Portsmouth on the
Piscataqua river, and its safe and deep harbour, which is
never frozen; a navy yard where the "North America,"
the first line of battle ship, built during the revolution,
was launched for the United States. These towns belong
to Massachusetts, and may be pointed out by the practised
eye, when sailing near to the shore; but our navigator
kept well off the land, outside of the Isle of Shoals, till he
came near to Portland. Here I landed for half an hour,
but deferred my visit to the town till my return from her
Majesty's dominions in New Brunswick. Toward night we
had little to see on shore, and when we reached Eastport
it was early in the morning. The scenery in adjacent
islands and in the territory of Great Britain is exceedingly
fine in the Passamaquoddy Bay.

The night was brilliant and calm; my cabin was on
deck, and my window opened to the side, so that I could
rest on my bed inhaling the pure sea air. I have often

been at sea, but never in such luxury. The speed of the vessel must have been at the rate of fourteen miles an hour, stopping only at Portland and Eastport till we reached St. John. Happily we encountered no fog, which often overshadows the shores of Fundy; the passage to St. John's Harbour was, therefore, displayed to us in all its beauty. At the entrance is a small island, called Partridge Island, occupied by a lighthouse, a signal-post, and a steam whistle, instead of a bell, to warn ships approaching during fogs. The town of Carlton, opposite to St. John, and Portland, a suburb on the city side, extend the dimensions, and surround the inner harbour. St. John stands on a rocky promontory and hill on the right entrance from the sea, so steep in some parts as to be fatiguing to the peripatetic,—the streets are laid out at right angles; King Street, the principal one, is a hundred feet wide; on the top of the hill is a terrace square of residences. The building of the city is dated so late as 1786. In 1763 the whole of what is now called New Brunswick was claimed by France, as the domain of New France. The river of St. John in the vicinity flows over rocks in powerful rapids, sometimes called falls; but there is only a gradual declivity at its mouth, which prevents ships or even boats from entering, except at the top of high water, when only it is smooth. The entire length of the river is 600 miles, of which 225 are in British territory from the Grand Falls. It is computed that, with its affluents, 1300 miles are afforded of navigable waters. Large tracts on its banks are wild forest and present upon its grand rocky hills pictures of great attraction. The Market House, the Custom House, and Court House, and fourteen churches of different denominations, show the enterprise of the population, which now exceeds 30,000. The Mechanics' Institute, grammar and other central schools, with literary society, show that the inhabitants delight in other pursuits than lumbering, ship-building, and engineering. Many of the habitations are constructed still of wood, and, therefore, the frequency of fires, which are notified by the fire-bell to the sudden dispersion of public assemblies at times when least desired.

I visited New Brunswick not anticipating any opportunity to plead the cause for which I had crossed the Atlantic. But friends of my relations there requested I would give them an address on some subject. I consented to give them some account of my mission to the United States, if they would convene a congregation. Arrangements were made in a manner satisfactory to all, and I gave a lecture in the Congregational Church. A good congregation assembled, and listened with seeming interest, till the *fire*-bell began to peal, when anxiety for the possible locality startled many, and induced not a few to go out. Some returned, and the proceedings were extended till between nine and ten o'clock. One of the local journals gave a report of the conclusion as follows:—

" An exceedingly interesting and well-timed address was delivered by Dr. Massie of London, to a good audience in the Congregational Chapel yesterday evening, the Rev. Wm. Alves, A.M., presiding. Dr. M. is one of the delegates (the other being a clergyman of the Church of England) from the clergy of Great Britain to Christian Ministers in the United States, on the subject of the Abolition of Slavery. Having taken the opportunity of visiting his friends in this city, he felt it to be his duty to respond to a request that he would make the people of this city acquainted with a history of the movement in France and in England. Dr. M. first gave a history of the rise, progress, and consummation of Emancipation in England. Subsequently to 1836, so strong had the anti-slavery feeling in England become, that when American clergymen came over, they were closely catechised as to their connection with slavery, their approval of it, and if they were not found opposed to it, they were shunned as if the blood of the negro had been on their hands. On one occasion the celebrated DANIEL O'CONNELL declined to shake hands with an Ame-

rican ambassador because he represented a slaveholding
nation. When Mrs. Stowe's popular novel appeared, it led
from 45,000 to 50,000 of the ladies of England, including
Lady Palmerston, and many ladies of high rank, to send an
address to the ladies of America, praying them to do what
they could to promote the abolition of slavery. When,
therefore, it came to pass that South Carolina, Alabama,
Texas, and Virginia seceded from the Union, and declared
in their instruments of secession that they did so in order
to perpetuate slavery, when Vice-President Stephens declared that in the new constitution slavery was to be the
corner-stone though it had been rejected by the first builders, the anti-slavery men of France and England felt that
a providential occasion was at hand, one in which it might
please God to work the ruin of that wicked system, which
treated men as brutes, and trampled on the requirements
of God's law in relation to the purity of the family institution.
They felt that they must encourage those who were opposed
to slavery, and could not sympathize with those who were
avowedly and irrevocably attached to it. British Christians
wished to strengthen their hands, and prevent a retrograde
movement. We have another object. We wish to ce-
ment friendly feelings between England and America, and
check irritation as arising out of the war. We wish to avoid
hostile collision between these two great countries, for no
darker day could dawn on the world, no day so sad to
Christian hearts, or so welcome to European despots, and
to the most wily and cunning fox of them all, than the day
that Saxon America and Anglo-Saxon England would draw
the sword against each other!

"The people of the Provinces and the Americans were
neighbours—'Live in peace,' continued Dr. Massie,
'Seek each other's good.' If they prosper, so will you.
If they suffer, you must suffer also. Let Protestant Christians, especially, in both countries live as a brotherhood—
thus God will bless you and make you a blessing.

"This is but a meagre account of a most impressive
address. On motion of Robert Sears, Esq., seconded by
Rev. N. McKay, a hearty vote of thanks was tendered to
Dr. M. for his instructive address."

At the close several persons who had lived in the

United States and other friends of the Union gathered around me, expressing their gratification. One gentleman, whose name or person I did not know, shook hands and left, despite of my resistance, in my hand what afterwards I found to be a ten-dollar note. Some of the *quondam* American citizens residing here proved exceedingly intelligent and conversible. I afterwards drove with my friends a few miles up the river bank, as far as the islands, popularly called the Magawagonish; having crossed by the suspension-bridge, a handsome and durable structure, which is contiguous to what have been known as The Rapids. The country has been cultivated, and is fertile. The rupture made by the river through the mass of rock that impeded its passage to the sea has left a great rugged chasm, which suggests some convulsion of nature. The cliffs on each side are lofty and perpendicular, and the breadth of the stream between them is not more than a quarter of a mile across, though only a few miles higher up the river is four or five miles broad.

I returned to the coast of Maine by the same magnificent steamer as I had sailed by on my voyage eastward, and was happy to meet on board gentlemen to whom I was not unknown, and who kindly introduced themselves to me. The coast was familiar to them, and I gleaned information which I valued. Professor Porter and his friend, as also their agreeable companions, added much to my passing pleasures, and not a little to my happy memories of transatlantic intercourse. We all enjoyed the adjacent island and mountain scenery, as we passed out from Passamaquoddy Bay near *Eastport*, sixty miles from St. John, and over the confines of British territory. This town, containing six or seven thousand people, is built on Moose Island, in a pleasant situation, and is bridged to the mainland of Perry; while more extended intercourse is maintained with Pembroke, Lubec, and adjoining British islands by ferries,

We were shown where the boundary line passes between British and United States. It may be longitudinal and latitudinarian, but it is an invisible continuation of imaginary points, which makes a veritable straight line. One man may have his farm on both territories, and be neither better nor worse. Our moving palace resumed her watery way, and about two o'clock in the morning her steward cast his cable ashore at Portland.

The hour at which we arrived was so unseasonable for family visitations, that, although I had been invited to the hospitality of Dr. Dwight, I preferred accompanying Dr. Porter to Preble House, as an open hospice. After a morning's rest, I went out to survey the city. It has been much and worthily praised as the commercial metropolis of Maine, " handsomely " situated, occupying a high point of land, and stretching along a ridge, which crowns a peninsula, at the extremity of Cusco Bay. The anchorage in the harbour is protected on every side by land, the water is deep, and communication with the ocean direct. The streets of the city, containing many good houses, are embellished with shady trees, so profusely that it is said there are 3000 trees within the city bounds. The main street, bearing the cognomen Congress, stretches along the ridge of the peninsula, from end to end. The City Hall, Court House, and the Athenæum are institutions which contribute to the ornament of the city, and the Society of Natural History, and the Portland Sacred Music Society, provide for the entertainment of the inhabitants. I attended a mass meeting of the citizens, when Vice-president Hamlin occupied the chair, in the City Hall ; General P. O. Howard, a hero and patriot, and an Hon. Mr. Davis from Washington, were the chief speakers for the day, in advocacy of the Union. The place was well filled, with ladies as well as all classes of men. The population of Portland was at last census 26,341, and had increased 5500 in ten years. The state seemed to vacillate toward the Democratic party last year—this year it has gone by a large majority for the Republican Union. In my rambles I met Dr. Dwight, and arranged to have my luggage conveyed to his dwelling. His courtesy and his urbane hospitality were unceasing, providing for my enjoyment by every means at his command. He had notified that I should preach in his pulpit on Sunday morning, and had arranged that my mission should be expounded in the evening. We called together on Dr. Carruthers, who has been for many years the honoured successor to the eminent Dr. Edward Payson. He assured me he had depended on me for his afternoon service. It was almost an Egyptian task to have three discourses to deliver on one such Sunday as were the hot days of August; but I would rather labour than disappoint. I therefore undertook to fulfil his wishes as far as I had ability. I must leave a local paper to report the proceedings of the evening :—

"Rev. Dr. Massie, the bearer of the address of 4000 clergymen of England to their brethren in America, expressive of their sympathy with the North in its efforts to suppress a causeless rebellion, having for its object the extension of slavery, and the degradation of white labour, held a meeting at Dr. Dwight's church, on Sunday evening last, for the purpose of defining the position of the people of Great Britain, and the object of his mission to this country.

" The body of the house was well filled, and the interest in the remarks of Dr. Massie was intense and unabated, from the beginning to the close, notwithstanding he occupied about an hour and a half. The desire was universally expressed to have the address repeated in the City Hall, when our citizens could more generally have the privilege of enjoying an intellectual treat.

"Dr. Massie read a select portion of Scripture, not, as he said, for the purpose of preaching a sermon, but as the foundation of the remarks he might make. He spoke of the wrong impression that had obtained in this country in relation to the position of Great Britain on the existing rebellion. He said the aristocracy of England, of which the London 'Times' is the organ, embracing a large propor-

P

tion of the Established Church, were generally in sympathy with the South. But the producing classes—the mechanics, the artizans, the labourers—were almost universally in sympathy with the North. The London 'Times' opposed Wilberforce and those noble men who laboured so ardently and successfully to emancipate the slaves of Jamaica, and other islands under the dominion of the British government. The 'Times' opposed the anti-corn law league until it became so popular that their opposition was harmless. It has never recognized in its columns, the Nonconformists, as a power, although they embrace more than half the worshipping assemblies of England. It speaks for the aristocracy of England, and cares for nothing except what may suit their taste and strike pleasantly on their ears. It does not give utterance to the voice of the people, who really have a controlling power in Great Britain at the present moment. He spoke of the large and enthusiastic meetings that had been held in different sections of Great Britain to give expression to the feelings of sympathy that everywhere existed for the North, in this struggle. An attempt had been made to enlist on the side of the South the feelings of starving thousands in Manchester and vicinity, and in other sections of Great Britain, who are out of employment in consequence of this rebellion, by endeavouring to make them believe that the North was the cause of their present misfortune; that it was owing to the blockade, ordered by the North to prevent cotton from coming to England. But these hard-handed mechanics raised their bony fingers toward the heavens and declared they would rather starve than throw any obstacle in the way of those who are endeavouring to put down slavery and elevate labour. After making these preliminary remarks and explanations, he read the address of the clergymen of France and England, which expressed their warmest sympathy in our attempts to elevate labour and overthrow the vile institution of slavery. It gave evidence of a thorough knowledge of the issues involved in the war; and while they did not propose in any objectionable manner to interfere with our movements, or to dictate to us the course we should pursue, they wished to give us the assurance that their sympathies were with us, and their prayers for our success were constantly going up to heaven.

" Dr. Massie is a very forcible and pleasing speaker, with the power of retaining the undivided attention of his audience. The gentlemen whose agent he is could not have selected a better man for the work assigned him. He leaves this city for the West, where we trust he will be kindly received and patiently listened to."

The editor of the " British Standard" published the following letter from Portland, which explains and fills up what would otherwise have been imperfect and obscure:—

" Sir,—The following address has received the signature of seventy ministers of this state, and would have received many more but for the unusual excitement attendant on our recent elections, which absorbed the attention both of editors and readers of our public papers:—

" TO THE MINISTERS OF GREAT BRITAIN ADOPTING AND CONCURRING IN THE ADDRESS OF JUNE 3, 1863.

" Reverend and Beloved Brethren,—The ' Address to Ministers and Pastors of all Christian Denominations throughout the States of America,' adopted by the Anti-Slavery Conference of Ministers of Religion, held in the city of Manchester on the 3rd of June, 1863, has been presented by the Rev. James W. Massie, D.D., one of the honoured brethren deputed for this purpose.

" It gives us Ministers in the State of Maine much satisfaction to know that so many ministers and pastors in Great Britain and France so fully concur and sympathize with us in judgment and feeling as to the bearing of recent and passing events on the cause of human freedom, and the destiny of millions so long held in unrighteous and oppressive bondage. These events have demanded and received our devout acknowledgments to God, whose wonder working providence has thus made the war undertaken for the purpose of perpetuating the thraldom of the negro, the means of loosening his chains, and letting him go free. We trust that legislative measures will soon provide for the utter extinction of slavery throughout our land.

" This, indeed, is not the only desired and expected issue of the war. The integrity of the Union we deem indispensable to the maintenance and perpetuation of our own liberty, and of the free institution of the country. The success of the Southern rebellion would not only have riveted the chains of the negro but have led to a further disintegration of the Republic, to perpetual civil wars, to social anarchy, and ultimately to a military despotism, involving our entire population in a bondage as galling and much more extensive than that from which, we trust, our coloured fellow-citizens will soon be universally and for ever free.

"We earnestly trust that the peace now so happily subsisting betwixt our own and other nations, will be preserved; and that the faithful disciples of Christ on both sides of the Atlantic will strive, by persevering prayer and mutual kindnesses, to counteract the spirit of hostility, and avert the calamities of war. As stewards of the manifold grace of God, let us be faithful to our trust. Let us exemplify and encourage the amenities of international goodwill. Let us follow after the things that make for peace, and whilst faithfully fulfilling every civil obligation to rulers and to fellow-citizens in our respective countries, let us remember that by claims and ties, higher, holier, and more enduring, 'One is our Master, even Christ, and all we are brethren.'"

"This document, you will observe by the accompanying notice, was to have been put into Dr. Massie's hands before his departure. My temporary absence from home prevented this; and now as the original which is now before me has been, whilst lying for signatures in the bookseller's store, seriously mutilated, accidentally or otherwise, by some unknown hand, it seems as well to retain it, and to send you the above copy with the statement that the document bears the signature of threescore and ten ministers, 'all honourable men,' and all loyal to the cause of human freedom. The visit of our mutual friend, Dr. Massie, has been of great service. His hearty addresses have everywhere ingratiated him with the American people, and have done much to disabuse certain classes of our citizens of impressions not altogether unnatural, and yet not authorized by the actual feelings of the English people. Your excellent representative has, I believe, no reason to complain of his reception; and has carried home with him such information and such views as may serve, by the blessing of the God of Peace, to strengthen the bond of international concord, and prevent at any future period a rupture which would convulse the world."

I remember the intercourse of Dr. Dwight and his excellent wife with much satisfaction, and regard as a high honour given by my mission, to have thus formed a domestic link with the honoured ancestry of this family. Jonathan Edwards and Timothy Dwight were New England apostles, and my host was a son of the latter in the line of succession, and a right worthy representative of the mighty dead. His wife inherited from her Pennsylvanian ancestry associations which intimately connected her with the service of the sanctuary. May the line of evangelical sanctity never be interrupted in their lineal descendants, and instead of the fathers, may the children continue to add honour to the name they bear. There were ministers in Portland whom I did not meet in their fatherland, some of them I had seen in England.

I left Maine for Massachusetts, where I had still one service to perform as part of my mission. To gratify friends I tarried a night at Lawrance, and proceeded again to Boston, and there became the guest of the Rev. Mr. Haskell, and through him was introduced to Mr. Stuart, originally from Britain, but now probably the largest shipbuilder in America. East Boston, where I sojourned on " Noddles Island," is connected with Old Boston by two ferries. The Cunard steamers have their own wharf here, 1000 feet long. The shipwrights and mechanics are a power in the place. I found my old tormentors, the mosquitoes, in great force here, from the water. The meeting was to be held in Tremont Temple. This is a building appropriated to public meetings and lectures. The peculiarity of its name is traced to the three elevations approaching to the height of hills, 130 feet above the level of the sea; and the earlier inhabitants used to call the district Trimountain, contracted to *Tremont*. The Indian word for the place was Shawmut, "living fountain," and perhaps fountains of good have flowed forth in this temple. The building is capacious, I should suppose about the size of Exeter Hall. It was not filled on the evening I was engaged there. This was ascribed to some other public attraction in the vicinity. But there was an assembly which would have crowded any ordinary church. It was my lot to deliver again what I had already before submitted to a Boston audience, a great trial to me, but this was compensated by the admirable response.

MEETING AT TREMONT TEMPLE.

A meeting of several hundred people was held last evening at Tremont Temple, to listen to the final address of Rev. James Massie, D.D., of London, one of the delegates from Christian ministers of Great Britain to the Christian public of the United States. Charles Stoddard of this city presided. Prayer was offered by Rev. Mr. Childs, Secretary of the American Tract Society. Rev. Dr. Massie was then introduced, and spoke for over an hour upon the same theme as he did a fortnight ago, his remarks being mainly confined to an expression of sympathy of his constituents with the loyal states in their struggle to maintain the integrity of the Government and remove the evils of slavery, and to promote right views, to avert the dangers of foreign intervention and war. He concluded by reading the address of those whom he represented. Rev. E. O. Haven, D.D., of this city, late editor of "Zion's Herald," read a reply prepared by a committee appointed at the previous meeting representing the Christian public of Boston and vicinity, to acknowledge the expressions of sympathy tendered by the English clergymen, and stating the facts pertaining to our present struggle. The meeting adopted the address unanimously, and adjourned about half-past nine o'clock.

RESPONSE TO THE MINISTERS OF THE GOSPEL IN ENGLAND.

To the Reverend Ministers of the Gospel, and all who love our Lord Jesus Christ in Great Britain :—The Christian pub-

lic of the city of Boston and vicinity, have received with
grateful pleasure the salutation and eloquent expressions of
sympathy tendered to them by the Rev. James W. Massie,
D.D., LL.D., and the Rev. J. L. Rylance, M.A., accredited
representatives of a large number of Ministers of the
Gospel in Great Britain.

The undersigned, a committee chosen for that purpose,
desire to return to you our grateful acknowledgments, and
deem it also a fitting occasion to present to you some
reasons that have impelled us to give our united support
and prayers to our Government in its present protracted
struggle to maintain, not only its own honour and existence, but, as we believe, the cause of humanity and of God.
The issue of this struggle will affect not only America, but
the whole Christian world. If our nation is politically
right, it is also morally right, and justly claims the prayers
and the approval of all who love the Lord Jesus Christ.
Christians in America do not ask for sympathy to strengthen
their own convictions of duty, but they do ask that Christians everywhere should acknowledge the Divine truth that
a rightful and righteous government is an ordinance of
God, and that an effort to establish or perpetuate human
slavery by rebellion, and fraud, and violence shall meet decisive and universal condemnation. Permit us, therefore,
to state the following facts :—

Supremacy of the U. S. Government.

The Government of the United States is, and from the
beginning has always been, the supreme authority of the
entire and one nation, denominated the United States of
America, and the Constitution of the United States of
America is the supreme law of this nation, a power ordained
of God, rebellion against which is resistance to the ordinance of God. All our officers, National and State, are
sworn, and all our citizens are bound to sustain it. It is to
us all that the Magna Charta, Sovereign, Lords and Commons can be to the people of Great Britain.

No Real Wrongs to Complain of.

This supreme authority of their and our common
nation has been repudiated and attacked, not by an
oppressed people, but by an oppressing caste of slave-

holders, confined to a portion of our territory, and embracing only a portion of that class who have not been able to show that they had been or could be wronged by the Government, prominent men among whom have confessed that they had no wrongs of which to complain, but that they desired to establish a rival system of Government, under which human slavery should be protected and rendered perpetual. The pretext that they had a right to rebel because the President, constitutionally chosen, was displeasing to them, is absurd, and the charge of unfairness to their interests in the imposition of tariffs is false.

Secret Plotting and False Statements of the Rebels.

In attempting to accomplish their bad design, the leaders of this rebellion have for a long time plotted in secret, while holding offices under the very Government, which they combined to overthrow, and, while solemnly bound by oft repeated oaths to sustain that Government; they have taken advantage of the confidence and leniency of the nation, to possess themselves, by stealth and violence, of large portions of the public property and the means of public defence; they have suppressed freedom of speech and action in the portions of the territory which they could control; they have overawed, or expelled, or imprisoned, or murdered, or forced into their own armies many thousands of the people; they have deluded the ignorant masses in the rebellious sections of the country, by false statements, and have succeeded for a time in producing an appearance of unanimity in their opposition to the National Government, which subsequent developments in large portions of the rebellious states have proved to be spurious and false; they have sent out emissaries to other nations, who, by untrue complaints of oppression, and by the use of large sounding words of liberty and independence, and extravagant promises of commercial intercourse and national alliances, and a pretence to aristocratic greatness, and worth, which has no foundation to rest upon, have appealed to the sympathy, the ambition, and the cupidity of foreign governments and peoples; they have even pretended to invoke the sympathy of Christians upon their designs; they have resisted the courts and magistracies of their own nation, and are therefore alone responsible before God and the world for the destruction of property at home, and the pain, and bloodshed, and deaths that have marked our great civil war, as well as for the disturbance of industry and the sufferings that have been occasioned by it in Great Britain and France.

No sanction for the Rebellion in any of the Revolutions of History.

For their course they find no sanction in any of the great revolutions among civilized nations which have received the approval of the best expounders of civil and moral law. The revolution to which our nation owes its independent origin was not undertaken for the support of slavery, nor any other confessedly bad institution, nor even primarily for territoral independence, but for the right, then denied, since granted by Great Britain to all her colonies, of some kind of representation in the bodies which had power to impose taxation ; it was also a struggle to maintain time-honoured privileges which had existed from the earliest settlement of these lands, then, for the first time, denied. As well might some disaffected counties of England, Scotland, or Ireland now throw off the authority of Sovereign or Parliament, call in a usurper to reign, and appeal to the example of William the Conqueror for a sanction, as these rebels against a just and impartial Government appeal for precedent to the story of this nation's birth.

The experiment of a voluntary confederacy of independent sovereignties was once tried, in a transitional period of our nation's history, and led the people to adopt the Federal Constitution, and become a consolidated power. To appeal to the hour of weakness in our history that preceded the perfection of its Government, for an example, is as wild as it would be for a horde of robbers or malcontents in England to seek to escape from the Government and set up a rival kingdom, appealing to the time when England, Scotland, and Ireland were independent sovereignties, or to the time when England itself was a Heptarchy.

The Case Summed up.

No, brethren and friends—reason and right, law and God require us to defend our national integrity. One

nation, peace will soon return to this country, and bind its
parts together in fraternal concord. The horrors of civil
war will soon be forgotten, when its primal cause, human
slavery, is completely removed. Were it possible permanently to divide this nation, frequent wars must result
between its parts, other nations would inevitably be involved in these struggles, the commerce and peace of the
world would be imperilled and diminished, the great missionary movements of Christian churches in this land, and,
perhaps, in Europe, would be interrupted, and our common
Christianity would be disgraced. The fearful war which
has arisen from this rebellion has been carried on, on our
part, in a patriotic and even Christian spirit, according to
the best usages of civilized nations ; and we believe that the
world has never seen an army in which so large a proportion of officers and soldiers have been impelled solely by a
regard for the cause of humanity and of God, as are found
in the army of the United States.

What the War has accomplished.

By divine Providence our Government has been led,
in its efforts to suppress this rebellion, to attack and
weaken the evils of slavery much more rapidly than
could have been constitutionally accomplished in a time of
peace. The abolition of slavery in the common territories
and in the district of Columbia, embracing Washington,
the capital of the nation ; the execution of a person convicted of being engaged in importing slaves from Africa,
and the entering into a treaty with Great Britain more
effectually to suppress this trade ; the recognition of Liberia
and Hayti as nations ; the immediate freedom of all the
slaves of rebels that come within the lines of our armies ;
the forbidding of our officers to return any fugitive slave to
bondage ; the Emancipation Proclamation of the President,
by which about three of the four millions of slaves in this
nation were pronounced free, large portions of whom are
now actually enjoying freedom ; the prospective and certain
abolishment of slavery in the two entire states, West Virginia and Missouri ; the urgent request of the President to
the other border and loyal states not affected by the Proclamation, to rid themselves of this barbarous institution,
and the earnest and open discussion of this proposition by

the people of those states; the employment of the emancipated slaves as free labourers by their former masters and others, in South Carolina, and Louisiana and elsewhere, under the supervision and protection of our Government; the earnest desire of loyal citizens in the rebel states, that when their respective states repudiate the rebellion, it may be as free states; and the means of education and religious improvement furnished to the emancipated slaves by voluntary Christian Associations from the loyal states, approved and aided by the Government; all show the genuine purpose of the Government to destroy slavery, and should awaken gratitude among all who oppose that relic of barbarism, and approve the Golden Rule.

Our Recent Successes.

Moreover the success which the Lord of Hosts and Great Arbiter of human events has given, and appears to promise to give to our arms, should awaken the most ardent praise. The capture of Vicksburg and Port Hudson, with all their military force and arms, thus opening the Mississippi river to commerce, and promising to suppress the rebellion in several states; the retreat of the strongest rebel army from Pennsylvania after a decided defeat at Gettysburg; the flight of the army under General Bragg in Tennessee; the defeat of General Price in Missouri; the discomfiture of General Johnston; the capture of General Morgan and his large band of marauders on free soil; the investment of Charleston and Mobile; the evident disheartening of the rebels, and the brightening prospect of success to the armies of the nation, together with the general recognition by the people of all these successes as the result of the Divine blessing, ought to unite the hearts of all philanthropists and Christians together in devout thanksgiving to Almighty God.

Injustice from Great Britain.

Since these things are so the friends of good government and of peace must regret that the representatives of American rebels, who have no national organization recognized at home or abroad, and no accredited ambassadors, have received so much attention, and been allowed to exert so much influence among the people of Great

Britain and France. They must regret that by a perversion of commercial freedom our enemies have been supplied with munitions of war, and that even armed ships have been launched from the docks and sailed from the port of England; and manned by British seamen, without visiting the ports of any other nation, but under the unrecognized flag which the rebels have chosen, have preyed upon our commerce, plundering our property, and destroying our ships. If these things loudly call for complaint, be it ours, as disciples of the Prince of Peace, now and ever to discourage warfare, and to exert all our powers to bring about such a common apprehension of the truth, and such a general respect for authority, and such an ardent desire for the coming kingdom of heaven on earth, as shall leap over national lines, bind our hearts in union, and preserve our respective countries from unholy strife.

Again we thank you for your fraternal sympathy, and especially for the expression of your abhorrence of slavery; and, praying that your country may never be called upon to suffer the ravages of civil war, but that whatever changes may be needed in your or our national institutions, may be brought about gradually and harmoniously, under the benign influences of the Gospel, and that the choicest blessings of heaven may rest upon you and the churches and people that you represent, we have the honour to be
Your friends and co-labourers in the cause of Christ.

EDWARD N. KIRK, EDWARD S. RAND, JOSEPH W. PARKER, ERASTUS O. HAVEN, ISRAEL P. WARREN, JOSEPH S. ROPES, JACOB SLEEPER, THOMAS N. HASKELL, CHARLES STODDARD, *Committee.*

I could not leave the locality till I had climbed Bunker Hill, and surveyed from it the shores of Charleston; both historically associated with the origin and progress of the revolutionary war. Boston is a city of bridges and causeways, rivers, canals, bays, and dams, and shows the enterprise of its citizens in its facilities for intercourse. One bridge is 1503, a second 1550, a third 1820, two others each exceeds 2750 feet, besides minor bridges of 503 and 1390 feet; two causeways measure, one 3432 feet, and the other a mile and a half in length. Other bridges connect roads which unite the city, called in geographical truth "a mountain city in the sea," with the main land as closely as if it were an integral part of the whole. Cars pass from Tremont Street to Bunker Street for five cents, and though the monument rises on the top of the hill, and ascends nearly three hundred steps to its flag staff, to one who wishes to survey the locality and ponder its historical associations, the journey will not be an obstacle. A magnificent view of land, water, and goodly structures is obtained. Below the base of the monument, on the hill side, in walks and banks, the form of the original temporary fortress is retained, and the position occupied by the citizen soldiers, here defending the liberties they had asserted, is traced. There is a monumental stone which marks where Warren fell. From this lofty point the waters of Charleston harbour, where the Bostonians cast the tea chests into the flood rather than pay an offensive tax imposed by the Government of George the Third is seen; and the sails and flags of vessels now floating on the same waters, prove how liberty lives when asserted against the usurpations of despotism or misgovernment. A blundering parallel has been drawn between the men of the American revolution and the rebels of Secession. They are as unlike as contraries. The men in 1774 had neither representative nor voice in the taxation imposed; the men associated as a Confederacy at Richmond were their own representatives and the rulers of others as fit to rule themselves; when they seceded to enforce taxation with the whip, and exaction of labour without reward from millions of their fellow-men; and they are still fighting for liberty to oppress.

I started from Boston by rail for Saratoga, Wednesday the 19th of August. Greatly to my comfort, by the way, the Rev. Dr. Blagden travelled by the same train, and kept me company till we arrived at our hotel. The country was known to him, while the route was new to me. The road we travelled led us through a great part of Massachusetts, over a section of New Hampshire, through Vermont, by the borders of Lake Champlain, not half a mile wide here, and into the State of New York; crossing the Connecticut river, the Otter Creek, and other meandering streamlets, we reached the magnificent Hudson flowing down in beauty and grandeur. I was indebted to the unceasing courtesy of my fellow-traveller for local information, as we passed Groton, Fitchburg, Bellows Falls, Rutland, and Whitehall. Fitchburg is fifty miles from Boston, and gives name to the railway route we preferred, as this would take us toward New Hampshire, a state which contains some of the grandest hill, valley, and lake scenery of New England. The white mountains lay to our rear, and we looked towards the green mountains of the sister state. The valley and river of Winooski wend toward Montpelier, till the Lake Champlain receives the tributary stream. The Otter Creek passes by Rutland, and is picturesque in its whole course, till about seven miles from Lake Chaplain, the brook, 500 feet wide, is divided by an island, on either side of which there is a fall of 30 or 40 feet; this and other cascades give attraction to the scenery. There are peaks and perpendicular ledges, which diversify the aspect of the country, Killington, Mount Ira, Mount Pico, and Castleton ridge intervene between Rutland and Champlain. The country is hilly in all the way through the State of Vermont; so that her inhabitants are designated the *Green Mountain Boys*. At Whitehall we were detained till the passengers, *via* Champlain, from Canada reached the central station. The accession was in numbers sufficient to prove that the intercourse is frequent and numerous. We waited for them more than an hour. Ticonderago Fort was near, though I did not turn aside to recall the historical

events, where in 1775 Colonel Allen surprised the unsus-
pecting garrison; having at the head of a Vermont
regiment penetrated within the walls, and at the bedside of
the commandant, whom he awoke, demanded the surrender
of the fort. "In whose name and to whom?" exclaimed
the startled sleeper; "in the name of the great Jehovah
and the continental Congress," replied the successful
aggressor. The valley regions through which we passed
have their memories peopled by French, Indian, and revolutionary scenes and incidents. Here are the battle
grounds of Bemis Heights, Stillwater, and Saratoga, leading to the defeat of Burgoyne and his army. The Mohawk
river and the "Last of the Mohicans," and the Cohoes
Falls and the Ballston Springs divide the traveller's
thoughts as he draws towards the metropolitan springs of
all America.

At Saratoga are four immense hotels, the United States,
the Union Hall, Congress Hall, and the Clarendon, each, to
look at, large enough to garrison a brigade. Yet are there
many other smaller establishments, and almost every private house used as auxiliaries, and accommodating the
surplus visitors with beds, under standing arrangements
with the proprietors of the principal hotels. The whole is
a maelstrom of pleasure.

The refreshment which all must find is *unrest*, the
repose of excitement, the reaction of universal commotion
and variety. Thousands of men and women at home in a
caravanserai and seeking the reinvigoration of their system
by tumblers of mineral waters, and such a whirl of intercourse, are a phenomenon. The Congress Spring is said to
contain chloride of sodium, carbonate of soda, carbonate of
lime, carbonate of magnesia, carbonate of iron, sulphate of
soda, iodine of sodium, bromide of potassium, silica, and
alumina mingled with carbonic acid and atmospheric air.
Besides this conglomerate, which is even bottled and sent

all over the world, are other springs called the Empire, the
Columbian, the High Rock, the Iodine, the Pavilion, and
Putnams. The sum of the whole matter is described by
"Appleton's Guide" in few words—"The Alpha and the
Omega of the daily Saratoga programme is to drink and
to dance; the one in the earliest possible morning, and the
other at the latest conceivable night." This pithy libel
may be a great truth with some; but it is a calumny upon
many others, as I can testify; and as I remember the Rev.
T. L. Cuyler very graphically represented in the columns
of the "Independent," I will borrow his sparkling eulogy
written under the effervescing influence of "High Rock."

  " Saratoga is to us a pool of Bethesda. When a year
of labour, pulpit and pastoral, has worn the machinery until
study becomes a weariness to the flesh, until the lazy liver
and the clogged digestion make the mind's chariot-wheels
drive heavily, then we always hasten to join the 'crowd of
impotent folk' who here wait beside those waters that need
no angel to trouble them. An eminent lawyer has told us
that after a twelve-month of exhausting toil, it only requires
forty-eight hours of Saratoga to make a new man of him.
  " To be sure, there is a deal of frivolity and folly here;
but it is a sober place, too, to the sober-minded. And here
in this quiet, sensible, well-ordered Columbian hotel—where
no frolics of fashion are enacted, and no mint-juleps are
compounded—where God is honoured every day by a large
family gathering for worship—we have got as much bodily
refitting in three days as Brother Beecher did after ten days
of purgatorial purgations on an ocean steamer.
  " Saratoga becomes more beautiful every year. This
year a new spring has been added to its attractions. Congress Spring for a long time had a monopoly of the cathartic waters. This is the oldest and most celebrated of all
the health-fountains in this valley.
  " None but a foolish or verdant man will touch one of
the tonic springs (like the ' Columbian') before breakfast,
or one of the cathartic springs after breakfast. The cool
morning walk is half the battle. To us an hour in the
Congress Park, between six and seven o'clock, is a luxury

beyond words. At that hour the fountain is mainly in possession of the sensible folk; for the herd of pleasure seekers who have over danced themselves the night before, have not yet quitted their pillows. After a brimming tumbler handed up by the dipping boy, then for a brisk walk through the park. At this early dewy hour the grass is sown with diamonds. A swath of new-mown hay fills the air with fragrance. A colony of squirrels, ignorant of guns and arrows, frolic before you in the paths; and my little girl counted forty robins in one circuit of the grounds. The grass has the *black green* of the English parks; at the upper end of the ravine the shadows of the departing night seem still to be lingering under the deep screen of pines and hemlocks. An hour of intermingled drinking in of scenery and Congress water, fits one for a hearty breakfast and a day of rational enjoyment. During the fashionable season a band is stationed near the spring, and then we drink to music, and a third sense finds sweet satisfaction.

"Delightful have been the hours passed among the great, the good, and the beautiful in these cool grounds, for fifteen summers past. Nothing takes the *tire* out of mind and body like it; no expenditure 'pays better' than the dozen or two of dollars spent in a week of sojourn in this pine air, and among the sparkling waters that 'spring from these valleys, and run among the hills.' As yet but few clergymen have sought recreation here this season."

I drank two or three tumblers of these wonderful vitalizing waters; but I suppose I was one of Mr. Cuyler's verdant visitors, as I had to pay somewhat sensibly in the consequences. But I went not there either to meet Miss Flora McFlimsey, or the mineral virtues of Saratoga. I was a month later than the date of the letter of Mr. C., and expected to meet a goodly company of clergymen from all parts. I was not disappointed. The Presbyterian minister to whom I had been advised to write, was from home, and a stranger occupied his pulpit. He had no power to interfere. My friend Dr. B., however, was indefatigable in helping me to personal intercourse with gentlemen who knew the place, and could exercise some influence. He

Q

had indeed no desire to be classed among the Abolitionists ; for of them he had a peculiar dread ; yet as a generous and courteous friend to a British stranger he exerted himself in all ways to minister to my personal comfort. There was a morning prayer-meeting conducted by a union of ministers, and to the president of the morning I was introduced, who kindly asked me to take part in the proceedings, and thus made me known to those present.

Arrangements were made to combine my mission with the service of the following morning. Notice was given from the pulpit and in the evening papers of Saratoga. The church was well filled, and the audience was representative of other towns and the higher classes. Generals, judges, governors, and senators mingled with reverend doctors and eminent lawyers, merchants, and medical practitioners, with their wives and daughters, and other ladies whose husbands were in the field of battle. Mrs. General Banks, both before and after my lecture, evinced her interest in my mission, as did other ladies in her circle. At the close of my address General Williams of Norwich was called to the chair, and a business meeting was constituted. Motions and lively discussion followed, and the following report appeared in the " New York Evangelist :"

" ENGLAND AND REV. DR. MASSIE.

" Several weeks since, the Rev. Dr. Massie, the messenger of the English Dissenting churches to this country, addressed a large audience at Saratoga, in the Baptist church, General Williams, of Norwich, Connecticut, presiding. After alluding to the early historic relations between England and her American colonies—to the character of the Puritans—the Old World and the New—to the Anglican Church and the Nonconformists—the large and influential bodies of dissenting Christians of various names in England, he came directly to the more important relations between England and the United States since the war began. He spoke of the earnest and friendly feelings which exist among immense numbers of intelligent and impartial men in England towards the Northern states of America. He traced the origin and rise of the Union and Emancipation Society of England, and its kindred societies, both of France and England, and the efforts and the influence which they had exerted to enlighten public opinion in that country, all resulting in the united request to send a special messenger to the United States with a memorial and address to the ministers, and pastors, and churches in the United States. He condemned in emphatic language all the sympathizers with secession, both in England and the United States.

"He was listened to with fixed attention for an hour and a half. He was frequently cheered, and his address, with all the interesting facts and statements, seemed to commend themselves to the approbation of all present.

"At the close of Dr. Massie's address, the Rev. Dr. Welsh, of Albany, rose, and after expressing his sympathy with much that had been said, made the pertinent inquiry why England did not put a stop to the fitting out of iron-clads to prey upon American commerce? A very spirited debate arose, and was continued for some time by a number of gentlemen. Dr. Massie explained that he was not there to defend the English Government, but to deliver his message of peace from the Churches of England. The discussion for the day terminated by the appointment of a committee, of which the Rev. Dr. Budington, of Brooklyn, was chairman, who, on the following day, offered the following preamble and resolutions:

"The Christian ministers and laymen met at Saratoga Springs from various sections of the country, and belonging to different portions of the Church, who have listened to the address of the Rev. Dr. Massie in presenting the letter of the French Protestant clergymen to their brethren in Great Britain regarding the civil war in this land, as also the letter of the ministers of the Gospel in Great Britain to the ministers of all evangelical denominations in the United States, unite in the following resolutions in response to these addresses:

"*Resolved*, That we acknowledge with pleasure the Christian and fraternal sentiments with which French and British ministers of the Gospel have expressed their sympathy with us in this time of our national trial and agony, and we receive it, with gratitude to God, as an expression of that unity of spirit which binds together in one the children of God in all lands.

"*Resolved*, That the moral support of European Christians is encouraging and grateful to us, because while striving for the maintenance of our Government and the integrity of our territory, we feel that we are contending for just government against revolutionary violence, and for republican institutions against an usurping oligarchy, and are therefore entitled to the sympathy of the loyal under all forms of government, especially to the co-operation of all the lovers of freedom throughout the world.

"*Resolved*, That while we are contending for the constitution transmitted to us by our fathers, and the insurgents to establish an empire whose corner-stone shall be human bondage, we acknowledge that slavery is the source of our misery, and cherish the hope that the suppression of the rebellion will issue in the abolition of this great evil.

"*Resolved*, That in view of the recent causes of irritation that have sprung up between Great Britain and the United States, in regard to which we feel that we have good reason to complain—we take especial pleasure in the arrival on our shores of this ambassage of peace and good-will, in the confident hope that by the interchange of Christian sentiments and the efforts of the Christian people of Great Britain to influence public opinion and the policy of their Government, alienations will not be suffered to grow into hostilities; but through forbearance and just counsels, England and America may, in the future as in the past, be united, not more for their mutual advantage, than for the welfare of all mankind.

"(Signed)   WM. WILLIAMS, Moderator.
    "WM. IVES BUDINGTON,
            Chairman of Committee."

Till the "Evangelist," containing this statement, was put into my hands, I knew not what had been the measure of acceptance or success, which attended my mission; but Dr. Welsh was the only senior minister whom I heard speak, in all America, under the influence of a feeling of antagonism or irritation. Yet he avowed himself a descend-

ant of the *Roundheads,* and affirmed that English blood
flowed in his veins, and tingled to his finger ends; and if
British policy could continue to tolerate the "*Alabamas,*"
and suffer "iron rams" to be sent forth to prey upon the
peaceful commerce of the American nation, he should be
willing to listen to the clangour of arms and try the hazard
of war. I saw in private many eminent citizens and prominent men in religious associations: Dr. Parker, late of
China; Dr. Hodge, of Princeton; Dr. Bidwell; Dr. Nadal;
Dr. Thompson, of Cincinnati, mingled in the circle, and in
discussions on questions involved in my message. It had
been regretted by many interested in my success, that in
some principal cities where public meetings were held,
some of the leading and most prominent clergymen were
absent on their summer vacations; my visit to Saratoga
served to compensate for this drawback, as there was a
large number of these men enjoying recreation and society
at the springs, while the proceedings reported in the "Evangelist" became known to hundreds who were in other
places.

CHAPTER VI.

THE western cities of America were now before me, where
correspondence and personal negotiations had opened the
path for my mission. To reach the direct route for the
rail, I must retrace my steps, *via* Ballston to Schenectady.
Ballston had its day for spas, and scenes, and fashion, but
Saratoga eclipsed it. The mineral waters were here discovered in 1769, and seated upon the stream bearing the
Indian name Kayaderosseros, and contiguous to lakes
abounding with attractions for the sportsman, Ballston
drew its annual concourse in early times. Schenectady lies
on the bank of the Mohawk, and where the Union College
now stands were, in bygone days, the Council Grounds of
the Mohawks. A party of French Canadians and Indians,
in 1690, fell upon the place like a midnight storm, killed
and made captive the people, and reduced the town to
ashes. But now Schenectady contains more than ten
thousand people, sustained by industry in machine shops
and other branches of manufacture, chiefly connected with
mechanical arts. Scotchmen gather here and thrive.
Aside from this town, but within a morning's walk, are
heights and cliffs with classic names: Mount Ida and
Mount Olympus find here a transatlantic home; while
Modern Troy lies along the river Hudson for three miles, in
depth from east to west more than a mile, and peopled
with men who wield powers greater than Grecian heroes

possessed, and perform feats far more useful to mankind than were achieved by Hector or Achilles. There is a population in it exceeding 40,000, who are busy with manufacturing industry, and who have adorned their city with magnificent churches, public buildings, and family mansions, as well as comfortable cottages for a prosperous community. Troy is also an *entrepôt* for railway travel in every direction. I had not literary leisure to search for a modern Parnassus. Mine was now an iron way, with its gradients. Still my progress conducted me to places of ancient name. My first resting-station was Utica, thence to Rome, but I could not explore its seven hills, and hastened forward to Syracuse. If there be no Cato to give laws to this Utica there are 22,000 inhabitants subject to the laws of the Republic. This Rome is more supplied with railways than it would have been had the Vatican been the legislature, and the Pontiff been supreme. You may travel thence by the iron road to Potsdam and Montreal, to Niagara or the Mississippi. Syracuse opens its ports to the puffing traveller with prompt hospitality. Twenty-six thousand people here profit from the manufacture of salt for the United States, and while they have salt in themselves, they are not left without Attic salt. This town is oft frequented by political and state conventions, when the tactics of party are matured. My route stretched onward, I had a choice of ways, through Canton, Jordan, Port Byron, Savannah, Clyde, Lyons, Palmyra, and Macedon, or by another course by Camillus, Marcellus, Auburn, Seneca Falls, Waterloo, Geneva, Vienna, Canandaigua, Victor, and Pittsford; all these towns lie between Syracuse and Rochester; but I did not stop to inquire by the way into the condition of any one, though I should have been glad to have examined Auburn state prison, of whose discipline and criminal statistics I have elsewhere read. I had not a day to spare, and hasted into Rochester.

Absence from home had prevented the efficient services
and mature arrangements of senior brethren. But the Rev.
Mr. Boardman, a son, by a former husband of the second
Mrs. Judson, his own father, also a missionary in the East,
showed me every possible attention, and arranged for a
public meeting in his own church. I never saw a place of
worship more entirely and systematically filled, and in the
most intensely heated atmosphere in which a man could
breathe, the audience gave a patient and earnest attention.
The New York response was accepted as the sentiment of
the ministers present. Many prominent citizens came forward to signify their concurrence, but the indisposition and
absence of leading pastors prevented a more organized
movement, beyond the shutting up of several churches that
the congregations might come to my address. I indulged
myself as a hearer in the morning services, and in the street
in which I worshipped there were five or six churches,
elegant and magnificent structures, two or three of them
with school-rooms as wings, giving the building a capacious
appearance. I had heard a scriptural and practically evangelical discourse from a Professor Hotchkins (I think that
was the name), and as the congregation under him was a
little sooner dismissed than some others, I passed in front
of other churches, and could look into two or three. The
congregations were large, and of the better class. Many
country vehicles, with their horses haltered to wayside
posts, stood waiting for their owners. Here were Presbyterian, Baptist, Episcopalian, Methodist Episcopalian, German, and Roman Catholic congregations; all the fruits of
voluntary zeal, and the promoters of its principles. There
were many other similarly worshipping assemblies in the
city. The Genesee and its falls give picturesque beauty
and commercial facilities to the place. The Mount Hope
Cemetery is in the midst of beauty. The streets pass out
to the suburbs in rows of self-contained villas, orna-

mented with trees and shrubbery, giving the appearance of solidity and comfort to the community. The sewage in some parts was in process of completion, by which I saw the depth and substantial style of their provision for health and cleanliness. Sixty years ago the whole county of Genesee was bought as an outlying forest region, for which some £800 were paid in purchase of the fee simple, by a calculating land speculator. The city alone contains more than fifty thousand inhabitants now, and the county participates in their prosperity. I think, however, this was the first city in America in which I saw pigs roaming at large, and enjoying the liberty of scavenging the garbage in the lower parts.

Though from Rochester to the Niagara Falls the distance was seventy-six miles, I shall not be charged with extravagant indulgence in turning aside to survey this cataract, and the wonders of nature which surrounded it. My road lay by Adam's Basin, Albion, Gosport, Pekin, and the Suspension Bridge. From the last I first caught a glimpse of the rushing torrent. I went to the International Hotel. It has since been consumed by fire. The situation was good, and the comforts many, and at moderate prices. I had occasion to consult a medical adviser here, and was wisely and economically counselled. I preferred pedestrian exploration, and passed along by the banks of the rushing waters above, and stood at the base of the rocks to admire the falling torrents from their incumbent precipitous ledge. There is a path down by steps, which one may walk. Carriages also, moved by a rope, await an order for less than sixpence up and down. I walked down, crossed to the Canadian side by boat just on the verge of the boiling pool, climbed the steep ascent toward the "Clifton," on British soil, and thence proceeded to the Fall on that side. I think the finest point of view is on the British side, facing the rapids in the channel from the Erie, down which the volumes of the overwhelming current rush with a ceaseless impetuosity, like ten thousand rolling buffaloes, tumbling one over another in mad confusion till all reach the steep place, 165 feet deep, where the final " battle charge of tempestuous waves" seems made into the troubled sky. I mean not to compete in picturesque descriptions with some writers as mad as Sam Patch was when he made a leap over the fall on the west side of Goat Island. I believe this monument of power needs to be seen to be appreciated, and I think it is better to see it first before any descriptions of it are perused. The great noise or sound of it is not its grandeur. One sentence of the sublime and *ridiculous* will show what man can do, " The torture of the rapids, the clinging curves with which they embrace the small rocky islands that live amid the surge, the sudden calmness at the brow of the cataract, and the infernal writhe and whiteness with which they reappear, powerless from the depths of the abyss, all seem to the excited imagination of the gazer like the natural effects of impending ruin, desperate resolution and fearful agony on the minds and frames of mortals" !! The points of interest selected for notice are " the Goat Island," the Rapids, Chapin's Island, the Toll-gate, the Cave of the Winds, Luna Island, Sam Patch's Leap, Biddle's Stairs, Prospect Tower, The Horse-Shoe Falls, Gull Island, Grand Island, the Whirlpool, the Devil's Hole, Chasm Tower, the Maid of the Mist, the Great Suspension Bridge, Bendor's Cave, Table Rock, and Termination Rock. Two historical incidents will illustrate better than a volume of description. About the year 1838, the American steamboat Caroline was set on fire, and sent over the Falls by the order of Colonel McNabb. Some fragments of the wreck remained on Goat Island till the following spring. Over the ledges of the Horse Shoe Falls it is computed that fifteen hundred millions of cubic feet of water pass every hour. A lake ship, the " Detroit," was condemned, and in 1829 she was drifted over this fall, but though she drew eighteen feet of water, she did not touch the *rocks* in passing over the brink of the precipice; showing, at least, some twenty feet of a fluent body of water above the ledge. The waters for which the Niagara is the outlet cover an area of 150,000 square miles—a fountain so inexhaustible as to manifest no perceptible loss though ninety millions of tons every hour be poured out, as they have been through succeeding centuries, over these stupendous precipices.

The distance from the Falls to Buffalo along the shores of the lake is twenty-two miles, and is gone over in an hour. A full view of the lake and its passage down to Niagara is here obtained, and deserves a patient survey. I was most hospitably received by Dr. Clark and the other clergymen of this city. As many as could be brought together in a brief space gathered in Dr. Clark's house to hear my representations, and confer on the most eligible mode of replying to my message. At the termination of the interview it was concluded most advisable that the clergymen of Buffalo should adhere to the New York address as they were in the State. But it was kindly pressed on my consideration if I could give a Sunday service to the people. Dr. Clark and his co-presbyters undertook to bring the English address before a presbyterial meeting soon to be held in the district. I promised to return from the west by Buffalo to preach and deliver my message, and in the mean time every opportunity was afforded for me looking round the town and its quays.

From a summary survey of the history of this town, as illustrating the progress of events, I extract a few passages from a "Half-Century Discourse," by Rev. Walter Clark, D.D. There is nothing like it in Europe. Fifty years ago there were 500 people in Buffalo. To-day there are 100,000. The assessor's roll, sixty years ago, put down the taxable property of the village at 2229 dollars; the assessed value of the property in 1862 was 42,000,000 of dollars. Fifty years ago the place contained five day schools, with less than 100 scholars; in 1862 there were thirty-three public schools, conducted by nearly 200 teachers, 13,000 children attending, at an annual cost of about 100,000 dollars. There was then one church, a membership of twenty-nine persons, and a congregation of less than 100; there are now forty-two Protestant, and thirteen Roman Catholic churches in the city. In the former time, one Sabbath school, managed by one teacher, had ten pupils; but now, in the Presbyterian body alone, are thirteen schools, 300 teachers, and 2000 scholars; but they are only a sixth part of the whole. The value of vessels on the lake might be 10,000 dollars fifty years ago; now there are 1400 vessels, with a tonnage of 6,000,000, employing 145,000 seamen, and valued at 13,500,000 dollars. In addition there are 1000 boats on the canal, having a tonnage of 500,000, and an estimated value of 3,500,000 dollars. The value of exports nothing in the first period: the value now, 57,834,888 dollars. It is asserted that the centre spring of all this fulness and growth is the religion of Christ, kept alive by the labours and prayers of the faithful. Gratitude dictates a further explanation, in reference to churches in New England. More than half of those who have sustained and carried forward the community, came from beyond the Hudson. The churches in Vermont, Rhode Island, Connecticut, and Massachusetts have been Christ's schools, where young men are trained for usefulness and power in distant and destitute fields. But while the community in Buffalo has been blessed in receiving, it has been blessed in giving. The first Presbyterian church of the city, in fifty years, has sent out as many as six hundred men and women to assist in founding or building up young churches and cities in the West.

All this is a truthful testimony of a venerated witness. In the historical comparison, one feature remains for notice. On the 30th December, 1813, in a terrible winter night, mothers, daughters, and men, some in waggons, some on foot, fled over the frozen ground into the sheltering woods, for a retreat from the war-whoop of invading *Christians*, who set fire to the wooden dwellings, and left a desolation as their memorial. These invaders were under British authority, on whose ravages the frightened inhabitants looked down from the nearest hill tops. Fifty years afterward, it was my special privilege to carry a message of fraternal concord and Christian peace, and to be welcomed by thousands, who gratefully flocked to the largest sanctuary in the United States, that they might receive and reciprocate the sympathies of kindred and fellow heirs of the most enduring inheritance. The apparatus which economizes and utilizes power in the most surprising manner, I saw first at Buffalo, the *Elevator*, employed for lading and unlading vessels—it works wonders. But not more wonderful are its facilities than has been the instrumentality by which the progress of this city has been effected.

The introduction of railway travel has diminished the demand for the magnificent and beautiful paddle-wheel steamers on the lakes; but still there are capacious screw steamers employed in the transport of merchandise, grain and minerals from above, and manufactures from the Eastern states. I wished to make the experiment of lake travelling, and after I had been conveyed along the majestic roads called streets, and into the suburbs, which expand Buffalo, in the certain expectation that as it has doubled in ten years, it will treble in ten years more : my kind friends went on board with me. Dr. Heacock had officiated at the marriage of the captain, and as I was Dr. Heacock's friend, I had a reward for his sake in the best room at the captain's disposal, and was entertained as his guest. He was a generous-hearted Irishman, though commanding a magnificent steamer on the American lakes. We proceeded up Lake Erie, touching in the afternoon at Cleveland, having previously sailed within sight of the shores of Ohio from Ashtabula, when we saw the tokens of manufacturing enterprise in towering chimneys and whirling locomotives. The river Cayahaga empties itself into the lake at Cleveland, and forms a convenient harbour. Our track lay onward to Detroit, and the farther voyage of the vessel was destined to Chicago. The time, however, required for the completion of the trip was more than I could expend, I therefore landed at Detroit, to proceed by rail. Detroit is in the state Michigan, though at the extremity of lakes Erie and St. Clair, on the banks of a river whose name it bears. It is only the breadth of half a mile across, an arm of the lake St. Clair, from Windsor in Canada. Water communication for large steamers extends by Lake Huron, and by the Straits of Mackinaw, into Lake Michigan. The voyage was such as I could gratefully enjoy, though for the most part out of sight of land, and as subject to storms and sometimes dangers as in the vast ocean. Hereby I had some idea of the extensive territory of the United States, along the inner borders of which there was so prolonged a region of water. I also observed phases of society in my fellow passengers which were novel and characteristic. Every class of American people are habituated to travel, delicate and young females and families, for hundreds of miles by themselves.

I landed at Detroit so early in the morning as to be unable to procure conveyances, and disinclined to intrude upon private families. I therefore availed myself of the civility of a watchman on one of the wharfs, to remain under shelter for an hour or two. Thus I learned more of the constitution of society than I could have done perhaps

in a higher circle of intercourse. The wealthy owner of
the warehouse I found to be a countryman, and one who
sympathized in sentiments which I had long cherished.
The gentlemen to whom I had letters of introduction were
also personally described, and my arrangements for the day
were facilitated by my early vigils on the water side.

Detroit has more than doubled its population between
1850 and 1860. At the latter date 45,619 was the census
return, and at my visit the increase was making rapid progress. It was founded by the French in 1670, and derives
its name from the language of that people in relation to
the strait of waters by which it stands. It is not now,
though it was once the capital of the state, and has standing in the midst of it the Old State House, with its dome
and tall steeple overlooking the town and its environs·
There is an open, spacious area, called the Grand Circus,
from which the avenues of that part of the town diverge
toward the river. The Campus Martius, a large public
square, indicates the military associations of its founders.
Jefferson and Woodward Avenues, and Congress Street,
the cemetery and the military barracks, in which horses
and horsemen are drilled for the United States army, the
Custom House and marine hospital show the kind of city
in which old General Cass delights to dwell. There is a
bank erected in a Grecian style of architecture : and a City
Hall in brick, with a façade a hundred feet in length,
proves that the French love for display has not departed.
Business activity, however, by land and water, and manufactories employing much industry, show that the rowdyism
of a large mass of Irishmen, ever ready for a brawl, cannot
repress the enterprise of the intelligent people of all nations.
Mr. D. Stewart opened his hospitable residence for my sojourn, and placed himself and influence at my disposal, and
for my introduction to gentlemen who could promote my
mission. Dr. Duffield, the Presbyterian, and Dr. Kitchell,

the Congregationalist, took the initiative in arranging for a
public meeting. The first gentleman has a choice cabinet
of some fine pictures, originals by old masters, and seems
to enjoy the *otium cum*—he gave his church for the meeting.
Dr. Kitchell and his family resided in the Russell House ;
and he was most assiduous in guiding me through the
localities to which I must go, and in preparation for the
meeting. The church bell sounding the invitation, and a
goodly company complied, so that the service was held in
the evening of the next day ; I felt I had done my work.
The response speaks for the men who signed and adopted
it with singular force and beauty :—

"TO THE REV. JAMES W. MASSIE, D.D.,

" Senior Member of the Anti-slavery Conference of Great
Britain, and Representative of the Protestant Clergy
of France.

DETROIT, *September 9th*, 1863.

" REV. AND DEAR BROTHER,—It is no more appropriate
than accordant with the emotions awakened by your Christian and eloquent address, delivered in the First Presbyterian church of this city, on Friday evening, the 28th ult.,
to offer this brief response to the letter of good will and
sympathy from the numerous friends of the United States
in England and France, in whose name you spoke, and
which, in concluding your remarks, you read to the
assembly.

" On behalf of my fellow citizens, and Christian and
ministerial brethren, there convened, and by the direction
of the committee then appointed, allow me to repeat the
salutations and welcome which it was my happiness, on
that occasion, to express to you ; and also our prayer for
your safe and prosperous return to your native land, where,
I doubt not, a glad reception and grateful appreciation of
your services—discharged so wisely and with such happy
results, in the fulfilment of your commission—await you.
The chords of Christian affection, under your skilful hand,
have vibrated in blissful unison. Stronger and more enduring are they, which unite Christian hearts, than those of

any social, civil, political, or mere earthly relation whatever. The love of the brotherhood in Christ sends its thrilling pulsations from his own living heart through all the members of his mystical body, inculcating the very 'life that is hid with (Him) in God.'

"Your mission, beloved brother, has not been in vain. A messenger of peace, with words of peace and love upon your lips, you have contributed, by exciting and invigorating fraternal affection, to preserve and promote reciprocal esteem and confidence among the people of two great nations, the only conservators of constitutional liberty in the world. The good Lord crown your efforts with great success!

"The general facts stated by you were not unknown to us. We have felt their power in preventing or abating irritation. But your visit and recital of them have excited a special soothing influence, in a season when there is danger of inflammatory excitement. We are happy to be assured that whatever may be the spirit of the governing authorities and aristocratic classes, in both the civil and ecclesiastical establishments of Great Britain, the mass of the people, who work, whether with head or hands, for a livelihood, are *not* in sympathy with the rebellion in the United States, which aims to establish here also a like privileged class, to hold the coloured race in a degraded and servile condition, to keep the free whites of the Southern states, that own not either slaves or real estate, in ignorance and dependence, to establish a monarchy upon the ruins of Republicanism, and to overthrow the freest government on earth. The Lord be praised, that the piety and just appreciation of liberty in your country prevent any envious wishes among the working masses for the destruction of our Federal Union, an asylum for the poor and oppressed of other lands. The false and malignant abusiveness of the London "Times" we regard as far from being a true exponent of the English mind and heart, as it is from being the chronicler of reliable history, or the representative of that country which should characterize the civil and social reciprocities of high-minded, honourable, and Christian nations.

"In reply to the letter of your constituents, expressing their views of slavery as it has existed in the United States,

R

we have only to say, that the evils of this pernicious system, morally, socially, and politically, transmitted from former generations, have been long regarded by the great body of Christian people in the Northern and Free states as a fretting sore, a cancer in the body politic, and a just ground of reproach; to remedy which, however, it was impracticable by mere human wisdom and benevolence, either immediately or ultimately, without the interposition and aid of a gracious Providence, earnestly and devoutly implored. That interposition has eventuated in a most unexpected way; and it is as marvellous in our eyes as it is severely righteous. Peremptory and pressing obligations have been suddenly and unmistakably devolved upon us by the providence of God, in the discharge of which a crisis in the history of American slavery has occurred, producing changes, which no force of moral suasion or governmental authorities of the Federal Union within their constitutional sphere could have secured. As Christian citizens our duty undeniably is to defend the Federal Government, whose constitution is the supreme civil and political law of the land, there being nothing in it requiring service or obedience from us contrary to the law of God and fidelity to Jesus Christ our only king. The reserved rights of citizens, in their several organized state governments, touching the respective internal, domestic, and social institutions and regulations, over which the constitution of the Federal Government and its officers had no delegated control—rendered emancipation impracticable, excepting by the several individual states having sole authority in these matters, to legislate within their own territorial boundaries. Thus the antagonisms of free and slave labour were counterpoised, and the friends of freedom and humanity were restricted to the use of moral power only, which always is more or less offensive to the perpetrators of evil. Moral power, to a great extent, by State legislation and schismatic divisions of churches North and South in different religious denominations had been rendered unavailable, and utterly repellent to the prejudices of society, of education, and even of religion in the slave states.

"It has pleased a righteous God to smite with blindness and madness the slaveholding population generally of the Southern states. Under the false pretext of a right of secession by individual states from the Federal Union, claiming not to be subordinate authorities under a national government but independent sovereignties—parties merely in a league or compact terminable at will—treason organized insurgent forces. Through the imbecility and fatuity of a former administration, to say the least, of which prominent instigators and leaders of treason were high co-ordinate functionaries, treachery succeeded to disarrange the finances, to impair the public credit, to rob the national treasury, to dismantle forts and armouries, and to disperse ' the regular army' and the navy so as to leave the capital defenceless, when rebellion should be prepared to unfurl its standard. The capture of Fort Sumter at Charleston proclaimed and initiated a war of treason and rebellion against the Federal Government.

" Its avowed aim was for the spread and perpetuation of slavery, and by the growth and commerce of cotton, to ally to its surreptitiously organized confederacy the manufacturing countries of Europe, especially Great Britain and France, whose recognition of its independence and intervention on its behalf were confidently anticipated.

" The patriotic, Christian, and heroic spirit of the North rallied promptly and mightily for the defence of its dishonoured flag and the support of the Federal Government. Thus far, by the blessings of Providence, success has attended the march of our armies, and the blockade of the Southern coasts by our fleets. We have sought to suppress a rebellion, which may well be characterized as one of the mightiest and most widely extended that ever attempted the overthrow of a free and benignant government. Nor have we sought in vain. If not routed entirely at the end of two years and a half it has been broken in twain, and flies before our invading armies, which have carried our victorious flag to wave in every state that attempted revolt.

In the prosecution of this war of defence against rebellion, the property in slaves according to the recognized and established rights and rules of war, has been extensively subjected to confiscation. Three million and upwards have been emancipated by the proclamation of the President; which, under the sanction of the high self-preserving power lodged by the Constitution in the hands of the chief magistrate, as the commander-in-chief in times and exigences of war, abides the irreversible law of the land. Thus the rebellion, while subjecting us as a people to much suffering, to enormous cost of treasure, and to great sacrifice of invaluable life, has been the occasion and the means which a righteous God, in his sovereign and adorable Providence, has employed to accomplish, more effectually and rapidly than the most hopeful and sanguine had ever imagined, the speedy, extensive, and prospectively entire extinction of that relic of a barbarous age, that foe to human happiness, that offence to God, and that dishonour to our glorious Redeemer, who came ' to proclaim liberty to the captive,' viz., the slavery now being extirpated from among us.

" Should that Divine providence continue propitious, and prevent the intervention of foreign governments in our affairs for the support of rebellion, we have no doubt of the ultimate and not far distant triumph of our arms, and of the re-establishment of the Federal Union and its government upon a basis more stable than at first. The rapid and extensive change of public sentiment of late in relation to the coloured race, the signal rebukes which have been administered to disloyal partizanship, the patriotism and heroism of our soldiery, the union in heart and effort in various ways among Christians of all denominations, for the temporal and spiritual comfort of our warring hosts, and the increasing and pervading spirit of prayer in our army and navy, and among the families, churches, and people of our country generally throughout the free states, together with the marked prosperity of our Northern and North-western states, to be seen in abundant crops and luxuriant fruits, in adequate revenue and undisturbed fiscal interests, in active and profitable commercial and industrial pursuits, and in the unexampled liberal contributions among all classes for sanatory and religious purposes in our ships, and camps, and hospitals, are features in the developments of providence, so clearly and strongly delineated, that we feel confident the favour of heaven will still attend and render triumphant the cause, as that of right and truth, of liberty and humanity, which unites, without distinction of party, the great masses of our population. What but the breath of the Almighty can have thus intensified the vital powers of this people? It is his Holy Spirit, we believe, that has stimulated the sense of Christian obligation among the people of this country, and made use of their zealous heroic discharge of the duty of defending their government, devoid of oppression, and of suppressing a rebellion without any reasonable pretext or shadow of excuse, the sure and obvious means of working out as its legitimate and inevitable result, deliverance from what once threatened, like some fatal virus, to destroy the health and life of the nation. It is the cause of justice, freedom, humanity, and of God; and, through the blessing of his providence we look with unwavering expectation to its final and glorious triumph.

"Let us have your continued and fervent prayers for this consummation.

"Rest assured that we appreciate them, and the assurances you have given us of sympathy from the heart of the mass of the people of Great Britain, and of their noble, generous, and Christian Queen.

"With sentiments of fraternal regard, we remain yours in the fellowship of the gospel,   GEO. DUFFIELD.

"As members of the committee we cordially adopt this reply of our chairman, Dr. Duffield. H. D. Kitchel, pastor of Congregational Church : Azariah Eldridge, pastor of the Fort Street Presbyterian Church ; J. M. Arnold, pastor of the First Methodist Episcopal Church ; J. Matthews, pastor of the Howard Street Baptist Church ; John P. Scott, pastor of the United Presbyterian Church ; James Inglis, pastor of the Baptist Tabernacle Church."

By the unremitting attentions of Mr. Stewart and his wife I was enabled to proceed to Chicago; though there had been reason to apprehend that I should be disabled by an affection in my ancle. I owe them many thanks for personal ministrations, as I also do to Mr. Stewart for helping me forward by free pass per rail to my next destination.

I had now before me 284 miles, over the whole length of Michigan, and to the principal city of Illinois. I started, after an early breakfast, and arrived at Chicago in about fourteen hours. The towns through which I passed were some of them of Greek or Indian names; some were Latin and some English, some French, and some a composition; but my readers will learn little from their insertion, further than that I passed through twenty-six places before I carried the *calumet* into Chicago. The country is a grain-producing region, and the inhabitants are thoroughly loyal to the Republic. Their regiments, in the field, have borne the name of the state into many conflicts. To illustrate the character of the men, I introduce an incident which afterward occurred. While sitting on the banks of the Ohio, and contemplating the events of the rebellion and its influence on the people around, a tall man in the garb of a sergeant, drew near, and readily answered to some casual observation I made. He bore the marks of having seen hard service; he said he was in the Michigan cavalry, and, at the time we were conversing, on the books of the hospital. He showed me his pass. I asked his age, and he answered in his sixty-third year. I inquired, was he a native of that state; he replied, his father was an Englishman, had brought him as a boy to New York State, where he had lived till he was a man, when he removed into Michigan. He had resided there several years, and never married. When the war broke out he volunteered. "Some people," he said, "might condemn me for doing so at sixty years of age; but I did so to help my country to put down slavery. I had seen it, when previously travelling through the slave states; but though I saw its horrors I was not allowed to speak against it. Now," he said, "I have marched through the same places, and I have not been prevented from denouncing it as the crime of man, and the curse of the land. I have had my sword in my hand. I may perhaps die from my present disease; but I shall not regret having done what I could." Our conversation turned to things of higher moment, and I found him no stranger to eternal realities, and the best preparation for them. Such was a sample of the Michigan cavalry.

In Michigan eight valuable ores of iron, five various forms of copper in vast quantity, silver and lead ores, bituminous and cannel coals, have been found, as well as sienite granite, marbles of great beauty, sand, and limestone and gypsum suited for ornament and architecture; all these valuable mineral treasures are in abundance and easily procurable. In 1861 an alteration in the law gave license to immigrant settlers to become the owners of eighty acres without price, and permission to purchase eighty acres more at a dollar and quarter per acre, and only the fourth of this sum to be paid down. The deed of the land is reserved only till the settler has bestowed some labour for the reclamation and improvement of the land: 40,147 acres were licensed to settlers under this law in 1861. What finer opportunity can be had for becoming an independent landowner?

I found on my arrival at the railway station in Chicago, Dr. Patten, the younger, with whom I had arranged for this visit, when we met in company with his father at New Haven. I had telegraphed from Detroit, and thus he was prepared to receive and take me to his house, in one of the remote streets or suburbs of the city. He had arranged for a service in the morning in his own church, and for a public meeting in the evening in Bryan Hall. His own church was a new building, and the fellowship not of long duration; but I was pleased to witness so respectable an assembly, and gratified in the communion which the truth and spirit of the Gospel assure. Here again I found the minister's study furnished and provided with a library under the same roof with his church; and, as far as I could observe, it is strictly a *sanctum*. In the evening, at first I apprehended the meeting would not equal others which had preceded; but, towards the time of commencement, a very large company had convened. Bryan Hall is an immense structure, and contains minor places of assembly; the hall in which we met would hold 2000 hearers. I pursued my usual course, and at the conclusion of the address the assembly under their chairman, agreed to an address in response.

"At a numerously-attended meeting to receive the Rev. Dr. Massie from England, held in Bryan Hall, Chicago, Illinois, on Sabbath evening, August 30th, 1861, Peter Page, Esq., was called to the chair. Prayer having been offered by the Rev. H. L. Hammond, the Rev. Dr. Massie addressed the audience and read a letter from an anti-slavery conference, pleading the cause of the slave. At the close of the address, the following resolutions were offered by the Rev. William W. Patton, D.D., and were unanimously adopted by the meeting, to wit:

"*Resolved.* 1. That so far as victory in the contest between the United States and the rebellious states is concerned, this nation neither asks nor needs the sympathy or aid of any other people, but, as events are rapidly demonstrating, is able to vindicate the justice of its cause and the strength of its government, by the success of its arms under the favour of Almighty God.

"*Resolved.* 2. That while thus confident of the preservation of our National Union, whatever may be the attitude of other nations towards us, we yet believe that our cause is the cause of personal liberty, stable government, free institutions, true civilization, and pure Christianity throughout the world, and therefore *deserves* the sympathy of good men in all lands.

"*Resolved.* 3. That we therefore deeply regret, for their sake more than for our own, the refusal of such sympathy by a part of the British nation, including many who had previously claimed to be the special foes of slavery and friends of the African race.

"*Resolved.* 4. That we on this account welcome the more cordially the letter of our British brethren, which tenders to us, on grounds of humanity and religion, the moral support of 4000 ministers of the Gospel of various ecclesiastical connections.

"*Resolved.* 5. That this meeting has listened with great pleasure to the able and eloquent address of the Rev. Dr. Massie of London, and to his expressions of personal sympathy with our country in its present struggle, and trust that his fraternal mission may link more closely the friends of liberty on both sides of the Atlantic."

This city is a stupendous monument of the energy and enterprise of man; in history it has not been surpassed. In 1831 the place was only an Indian trading port; nine years afterwards it had gathered only 5000 inhabitants. In 1850 the population had swelled to 29,963, and during the following ten years by the census its numbers had exceeded *a hundred and nine thousand.* The rapidity of its increase had been continued till the time of my visit. The situation has probably much to do in attracting these thousands; but there must be wisdom in the local or municipal government to take advantage of its natural and unrivalled position. The lake provides a pathway, but it seemed to me to have been an encroaching neighbour; the railway track for miles passes through water, and the margin of the water appeared to be a marshy soil, notwithstanding the town or city stands fifteen to eighteen feet above the level of the lake, and I learned that the city was well drained. There is a river bearing the same name which passes through the most populous district, dividing it into two branches, and crossed by swinging bridges, which allow the passage of vessels. The streets are wider than those of any other American city, and cross each other at right angles, for the most part paved, and in process of being levelled as I passed through. For five miles the river serves as a town-harbour for the largest vessels, which are engaged in the grain and lumber trade. In 1838 the exports of Chicago were 78 bushels of wheat, and no other grain was exported. In 1842 they had increased to 586,907 bushels of grain, in 1852 they were 5,873,141 bushels, and in 1862 they had increased to 55,720,760 bushels, tenfold more every ten years! Lake Street corresponds to the Broadway in New York, and Michigan and Wabash Avenues are adorned with magnificent residences and rows of wide-spreading trees. Already the city boasts of Court House, Custom House, Armoury; spacious and elegant churches for all sects. The cream-coloured marble of Chicago supplies material for building. Happily there are agencies engaged for the moral and intellectual culture of the minds of the younger members of society. A Young Men's Association Library and the Chicago Historical Library are the incipient tokens of literary and mental ambition. The city has come to its rapid development under auspices which may render it a rival with Cincinnati to the west or Boston in the east; much will depend on the religious organizations and ministerial instrumentalities of the present day. It is said that in no part of the Union have towns and cities sprung up so rapidly and in such wonderful growth as in Illinois. How vastly important must it be, therefore, that in Chicago there should be a model for all others! Mine host showed me every attention, and afforded me every facility for surveying and comprehending the gourd-like structures of the place. I suppose he could not assemble ministerial brethren, so many of them being, as he himself had been, from home for their summer vacation. My mission would have had more scope had more brethren been interested in it, and the response would have spoken in more various tones in our international sympathies.

The extent of Illinois—380 miles its greatest length northward, and 200 its greatest width westward—renders it one of the most influential in the Union, combined with its wealth in water, its mineral resources, and agricultural capabilities. The Mississippi, Ohio, and Illinois are the principal rivers; but to them may be added the Wabash,

the Rock River, the Sangamon, Kaukakee, the Des Plains,
and the Fox River. Other states border on some of these,
and share the blessings, but the state of Illinois monopolizes
some, and has a portion in all the others. Her prairies,
too, are sources of her wealth and prosperity; within her
borders, after leaving Chicago, I first saw this American
feature of nature. Immensity as in the boundless ocean im-
presses the beholder; far as the vision stretches the vast un-
dulating plain spreads abroad; occasional groups of trees
standing in comparative solitude, like a ship in the open sea.
Here and there toward the west I observed a fringe of forest,
and everywhere vegetation spread its gay carpet on the
measureless lawn; but miles and miles were passed without
a habitation or trace of man, except in the cultured fields
and the railed enclosures, which seemed only to restrain
the cattle from exposure to passing trains. The uniform
level of the prairie is by some ascribed to the deposits of
water which long covered the surface. The soil is entirely
free from stones, and richly fertile. Under the hand of man
rank grasses and flowers soon give place to Indian corn and
luxuriant wheat. The soil in some places is often twenty-five
feet deep, and even on the highest plains the fertility of the
soil is almost spontaneous in its productiveness. The towns
are numerous when the whole state is surveyed, and this
growth is rapid almost in proportion to the vegetation of her
Indian wheat.

The population of Illinois has been mingled with accessions from the Eastern states and from Britain, but they
have been chiefly single men. The excess of males over
females is large, numbering 93,281 in the majority in the
census of 1860. It may be expected, however, that this
excess has been decreased by the casualties of the war.
On the 31st of December, 1862, Illinois had sent into the
field 135,000 men, of whom there were 130 infantry, 16
cavalry regiments, and two regiments and seven batteries

of artillery. In this state, horses and mules are bred in great numbers. The latter rise, many of them, as high as ordinary horses, and are both more easily fed, and more useful for agriculture and draft. Springfield is the capital, and has enlarged its bounds in a few years. I passed this way the day before the State mass meeting assembled to receive Mr. Lincoln's singular letter. The town called Lincoln, in honour of him, promises soon to equal many older towns. Peoria and its lake attract thousands every year, and Alton contains already 10,000, though its foundations trace back only to 1832. My route took me past thirty-eight stations, as I journeyed from Chicago to Alton. Three miles farther down on the Mississippi than Alton the Missouri comes on the other side, and unites with her more majestic rival for better and for worse, and for many miles they flow down in the same channel more as twins than antagonists. The difference of the colour and even of purity, displays the original uncongeniality of the union. The entire railway from Chicago to St. Louis is 283 miles, without any relieving interludes in the route, and becomes monotonous and wearying at the close of the day. Before I cross the boundary into Missouri from Illinois, I must record what truth exacts and philanthropy mourns. A revised constitution, prepared by a convention of the state, was submitted to the popular vote in June, 1862. It was rejected by a majority of 25,000. I mention these circumstances and numbers to prove that the attention of all the citizens was directed to what yet follows. Two articles were separately voted on, one denying the right of suffrage to negroes, and the other prohibiting them from settling in the state; for these a majority of the votes were cast, and they have been incorporated into the old constitution: where they will work as doth a canker, till God's judgments for the poor shall avenge them, and lead a penitent people to reverse the decision.

Passengers from Illinois by the Chicago railway pass along the banks of the Mississippi from Alton to Illinois town, and their luggage packed on waggons, and passengers seated in omnibuses, are conveyed across the river in a floating bridge propelled by steam. At night it seems perilous to a stranger, but the glare of gas and the lights on the St. Louis side give an appearance of picturesque adventure to the brief voyage. Each passenger gave the address where he wished to be set down to the conductor, and on landing each vehicle started for their several destinations. I had informed Dr. Post by telegraph that I should that day travel from Chicago, and wished a room to be secured for me at Barnum's Hotel. I found provision made, and soon retired to rest. In the morning my arrival was heralded by a paragraph in the " Daily Missouri Democrat," of which the following is a copy :—

" ENGLISH SYMPATHY WITH AMERICA.

" By a private telegram from Chicago we learn that the Rev. Dr. Massie, of London, was expected to arrive here last night, and take apartments at Barnum's.

" As he comes to our city on a special mission, a few words as to its nature would add much to the public interest in his visit. On the 12th of February of this year the Protestant clergy of France, to the number of 750, addressed to the Protestant clergy of England a letter designed to urge them 'to take the lead in a great and peaceful manifestation of sympathy for the coloured race, so long oppressed and debased by Christian nations.' They desired by this means to ' discourage the partizans of slavery,' and ' encourage and strengthen those who wish to abolish it, at the same time persuading them to listen to friendly suggestions.' This letter was brought under the consideration of a conference of ministers, who issued a reply since, signed by over 4000 names of clergymen, which, with the letter from France, it was designed should be sent to the loyal ministers of this country. It was afterwards determined, in order to make the address

more forcible, and to better attain its object, to send a delegate to this country to set forth the views of the signers,
and express the sympathy of a large portion of the British
people with the cause of the North, greatly increased as it
has been by the President's proclamation of emancipation.
Dr. Massie was chosen as such delegate, and with this
object in view has travelled as far as Chicago, and was
expected to reach St. Louis last evening. We suppose he
will take some occasion to address our citizens in regard to
the special object of his mission; and aside from the merits
of that object the dignity and influential character of the
body he represents, entitle him to an attentive and
thoughtful hearing.

"We shall hope to announce in a day or so some opportunity when the public may hope to hear Dr. Massie
upon the topics alluded to."

I had not finished my breakfast, when I was informed
some gentlemen awaited me in the parlour. Here I found
Dr. Post's son, in his father's absence from home, and a
friend of his, who claimed a personal knowledge of me
from intercourse to which we had been introduced thirty
years ago by the late Dr. Bennet, of London. I remembered the occasion of our interview, and felt relieved to
have such a friendly coadjutor. We were engaged in conversation, when four or five other gentlemen were announced and introduced. I left them to constitute a local
committee of arrangement, and placed myself at their
disposal for a public meeting. Their first apprehension
was that, in a time so brief as I allowed, efficient arrangements could not be made; and then it appeared that some of
the senior ministers were absent, and again that the evening
eligible for me interfered with some local engagements. I
expressed my willingness to do any work and accept any
meeting, but I must reach Cincinnati for the following
Sunday. Their object had been to defer my services till
Sunday, but as I was determined to follow my programme,
earnest and vigorous measures were adopted to gather a

demonstrative meeting. The Illinois convention on that day at Springfield, and a convention being in progress in their own State to denounce the continuance of slavery any longer in Missouri, gave, in their mind, importance to my mission. It was agreed that application should be made to the chairman and committee of the Chamber of Commerce or Exchange to admit me at the hour when the attendance would be greatest, as soon as business would permit, that I might explain the purport of my message, and induce them to encourage their families to attend the meeting in the Methodist Episcopal Church. The consent of the authorities was obtained, and a deputation sent to invite me. I took my place, surrounded by many gentlemen, on the raised daïs, from which I spoke. The interview lasted half an hour, and a complimentary resolution was carried pledging their co-operation. In the evening the audience was beyond all expectation, filling the area of the church with an attentive congregation. I was as free to utter my anti-slavery sentiments in Missouri, as I had been in Connecticut. The Rev. H. Cox, at whose church I spoke, affirmed that such an address would not have passed without a mob, and the probable destruction of the place, only one year before ; but now it was cheered, and accepted by the most cordial demonstrations. The response was prepared afterwards by a committee chosen at the meeting, and I have received it since my return to England, accompanied by an apologetic letter.

" RESPONSE OF THE CLERGY OF ST. LOUIS, MISSOURI, TO THE REV. DR. MASSIE OF LONDON, ENGLAND, ON THE RECEIPT OF THE ADDRESS OF THE FRENCH AND ENGLISH CLERGYMEN.

" REV. AND DEAR BRETHREN,—We have received the ' Address to Ministers and Pastors of all Denominations in the United States of America,' adopted by the conference held at Manchester, England, June, 1863, and brought to us by Rev. Dr. Massie. We have listened with great satisfaction to his expositions of the sentiments of the people of England, and also to his assurance of their deep and hearty sympathy with the people of the United States in the fearful struggle in which we are called to act against a rebellion which aims to overthrow our national government, and seeks the establishment of a government resting upon *human slavery* as its.'CHIEF CORNER-STONE.'

" We have ever believed the heart of the people of Great Britain to be true to law and liberty, and beg to assure our brethren that however much we deplore the lapse of time during which we were permitted to struggle without any *public* manifestation of sympathy from those who had occupied a prominence so noble and glorious in the effort to rid the world of human slavery, yet we are now especially gratified by the reception of a sympathy so earnest and encouraging from thousands of the best and most prominent men in Great Britain and France.

" It is to us a source of profound gratitude and rejoicing that, notwithstanding the many pecuniary interests of both nations which are involved in and jeopardized by the prosecution of this war, so large a number have had the courage to avow such convictions as secure to us in all our conflicts and trials a sympathy which, resting on *moral* grounds, will of necessity be enduring; and sharing, as we do, so largely in these moral convictions we feel their full force, impelling us to move forward in the national struggle until the smoke of the conflict shall have passed from the land, and our nation stands as she was designed to be, *a nation of free men.*

" Living in a state in which the desolations of the war have been signally experienced, and which, during all its history, has been *burdened* and *cursed* by the institution of human slavery, we have the *strongest* reasons for welcoming cordially and gratefully these words of encouragement and sympathy from the friends of liberty in other lands,— words which, we trust, will strengthen our government in its great struggle, and add to those moral forces, whereby our nation must be delivered, not only from the perils of rebellion, but from that *monstrous* iniquity from which the rebellion has sprung.

" We heartily unite with our brethren in other cities in the earnest prayer that the power and influence of England

and America, may always be united in favour of the sacred interests of truth, liberty, and humanity.

"H. Cox,
H. A. Nelson, } Committee."

"St. Louis, Missouri,
"To Thomas B. Potter, Esq.,   October 30th, 1863.
Manchester, England.

"My dear Sir,—A few days ago, I received from Dr. Massie's friend, W. B. Brown of Newark, New Jersey, a request for the copy of the address of the clergymen of this city responsive to the one received through Dr. Massie from the ministers of England and France. I regret the imperfect character of our response, but Dr. Massie remained so few hours with us, and all our movements were so hurried, as to render it impossible for us to do more than merely allude, in a very brief manner, to matters and thoughts which properly demanded more care and deliberation. This must be our apology, if you please. Please present to Dr. Massie our most earnest sympathy and we wishes. We shall remember his visit to our city with grea pleasure.

"Our state is now as much excited as possible. *Freedom must win*, but the slave power will die hard. The logic of events has done much, revolutionized the opinion and feelings of most of our people, and we work and pray for *universal* freedom. God bless you and your society.

"Yours for America and Universal Freedom,

"H. Cox."

To me, a visit to Missouri had peculiar interest, as I had watched the struggle in Kansas, and had long mourned the "Missouri Compromise," and equally deplored the spirit which had prompted its repudiation by the party who carried it. I was prepared to anticipate instruction and matter for thoughtful reflection in personal examination of the features of St. Louis. I thankfully availed myself of the personal attentions and guidance of Mr. Post, Mr. Cox, and other friends who conducted me through the city to its environs. It is a magnificent city, and continues to enlarge,

s

it prospers even more since slavery began to hide its head.
Prior to the war, in the whole state, the number of slaves
in 1860 was 114,931. Governor Gamble estimated, in 1862,
that they did not exceed 50,000. In 1850, the population
of St. Louis was 77,860, and it had risen, in 1860, to
160,773; but the increase had not abated, three years afterward. When I was here, there were adventitious accessions to the inhabitants, in poor fugitives whose homes
had been desolated by rebellious armies and guerilla bands.
There were also prisoners in thousands who had been captured in the field, and soldiers who were there to guard
them; and sick and wounded men from the army in convalescent hospitals. Some of the premises now occupied
as prisons or hospitals were formerly inhabited by men at
present in rebellion, and who had instigated others to conspiracy and treason. They are some of them wandering
in England now, not well pleased that their confiscated
because forfeited property should be applied to the service
of the state. I met one of these vagrant secessionist rebels
in Scotland, craving an *obolum* of Southern sympathy, and
threatening, if he should ever meet Governor Gamble, he
"*would cut his weasel.*" This hero affirmed he had *breasted*
the bullets in the present war, and would do so again; for
the South would *lick* the Yankees yet. I presume, however,
he would rather breast a *dead* negro on the dissecting-table.
He boasted that he had dissected the head and brain of
every nation of men, and he could demonstrate that the
black race were not able to govern themselves, and were
made to be slaves. It is glibly stated by the " Literary
Churchman" that—

" Englishmen, filled to overflowing with even a fanatical love of liberty, can now listen with equanimity, and it
is said with applause, to the following statements of a man
of science at an important meeting :—
" '1st, the skin of the negro is structurally different

from ours; 2ndly, his bones are heavier; 3rdly, his arms are longer, even reaching below the knees; 4thly, his legs are bent; 5thly, his heel protrudes behind his foot; 6thly, his great toe is rather a kind of thumb, separated from the other toes; 7thly, the skull is thicker; 8thly, the forehead is flattened, and recedes; 9thly, the jaw projects largely (?); 10thly, the facial angle is widely different from the usual European type; 11thly, the pure negro has no intellectual development after mere childhood; 12thly, all cases of 'so-called intelligent negroes' have been of mixed European and African blood!'

"As these are all questions of fact, and not of opinion, it is useless, of course, to be impatient about them."

Such was the profound anatomical argumentation of Dr. McDowell, Professor of Medicine in St. Louis for twenty-five years, Surgeon and Inspector-General of Hospitals in the Confederate Army of the South, with many other titles and distinctions, which he *had* hoped would have been his passport to deliver a course of lectures on the physical history of man in some learned university city. He assured me the North had set a price upon his head in reward for his capture. It must have been because they did not know what it was made of, or what was in it. But with several surplus oaths, he affirmed that his house, lecture-room, and museum had been converted into a prison for Secession soldiers in St. Louis. He intimated that he had 5000 acres of land in one state, 19,000 in another, and an equally fabulous extent of land in some others. I could only reply that he must have got it *cheap*, and if he were so conscientious a patriot, he need not talk so largely about his losses. He was as rich now as he was when he was born of parents partly Irish and partly French. I believe I saw the premises of which he spoke, he is not unknown in the place.

St. Louis has all the elements of an elegant and magnificent city in her site and the conformation of the ground within, and round about in the suburbs. It lies upon the

right bank of the Mississippi below the entrance of the
Missouri twenty miles, and above the entrance of the Ohio
174 miles. It is 1194 miles above the city of New Orleans.
Two limestone plateaus, rising one above the other forty
feet, and the lower above the river twenty feet, are occupied by St. Louis. The upper terrace widens into a plain,
from which fine views of the city are obtained, the entire
extent of which along the curves of the river is about seven
miles, and three miles back from the river. The denser
portion of the habitations covers about one third of this
space. The streets are wide and regular, the MAIN and
SECOND streets and the FRONT street are great thoroughfares.
Lafayette Square is a kind of public park; but it is in the
environs and streets leading to them where the elegant
magnificence of St. Louis is seen. There are private
grounds which the owner opens to the public in gardens,
walks, and adorned with botanical exotics, which are
greatly admired. The City Hall, Custom House, Court
House, and hotels; the churches, and the United States'
Arsenal, show the wealth expended in the structure of the
city. I was interested in the branch of the Sanitary Commission working here, and found its chairman, Mr. Yeat-
man, a man of position, born and brought up in a slave
state, working at his desk daily with as much assiduity as
if his living were derived from it. The benevolence developed by this association in all America will tell hereafter
in her history. A word on the *history* of this great centre
of the West. Laclede chose the present site of St. Louis in
1764. It was settled as a trading station for trappers, and
the annual value of furs brought in till 1804 was on an
average 203,750 dollars for fifteen years. At this period
the population was under 2000, half of whom were wandering in quest of furs among the Indians. A band of
Spanish soldiers under a leader named Rious had seized
the place in 1768 in the name of the Spanish monarch, but

it was transferred to the United States in 1804. The first brick house was built in 1813. As a *city* its history began in 1822; it had been called St. Louis in honour of the King of France, Louis XV. Emigration from Illinois began to flow in 1825. In 1830 it had inhabitants 6694; in 1840 it had 16,469, in 1850 the number had risen to 77,850, but now it is near to 200,000.

It is with regret I now turn my back upon the West, but I must look into the borders of the South, and touch upon an actual slave state. To reach Kentucky my route lay across the "mother of waters," and again I should cross the Kaskaskia and the Wabash, till I should come to the banks of the Ohio, through the states of Illinois and Indiana. Not one of the towns through which I had to travel would be known to more than one of twenty in any company of English people, though their number is probably forty: Xenia, and Flora, and Odin, and Sandoval, and thirty others, would not, in the mention of them, contribute to the precise information of my reader. I will, therefore, look only into my compartment of the train. Every separate carriage, in length perhaps forty feet, is furnished with cushioned seats and backs; the latter being moveable so that the occupant can sit as he pleases, looking forward or backward on the route. These several seats are *close enough* for the convenience of a tall or stout person; only two can sit on each seat from the side to the centre of the carriage. There is a clear pathway in the middle, the whole length, and a door at each end. The conductor or other person can and may move up and down every minute, no restraint. Arrangements are made in most carriages for a large jar of water with cock and dish for drink, and for a stove in winter. There is a convenient closet in one corner, with suitable arrangements for the comfort of travellers. I seldom saw second-class carriages. Generally all, rough and smooth, vulgar and refined, rich and poor, travel together; except that often one carriage is set apart for ladies, into which all females, their husbands, and children, may also go. I have seen an invalid soldier carried by his father and laid upon the floor; and I have seen, when the sick man could provide it, a mattress laid on the top of two seats, so that he might be stretched on it. There are also sleeping cars in night trains, which may be engaged before starting, by paying an additional charge in proportion, for a single or a double bed. I have rarely seen rudeness or offensive behaviour, or even persistence in smoking when declared to be offensive. The only ill-behaved man I saw was a rude *drover sort* of Irishman; and when told he was a reproach to his country, by one who, he thought, was from the same land, his manners improved. I travelled in the midst of many soldiers, in the ranks and in commission, and availed myself of free conversation with them. A large proportion was of young men. I did not meet one who was an Irishman; some might be the sons of Irish immigrants, but they had not the sibboleth; some were English, who had become citizens; but my hap was not to recognize a single Irishman, so far as his tongue or intercourse would lead me to conclude. Some whom I met, even of the lower rank of officers, uttered profane language so frequently as to prompt me to remonstrate. I dealt thus with two who sat close to me. "Jesus Christ," "by Jesus," "God Almighty," and such profane expletives being their choice. I asked them if they would take the name of their mother or father thus familiarly, or the name of any friend whom they honoured, in their mouths; would they use his name in any expression of surprise? Now, I said, *Jesus Christ* is a friend whom I highly honour, and I reverence his name as I do the name of God, and it was not pleasant to hear these names so thoughtlessly uttered. They apologized most softly, and without being offended, nor did I hear them do so again. Among a number of young soldiers who were amusing themselves and too freely mentioning the *devil*, I said I never liked to hear him familiarly spoken of, because then I thought he was sure to be present. They heard the reproof kindly, and, though in joke, referred to their *Sabbath school* lessons. I was thus informed of their early associations, and learned how to deal with them. But after all the army is a sorry school for young and inexperienced lads.

As we approached the end of the journey, we reached New Albany, four miles north-west from Louisville, and on the Indiana side of the Ohio. It is within the borders of a free state, and contains 10,000 inhabitants, though only laid out in 1813. Churches, schools, and a Lyceum provide for its population intellectual and spiritual instruction. Our road lay along the banks of the Ohio. The ferry at Jeffersonville supplies a passage for railway companies. It is in the same State with New Albany, and increases as the cities of the State do elsewhere. The public buildings, warehouses, and hotels have risen with the station, and there are numerous handsome private dwellings. The Ohio river is here about a mile wide, and has a more rapid current in consequence of a gradual fall of twenty-two feet in two miles. Some writers are magniloquent about the *falls*, and speak of a "great many broken rivers of foam making their way over the falls;" but these are visions reserved only for the privileged. I walked along the banks and crossed beside the "fine island which adds to the beauty of the scene." Yet none of these features of the fall appeared; perhaps the water was in "a high stage," and denied the pleasure to me. Portland presented a pretty aspect as a village by the river brink. I was advised by a fellow traveller to put up at the Galt House. Here I was in the midst of slavery—the servants of the house were bondmen, and it was manifest by their indifferent attendance. Every man in the saloon, or hall, or retiring rooms, or in the vestibule of the house, clerks at the desk, or proprietors, or visitors, or town's men, who came in on business, or for pleasure—all rolled as a sweet morsel, under or over their tongue, or in their cheek, or from one side of the mouth to another, the everlasting tobacco, and squirted its juice wherever they sat, at your feet, or over your knee, before your face, or behind you, on the floor, or ground, without deference or apology. I never was in a house among so many men where the appearance of women was so dispensed with ; and I wonder not that women should have spurned such a salivarian current and such an odour as must have been put forth from every man's mouth. I sought out anywhere a place of retreat, but hesitated to change my quarters, as I might make bad worse, and rather add to my misery. The town had an aspect of declension ; houses standing unoccupied, half built, and ready to fall, and warehouses to let. I was told the population had decreased 10,000 since 1860, when it was 68,039. The merchandise which I saw was principally tobacco ; and the carts driven by negro slaves were employed in conveying its preparations in hogsheads. The only pleasant sight I witnessed was the fruit-market— peaches, apples, and melons, etc.

Two gentlemen I inquired for and ultimately found. I suppose my inquiries for them suggested to those around me a mistaken *notion*. I called on the editor of the "Louisville Journal." Mr. Prentice is well known far and near ; and when he knew my name, and identified my object in visiting the place, he received me with the cordial courtesy of a gentleman. We were wide as the poles asunder, but not the less gratified in our interview. He is a strenuous advocate of the Union against the Secession ; but avows not any sympathy with those who call for emancipation. He knows the secrets of the system, and its bondage for more than the sable sufferers. I called with an introductory letter on Bishop Smith, the Episcopal ruler of all Kentucky, and who is intimately conversant with every part of his diocese. A bishop, more unpretending and yet gentlemanly, informed, and communicative, I could not desire to meet. He is known to desiderate the removal of slavery, and to deplore its constitutional evils in society, and he has freely conferred with clergy and laity over all the State on the question. He has sought by writing and other means to convince others that it is an evil, of contagious influence and fearful operation; and welcomed me as a messenger come to stimulate, where it could be wisely done, in his judgment, all who could work for the *removal* of slavery. But he was not an Abolitionist or Emancipationist, and he could think of no measure of co-operation for me in that state. He believed that before the present war nearly two-thirds of the Kentuckians were for gradual emancipation. I suppose after they were themselves all dead. He feared there might not be so many now. If, however, any foreign influence were attempted to promote anti-slavery sentiment in the state, he believed most of them would so resent the interference as to become more pro-slavery than ever, and it would only end in convulsion. Bishop Smith is a most excellent, mild man, and can only advocate gentle persuasives, and imperceptible tonics, in infinitesmal doses. Luther, and Knox, and the Puritans, did not study in his school, yet I was greatly gratified by the venerable man's friendly and enlightened converse. There is a canal cut through the solid rock, I fear the work of slaves, for the most part of two miles, which serves the navigation of vessels, which cannot brave the falls. The extent of the city is along the river, two miles; the leading streets lie in the same direction. I walked through almost all of them; many of them are adorned with trees, and numerous sumptuous houses prove there has been wealth and indulgence of pleasure in times gone by. There is a lull in the operation of the slave system.

I conversed with one of the government contrabands employed at work by the day's wage, who had a pretty correct apprehension of the present state of affairs. He had been the chattel of a rebel colonel, and hence his freedom. His father's family had been large; two brothers had worked out their own freedom, another was still a slave, the property of some other master, but apparently in circumstances more favourable than that of many slaves as long as he is content and has no children to sell. This poor fellow had disease brought on by slave work in a rupture, and was the less able to provide for himself. There were wooden buildings in process of erection for the States Government for warlike stores; and, as I sat surveying them, a Welshman approached to speak to one who seemed a stranger. He had imbibed slaveholding ideas of the negroes, though he assured me he was anti-slavery. He had also assimilated his notions of strong language with oaths and swearing, and the use of the Divine name. His sympathies were expressed in *expectations* that the South would succeed, etc. I was disposed to shake off the dust of my feet on the banks of the Ohio as soon as I could arrange for a train, which would convey me back to freedom, and away from the sight of slavery. There are seven religious colleges in Kentucky, two each for Baptists, Presbyterians, and Roman Catholics, and one for the Campbellites; three theological schools are sustained, one each for Baptist, Presbyterian, and Roman Catholic. In the number of asses and mules there is only one state which exceeds this state in productiveness, and in number of swine it is nearly equal to either of the three largest—Indiana, Tennessee, and Missouri—swine-producing states. It is second in tobacco and first in hemp, but in grain it is inferior to many. The state was invaded by the Confederate bands September 5th, 1861, and thenceforth all parties were tested. Severe battles were fought at Wild

Cat, Mill Spring, Mumfordsville, Perryville, and Richmond, but now the Confederates have not a foothold in the state.

I proceeded by the Jeffersonville Railway to Seymour, and thence to Cincinnati to fulfil an engagement made a month previously, and reached that city a little after ten o'clock p.m., having travelled 146 miles. A friend met me at the station, and conducted me to the Burnet House. My mission was now in the "Queen city of the West;" her population was reported in the census of 1860 as 161,044. Perhaps some writers include contiguous villages in their estimate, as I see the population numbered by some as high as 250,000. Covington, though in Kentucky, is only across the Ohio, which steam vessels, as ferry boats, traverse every five minutes. A bridge connecting the places is in process of erection. Mount Auburn is in the environs, and so is Walnut Hill, where Lane Seminary is situate. In both these suburbs persons having business in the city have luxurious country seats. I was engaged by Professor Day to visit this latter village, and preach at the chapel of Lane Seminary on the morning of Sunday. The residence of Mrs. Beecher Stowe, and probably the cradle of "Uncle Tom," while her husband was one of the professors, was close by. The drive to this place was exceedingly agreeable in the quiet of a Sabbath morning, in the midst of such enchanting scenery. The repose and sweetness of the academic retreat, where I had the privilege to commune with loving kindred spirits in Divine service, were exceedingly refreshing to my mind after the miscellaneous but varied pressing engagements of the preceding week. I was told some of my hearers had pleasurable emotions in the service, and so had I, and doubtless it was good to be separated from the world awhile. Professor Day escorted me to the city in the afternoon by another way than that by which we had gone. I was shown before we started his last monthly parcel of periodicals, containing one of each leading denominational class published in England. American men of letters are as familiar with English literature as are most of our own respectable journalists. Looking down, as we wended our way from Walnut Hill, and left Mount Adams behind us, as well as Mount Auburn, we passed within view of Mr. Longworth's residence, known in the West not only for his gardens, conservatories, and art treasures, but also for his vineyards and his culture of the grape, from which the "sparkling Catawba" is produced. The survey was enchanting and expansive, of the valley in which the city is built, three miles in extent, and enclosed by rising grounds, which give an elevation of 400 feet above the river. The summits are reached by a gentle ascent, from which commanding views of the whole amphitheatre are everywhere presented. A subsequent day was spent in company with Dr. Thompson and his friend, exploring the valley of Mill Creek, five or six miles to the north-west of the city; on the sloping banks round which the most picturesque views of beautiful scenery and landscape are obtained. The demesnes of city merchants here are usually open for drives to the casual visitor. The "Spring Grove Cemetery" is situated here; its undulations, knolls, and valleys for 168 acres have been made available for the purposes of the discerning ground architect, who has laboured successfully to rob "the house appointed for all living" as the mansion of the dead, of many of its terrors, and has smoothed the earth sod as a pillow for many an aching head. He has not given the hope of the resurrection of the just, which can be assured only by ONE; but he has prepared a bed for the repose of the dust of many who may by previous faith sleep in Jesus.

I inquired for the noted pork shambles of Cincinnati. Once there was rather a boast of these. The same processes are still pursued, and the same trade continues profitable; but there is not much poetry about the occupation.

Formerly the DEER CREEK was a green-margined, pebbly stream, gurgling along the base of *Mount Adams*, and inviting the wayfarer to ramble on its sunny banks; but now it is an *underground sewer*, carrying off the blood and offal of extensive pork-killing and packing establishments. One enterprise characteristic of local energy deserves attention for a moment—THE SUSPENSION BRIDGE across the Ohio. The foundations, 80 feet by 52 at the base, from which the towers rise 230 feet high, and 1000 feet apart, indicate their strength. The cables, anchored 300 feet back on each side of the river, passing over the towers, show the length of spring by which the weight of the bridge is sustained. The span, about the third of a mile long, and 122 feet higher than low-water mark, above which the highest freshet has risen only 62 feet, leaves space enough for any river steamer to pass under. Rail trains, and other conveyances, have in the grade of ascent abundant power of transit. MAIN STREET, the great business thoroughfare, is five and a half miles long. The leading streets after this are named " First," " Second," " Third," etc. Pearl Street is parallel with the river, and Fourth Street is a long, wide, elegant, and fashionable promenade, on the brow of the First Terrace. The Cincinnati Observatory is remarked for its beautiful situation, commanding view, and celebrated telescope. The Merchants' Exchange, with its reading-room, and Mercantile Library Association; the Medical College; the Cathedral, its altar, organ, and pictures : the Episcopal Church ; Presbyterian Churches, and Educational Institutions, show what has been done in less than forty years by western energy. The whole State is no less a monument of enterprise. It has twenty-three colleges and nine theological schools ; of each, the following is the denominational distribution : the Methodists have six and one ; the Presbyterians of three sects, five and three ; the Roman Catholics, three and two ; Lutherans, two and one ; Episcopalians and Congregationalists, one of each; the Baptists, one college; Unitarians, one; United Brethren, one; and the New Jerusalem Church, one. Medical Schools are four, and there is one Law School. The total amount of school fund for the state is above 2,796,241 dollars, and its annual interest is 168,362 dollars; while this fund and taxation provided for common schools, 2,834,066 dollars for 1861.

Arrangements had been made that a united public meeting should be held for my mission on Sunday afternoon at four o'clock, in the First Old School Presbyterian Church. The Rev. Mr. Annan, pastor, took a lively interest in the proceedings, and many of the city clergy were present. The meeting lasted till nearly six o'clock, when a committee was appointed—Dr. Thompson, chairman—to consider the form and matter of a response. This committee assembled for deliberation, and adopted unanimously the address which had emanated from New York. I will make a single extract from the " Cincinnati Gazette" of the following morning :—

"The first Presbyterian church of this city was densely crowded, last Sabbath afternoon, by a congregation comprising members of all denominations, who had assembled to listen to the remarks of Dr. Massie of London, who is now on a visit to this country, travelling through and speaking in all the principal cities of the loyal states, as the representative of the ' Union and the Emancipation Society' of the English nation. We give the following paragraphs from the report of the ' Daily Gazette' of Monday:

" In commencing his remarks the Doctor said that he did not think it was incompatible with the sacred character of the day to speak to them of the struggle in which they were engaged, and of the sympathy which England felt in that struggle.

" He did not know when he left England that there was so much need for the interchange of sympathies and confidential communication between the people of England and America. He did not know how deeply had entered into the heart of the people of this land, the feeling of sorrow and disappointment which he now found to prevail, because of misapprehension and misrepresentation concerning England in America, and concerning America in England. The first object of his mission was to strengthen the hands of those who were seeking to destroy the source of the present war, the spring of the rebellion, and the power of those who are acting as rebels against that government by which they themselves had previously enjoyed the highest rights that man can enjoy.

" We believe that America, if she continued to prosper, would prove a blessing at least to the transatlantic world, and that gradually her institutions, her liberties, and her religion would spread over the other parts of the continent of America, and we have wished her God speed in such prevalence—prevalence by reason, by righteousness, by justice, by law, and by an equitable government. We look to the people of America as a kindred people, that had sprung from our own ancestors.

" The speaker then enlarged on the proceedings of the Evangelical Alliance of England, and the Union and Emancipation Society of Manchester, recounting at length the history of each, and reading in full the address issued by the Emancipation Society to the ministers and pastors of the United States. This address, with a letter, had been delivered to the President, Abraham Lincoln. When he was in Washington he had called on the President and asked him if he had read the letter. The President replied that he had, but would read it again before him—which he did, reading it aloud. It is not my duty, the speaker said, to tell you what passed between us, but I will tell you what is my impression concerning him. He is the enemy of slavery and wishes its abolition. He is the friend of the slave, and wishes him liberty. He has issued his proclamation of liberty and will not retract one syllable of it. He is as pure a patriot as probably ever sat in the Presidential chair. He is a true Christian and a man to be trusted as honest and worthy of all praise."

It had been deemed important I should visit Columbus, the capital of the state; and a correspondence between friends interested in the mission had been delayed by the absence of clergymen in whom they relied. It was feared

my time would be too brief from other forward engagements for suitable arrangements to be made. As, however,
I had two days which could be thus appropriated, I pushed
forward, by a free pass, on the rail. The distance was 120
miles. The line passed through Miamiville, Loveland,
Morrow, Xenia, Cedarville, Florence, and London. Miami
is the name given to a college chartered to grant degrees;
but I have understood it expired almost as soon as it produced one such creation, which for years after adorned a
Scottish minister's name. Xenia is the capital of a
county, well planned with some substantial private residences and a handsome courthouse. In the township are
12,000 inhabitants. It is within ten miles of Yellow
Springs, the seat of Antioch College, occupying an area of
twenty acres with its academic buildings, and designed for
the literary education of females as well as males. In the
midst of picturesque scenery the spring pours out from a
limestone rock a hundred gallons every minute of sulphur-
ous waters, possessing certain medicinal qualities. London
is a village with some 2500 inhabitants, many of whose
houses, stores, and churches were consumed by a great
conflagration in January, 1850. I had furnished myself, in
my handbag, for a single night, and on arrival at the
Columbus Terminus I took a street car to proceed to some
central hotel. As soon as I had washed and refreshed
myself by shaking off the dust of the way, I studied the
" City Directory" for ministers' names and residences, and
found Mr. Goodwin, a Congregational clergyman, was not
far off from my centre. I found him accessible, gentlemanly, and hospitable, and he would not suffer me to
return to my hotel. In brief time he went forth to consult
such other ministers as were at home. His own church
was under repair, he therefore obtained the Presbyterian
church of a hearty and well-educated Welsh brother. Mr.
Evans and Mr. Goodwin conferred with an invalid senior

minister, and announced in the local press the arrangement for a meeting on the following evening. The interval
was spent waiting on gentlemen likely to take an interest
in the movement. I was introduced to Governor Todd at
his office, in the capitol, and gave him such information
as he desired in a lengthened interview. He has since
been succeeded by a truly Union candidate, who was in
vain opposed by Vallandigham and his party. Dr. Ides,
an active citizen, introduced me to view the state prison,
in which Morgan' and his marauding band were held in
durance after their sanguinary raids and plunderings in
and around Ohio. I was pleased to see the wise and
economical arrangements of the prison; every criminal
working for his food, and even providing a fund for his
own advantage when his term had expired. Some of them,
poor fellows, were there for life; but even they had the
happiness of doing something which added to their own
comforts. I saw some life long prisoners under sentence
for murder, who appeared innocent enough in their prison
occupations; and who had opportunity for reflection and
contrition. Morgan's band were not *made* to work; their
imprisonment would have passed more lightly as workmen
than as gentlemen prisoners of war. Hardened and insub-
ordinate offenders had their doom in solitary cells; poor
wretches! they were their own worst punishment and tormentors. The sentinels had their promenade upon a platform on the wall: hence Morgan's subsequent escape. The
food, work, and punishment of this prison seemed to me
worthy of imitation. The year 1860 and 1861 returns, give,
November 1, in prison 932; subsequently received 355 +
1287. The number discharged, 365; residue, 924. Those
who left were, 246 by expiry of their term, 87 by pardon,
11 sent to reform school; 9 discharged on writ of error;
4 escaped, and 6 died. There were 16 female prisoners;
109 coloured males; and 799 white males at the close of

T

the year. The convict labour produced during the year 77,318 dollars, besides what labour was expended on the repair and enlargement of the prison. The capitol is a large demonstrative building of marble like limestone, has a façade of 300 feet, and an elevation to the top of the rotunda of 157 feet. The halls and adjoining chambers were convenient rather than gaudy. The population is said to have been 25,000 in 1853. This is a mistake. The census in 1850 was 17,882, and in 1860 only 18,629. The principal streets are wide and long, and the houses are many of them elegantly built, and I have no doubt well furnished. Wealthy persons reside in Columbus.

The meeting convened to hear my message was respectable, not so large as in some places; but the responsive sympathy both from the mass and by individuals quite compensated me for my journey and labour. I expected a formal response in the name of the ministers, but I believe they resolved to adhere to the New York reply. The visit gratified me.

My kind host drove me to the station, and, with a patience which seemed exhaustless, waited to see me start for Cleveland, by a through train from Cincinnati. It was more than an hour beyond its time, during which we had leisure to study character. A most conspicuous *hero of the stump*, ready to speak at any time on any subject, and for any party, was pushing hither and thither, as a man of the greatest importance; a budget of papers in his pockets which waved to the wind, and a forest of hair on his head which hung like pine branches over his shoulders; he seemed in search of constituents, or occasions on which to engage his natural powers. He was one of those New World geniuses who could fabricate a story, which, if not true, would yet tell *well;* and who had a few *saws* and extracts of poetry ready to be dovetailed into any mass of talk, and could undertake to make " the worse appear the better reason." While I stood watching the moving mass, one of my fellow-passengers across the Atlantic recognized me, and acknowledged he had not yet found employment in what he would like, and thought he should return to England. He had promise of situations, and could work and get wages, but nothing that suited his fancy or ambition.

One of the American railway agents stands out before me. He is called the *baggage* agent; he has hanging on his arm a hundred short chains, at the end of each a brass plate, bearing a number, a duplicate of which he has ready to give when required. He passes through the whole train of carriages as they approach the principal terminus, and asks every passenger if he has any baggage to care for. When the train starts, a check clerk gives for every separate package a check. This man will take the passenger's check or checks, and a minute of his address, if agreeable, and give in return for each a brass plate or written card, charging a quarter of a dollar, equal to a shilling; which entitles the holder to a seat in the omnibus, and the delivery of the baggage at the address. But now my train has come, and I proceed. Twenty-four towns or stations lie between Columbus and Cleveland. The names are still a memorial of the past: "Worthington, Berlin, Delaware, Eden, Gilead, Iberia, Salem, Greenwich, New London, Rochester, Wellington, Grafton, and Berea," passing by others of local association. Population is found along the whole 120 miles, all in the state of Ohio.

Cleveland ranks next to Cincinnati in importance and population. It had more than doubled from 1850 till 1860. In the first year 17,034, in the next decade 43,417. It is probably 50,000 now. It is placed on a commanding bluff overlooking the lake, having broad, well-paved streets, and open squares. It was laid out in 1796, and named in honour of a Connecticut general. The first site was on the eastern shore of the Cuyahoga; but, on the opposite side of the river, Ohio city has grown a place of importance, and both are united under one municipality—several bridges crossing the river.

The view upon Lake Erie is good, but better from the higher parts of the city, and also from Brooklyn on the other side of the river. The square in which Commodore Perry's statue stands is spacious, and the post-office recently erected on its higher side, is respectable. Other public buildings evince progress. But the *churches* are the most notable proofs of liberality and wisdom to which I can point. I preached in a fine stone building, called the First Presbyterian Church, which surpasses many metropolitan structures in England. This was the second which had been erected by the same congregation. The first was destroyed by fire. The second church, in which my *message* was delivered on Monday evening, was almost as good, and was better for the speaker. The Plymouth church (Congregationalist) was smaller, but most substantially constructed. Here I preached on Sunday evening to a congregation which overflowed. Two or three Episcopalian and a large Romish church in the upper part of the town, were all equally well constructed and suitable for their purposes. There was a mass political meeting in the town on the day fixed for the delivery of my message. But the class of persons who attended in the second Presbyterian Church were possessed of local influence, and represented the worth, wealth, and piety of the town. The church was well filled, and the proceedings animated. The whole course of proceedings is narrated by Dr. Wolcott, in his communication, which will show the general interest taken in the mission. The gentlemen who afterwards came forward and manifested their personal sympathy and interest, represented the commercial as well as the retired classes. The brother of the late Admiral Foote, several bankers, and directors of railway companies, and active office bearers in the several churches, principally of the Presbyterian, Congregationalist, and Baptist orders, and all the pastors of these churches *able* to attend, cordially sustained the demonstration, besides those who uttered their sentiments in the meeting. I afterwards received tokens of personal kindness in being conveyed through the town and beyond it into the suburbs, as well as the free pass which conveyed me to Pittsburg, and afterwards to Buffalo, besides unceasing and vigilant hospitality from the Rev. T. H. Hawks and his admirable wife, which I must ever retain in a grateful remembrance.

"CLEVELAND, OHIO, *Sept.*, 1863.

"At a meeting of ministers of the gospel in the city of Cleveland, held in the Lecture Room of the First Baptist Church at the close of the daily morning prayer-meeting, the Rev. T. H. Hawks, pastor of the Second Presbyterian Church, was called to the chair.

"The Rev. W. H. Goodrich, pastor of the First Presbyterian Church, reported to the meeting a correspondence which he had with the Rev. Dr. Massie, of the British deputation, and that the latter had consented to address the churches of Cleveland. On his motion, a committee was appointed, consisting of the Rev. S. C. Aiken, D.D. (Presbyterian), the Rev. S. W. Adams, D.D. (Baptist), and the Rev. Samuel Wolcott, D.D. (Congregational), to make arrangements for a public meeting, and to prepare a reply to the addresses of the British and French ministers and pastors.

"Monday evening, 14th September, in response to a published invitation from the committee, ministers and pastors in Cleveland and other towns of Northern Ohio of different denominations, held a meeting in the Conference Room of the Second Presbyterian Church, at half-past six o'clock, preliminary to the public meeting. The Rev. Mr. Hawks was appointed chairman.

"Dr. Wolcott, in behalf of the committee, presented the reply which had been prepared, and which, after discussion, was unanimously adopted. The meeting then adjourned to the public meeting.

" A large audience assembled in the church, and after an appropriate opening anthem by the choir, prayer was offered by Dr. Adams.

" The chairman explained the object of the meeting, and introduced Dr. Massie, who for an hour and a half held the close attention of the audience, while he set forth the nature of his mission, the circumstances under which it originated, and the state of public sentiment in Great Britain respecting our affairs, especially on the part of those whom he directly represented, and closed by reading the Address, which he had been commissioned to bring. His remarks throughout were earnest and eloquent, and the effect of his statements on the meeting was exceedingly happy.

" Dr. Wolcott followed with a few remarks, assuring the deputation that the heart of the entire assembly beat responsive to all the kind expressions which had been uttered, and with a warm appreciation both of the spirit which prompted the message and the sentiments which it embodied; and expressing the hope that visits like this, and kindred influences, would secure a good understanding between the two nations, united by so many ties, and result in their more complete and mutual consecration to the peaceful and lofty mission which the God of nations had assigned them on the grand theatre of the world's history. He then read the Reply which had been adopted at the ministers' meeting.

" The hymn commencing—

> ' My country, 'tis of thee,
> Sweet land of liberty,
> Of thee I sing '—

was then sung by the congregation, after which the Benediction was pronounced by Dr. Massie.

" No roll of the ministers present was made. Among those who participated in the meeting were Rev. Messrs. Monteith, Hoye, and Palmer, of Cleveland; Rev. Mr. Webster, of Princesville; Rev. Mr. Sharpe, of Collamor; Rev. Mr. Turner, of Newburgh; Rev. Mr. Sharpe, of Huntsburgh; and Rev. Mr. Potter, of Freedom.

" REPLY.

" The Ministers of the Gospel in the City of Cleveland and
vicinity, to Christian Ministers and Pastors in Great
Britain and France, send greeting :

" REVEREND AND BELOVED.—At a public meeting called
for the purpose, we have listened to your addresses, com-
municated by the senior member of your deputation, the
Rev. Dr. Massie.

" Permit us to say in reply, that we accept, with lively
sensibility, the grateful assurance of sympathy from our
brethren abroad, in the great struggle which now convulses our land, and which is the fruit of a conspiracy and
revolt, instigated by leading slaveholders in the Southern
states for the purpose of saving the institution of slavery
from certain destruction through the legitimate and peaceful action of moral and political causes, and perpetuating
its evil sway on this continent by the power of the sword.
No other pretext for the rebellion has ever been honestly
assigned.

" We fully and unanimously endorse your avowed abhorrence of human bondage, regarding it as a sin against
God and a crime against man ; and we join in your earnest
expression of sympathy with our coloured brethren, and
recognition of their claims as members of the same great
family with ourselves, invested with the sacred rights of
humanity, and having a common Father in heaven.

" We rejoice with you, and render thanks to God, that
through his overruling Providence, this wicked rebellion is
resulting in the liberation of the slave and the elevation of
the coloured freeman ; and it is our fervent prayer that
universal emancipation may be ushered in with the return
of peace. We are pledged not to rest from our labours
until our whole country has been redeemed from the spirit
of barbarism, treason, and oppression ; and we joyfully
anticipate the day when the Republic, founded on the
principles of justice, liberty, and humanity, shall be relieved
of the stain which has tarnished her glory, and her flag be
recognized on all shores as the symbol of a free and powerful Christian commonwealth, harbouring no tyrant and no
bondman. Believing that the effectual suppression of this
slaveholders' rebellion by the strong arm of the Federal
Government, will conduce to this end, we shrink not from

the burdens and sacrifices which the patriotic cause imposes, comforted by the reflection that treasure and precious life freely laid upon the altar of our country, in defence of our common laws and liberties, are not unavailingly offered.

" We would respectfully remind you, dear brethren, that the enfranchisement of those in bonds, dear as that object justly is to you and to us, and the only one presented in your addresses, is not the only, nor even the primary issue involved in our present contest. The sentiment directly assailed and wounded in this rebellion is the sentiment of loyalty, of nationality, of allegiance to lawful authority ordained by God. The leading question to be decided is, whether we have a country or not. It is a question of government, or of no government; nay, it may be truth-fully stated in a stronger form than this. It is a question of the best kind of government—the most benign, just and liberal, in some respects the most favourable, of any to human development and progress, on the one hand; and, on the other hand, of a state of anarchy or of des-potism, bearing a closer resemblance than any other form of society to a hell on earth. This is our situation, and it leaves us but one alternative. The men who are lifting a parricidal hand against the country to which their filial reverence and love are due, profaning a divine ordinance, must be crushed in their criminal attempt to strike down, without provocation, and in the interest of slavery, an established and equitable government. We are fighting the battle of constitutional government for all races, not less than that of personal freedom for the coloured race; and we are entitled to the moral support and active sympathy of the friends of law and order, the lovers of well-regulated civil liberty, in all lands. We have been deeply pained by the countenance which the rebels have received · abroad from those from whom previous acts and professions led us to expect at their hands a very different treatment, and especially by the facilities which have been furnished in British ports for the fitting out of ships to cruise as pirates upon the high seas, under false colours, and prey upon our commerce; and we feel that the utmost efforts of the friends of peace in the two countries will be needed to adjust satisfactorily the international question which has thus sprung up between the two governments, and prevent pre-sent exasperation from ripening into open hostility. But

with reference to the single topic which you have kindly
brought before us, be assured, brethren, that we do not
mean to overlook, nor permit our rulers to disregard, the
righteous claims of our coloured brother—knowing that
the Republic, in this crisis, must find her salvation, under
God, in the spirit of liberty and equity, in which she had
her birth.

"In responding to the faithful appeals of our dear
brethren in Great Britain and France, it is pleasant to be
reminded of the strength of that spiritual bond which
unites us, belonging to different and distant nations, and
dwelling under different forms of government, in the sound
and refreshing fellowship of a kingdom which is not of this
world. With the reverend brother who comes among us
as your representative, bringing your Christian salutations,
we have formed a brief but delightful acquaintance, and we
bear a willing testimony to the happy influence of his
Christlike spirit and mission. Through him we send back
our fraternal greetings, addressing to our brethren across
the waters, in these troublous times, that exhortation of the
apostle which embraces us all as believers in Christ:—
'Wherefore we, receiving a kingdom which cannot be
moved, let us have grace whereby we may serve God
acceptably, with reverence and godly fear.'

"Wishing you grace, mercy, and peace, we remain,
beloved,

"Yours in the faith and fellowship of the Gospel,

"T. H. HAWKS, Chairman.

"CLEVELAND, OHIO, Sept. 14, 1863."

While I was anticipating the duties of the Sabbath a
gentleman kindly conveyed me about five miles into what
is called the Western Reserve, to the residence of a Frenchman, M. Mattithieu, who has cultivated an extensive vine-
yard, and has erected the apparatus necessary for making,
preserving, and bottling wine from the Catawba grape. I
tasted several of his casks. The best of his samples was
not unlike French Sauterne, but had, perhaps, more body.
His vines grew with great fertility and productiveness;
but I did not see in many houses any use of wine, European
or American. As I returned from this drive a telegraphic

message from New York was put into my hands, informing me of my brother, the Rev. Robert Massie's sudden death at Atherstone, in Warwickshire. He was a faithful and loving servant of a Divine and gracious Master, who had reserved for him in a better world his enduring reward. The shock was sudden, and was followed by partial and lingering indisposition to myself.

The route which I had to take, when starting from Cleveland for Pittsburg, was by towns and stations mingling, as names, Bedford and Macedonia, Ravenna and Lima, Winchester and Hanover, Salineville and Yellow Creek, New Salisbury and Wellsville, Liverpool and Rochester, Smith's Ferry and Industry, Economy, Sewickly and Alleghany. The distance is about 150 miles, and the country through which we pass is well peopled. Till we approach Alliance we pass through the Western Reserve, a district which belonged to one of the older states, but was allotted to Ohio in recent times. Ravenna has had trade in agricultural produce by canal with Pennsylvania. At Summitville and Salineville mineral wealth employs the capital and industry of multitudes. Coke and coal are here produced in abundance for the forge, the furnace, and the machine-shop. These places lie on a line of rail which serves as a connecting rod with two others, and hence delays at both terminations. From Yellow Creek and Wellsville the Ohio is in sight till we arrive in Alleghany city. The presence of this beautiful stream enlivens the journey, while the opposite banks are occupied by towns and villas seated in the midst of great variety, hill and dale, land and water.

As we approach the blazing furnaces and smoky chimneys around Pittsburg we have Birmingham, and Manchester, and Lawrenceville claiming notice. Above Pittsburg the rivers are designated by Indian names, the Alleghany and the Monongahela, the latter " the yellow

muddy," the former the "pure clear water." Below the
city they flow on united, cleared, and sparkling, the Ohio.
My space will not permit such descriptions as the scene
invites. The mineral wealth of the land, and the enterprise and manufacturing skill of the people, have been
developed with energy and success. While I was here the
son of the Duke of Newcastle and other travellers were
witnessing and admiring the productions in steel which
issued from the workshops. The city is situated on a
triangle, a point at the confluence of the two rivers. Alleghany city is on the opposite bank. Birmingham, to the
south side of the Monongahela, is a mile from the centre;
and Manchester is two miles below, on the Ohio. The
two cities by last census contained about 80,000, and no
doubt the other suburbs added will give 20,000 more.
This, however, is not the place for rest, only for work.
The first two nights I was here mosquitoes within, and
the rolling mills and fiery furnaces without, kept me vigilant till the sun rose. The smoke beyond the river, before
the Monongahela Hotel, did not invite the lover of the
picturesque. However, above the Alleghany river, there
are elegant residences on commanding situations. Here
are located the " Western Theological Seminary" of the
Presbyterian Church, the " Theological Seminary" of the
Associated Reformed Church, and the " Alleghany Theological Institute," the last organized in 1840, and the two
former in 1826 and 1827. I suppose there is more Presbyterial power in and around Pittsburg than in any similar
amount of population in the United States. Many residents here came in the early years of the century from the
north of Ireland and Scotland. The city was laid out in
1765 on the site of Fort Du Quesne, and the name was
afterwards changed to Fort Pitt. A large STATE mass meeting was held in a field beyond Alleghany City to receive
Governor Curtin, who stood as a candidate for re-election

during my visit. I had a conversation with him on my
mission, and I attended on the hustings during the early
proceedings of the public meeting; but I could not stand
the heat and pressure. The business was opened by a
long and evangelical prayer by Dr. Douglas. Pittsburg
looks as we pass along its populous streets like an antique,
industrious, well-doing town of the old country, but it shows
neither the rags nor the wretchedness of the Irish parts
of Glasgow. The churches are large and comfortable
places of worship. Preliminary arrangements were advertised for a meeting to receive my mission, in Dr. Paxton's
Church. A newspaper paragraph was afterwards sent to
me by Dr. Douglas, which details proceedings. I leave it
to introduce the response which followed. Other reports
appeared in several newspapers at Pittsburg, which,
through the courtesy of their editors, were also sent to
me. One of them I will place in the appendix.

"MINISTERS OF GREAT BRITAIN TO AMERICAN CHRISTIANS ON
THE SUBJECT OF SLAVERY.

"A meeting of members of different denominations of
Christians in Pittsburg and Alleghany was held in the
First Presbyterian Church (Dr. Paxton's) last evening, to
hear an 'Address to Ministers and Pastors of all Denominations throughout the States of America,' adopted by
an anti-slavery conference in Manchester, England, on the
3rd of June, 1863, in England, and sent to this country by
the hands of the Rev. Dr. Massie, of London. The Rev.
Dr. McKinney introduced the exercises by giving out a
portion of Psalmody, and leading in prayer at a throne of
grace.

"The Rev. John Douglas, D.D. then introduced Dr.
Massie in a few words, remarking that he was a man of
high moral character and social position—not a deputy
from the English nobility, nor an accredited ambassador
from the English government, but a representative from
the English *people*. He comes from the land of Wilberforce
and Clarkson, and filled with their spirit.

"Dr. Massie then delivered a very interesting address, in

which he showed that the masses of the working population of England sympathize with the United States Government in its present struggles.

"He cautioned the people of this country against believing the London 'Times' as the organ either of the English Government, or the English people. It speaks for itself. It would say black is white to-day, and to-morrow affirm that white is black, without giving any reason for its change of opinion At first the 'Times' said it was eminently proper for English ship-builders to construct ships to prey upon American commerce. Now it thinks it not altogether *moral*, because Americans may treat England in the same way at some future day.

"It is to be regretted that there was not timely notice given of the meeting, so that more of our citizens might have had an opportunity of hearing the admirable lecture of Dr. Massie, as well as the address of the Conference.

"At the conclusion of the address the meeting organized by calling General William Robinson, jun., to the chair, and appointing Dr. McKinney secretary.

"On motion of Rev. Mr. Smith the chairman was authorized to appoint a committee of five to prepare a response to the address. The chairman nominated the following: Rev. Dr. Douglas, Rev. Mr. Smith, Dr. Jacobus, Rev. Mr. Eells, and Dr. McKinney.

"On motion of Dr. Douglas, Rev. James Prestley, D.D., was added to the committee.

"The meeting then adjourned, Dr. Massie pronouncing the benediction."

REPLY TO THE ENGLISH AND FRENCH CLERGY.

"The committee appointed at the late meeting in Dr. Paxton's Church to prepare a reply to the Address of the Manchester Anti-Slavery Conference, suggested by addresses of 750 French and 4,008 English clergymen, have unanimously agreed to forward the following:—

"Reply of Ministers in Pittsburg and Alleghany to an 'Address to Ministers and Pastors of all Christian Denominations throughout the States of America,' from an Anti-Slavery Conference held in Manchester, England, June 3rd, 1863.

"REVEREND AND DEAR BRETHREN,—At a meeting of

ministers and members of different denominations of Christians convened in the First Presbyterian Church, Pittsburg, United States, on the evening of September 16th, 1863, to hear an 'Address to Ministers and Pastors of all Christian denominations throughout the States of America,' adopted by an 'Anti-Slavery Conference of Ministers of Religion,' held in the city of Manchester on the 3rd of June, 1863, and presented to the churches in these cities by the Rev. J. W. Massie, D.D., LL.D., the senior member of a deputation sent out for that purpose, the undersigned were appointed a Committee, to prepare and return a suitable reply.

"We most cordially reciprocate, dear brethren, the kind and fraternal sentiments expressed in your excellent Address, and join most heartily with you in your earnest denunciation of *American Slavery*, the prolific source—whatever may be the complications that have arisen in the meantime—of all those mighty agitations that are now convulsing our land, and threatening the very existence of our national life. We agree with you in the main, when you state that no other cause than that of human slavery has been assigned by the rebels themselves, for their revolt against their government. Their avowed object is to found a Confederacy, the 'corner-stone' of which shall be chattel-slavery, as it now exists in the South. Such an object, in the midst of all the evangelical light and civilization of the latter part of the nineteenth century, can meet with nothing but merited scorn and rebuke from every lover of Christianity, and the well-being of the human race.

"It has, therefore, been a matter of no little astonishment to us that in England especially, which claims the glory of being the first among the civilized nations of the world that abolished both slavery and the slave trade, and of having spent, within the last half century, two hundred and fifty millions of dollars in the general suppression of both—the cause of the slaveholders' rebellion—so much at variance with the genius and spirit of her free institutions—should have met with so much sympathy, if not support.

"We do not wish to argue the question here, but we have read history to no purpose if so hasty a concession of belligerent rights to insurrectionists and rebels against an organized and friendly government, endeavouring to maintain its traditional honour, prestige, and power, is not only unprecedented, but an anomaly in the annals of international comity and law.

"But we are still more astonished that, despite the friendly remonstrances of the United States Government, they should be allowed to construct and fit out, within the English realm, vessels for the purpose of preying upon our commerce, assailing us in the defence of Constitutional liberty, and aiding in the establishment of a despotic slave power.

"But amidst all this, it affords us no little gratification, dear brethren, to receive your words of sympathy and encouragement, and to know that you and kindred associations in Great Britain have earnestly protested to your government against those grievances and violations of international courtesy, of which we justly complain. This is as it should be; for, in pouring out the blood and treasure of our nation so profusely as we are now doing, we are not merely vindicating our traditional power and glory, but are subserving the cause of universal freedom throughout the world. We are happy to say that the blessings of civil and religious liberty are everywhere following in the path of our victorious armies. Under the favouring smiles of a righteous God, who executes just judgment for all that are oppressed, we have no fear of the final success of our government in suppressing this wicked rebellion; and with it must fall its hateful, debasing, and demoralizing inspiration.

"We can, most fervently and unfeignedly, unite with you in earnest prayer to the God of nations for the universal emancipation in his own time and way of the coloured race, and for the recognition of their claims to the rights of humanity.

"Your address has been greatly enhanced in our estimation, not only by the worthy brother (Dr. Massie) who presented it, and has been endearing himself to our people, wherever he has gone, by his Christian counsels and exhortations, but also from the fact that it is the offspring of two addresses on the same subject, signed respectively by 750 ministers in France, and 4008 ministers in Great Britain and Ireland.

"In conclusion, dear brethren, we assure you that it will be our constant care, and be esteemed our delightful province, to cultivate the most amicable relations with the Government and people of Great Britain, in all circumstances and occurrences which do not involve a compromise of the dignity and honour of our country; and it shall be our constant prayer that we may never be brought into deadly conflict with a nation to which we are so closely related by ties of kindred, lineage, and religion.

"Yours in the cause of Christ and humanity,

"JOHN DOUGLAS, chairman; DAVID McKINNEY, secretary; M. W. JACOBUS, J. M. SMITH, W. W. EELLS, JAMES PRESTLEY, Committee."

I returned again for a day to Cleveland, and again was welcomed by Mrs. and Mr. Hawks, in whose family circle I had continued to enjoy so much of unremitting and sedulous hospitality, the more especially as indisposition interfered with my freedom of intercourse. I left Cleveland by the Erie Railway by express in the afternoon, and was received by Dr. Heacock, in accordance with his kind arrangements previously made. The distance was 183 miles, but this was the most expeditious travelling I had had in America. We accomplished it in seven hours, passing at least thirty-five towns or stations on the route, including Euclid, Wickliffe, Geneva, Erie, Wesleyville, Quincey, Dunkirk, Silver Creek, Mile Creek, and Hamburg. I mention the number of stations, as showing the centres of population over this vast continent. However scattered they may be now, the anticipation is not a dream when a denser mass will inhabit these lands; and if stimulated by the spirit of the present age, the American nation will be powerful for good or evil. As pervaded by an enlightened religion, and leavened with the sympathy of many families whose roots are spread out in the mother country, it may be hoped their strength will be added to the power of Britain, speaking the same language, and inheriting the same principles of liberty and religion; and both animated by generous impulses for the welfare of mankind, their mutual prosperity will be a mutual joy, and a means of diffusing truth, liberty, and religion. 1 am again within the bounds of New York State, and have only rested here to complete what the resident ministers sought to persuade me to do before I should leave America.

The appointment had been locally made, before my arrival, that I should preach in the morning in the First Methodist Episcopal Church, and that there should be in the evening a united meeting in the Central Presbyterian Church. Ministers of all the Christian denominations were on the platform or around it in the church. The house was literally crammed, and I was assured hundreds went away, though the rain was falling in heavy showers at the time of service. I was rewarded for my desire and efforts to serve the cause of international peace and liberty. I find in one of the newspapers which followed me, a friendly notice of the two services, which will serve better than any description of mine. I left Buffalo with a heart full of love to the open-hearted and generous brethren who labour in word and doctrine. I learned from private intercourse to hold in admiration Drs. Walter Clark, Heacock, and Smith. My only regret is that it is not likely I shall ever be able to visit them again.

" In accordance with an arrangement made when Dr. Massie passed through our city a few weeks since, he spent last Sabbath with us. As is well known, he comes as the representative of the churches in England and France, to the churches of the United States, bearing a fraternal address from them, to us, expressive of their sympathy with us, in our loyalty and religion. Personally, Dr. Massie deserves the gratitude of the American public, for his deep and intelligent interest in our affairs, and for his earnest and continued labours to promote our cause in England and France. We are satisfied that if the loyal people of these states knew how much the Doctor has done for them, and at what cost of effort, time, and money,

U

they would give unmistakable manifestation of their high appreciation of his services. Dr. Massie has served us long and has served us well.

"On Sabbath morning Dr. Massie preached in the Grace Methodist Episcopal Church. His sermon was highly evangelical and profitable to those who heard. The subject was the 'Direct witness of the Holy Spirit to our personal acceptance as children of God.'

"In the evening, the Union meeting was held in the Central Presbyterian Church, to hear him in regard to his special mission. The house was filled. There were not less than *two thousand* persons assembled. It was really an imposing spectacle, one worthy of the occasion, and only worthy. For surely if European Christians take so deep an interest in our situation, as to send a delegate to express their regard, we ought to assemble in large numbers to hear.

"The Doctor spoke an hour and forty minutes. He recounted our national and Christian affinities with England—he acknowledged that there were those in England who did not sympathize with us in this struggle; belonging principally to the aristocracy and the 'apes of aristocracy' —he apologized for the errors of judgment in many of his countrymen because of their ignorance of our geography, our State Constitutions, and Federal Compact; the power of our President, and Commander-in-Chief of our armies; of our political parties and local interests. He warned us against accepting the "Standard" and "Times" as exponents of English opinion. He assured us of the sympathy of the working and middling classes, and of the Dissenting Christians, and gave instances perfectly convincing. He detailed the efforts of the 'Union and Emancipation Society' in forming public opinion, printing and circulating tracts and papers, containing facts and true issues connected with the rebellion, by public meetings and speeches, and the adoption of addresses and resolutions expressive of sympathy and approval of the cause of the North. He described the sufferings of the Lancashire operatives, 1,500,000 of whom had been more or less dependent upon the supply of cotton. Many had been reduced to naked beggary, and were fed from the poor rates, and yet refused to unite in asking their government to break the blockades. No, said they, the North is right, the South is wrong, and we will suffer on. He closed with an eloquent appeal, that we should be patient with England, not exacting, even where we had cause, but to strive to avoid a war between the two great Protestant nations of the earth, lest the enemies of God and man should triumph.

"The above is but a meagre sketch of the manly, generous, Christian, and eloquent address on the occasion. It must do good. Such addresses, delivered as they have been all over our country, must prove like oil on the troubled waters. The Doctor is now on his return to the seaboard, whence he will soon sail for his native land. May his voyage be prosperous, and his life long be spared for usefulness, and be brightened to its close by the recollections of his visit to his American brethren."

My journey was from Buffalo by sleeping car to Albany. I had declined this mode of travel previously, having an impression it would not be comfortable. In this I was mistaken; under the guidance of Dr. Heacock I went an hour before starting time and arranged for and occupied a double berth. There was, therefore, air and space, and I slept and rested till we approached Albany. I might have been even more composed and comfortable. I had not spent any time at Albany prior to this visit. I was surprised at its size, and disappointed at the want of enterprise and faith among certain prominent, I cannot call them leading men. The Rev. Mr. Bridgman, Baptist minister in the First Church of that denomination, had heard me at Rochester, and pressed me to come to Albany for a like purpose, making request I would come to his house, and write apprising him when my time drew near. I did write, and then he renewed his invitation to take up my abode at his house, but apprehended a week meeting would be a failure, and he would suggest a private meeting of ministers at his house as preferable. I replied by telegraph in time for Sunday notices, that I was willing to accept of any meeting, but should prefer one in which the

public would be interested.   I could not appropriate a
Sunday to Albany.

I found this city with a population, at last census, of
62,367, having increased nearly 12,000 since 1850.   It has
the Capitol, State Hall, City Hall, hospital, forty church
edifices, the Dudley Observatory, the University, with a
law department the best in the Union, a medical college, a
state normal school, the Albany Institute, the Young Men's
Association, and the Apprentice's Library, these three last
having between them 16,000 volumes; while the State
Library has 46,000 volumes.   There is one edifice in State
Street, where are deposited most interesting public collec-
tions in natural history, in geology, and in agriculture.
There is a large commerce maintained by the Hudson, the
Erie Canal, and the Champlain Canal, with every facility
for river and canal navigation.   The state legislature meets
here, and many public officers and prominent men in the
state reside in Albany.   Some kind of notification was
given that there would be a meeting in the First Baptist
Church.   I went and found a congregation of three hundred.   I pursued my usual course, modified my extempore
address to what I supposed the audience might require.
At the close, the postmaster, Mr. Dawson, who is also
editor of one of the most respectable local journals, Governor, or Judge Harris, who is, I think, Senator for the state,
and some others, came forward, expressing their extreme
regret that the notice had been so inefficient, and the
attendance so small; and urging that I should renew my
visit and repeat the same address.   I objected that already
I had delivered what, in substance, I must again speak, and
that I should feel as if the cream had already been taken
off, and it would afterwards be found very stale to them
who had already heard it.   Senator Harris answered, "I
could sit down and hear every word again *now*, and I should
like the whole to be delivered to members of Congress at

Washington." The next day the same subject was introduced by some of the office-bearers of another church, and I consented to endeavour to comply, if a reasonable effort were made to secure an attendance. But my ultimate engagements, prior to sailing for Europe, were so precisely fixed, that I could not defer on a contingency their due notification for other places. Thus Albany was the only city in which the mission was attempted and left incomplete. There was no response, though, I presume, some of the clergymen adhered to the answer adopted in the city of New York. I was much gratified by the tone and conduct of a prayer meeting I attended in the congregation of Dr. Palmer of the First Congregational Church. From him I received much kindness.

A letter from Dr. Thompson of New York, was received, inviting me to a meeting of the *General Association of New York*, to be held at Gloversville, about fifty miles up from Albany, beyond Fonda. The sessions were to continue for the week, and arrangements would be made for me to address the assembled ministers. I repaired by train to Fonda from Albany, and thence by coach along a picturesque road, and upon a timber track for a great part of the way. I reached the place about mid-day, and was introduced in due form by Dr. Thompson. The chairman, in the name of the association, welcomed me, and I listened with much interest to their discussion. The place of worship was an elegant country church; the assembled congregation consisted of members of the community living in the place, or who had come as delegates or visitors. The village and its vicinity were superior to any rural village in England, in the style of the houses, and in the verdure and shade of the trees which lined the roads and paths. I was told the population was 5000, and almost all, directly or indirectly, employed in or depending on the manufacture of gloves, which were cut up into shape and

sent out daily by horse conveyance; with thread, etc., to
the houses of the people, while the work of the previous
day was regularly brought to the warehouse by the same
messenger. I never attended a meeting in which my
sympathies were more enlisted, or in which, as participat-
ing the services, I felt more identified with all who were
engaged with me. I am glad to have a report which appeared in a New York paper, to embody here.

"The Rev. Doctor Massie of London was present during a part of two sessions of the above meeting.

"By invitation he stated the object of his visit to the
United States, and read a brief extract of the letter of
which he was the bearer. In the course of his remarks, in
language that touched every heart, and brought tears to
almost every eye, he described his life-long sympathy with
the United States, intensified by our struggle against a rebellion in behalf of slavery. His statement of the action of
the Manchester workmen in favour of the American Union,
and against any recognition of the slaveholders' proposed
Confederacy, or compromise therewith, notwithstanding
the continuance of the war was producing starvation
among them, produced deep feeling.

"At the close of Dr. Massie's address, the following
resolution was adopted :—

"'Resolved, that the Rev. Dr. Massie be requested to
accept for himself and his associate signers of the letter of
which he is the bearer, the assurances of our sincere esteem
and our pledge of co-operation with them for the preservation of fraternal feeling in behalf of Christianity and of personal and constitutional liberty.'

"Rev. H. G. Ludlow, who had been announced to preach
preparatory to the administration of the Lord's Supper,
arose and gracefully declined, as we had had, in Dr. Massie's discourse, an admirable preparation for the Communion. He requested that Dr. M. might take part in the
administration of the ordinance, which he did.

"After the 'Supper,' Dr. Thompson read the reply to
the address of the English brethren prepared by an assemblage of clergymen in New York. This was adopted by

the Association, and laid on the table for the signatures of the members, and others present."

I do not know, but there *might be* eighty ministers present, with delegates from all parts of the state of New York, and some who, by correspondence, were introduced from other states. All did not remain for the week, but the communion was large, and pervaded by a deep spirit of devotion. I determined to sail down the Hudson to New York by one of the magnificent steam vessels which regularly make the voyage as passage boats, and Mr. Bridgeman, who manifested great kindness, accompanied me to the ship; where an immense organ was played by the power of steam.

The sail down the Hudson is an ever-varying panorama on both banks. The river is majestic, and its shores, enriched with towns and villages. Garden walks and forest clumps, capped by distant mountains or nearer craggy heights, continually attract the admiration of the traveller. The numerous vessels, large and small, which pursue their watery highway, indicate the commercial wealth possessed by its traders. I might fill my page with names of the towns on either side, and in vain attempt to delineate the features of the Catskill peaks and ridges, from Mount Merino downwards to the highlands, their storm king, and Cronest,—

"Where Hudson's waves o'er silvery sands
  Wind through the hills afar,
And Cronest, like a monarch stands,
  Crowned with a single star."

West Point presents surpassing attractions beyond the fact that here the edifices of the United States' Military Academy stand in full view. It was established by Congress in 1802. From the ruins of fortresses on the loftiest summits the eye may from all points drink in an enchanting panorama of the river and country. Anthony's Nose, 1128 feet above the water, throws the Sugar Loaf into the shade.

Dunderburg's Mountain, and Peekskills Glen, and Verplank's Point, the portals of the lower gateway of the Hudson, warrant me to pause and transcribe the lines of Theodore Fay,—

" By wooded bluff we steal, by leaning lawn,
    By palace, village, cot, a sweet surprise,
At every turn the vision breaks upon,
    Till to our wandering and uplifted eyes,
The highland rocks and hills in solemn grandeur rise."

Verdritege's Hook and Sing Sing's hill-slope stand apart to give the Hudson the widest stretch of its course, four miles in width here. Irving's Sunnyside and Yonker's Villas indicate a nearer approach to the empire city; and Fort Washington and the Palisades stand by, while our steamer bangs her music with engine power, and draws toward her berth; where her passengers are landed.

I had telegraphed from *Hudson* to Orange Valley in New Jersey that I was on my way by water, but as I feared the steamer would be later than her time, I would travel express on my landing at Jersey city. I, therefore, started by the first train for Newark, and thence by horse conveyance to Orange. My arrival and proceedings are narrated in the following paragraphs :—

" THE ADDRESS OF DR. MASSIE.

" We noticed very briefly in our last week's issue, the visit of the Rev. Dr. Massie to Orange, and the address which he gave in the First Presbyterian Church on Tuesday evening of last week. A large and intelligent audience, including many clergymen of Orange and vicinity, assembled at the hour appointed, but were obliged to wait nearly an hour before Dr. Massie arrived, as he had been detained by the delay both of the steamboat and of the cars. A telegram was received from him and read by Rev. Mr. Bacon, and the audience with great patience and good nature determined to await the chances of his arrival, the interval being occupied with patriotic music by the choir,

and brief remarks by Rev. Mr. Hoyt and others. At half-
past eight, Rev. Dr. Massie entered the church, and was
greeted with cordial applause. Without waiting for refreshment, though greatly fatigued and exhausted, he was
at once introduced by Rev. Mr. Bacon, and for more than
an hour held the fixed attention of the audience, interrupted frequently by hearty manifestations of delight and
approbation. He showed that though the government of
Great Britain and a large part of the aristocratic class had
been unfriendly towards us in our present conflict, yet the
great heart of the English people, the working men, especially, was sound and right. Nothing in all the history of
the three past years has been more heroic than the patient
endurance of the people of Lancashire, as Dr. Massie described it; and the earnestness and vigour with which the
friends of the Union have defended and maintained the
cause of liberty and of the Republic, against many obstacles and bitter opposition was eloquently set forth. At the
close of his address, Dr. Massie read the letter signed by
upwards of four thousand ministers of all denominations,
and the message from the Anti-Slavery Conference, expressing their conviction of the iniquity of a Confederacy
based on slavery for its corner-stone, and their earnest wish
for its overthrow and for our success. Dr. Massie's visit
to America has done, we are assured, great good, and we
feel that the Christian public in this place owe him hearty
gratitude for the good words he has spoken to us.

"At the close of Dr. Massie's message, Rev. Mr. Hoyt
stated that at the request of several of the clergy an address
in response to the English message had been prepared by
Rev. Mr. Mulford, of South Orange, but that as the hour
was very late he was unwilling to read it, unless it should
be called for by the audience. The audience having unanimously voted to remain and listen to it, it was read as
follows :--

"'We have received the address signed by more than
4000 Ministers of the Gospel in England, and 750 in France,
through your representatives, the Rev. Drs. Massie and
Rylance.

"'We desire them to carry back to you the expression
of the deep and affectionate regard with which we listen to
your words of high cheer and sympathy.

"'We had learned to read alike in prophecy and in history, that though you were long separated from us in that free and living sympathy, you might yet be brought near in suffering and in struggle. Lancashire is not very far from Bristol. The roots of the system of American slavery reach beyond the sea. They are of an older growth than our history. They have gained sustenance from a foreign soil. We must bow together in the day of judgment that has broken upon it, in the "awful dawn" of battle fields.

"'But we receive your words, not as addressed to us, as individuals, but as the expression of a national sympathy. In that higher and wider issue which involves the sacrifice of the individual for the life of the nation, all other issues are gathered up. A nation is not an empire. To fight for a nation is not fighting for an empire. They who have learned from St. Paul, that "God has appointed the boundaries of all nations," will hold them reverently, and guard them steadfastly, and we need not say to you, after those years of battle, that the integral unity of the nation is written upon our hearts, in the lines of these mountains, and rivers, and hills.

"'And we have learned to read with deeper reverence those lessons of ancient political wisdom, whose application is not limited by centuries, as with the closest significance, the warning has been repeated for us, "say ye not a confederacy to all those to whom this people shall say a confederacy." For we have gone into battle, in ranks which bore its old ensigns for the nation's life, for its order and organic law, for the security of its capital, for the maintenance of its ordained succession of executive and legislative authority. And we have read with clearer light the words, not measured in the theories of modern political sciolism, "as the days of a tree, are the days of my people," for the worth and glory of a people has been derived not from its eradicating, but from its maintaining the works of its ancestors. The struggle has been with Confederate forces. The long strife which the prophets revealed has been repeated here, of unity and life with the principle of secession and the lord of division, of order with anarchy, of freedom with slavery, of Judea with Babylon, of a nation with a confederacy.

"'And we have learned more clearly and firmly to hold the nation's life as the gift of God, to rest in the ancient creed of prophets and heroes, that its origin is in God, and its calling from God. The only covenant that we have recognized has been the divine covenant with our fathers, sealed by years of blessing unto their children. The only compact has been of the generations that were with the generations that are and the generations that are to come in the transmission of a sacred and unimpaired heritage. And on battle-fields, where sleep our brothers and sons, mingling with the soil, that they have made for us more sacred, we have learned that in sacrifice is laid the life of nations, as is laid every form of divine life, and for them the words are verified, "He that loseth his life shall find it." Therefore do we reply to your words as those who though "sorrowful are always rejoicing." And the future rises fairer and clearer, for if we have learned with you that there can be no union without liberty, we have learned as well that deeper truth, that there can be no liberty without union. We may look, then, together, to the overthrow of all systems that are laid in falsehood and oppression, and for the coming of a civilization of social order and freedom, which is built upon that "foundation other than which no man can lay," and which rests not upon slavery as its corner-stone, but upon the corner-stone of the Divine Person, who for mankind gave his life to be crucified as a slave. In his kingdom we look for the glory of these nations to be gathered in, firm in the faith that in that kingdom no sacrifice laid upon the altar of the nation will be counted vain, and no battle fought for liberty and humanity, but will have been led by his confessors and martyrs.

"'Again we thank you for your words of cheer and sympathy sent to us in the nation's struggle. We look alike to the coming of a kingdom into which we have striven to bear the nation's glory. We acknowledge no security save in righteousness. We trust in the maintenance of peace, and as we believe that to be alone the fruit of righteousness we would make earnest our closing words. There is no court for the decision of international law but the arbitrament of Christian public opinion. The bond, not of local, nor of civil, nor of municipal law, is the foundation of peace between nations, but the bond of righteousness. And words of sympathy, however deep and noble, must seem those of few and solitary men, when the message of our success or disaster shall be borne back by the "Florida," or "Alabama," or ships that sail from Liverpool.

" 'With you may we strive for the things that make for peace. We stand together in the brotherhood of Christ. We rejoice in the communion of saints. In the union of that brotherhood, and with the prayer that we may work together in the elect purposes of that communion,

" 'We are yours,

" ' E. Mulford, James Hoyt, F. A. Adams, Geo. B. Bacon, Jas. S. Bush, Geo. E. Horr, B. F. Barrett, John Crowell.'

" The exercises were then closed by a fervent prayer of benediction from the Rev. Dr. Massie."

At Orange Valley I received a telegraphic message, intimating that my friend Dr. Thompson had promised I would take a service in Jersey City on Sunday morning. I obeyed the summons, and, as I was expected, directed my discourse to the object of my mission, and offered the substance of my message to a large and patriotic assembly in the Congregational Tabernacle. I was here, as I had been in Orange Valley, most hospitably entertained. I shall remember the household kindnesses of Mr. and Mrs. G. B. Bacon, and the Hon. Mr. Gregory and his numerous family. Once more I could not resist the importunities of the Rev. W. B. Brown and his friends in Newark, and, in compliance, attended at an immense congregation assembled there to honour my mission and hear my message. I consented the more readily to this additional service, as Newark is a city of more than 70,000 inhabitants, and New Jersey is widely leavened with sympathy toward the Southerns. Among them a large portion of its manufacturing trade was formerly conducted; and although accounts were repudiated at the beginning of the rebellion, who knows, if the rebel states were restored, but they would remember

their friends and repay their losses? When my address
was concluded, a response was presented in the following
language :—

"NEWARK, NEW JERSEY, *October* 2, 1863.

"REVEREND AND DEAR BROTHER,—Your mission to us as
bearer of the 'Address to Ministers and Pastors of all
denominations throughout the States of America,' founded
upon addresses from ministers and pastors in France and
Great Britain, is heartily welcomed, and its words of kindness and its spirit of true Christian sympathy are heartily
reciprocated.

"The high character of the gentlemen who are deputed
to bear the address to us, on behalf of their brethren, *alone*
entitle it to respectful consideration. But when we find
affixed to the accompanying documents the signatures of
4000 ministers of all denominations in Great Britain, and
750 pastors in France, it comes with greatly-increased
claims to our regard.

"We thank you for your sympathy with us in the time
of our trials, and hope and pray with you that the result
of the struggle in which we are engaged may be the utter
and final extinction of that great system of human
bondage which has so long cursed our country and disgraced the Christianity of the age in which we live—the
legitimate results of which have culminated in the present
terrible conflict that convulses our beloved country.

"We agree with you (using your own words) 'that no
darker nor more dreary calamity could threaten any nation
or people on earth, than the successful establishment of a
Republic, whose corner-stone is the slavery of the working
man.'

"No language can adequately convey our detestation
of the system in its causes and effects, and in all its relations, socially and politically. We confidently anticipate
its speedy destruction as an inevitable incident of the war,
and hail the expected result with joy, and bless and recognize God's hand in it.

"But our struggle is for the *nation's life* against a
parricidal hand, and to maintain our existence as a people.
We think, moreover, that our contest is the common cause
of a true civilization and of humanity itself. Every vir-

tuous and every pious principle of our bosoms is arrayed in
this conflict, and we see no proper termination than that of
the entire restoration of the integrity of the Union, and
the complete vindication of the injured majesty of law.
Our religion and our philanthropy mark out for us this clear
line of conduct.

"We consider that on the issue of this contest depend the
cause of human liberty everywhere, and obedience to Constitutional law, and interests that involve the whole family
of man.   We have no fear, under God, of the final result.

"We thank you for the word of encouragement uttered
in our ears, and for the assurance of the good wishes of
the wise and virtuous of mankind.   We joyfully join
hands with our beloved Christian brethren of other nations
in foreign lands, and unitedly pray that our peace with
them may never be broken ; and in order to this, that we
may ever cultivate right sentiments of international justice
and comity, and feelings of mutual kindness and goodwill,
and look forward to the time when a practical Christianity
shall diffuse the blessings of peace everywhere, and the
sceptre of Messiah be swayed over all the earth.

"WILLIAM B. BROWN, of the Congregational Church and
Secretary of the Meeting ; R. B. CAMPFIELD, Chairman ;
Robert Atkinson, North Baptist Church ; M. E. Ellison, of
the Methodist Evangelical Church ; J. T. Crane, of the
Methodist Evangelical Church ; Samuel Hutchings, of the
Presbyterian Church; Henry Clay Fish, First Baptist Church;
Samuel H. Hall, Pastor Presbyterian Church, Oswego,
New York ; E. A. Osborne, of the Presbyterian Church ;
J. Few Smith, Pastor Second Presbyterian Church ; James
P. Wilson, Pastor of South Park Church ; Isaac M'Ilvaine,
Chaplain ; John Kitchill ; S. S. Hughson, New York ;
Robert H. Tozer, Naples, New York ; E. M. Griffith, of the
Methodist Evangelical Church ; Edgar M. Levy, Pastor of
the South Baptist Church, Newark, New Jersey, formerly of
the State of Georgia ; John C. Eccleston, Rector of Trinity
Church, Newark ; James M. Tuttle ; H. Harris ; Benjamin
C. Dutcher."

My mission had been directed to ministers and pastors
in the United States ; but I had, in all the principal cities,
seen gather round me gentlemen in commercial, and offi-

cial, as well as professional stations of society. I had met them occasionally as members of the Union League, and was indebted to the co-operation and countenance of such friends of this country in arrangements and facilities prepared for my journey. Many of them had, without intercourse with myself, cherished a warm sympathy in the events of my progress. It was repeatedly suggested that a visit to the Union League Club, at their club rooms, would be gratifying. I expressed a readiness to attend, the only evening I had free, the 1st of October. In several papers of that morning a paragraph appeared, intimating to the members that such an arrangement had been made. I dined that day with one of the members, who escorted me to the " Rooms." There were from a hundred to a hundred and fifty present. The club was called to order, and Jonathan Sturges, Esq., vice-president, in the absence of the president, then an invalid, took the chair. He introduced me, and then invited me to give some account of my mission and impressions as I had passed through the States. I spoke about an hour, detailing my progress and describing my general reception. The chairman then requested the Rev. Asa D. Smith, D.D., President elect of Dartmouth College, to make the acknowledgments of the club to me. Dr. Smith's cordial personal friendship prompted many kind words in commendation of my services; and then, in the name of the members of the club, he assured me that there were present mercantile and professional gentlemen of the most eminent firms and positions in the community; and that they were resolved, at the most costly sacrifice, to maintain the present conflict until rebellion and slavery were buried in the same tomb. The chairman rose and confirmed this sentiment by calling for *three cheers*, which were given with the most demonstrative effect. At the close, a resolution was presented to me, signed by chairman and secretary, in the following terms :—

" At a meeting of the ' Union League Club' of the city
of New York, held at the club rooms, Thursday evening,
October 1, 1863, for the purpose of receiving James W.
Massie, D.D., LL.D., the following resolutions were unanimously adopted :—

" *Resolved*, That.the thanks of the Union League Club
are due, and are hereby most cordially tendered, to James
W. Massie, D.D., LL.D., of England, for the eloquent and
instructive address delivered by him this evening.

" *Resolved*, That the Union League Club do most heartily
approve of the objects, for the attainment of which Doctor
Massie was induced to visit the United States of America.

" Jon. STURGES, *Vice-President.*
OH. D. SWAN, *Secretary.*"

Though the meeting at Newark was held on the 2nd of
October, the evening before I sailed from New York, the
service in the Tabernacle, Broadway, was designed as my
farewell to the friends of my mission ; other friends, too,
besides those present were debarred by previous engagements and the want of precise information, from giving
their presence and co-operation. Among these was Dr.
Tyng, Rector of St. George's. He wrote a letter of explanation ; and, as from the beginning he was so heartily
identified in my success, I give it a place, as a preliminary
to the report from the pen of Dr. J. P. Thompson, which
appeared in the " Patriot" of London, Thursday, October
22nd, 1863.

" ST. GEORGE's RECTORY, *September* 29, 1863.

" THE REV. JAMES W. MASSIE, D.D.

" REVEREND AND DEAR FRIEND,—The meeting held on
Sunday evening was without my previous knowledge, and
unnoticed by me, until it was too late for me to make any
arrangement to attend it.

" It would have given me pleasure to have expressed
in public the cordial feeling with which I welcomed your
whole mission, and the sincere respect which I have learned
to cherish for you, in your personal fulfilment of it.

"Though I cordially agreed to the reply which you carry with you from New York, adopted by the meeting of ministers, and read on Sunday evening last, you well know that I should have desired to welcome your mission in much more emphatic terms of brotherly love, and to have expressed in a reply a much more distinct estimation of the earnest faithfulness which prompted the address brought by you, and of the interest and effort from which it proceeded.

"I trust your own observations will have tended to impress you with the conviction that the people of the United States will never consent again to yield their territory to the acknowledged dominion of slavery, whatever may be the cost of life or treasure which shall be required to prevent it.

"If it be only by a prolonged contest that we can secure and maintain an universal and established freedom in our land, then must we fight until this triumph be obtained. Neither the Southern rebellion nor European intervention in any form, will ever be permitted to force upon us the acknowledgment of the renewed rule of slavery, until, as a people, we shall be impoverished and overcome beyond the power of farther resistance.

"I trust that our English and French brethren will be made to realize through your accurate expositions, the fact that however we may have been misrepresented and maligned in this contest, we are perfectly sincere in our determination, never to yield it until this great end has been attained, or ourselves have been destroyed.

"I trust our gracious Lord will carry you, my dear friend, safely to your home, and make your remembrance of your visit among us as agreeable and encouraging.

"I am, with very great respect,
"My dear Dr. Massie,
"Your friend and brother in the Lord,
"STEPHEN H. TYNG."

THE REV. DR. MASSIE'S VISIT TO AMERICA.

To the Editor of the "Patriot."

"SIR,—Our honoured guest, Rev. J. W. Massie, D.D., the representative of British sympathies with our national cause, leaves us to-day after an extensive and highly-favoured tour in the Northern and Western states. Dr. Massie arrived in New York at a time the most inopportune for his object—just as our citizens were scattering to their country retreats, when, too, a great battle was impending in Pennsylvania, and when the air was again full of rumours of British recognition of the Southern slave-drivers as an independent power. There was hardly anybody here of our representative citizens to greet such an embassy, and the public mind was intensely preoccupied with domestic affairs, and particularly sensitive toward England. But Dr. Massie's good sense and tact, and his kindly spirit, did much to overcome the latter obstacle, while the readiness of Christian ministers to promote international peace and to reciprocate fraternal courtesies in a measure obviated the former.

"Dr. Massie having laid his object privately before Drs. S. H. Tyng, of the Episcopal Church; A. D. Smith, of the Presbyterian; and J. P. Thompson, Congregationalist; a large and influential meeting of ministers was promptly convened by those gentlemen, at which the address of the Manchester Conference was formally received, and a suitable reply was adopted. This reply has since been signed by a large number of ministers, chiefly of the State of New York, and distinct replies have been adopted in Boston, Cleveland, and other places visited by your delegate.

"Dr. Massie was introduced to the Christian public of New York in my own church, the Broadway Tabernacle, on the evening of July 5, and was cordially received by a large assembly. He preached also in two or three other churches during his first sojourn in the city. Since then he has visited Washington, Philadelphia, Boston, Portland, Worcester, Springfield, Providence, Hartford, New Haven, indeed, nearly all the leading towns of New England, and has extended his tour westward to Albany, Rochester, Buffalo, Pittsburgh, Cleveland, Cincinnati, Chicago, St. Louis, and Louisville, the last two towns being in slave states, or rather, states now in transition from slavery to freedom.

"What observations Dr. Massie has made upon our country and its institutions in this wide survey, and what opinions he has formed concerning us and our cause, he may well be trusted to report with his own lips. I doubt not that he has observed with discrimination and has judged with candour, and that in all he may deem it his duty to say of us as a people, in this grave crisis of our affairs, the law of Christian kindness will govern his speech. He will not disguise from you the fact that while he has been everywhere received with courtesy, and his mission has been entertained with favour, he has found among our best citizens not a popular political rancour against England, not a reckless tone of belligerance, but a feeling of disappointment and sorrow that the freest nation of Europe, allied to us by language, by religion, by history, and by institutional liberty, should have been so backward to appreciate our cause, and so willing to let her moral influence slide into the scale of rebellion against free government in the sole interest of slavery. It is well that Englishmen should understand what I am sure Dr. Massie now fully understands—that England has lost immeasurably in moral *prestige* in the view of American Christians.

"Only yesterday, New York rendered to the officers of the Russian fleet now in our harbour a civic and popular ovation like that rendered to the Prince of Wales. This was done with right good-will and for a purpose; for Russia, autocratic Russia, has been more just, honourable, and friendly in her attitude toward our national Government than has constitutional England or our ancient ally, France. The popular feeling in our loyal states is far more cordial toward Russia than toward England. The reasons for this Englishmen should not blindly overlook. The fact itself they cannot afford to ignore. Dr Massie can shed some light upon it. At the same time he can assure you that there is a general disposition in this country to cultivate amicable relations with Great Britain, and even to study the things that make for peace. The visit of Dr. Massie has had a happy influence in this direction. His frank, intelligent, and earnest sympathy with our cause, not only in its anti-slavery aspects, but in its wider relations to that constitutional liberty which Englishmen ought to value no less than we, his candour in condemning the violations of neutrality by British ship-builders, the pro-slavery tendencies of some of your public men and leading journals, and the apostasy of many Englishmen from the anti-slavery faith of their fathers, together with his uniform kindness of heart and warmth of Christian fellowship, have won for his 'mission, and for the England which that represents, the respect and confidence of a wide circle of Christians in America. It is due, also, to Dr. Massie to say that he has borne himself everywhere as a true Englishman; that he has spoken no word here that will not bear to be published at home; that he has been particularly careful not to compromise his constituents by his individual opinions, and not to mingle the object of his mission with any minor political, ecclesiastical, or reformatory measures, or with any partisan characters among ourselves. Having heard him upon several occasions, I can truly say that no one could have carried himself with more dignity, prudence, suavity, and integrity than has this ambassador of the Manchester Conference.

"On last Sabbath evening a farewell service for Dr. Massie was held at the Broadway Tabernacle Church, in which several ministers of different denominations participated. This is the largest church edifice in the city, with the exception of St. George's (Rev. Dr. Tyng's), and every nook and cranny of the building was occupied. Hundreds went away unable to gain admittance, and hundreds stood patiently in the aisles and the vestibule throughout a service of three hours. The tone of the meeting for liberty to mankind, for fraternity with England, for fellowship with all good and true men in Christ's work, would have warmed and cheered your hearts. I queried whether so respectful, so cordial, so sympathetic a hearing would have been accorded to an American speaking freely of our affairs in your Congregational Union as was there accorded to Dr. Massie, in spite of piratical British cruisers and British rebel rams. As the proceedings of this meeting will soon be published in pamphlet form, I forbear any detailed report."

CHAPTER VII.

THE COLOURED PEOPLE—PREJUDICES AGAINST COLOUR IN THE NORTH—RIOTS IN NEW YORK, JULY, 1863.

We have here a subject replete with interest to the philosophical and philanthropic statesman or scholar. International polity and physiology are alike concerned in the practical conclusion. The sympathies and rights, divinely bestowed on the negro as on every child of the human family, are equally embraced. When I first proposed to myself the *heading* of this chapter, all that it involves did not present itself. The international destiny, the reproduction and final *habitans* of this people, often recurred in my converse with Americans; and I am not prepared yet to dismiss the inquiry, as if I had settled the problem. In the Northern States there has been a strong prejudice against people of colour. There still remains a lingering, though I hope diminishing, sympathy with that prejudice. In England, the prejudice is as strong. Except where slavery presents to the coloured person licentious allurements and facilities, or a temptation to claim kindred with the dominant race, there may be an equal repugnance to the pale-faced alliance in pure coloured people. It is not probable that the one will ever absorb the other, and it is not in Christianity or ethics to desire a war of races for the utter extinction of one of them. There are more coloured people than palefaces on the earth, and the lands where coloured nations are aboriginal are more adapted to their constitution and habits than to other tribes. Northern latitudes and colder regions, whether for labour or for health, are less congenial and desired to those of fleecy hair and dark complexion.

Four hundred thousand, perhaps, may have been acclimatized in the free states, but the families of these free coloured people do not perceptibly increase. The adults do not reach an old age generally, and their offspring often suffer from bronchial diseases, from phthisis and scrofula. They are attached to the North because it is a *free soil*, not because they find its climate genial. Yet would it be a violation of human rights were the legislatures of these states to decree for them involuntary exile, or, as has been done by some of them, to disfranchise and brand them with any discriminating disqualification. The feeling of persecution, because of a law of their Creator, should not be engendered in the white man's breast, nor suggested in the coloured man's experience. It is well, therefore, that the colonization theory, proposed in President Lincoln's former Message, has not further been agitated, or revived for consideration.

Besides those hundreds of thousands who *were* free coloured, of whom we have spoken, there are the four millions who have been slaves, and whose birthplaces have been in the South. Few, indeed, of those living, now know any other land. They cannot be transported. Their progeny every year, in life statistics, should be *sixty thousand*. One hundred and twenty ship loads for transport every year! leaving the four millions behind. But the coloured race is necessary in the South, not as *slaves*, though they may prove free labourers. For the past two hundred years they have been the productive force. There is no other element prepared to take their place, and were it possible to abstract it from the country, it would only add poverty and ruin to the community. In other lands the scheme was tried to remove obnoxious labourers, and

the exiled carried the wealth of labour to other lands, and
left ruin behind them, as when the Moors were driven
from Castile, and the Huguenots were murdered or
banished from France. The native born coloured people
are needed in the South, and natural laws over-ride all
temporary expedients. They have done the work even by
a vicious system, they can do it much better by a healthy
and natural organization; and, therefore, the power of an
economic necessity will enforce their permanent settlement
as freemen.

Does the fact of colour and constitutional congeniality
with a warm atmosphere, include the inferiority of the race
and its impossibility of ever living on an equality with the
white ? Would it suffice as answer for the African negro,
or the Southern brahmin, to reason from similar premises
vice versa? An eloquent writer from Delaware has concluded that it is " impossible that the two races can ever
abide on that continent on terms of equality." He says
this without meaning to be an enemy to the negro. He
does not press emigration, and yet *his* America is not to be
the ultimate home of the coloured race. They are to *go*
out from it. He finds something in the character of the
African race, which "*perhaps*" renders this probable. His
idea is that " in the strange workings of Divine Providence
this race has in a marvellous manner been brought to this
land (America), and put under a tutelage for a great future ;
and that Africa, its home, may become the recipient of
blessings, the foundation and preparation for which were
made in this country." He pursues a parallel in *the
Egyptian bondage of Israel, and the American bondage of the
negro,* the *destiny* of Israel and the negro. He explores
Africa and finds many *lands* of promise there, and spheres
of Christian enterprise in which the American negro is to
engage. I think it is possible that there may be work of
this kind for hundreds, or even a thousand, but other

thousands will rise in their stead. I am more attracted by his generous defence of the negro characteristics as they may be developed in a state of freedom, which is herewith presented somewhat abridged.

"The world has always seen the African race in its lowest form. This seems true as far back as Egyptian monumental times. One is struck, when looking at copies of ancient hieroglyphics, with the degraded type of negro feature which always appears when these captive people are delineated. The African race seems under human policy to have been fated to be always represented by a slave, and, as was inevitable, it has been judged by the example seen. But the researches of travellers have of late compelled us to reverse many, if not all these conceptions. Africa gives us, indeed, perhaps the lowest types of humanity in the Bushman or Hottentot, yet the explorations of travellers have also shown these are not the true and normal examples of the African stock. It can readily be seen that wherever the African character is measured by the standard of an African slave, the judgment must necessarily be an erroneous one. The best tribes are not, in the nature of things, those out of which slaves are made. War and conquest are the fruitful sources of slavery! But the abler tribes are the warriors and the conquerors, while the weaker and the lower are the captives. Thus at the outset the slave declares by the fact of his servitude his inferiority of lineage. To this we are also to add the pretty well-known fact that the poorest of these captives are those who come into the hands of the slave-dealer on the coast, while the better made and the more intelligent are reserved for the service of their captors. Thus, with this further reduction, you have in the African as he comes to the slave-ship the lowest specimen of an inferior type of his people. But just these have been the exponents of the African race, and it is not only not surprising, but entirely natural that a false estimate should have been made of the whole negro family.

"What we would infer, the explorations of recent travellers show to be actually the case. We might refer to the Kaffirs in the south, close upon the regions where the Hottentot is found, a race of stalwart and noble men, who have had skill and bravery enough to resist the power of the Dutch, and even to wage a determined war with the English power itself. To the east of these Dr. Lindley, one of the missionaries of the American Board found tribes among whom he lived for a quarter of a century, and whom he describes as being physically inferior to no race, the men in some districts averaging nearly six feet in height. 'They might be called stupid,' says Livingstone, (p. 21), speaking of Bakwains, a people with whom he was much associated in South Africa, in 'matters which had not come within the sphere of their own observation, but in other things they showed more intelligence than is to be met with in our own uneducated peasantry.' Two of the missionaries of the American Board, Messrs. Preston and Adams, speaking of a visit to the Pangwees, a tribe of people living just under the Equator and back from the coast, and who are described by other writers as an every way superior race, tell us of natives whom they saw from places still further inland 'which we had heard of, but as yet had been unable to reach.' 'The variety,' say they, 'of complexion presented to us was quite an object of curiosity. Some were of a jet black, others with their braids of soft black hair, one and a half or two feet in length, might be easily taken for quadroons.' The 'New American Encyclopædia' treating of the Mandingoes, says : 'They are remarkable for their industry ; they are mostly Mohammedans. The principal trade of that part of West Africa which lies between the equator and the great desert is in their hands. They are not only active and shrewd merchants, but industrious agriculturists, and breeders of good stock of cattle, sheep, and goats. They are black in colour, tall, well-shaped, with regular features and woolly hair. In character they are amiable, hospitable, imaginative, credulous, truthful, fond of music, dancing, and poetry. They are adventurous travellers, extending their commercial journeys over a greater part of Africa. The Mandingoes are the most numerous race of West Africa, and have spread themselves to a great distance from their original seat, being found all over the valleys of the Gambia, Senegal, and Niger.' Such quotations and testimonies demonstrate the fact that there are superior races of men in Africa, that these are even the charac-

teristic races of the continent. Every new discovery
exhibits this more clearly.

"Though the negro of this country may not be of the
best races of Africa, yet he is not of the worst, and has had
influences exerted, both as to race and character, which
much more than compensate for any possible inferiority of
descent. We may fairly take the estimate of the native
African as we find him at his best estate at home, and
build a promise of the future of the African here upon it.
The African character has its own marked and distinctive
peculiarities. It is tropical. It has passion deep and per-
vasive, slumbering within a rounded form and in deep,
dreamy eyes. It is ductile and plastic, ready to receive
impressions, and to be shapen by them. It does not possess
the hard, aggressive features of the character of the tribes of
Northern Europe; it does not seek by conquest to extend
its power, or to mould other people to its form. It is
adapted to receive rather than to give. It is therefore
essentially imitative. From this comes the rapidity with
which, under favourable circumstances, the African
advances in civilization yields to them with marvellous
rapidity.

"There is, perhaps, no race that gives up so readily and
fully old habits and associations. We find no granite
formations of character underlying the race, such as are
met with in the tribes and peoples of Asia. Compare, for
instance, the plastic mobility of the Pangwee and Bakwain
with the rigidity of the Hindoo or Chinese. Or, where the
case may be seen in even a more striking way, compare the
African negro with the American Indian; take the one
from his tropical wilds, the other from his forest home, and
place them both under the same civilizing influences, and
in a single generation the one is nearly at your side, the
other is simply a savage still. The rapid rise of the negro
race in the West India Islands, Jamaica, for example,
when made free by the British Government, is an illustration,
though the time has been too short to bring it out to the
full. Taking all the facts as they are given us, we find the
people rising almost at once (for thirty years are usually as
nothing in the life of a people), out of the barbarism of
slavery into a nation self-supporting, self-governing to a
considerable extent, moral and religious; not, indeed, in

the highest degree, but still wonderfully advanced. Sewell's 'West Indies, or the Ordeal of Free Labour in the British West India Islands' presents an evidently dispassionate and disinterested view of the condition of these islands. An attentive consideration of his statements would go far to relieve the matter of emancipation of some of the difficulties with which to many it seems environed. 'These people,' he remarks, 'who live comfortably and independently, own houses and stock, pay taxes and poll votes, and pay their money to build churches, are the same people whom we have heard represented as idle, worthless fellows, obstinately opposed to work, and ready to live on an orange or banana rather than earn their daily bread.'

"Together with this plastic docility the African has another characteristic—the race has a peculiar power of resistance and permanence. It is said that no race has ever been able to abide a close contact with the Anglo-Saxon. One of two results has always followed,—either it has been swallowed up and lost as a river in an ocean, or it has gone down and been swept away. But this race has neither been absorbed nor destroyed. It has grown under the most adverse influences, and asserts itself in all its peculiar characteristics under foreign skies, and after the lapse of two centuries the negro of America is a true African still. This race has not greatly mingled with other races. It is rather a characteristic of it not to seek an amalgamation with another people, its tendency is to remain apart. We are well aware, indeed, that this is exactly contrary to the views of many who have built their opinions on popular assertions and prejudice rather than on observed facts. The assumption is that the negro desires to mingle his blood with that of the white races. The reverse is the fact. There is, though it may seem to some unaccountable, a certain pride of race which leads the negro to exult in the purity of his blood, and to regard a foreign element in it as not only not desirable, but even objectionable. This feeling does not belong simply to the negro on his own continent; it perpetuates, perhaps magnifies itself when surrounded by another people. Among them in this country a pure-blooded negro will, with biting sarcasm, taunt the mulatto with the fact that the blood of another race is in his veins. This feeling leads the race to remain by itself; and when left to its natural course, such is the result. The statistics of this country show that the free black does not mingle with the white race; no elevation or freedom can popularize such an inter-mixture. Here and there, but so seldom as to present but, perhaps, a single case only in widely-separated communi-ties, there is an inter-marriage. This seeming want of inclination, coupled with a repugnance on the part of the white, must ever keep the two races apart when they stand on an equal footing of freedom.

"The often repeated argument against emancipation, founded on the notion that it would be necessarily followed by amalgamation, is the product of the grossest ignorance and thoughtlessness, while at the same time it betrays a shameful want of confidence in the white race itself. It surely argues no great power or stability in a people when they are not able to keep themselves from being mixed up with a proverbially inferior race. But facts point in a wholly different direction: so far from freedom promoting this intermixture, the only condition in which these two races are found mingling is where the negro is in a state of servitude. Here the process goes on freely, and under the working of natural causes. The influences which on either side under other circumstances make it infrequent, here become inoperative, and are overborne by other and more powerful ones. The close intimacies, beginning with infancy and extending over the whole life, destroying what under other circumstances might seem to be a natural separation; a servile desire to please on the part of the slave, lust and cupidity on the part of the master—all combine to make the blood of the two races flow in the same veins. Slavery is the source of amalgamation. The mulatto and the quadroon tell you unerringly of a present or a former servitude.

"With this pliant ductility and this permanence of race there is another striking characteristic—the negro's attach-ment to place. It is probably a natural trait, but from easily perceived causes it is perhaps intensified in the case of the American negro. He loves his home, and seldom goes willingly away from it, whether slave or free. The number of fugitives from bondage would be prodigiously multiplied were this feeling more easily overcome. Many a poor bondman has turned back to slavery when the hard alternative has been forced upon him to remain in it or go for ever away from the familiar and dear scenes of his childhood's home. It is a necessity scarcely less powerful than death that compels him to leave them behind. The efforts which philanthropy has made to promote their colonization have met with an insuperable obstacle here, and will be compelled to contend, more or less unsuccessfully with it, till there shall be strength and education enough given the black to rise above it. Among the many objections which have been urged against emancipation, this has been a very common one, and has had great force in the popular mind,—it will flood the Northern States with free *blacks. The objection is vulgar and thoughtless; if the simple economic law of supply and demand, as powerful over men as material, were not sufficient to keep this people where they are needed, and to prevent them from going where they are not, the love of home would be strong enough to bar such a result. The slave needs all the mighty stimulus of a prospective deliverance from slavery to induce him to leave the place of his birth, and that even is often not enough; why, then, when he has that boon in his hand, and walks the old haunts a free man, with work requited and enough, why should he now go away to strangers and a strange land? No, the States which have meanly and disgracefully passed their laws excluding the freed black from a home within their borders, might have spared themselves the dishonour. The dreaded calamity would never have occurred.

"The effect of emancipation will be the reverse of this fear; the free blacks of the North will gradually go South; in place of Northern states being overrun with the one, they will, in process of time, be stripped of the other. With slavery out of the way, the black will naturally bend his steps to the region where climate, congenial employment, habits, associations, all welcome him; he will go away from a people who do not understand him, and whose prejudices keep him down, to be near a people who have grown up with him, who know him, and are better able to do him good. This consolidation of the race in one part of the land will have an important bearing on its future. Emancipation only will fully accomplish it.

"Passing these characteristics, common to the race both in Africa and in this country, let us consider others, which have been superadded by the residence of the negro in America. These are marked and important. Strangely enough, one of the marked effects of the residence of the black in this country has been to give a new and foreign element to the mental and physical structure of the negro. It has created an admixture of blood with a superior race. The natural effect of slavery has been to infuse the best blood of the master in the veins of the slave. This fact has not, perhaps, received the attention which it deserves as having an influence upon the future of the negro race. We do not speak of it in the way of sarcasm or reproach, but as something which, while it cannot be concealed or denied, ought not to be overlooked. It cannot be when the coming history of this people is under consideration.

"The intermingling of race has been extensive; so much so, that in many places the pure-blooded negro is in the minority of the whole coloured population. Here is not the place to make any extended observations on the intellectual and physiological effects of the union of different races in the same people, to elevate and give them tone and character. The facts are very familiar. We can see that in the case before us these effects will be of the same general character. In the new social order which will come into being on the abolition of slavery, this intermixture of race will be less and less frequent, but what has already taken place will tend greatly to hasten the elevation and advancement of the black. The energy, the fire, and activity, the ingenuity and perseverance of the Anglo-Saxon, joined to the plastic docility of the African, is a strange combination, yet one which may be seen every day, and which when made free and permitted to exert its unrestrained power, will be of unmeasured value. The mulatto makes a very bad slave, but will be a noble freed man.

"It need not be a perpetuated intermingling of race. It will not be when slavery has gone, and it is well. Physically the mulattoes are a feeble people, and destined usually to an early death ; nor are they prolific. By the force of merely natural causes, in process of time, they will almost wholly disappear. The immobility of the race will assert itself. But in the meanwhile they will have done their work in assisting the rise of their brethren. It is a force imparted for a special occasion, strangely given, but not in vain. It is a spoil taken from the enemy, one of the marvellous instances in which human passions and crime go to help human progress; it is the blood of the master given to make, by and by, a speedier elevation and a more perfect manhood for the slave.

" Together with this transfusion of lineage in a part of the coloured population, the actual contact of the whole with the white race is another fact which must be attentively regarded. This otherwise isolated people, isolated not only by continental separation, but by colour from the rest of the human family, have been brought into the closest possible relationship with one of the foremost people of the world. They have been introduced into families, making part of the household; have, to a certain extent, been brought under the influences of the civilization and enlightenment of this white race. Upon such a susceptible people, receiving impressions so easily, and being moulded so completely by them, this association cannot but have an influence, whenever the time of freedom comes. In a state of slavery, while these influences are exerted and their power is given, yet it must be more or less a latent power. Slavery gives no opportunity for its exhibition. It is like throwing electric sparks into the Leyden jar; it might seem that as they flash and disappear, that all the power is lost, but when the proper conditions are fulfilled the unseen force, slowly gathered, puts itself forth with prodigious energy. When the impulse and opportunity is given by freedom to the American negro for advancement, the probabilities are that an example of rapid elevation will be given by them such as the world has never seen. The elements which have been working in and around them are such as have never been combined in any people before. Here is an imitative and plastic people dwelling in the most intimate associations with an enlightened, energetic race, surrounded by the light of civilization, learning, art, science; it is simply impossible that they shall not partake in some degree of these great benefits. They may be seemingly excluded from them all, but a subtile power is the while going forth and is silently laying itself up in store, by and by to appear in their sudden development.

"But beyond and above all, the negro race in America is a *quasi* Christian race. Here are four millions of Christians. We mean, of course, nominal Christian in contradistinction from any other form of religious belief. Before this one fact we may stand in silent wonder and admiration at the processes of God's great providence. If anywhere on earth the night of heathenism is dark, and the darkness is palpable, it is in the negro's native home. Yet here are millions of the same race maintaining their peculiar characteristics with great distinctness, yet in many points a Christian people, infinitely above their brethren in their original seat. The contrast in this regard between the race here and there, is simply immeasurable. They have been taken out of the blackness of idolatry, and reared for two centuries in the presence of Christianity, so that heathenism has passed almost out of their traditions. All this great result has been occasioned by slavery, sprung from cupidity and the origin of unnumbered crimes! Perhaps human history presents nowhere a more striking example of God's power to make the wickedness of man bring honour to his name.

"Here, then, are a people, with very much of superstition, with very much of ignorance, with, you may say, a low type of piety, but yet, after all, many of them a Christian people. They are a *Protestant* people. Romanism has never obtained any extensive hold on them here. May we not say that in this, that these four millions of blacks are a Protestant people, there is an element of unbounded promise?

"If we throw together these characteristics and facts in regard to the negro race, we have this :—Here is a nation with good mental endowments, peculiarly distinct and seemingly destined to remain so, yet docile and ready to receive the impression of all influences surrounding them, brought not only in closest contact with one of the ruling races of the world, but actually receiving a transfusion of its blood, made at least in part partakers of civilization, and already Christianized in a form where there is the least play of superstition or error. Is it difficult to predict the future of such a people? Is it certainly absurd to say that there is a history before it, if not of the highest style, yet one good and even excellent; if not the noblest as aggressive in its good upon the world, yet one sufficiently glorious for itself?

" Whatever may be the ultimate destiny of this people
we think that we are justified when we say, looking over
the facts in the case, that when the incubus of slavery is
removed, and they start forth on a career of freedom, their
rise will be extremely rapid. Indeed, taking all the elements of progress which they possess into consideration,
it is simply impossible that it should be otherwise. The
legitimate effect of slavery is, to thrust the victim as far
down in the scale of being as is possible. *The nearer the
brute the better the slave*, is the true law of slavery. Slavery
is the cause of ignorance, degradation, and crime. It
would, by a dreadful necessity, strip the slave of every attribute of manhood; neither soul nor body is his own, the
one is kept in darkness as the other is sold in the shambles. What can a system that locks up all human knowledge, stalks through the soul trampling down all that
constitutes the man, not accidentally, but by the necessity of its existence, what can such a system do for its
victim?

" There may be benefits such as we are now speaking
of coming to the slave in his slavery, but slavery does not
give them. The laws which create slavery would shut out
everything, but they cannot. In spite of them all, the
good will come. So it has been with the coloured race in
this country. This good can only be made to appear in a
state of freedom. Just here there is forced upon us another
thought of tremendous significance. This gradual unseen,
but mighty gathering of power in the slave in this land,
cannot be for ever without one day coming into form. You
cannot be evermore throwing electricity' into the jar; by
and by its overcharged contents will burst out in sudden explosion. While you may, let the conductor take them safely
and usefully away! No one cares to follow in imagination
where the thought leads him. Emancipation must be
given sooner or later, or all goes down in a hideous ruin,
and no experience can calculate nicely when the last moment of safety is reached. It may come, and the crashing
thunderbolt tell that it has gone."

The *possible* of what the coloured citizen in America
may reach can be argued *à priori*, or from facts in other

Y

lands; but the actual progress which has been made in a
few months is far more satisfactory: and by evidence of
exceeding value, the Commissioners, appointed by government to inquire into the condition of freedmen, have demonstrated the powers of the negro, and his susceptibilities
of improvement.   I know not on the present aspect of
America for the future, a more valuable document than is
the "Preliminary Report touching the condition and
management of emancipated refugees," presented by Messrs,
"Robert Dale Owen, James McKay, and Samuel G. Howe,
Commissioners."   They advise many admirable measures,
and exercise a dispassionate and enlightened judgment on
facts which have come before them, which must be of in-
calculable service to the government; on "the employment
of negroes" as "military labourers" and as "soldiers."
They say they are "confirmed in the conviction that if the
government can, before the end of the present year, bring
200,000 or more coloured troops into the field to serve
during the war, the result will be alike advantageous to
the cause of the Union and to the race to which these
troops belong.   Docility, earnestness, the instinct of obedience, are characteristics, as a general rule, of the coloured
refugees, who enter our lines."   Their testimony concerning the bravery of coloured troops, shows how valiant they
have proved themselves in the hour of battle.   The observations of the Commission, in the sections of country
visited by them, together with the evidence obtained from
those having most experience among freedmen, justify their
conclusion, that "the African race, as found among us,
lacks no essential aptitude for civilization.   In a general
way the negro yields willingly to its restraints, and enters
upon its duties, not with alacrity only, but with evident
pride and increase of self-respect.   His personal rights, as
a freedman, once recognized in law, and assured in practice,
there is little reason to doubt that he will become a useful

member of the great industrial family of nations. Once released from the disabilities of bondage, he will somewhere find, and will maintain his own appropriate social position." It will interest the reader to trace the outline of facts on which the Commissioners based their conclusions. The following extract from their report submitted to government is exceedingly gratifying to the negro's friend :—

" NEGROES AS REFUGEES.

" *From the Freedmen's Inquiry Commission Report.*

" (District of Columbia, Eastern Virginia, and North Carolina.)

" All the investigations and inquiries the Commission have made throughout the above sections of country, all the evidence they have there collected in connection with the character and condition of the negro population who, from all quarters, find refuge within our lines, tend to this, that these refugees need not be, except for a very brief period, any burden whatever on the government ; but that, on the contrary, they may speedily become, under a system of supervision not difficult either to arrange or to conduct, provided the proper persons be employed, auxiliaries to the government in its prosecution of the war, to the full as efficient as if the same number of loyal whites had emigrated into the Northern States.

" The evidence before the Commission establishes, beyond cavil, the fact that these refugees are, with rare exceptions, loyal men, putting faith in the government, looking to it for guidance and protection, willing to work for moderate wages if promptly paid, docile and easily managed, not given to quarrelling among themselves, of temperate habits, cheerful and uncomplaining under hard labour, whenever they are treated with justice and common humanity, and (in the Southern climate) able and willing, on the average, to work as long and as hard as white labourers, whether foreign or native born.

" The circumstances which have thrown them, for a time, on the care of the government for support, are such as operate equally upon indigent whites arrested in their ordinary course of labour by the operations of the war, and it is a mistake to suppose that assistance has been needed or obtained exclusively by persons of colour in consequence of such disturbance. In some places the number of poor whites succoured has been greater than that of poor blacks. In November last, Major-General Butler was feeding, in New Orleans, thirty-two thousand whites, seventeen thousand of whom were British-born subjects, and only ten thousand negroes; these last chiefly women and children, the able-bodied negro men being usually employed on abandoned plantations.

"Nor, where relief has been required by both whites and blacks, have the latter usually applied for or received, in proportion to numbers, nearly as much as the former. Mr. Vincent Colyer, appointed by General Burnside, at Newbern, N. C., superintendent of the poor, white and black, reports that while seven thousand five hundred coloured persons and eighteen hundred white persons received relief through his instrumentality, the average proportion dealt out in each of the staple articles of food—as flour, beef, bacon, bread, etc.—was about as one for each coloured person relieved to sixteen for each white person to whom such relief was granted. At the time this occurred, work was offered to both blacks and whites; to the whites at the rate of twelve dollars a month, and to the blacks at the rate of eight dollars a month.

"Under any circumstances, and in all large societies, even during a normal and peaceful condition of things, there will be found a certain amount of vagrancy and a certain number of indigent poor, disabled or improvident, to whom it is a custom and a duty to extend relief. Beyond this, except as an expedient for the time being, the Commission believe that the refugee freedmen need no charitable assistance. In the city of Washington, containing sixteen thousand free coloured persons, these support their own poor without almshouse aid, and scarcely a beggar is found among them.

"The vices chiefly apparent in these refugees are such as appertain to their former social condition. Men who are allowed no property do not learn to respect the rights of property. Men who are subjected to despotic rule acquire the habit of shielding themselves from arbitrary punishment by subterfuges, or by a direct departure from the truth. In the case of women living under a system in which the conjugal relation is virtually set at naught, the natural result is that the instinct of chastity remains undeveloped or becomes obscured.

" Thus, stealing is a common vice among these people, when temptation occurs. Thus, they have the habit of lying when they deem a lie necessary to please a white superior, or a defence against blame or punishment: under other circumstances, they are as truthful as the average of uneducated white people. Thus, too, many coloured women think it more disgraceful to be black than to be illegitimate; for it is especially in regard to white men that their ideas and habits as to this matter are perverted. A case came to the knowledge of the Commission, in which a mulatto girl deemed it beneath her to associate with her half-sister, a black, and the daughter of her mother's husband, her own father being a white man. Such ideas, and the habits thereby engendered, render it highly important that freedmen's villages, particularly when they are chiefly inhabited by women and children, should be at a distance from any military encampment, and should be strictly guarded. And as there are no sentinels so strict as the negroes themselves, the Commission believe, for this and other reasons, that coloured guards will be found the most suitable and efficient for such service; and they recommend that, in every case, they be substituted for whites.

" The testimony of the more intelligent among the superintendents is to the effect that the vices above referred to are not obstinately rooted, and that each one of them may be gradually eradicated by a proper appeal to the self-respect of the newly made freedman, and by a strict recognition of his rights. He is found quite ready to copy whatever he believes are the rights and obligations of what he looks up to as the superior race; even if these prove a restraint upon the habits of license belonging to his former condition.

" An officer on General Dix's staff, acting as provost judge at Fortress Monroe, related to the Commission, in graphic terms, with what earnestness and conscious pride

of his new position a negro, sworn as witness for the first
time in his life, stood up to take the oath and deliver his
testimony.

"As to the false ideas touching chastity above referred
to, the Commission believe that these can be in a great
measure corrected by bringing practically to the notice of
the refugees, as soon as they come under the care of the
superintendent, the obligations of the married state in
civilized life. Debarred, as slaves, from any legal union—
often from any permanent connection—unable to contract
a marriage that is not liable to be broken up at the will
of a master—they usually regard it as a privilege apper-
taining to emancipation to be married 'as white folks are.'
The Commission think that, while compulsion in regard to
this matter should be avoided, a judicious superintendent
will, as a general rule, find no difficulty in inducing refugees,
when bringing with them those whom they acknowledge to
be their wives and children, to consent to a ceremony which,
while it legitimizes these relations, imposes upon the husband and father the legal obligation to support his family.
This obligation, and the duties connected with the family
relation of civilized life, should be carefully explained to
these people, and, while they remain under our care, should
be strictly maintained among them. The evidence before
the Commission proves that, with few exceptions, they
show themselves prompt to acknowledge and ready to
fulfil such obligations.

"Sufficient evidence is before the Commission that
coloured refugees in general place a high value both on
education for their children, and religious instruction for
themselves. In Alexandria, and in various other places, it
came to the knowledge of the Commission that one of the
first acts of the negroes, when they found themselves free,
was to establish schools at their own expense; and in
every instance where schools and churches have been provided for them, they have shown lively gratitude and the
greatest eagerness to avail themselves of such opportunities of improvement.

"As a general rule, they are more zealously devotional
than the white race; they have more resignation and more
reliance on Divine Providence. They have, also, more
superstition. This, however, the Commission think,

should not be harshly dealt with. It is of more importance sympathizingly to meet and encourage, in these untaught people, the religious sentiment which sways them, than to endeavour, in a spirit of proselytism, to replace their simple faith in the Divine goodness and protection by dogmas of a more elaborate and polemical character. Practically, as regards the Christian graces of kindness and humility, we have as much to learn from them as they from us.

"It is desirable that, as soon as possible, their schools and their churches be supported, in whole or in part, by themselves.

"Medical aid they need, in the outset, and it should be provided for them; but here, too, the principle of self-support should be introduced as soon as circumstances permit. Vaccination ought to be strictly attended to."

"(South Carolina and Florida.)

"What has been stated in the foregoing pages as to the refugees that have crossed our lines from Eastern Virginia and North Carolina, though true in the main also of South Carolina and Florida negroes, is to be received with some modification as regards the former slave population of these two last named states, especially South Carolina.

"This is one of the states in which the system of negro slavery seems to have reached its furthest development, with the least modification from contact with external civilization. There it appears to have run out nearer to its logical consequences than in any other we have visited. There it has been darkening in its shades of inhumanity and moral degradation from year to year, exhibiting more and more increased cruelty, a more marked crushing out, in the case of the negro race, of the humanizing relations of civilized life, and a closer approach, in practice, to a monstrous maxim; the same which a Chief Justice of the Supreme Court, perverting history, alleges to have been the sentiment of the civilized world when the United States Constitution was adopted, and in the spirit of which he assumes (in virtue of such perversion) that Constitution to have been framed; namely, that 'the negro has no rights which the white man is bound to respect.' The evidence before the Commission shows that, half a century ago, its phase was much milder than on the day when South Carolina seceded. It is the uniform testimony of all emancipated South Carolinian slaves above the age of sixty, that their youth was spent under a state of things, which, compared to that of the last thirty years, was merciful and considerate. As a general rule, these old men are more bright and intelligent than the younger field hands; in many of whom a stolid, sullen despondency attests the stupefying influence of slave-driving under its more recent phase.

"The disintegration of the family relation is one of the most striking and most melancholy indications of this progress of barbarism. The slave was not permitted to own a family name; instances occurred in which he was flogged for presuming to use one. He did not eat with his children or with their mother; 'there was no time for that.' In portions of this state, at least, a family breakfast or dinner table was a thing so little known among these people that, ever since their enfranchisement, it has been very difficult to break them of the life long habit that each should clutch the dish containing his portion and skulk off into a corner, there to devour it in solitude. The entire day, until after sunset, was spent in the field; the night in huts of a single room, where all ages and both sexes herded promiscuously. Young girls of fifteen—some of an earlier age—became mothers, not only without marriage, but often without any pretence of fidelity to which even a slave could give that name. The Church, it is true, interposed her protest; but the master, save in exceptional cases, did not sustain it, tacitly sanctioning a state of morality under which ties of habitual affection could not assume a form dangerous or inconvenient to despotic rule.

"The men, indeed, frequently asked from their masters the privilege of appropriating to themselves those of the other sex. Sometimes it was granted; sometimes, when the arrangement was deemed unprofitable, it was refused. Some cases there were in which a slaveholder, prompted by his own sense of morality, or religion, or urged thereto by a pious wife, suffered these connections of his slaves to have the sanction of religious ceremony. But it is evident that to connect even with such a *quasi*-marriage the idea of sacredness or religious duty was inconsistent with that legal policy of the slave states which forbade to render indissoluble among slaves a relation which to-morrow it might be for the interest of their owner to break up.

"The maternal relation was often as little respected as the marital. On many plantations, where the system was most thoroughly carried out, pregnancy neither exempted from corporal punishment nor procured a diminution of the daily task; and it was a matter of occasional occurrence that the woman was overtaken by the pains of labour in the field, and the child born between the cotton rows. Humane masters, however, were wont to diminish the task as pregnancy advanced, and commonly gave three, occasionally four weeks' exemption from labour after childbirth. The mother was usually permitted to suckle her child during three months only; and the cases, were rare in which relaxation from labour was allowed during that brief period. On the other hand, instances have occurred in which the more severe drove the negress into the field within forty-eight hours after she became a mother, there to toil until the day of the next birth.

"A noble exception, among others, to such a system of inhumanity, gratefully testified to by the negroes who enjoyed it, was to be found on the plantation of ex-Governor Aiken, one of the largest and most influential planters in the state. His habitual clemency, it is said, gave umbrage to many of his neighbour planters, as endangering their authority under a severer rule.

"Under such a slave system as this, where humanity is the exception, the iron enters deep into the soul. Popular songs are the expression of the inner life; and the negro songs of South Carolina, are, with scarcely an exception, plaintive, despondent, and religious. When there mingles a tone of mournful exaltation, it has reference to the future glories of Zion, not to worldly hopes.

"If to the above details touching slave life in this state we add the fact that, because of the unhealthy climate of the Sea Islands off the South Carolinian coast (chiefly due, it is said, to causes which may be removed), the least valuable and intelligent slaves were usually placed there; further, that being much isolated in small communities, these slaves frequently had children of whom the father and mother were near blood relatives, producing deterioration of the

race, it can excite no surprise that the negroes of South
Carolina, as a class, are inferior to those from more Northern states. An intelligent negro from a northern county of
North Carolina, who had there learned the blacksmith's
trade, and had been hired to work on a railroad in South
Carolina, stated to the Commission that he never knew
what slavery really was until he left his native state.
While there, he was comparatively contented. Within a
month after he reached South Carolina, he determined to
risk his life in an attempt to escape.

"Yet the negro of South Carolina may be reached, and,
with rare exceptions, he may, in a comparatively brief
period, be in a measure reformed by judicious management.
A chief agency in effecting such reform is the regular payment of wages for work done. Captain Hooper, the acting
Superintendent at Port Royal, under General Saxton,
having charge of some seventeen thousand refugees, testifies as follows :

"*Question*—Do these persons work willingly for wages?
"*Answer*—I never knew a case in which a coloured man
had reasonable security for getting wages—even moderate
wages—that he was not ready to work.

"Such cases however occur, as other witnesses testify;
but the general rule is as Captain Hooper states it.
"Mr. Frederick A. Eustis, son of General Eustis, who
owned the plantation on Ladies' Island, and who has
returned to cultivate that plantation by hired labour, while
expressing the opinion that the new system of labour in
South Carolina was too lenient, and that 'the negro should
have no appeal, except in cases of extreme cruelty on the
part of the superintendent,' gave the following testimony
as to the people now working on his own plantation :

"'I never knew, during forty years of plantation life, so
little sickness. Formerly, every man had a fever of some
kind, and now the veriest old cripple, who did nothing
under secesh rule, will row a boat three nights in succession to Edisto, or will pick up the corn about the corn-
house. There are twenty people whom I know who were
considered worn out and too old to work under the slave
system, who are now working cotton, as well as their two

acres of provisions ; and their crops look very well. I have an old woman who has taken six tasks (that is, an acre and a half) of cotton, and last year she would do nothing.'

" But the great school for giving character to the race, in this state and elsewhere, is military discipline. Colonel Higginson, commanding a coloured regiment at Port Royal, was asked:

" *Question*—Do you think that, as preparation for the life of a citizen, the organization of negroes into military bodies is important ?

" *Answer*—I should say, of unspeakable value.

" Judge Smith, chairman of Tax Commissioners for the State of South Carolina, deposes:

" *Question*—What is your idea about enlisting negroes as soldiers ?

" *Answer*—It is the best school in the world. If you could have seen the men who now compose the coloured regiments here as they were before, lounging about with a shuffling gait, looking sideways with suspicious manner, and could have contrasted their appearance then with their present bold, erect carriage and free bearing, I am sure you would agree with me. It makes men of them at once.

" The Commission bear emphatic testimony, so far as their researches have yet extended, to the truth of these remarks. The negro has a strong sense of the obligation of law and of the stringency of any duty legally imposed upon him. The law, in the shape of military rule, takes for him the place of his master, with this difference—that he submits to it heartily and cheerfully, without any sense of degradation. The Commission believe that, of all present agencies for elevating the character of the coloured race, for cultivating in them self-respect and self-reliance, military training under judicious officers, who will treat them firmly and kindly, is at once the most prompt and the most efficacious. In this respect the war, if the negro be employed by us as a soldier, becomes a blessing to him, cheaply bought at any price.

" Under proper treatment public opinion among these people sets in in favour of military duty. No difficulty is anticipated in procuring coloured men to enlist, provided those now in the field shall be regularly paid, and provided the determination of the government to protect them in all the rights of the white soldier shall be clearly made known to them, especially if this latter determination shall be signified to them by the President in his own name. Our Chief Magistrate would probably be surprised to learn with what reverence, bordering on superstition, he is regarded by these poor people. Recently at Beaufort a gang of coloured men in the service of the Quartermaster, at work on the wharf, were discussing the qualifications of the President—his wonderful power, how he had dispersed their masters, and what he would undoubtedly do hereafter for the coloured race—when an aged, white-headed negro—a 'praise-man' (as the phrase is) amongst them—with all the solemnity and earnestness of an old prophet, broke forth : 'What do you know 'bout Massa Linkum ? Massa Linkum be ebrewhere ; he walk de earth like de Lord.'

General Saxton deposed :

"*Question*—Were the women, under the slave system, taught chastity as a religious duty ?

"*Answer*—No, sir. They were taught that they must have a child once a year.

"*Question*—Has your observation led you to believe that the refugees pay regard to the marriage ceremony ?

"*Answer*—Yes, sir. Whenever it is solemnized, I think that they do.

"It is here to be remarked that, in the cities, there appears to have been a nearer approach to recognized marriage and to conjugal fidelity than in the country, and that there the Church succeeded better in repressing juvenile incontinence.

"As a general rule, however, the religion of the South Carolinian slave was emotional, and did not necessarily connect itself with the suppression of vicious habits, but rather with church observances. It produced, indeed, submission, humility, resignation, reliance on Providence, obedience to masters ; but its effect in checking lying, thieving, incontinence, and similar offences, was feeble and uncertain. A slave has seldom any distinct moral perception that he ought to speak the truth, or to respect private property, in the case of a person he dislikes ; but these people are easily reached through their affections.

"Whether because the race is not addicted to intemperance, or that they were here cut off from its temptation, drunkenness is an almost unknown vice. Captain Hooper testified:

"'I never saw a negro drunk, and I heard of but one case, and that was of a man working on a vessel at Bay Point, who got whisky on board.'

"There is no disposition in these people to go North. General Saxton offered them papers for that purpose, but no one availed himself of the offer. They are equally averse to the idea of emigrating to Africa. These feelings are universal among them. The local attachments of the negro are eminently strong, and the Southern climate suits him far better than ours. If slavery be re-established in the insurrectionary states, the North will indeed be flooded with fugitives fleeing from bondage, and the fears of competition in labour sought to be excited in the minds of Northern working men, will then have some plausible foundation. But if emancipation be carried out, the stream of negro emigration will be from the North to the South, not from the South to the Northern states. The only attraction which the North, with its winters of snow and ice, offers to the negro, is that it is free soil. Let the South once offer the same attraction, and the temptation of its genial climate, coupled with the fact that there the blacks almost equal the whites in number, will be irresistible. A few years will probably see half the free negro population now residing among us, crossing Mason and Dixon's line to join the emancipated freedmen of the South.

"The chief object of ambition among the refugees is to own property, especially to possess land, if it be only a few acres, in their own state. Colonel Higginson testified to his conviction that the effect of bounty land would be much greater on the coloured than on the white soldier. They delight in the idea.

"Working for wages, they soon get an idea of accumulating. Savings' banks will be popular with them whenever their confidence is won.

"The negro of Florida occupies an intermediate place between the slaves of North Carolina and those of South Carolina. He is more enterprising and more self-reliant

than the latter. As a general rule, he enlists more willingly, and makes an excellent soldier. Many of them were
employed as lumbermen, and in other vocations better
calculated to call out their intelligence than the monotonous labour of the cotton field."

The tide was strong in the spirit and influence of the
slave-holding power upon the religious organizations of
America twenty years ago. Even the Bible Society was
restrained ; the truth was fettered and cast out from Tract
Society publications in reference to the claim or cause of the
slave, and the operations of the Boards of Missions in
American spheres were perverted or misrepresented.
Therefore some earnest and conscientious anti-slavery
members of these organizations repeatedly agitated in their
assemblies or committee rooms the questions involved.
Minorities were repelled and individuals were thrown off
or withdrew. Seventeen years ago the American Missionary Association was formed, and tract societies with
anti-slavery freedom sprung up. The Missionary Association had home spheres in Western States, and embraced
opportunities to diffuse the gospel among people of colour.
The principles embodied in this organization distinctly
pledged its executive, " that in selecting its fields of labour,
conducting the missionary work, appointing its officers,
agents, and missionaries, it would endeavour particularly
to discountenance slavery." From its commencement it
never bowed the knee to this Baal ; during the eventful
years of its existence it has held fast and disseminated its
faith ; and on this basis has earnestly and successfully prosecuted the work, so that they were regarded as fanatically
earnest for the extinction of slavery. In the new attitude
of the country, they have reasoned that, as God sendeth
the lightning to make a way for his rain, so He has sent
judgments upon their land for the sins of the people, that
his mercy may descend ; his crushed children are being

delivered, and tens of thousands of freedmen are now accessible to their missionaries. Twelve missionaries were therefore withdrawn from the north-west, and as an association they have left that region to the care of the churches which have sprung up, that they may devote the more energy to the South. And here they feel " the present life and the eternal salvation of millions may depend upon the advocacy of a righteous policy *just now.*" " Let us," they exclaim, still demand " emancipation immediate and universal, the breaking of every yoke as a matter of justice. Were we permitted, as we are not, to regard the work in relation to its *necessity* only, then we should see that God holds us bound, in view of the rivers of blood flowing, because slavery is not effectually smitten, to press on to *its* death, determined to open the doors of liberty to its suffering victims, as we would have heaven's doors opened to us." At their annual meeting, October 1862, they adopted and took measures to make effectual the following resolution:—

" That we rejoice that God in his Providence has begun to burst open the gates of the Bastile in which four millions of our brethren have so long lain bound; that several thousands have already emerged to life and liberty, and other thousands and millions are hopefully coming; that among these thousands a door is open for missionary labour at once so wide and so hopeful of the choicest fruits, that this Association feels pressed for many reasons to enter and occupy this field with their utmost ability— the emancipated being eminently ripe for the gospel, eager for a knowledge of the Bible and for ability to read it, and their social and moral elevation being beyond measure valuable as a testimony against slavery, and against the fallacies and falsehoods alleged in its justification. The Association also regard this missionary work as due to the spirit of a pure Christianity, as adapted eminently to honour the gospel and its Author, and as one which peculiarly belongs to the American people, being one of the works meet for repentance of their long and guilty oppression of the coloured race."

The work which is in progress among the *freedmen* is best exhibited by the course of action among their agents. The schools deserve pre-eminent notice.

MRS. PEAKE'S SCHOOL.

Under date of October 1st, Mr. Lockwood writes :—

"I have just visited the school of Mrs. Peake (the coloured teacher) near the seminary, with great satisfaction. Am delighted at the good order and rapid improvement in so short a time. The school numbers forty-five children, and others are expected. She offers to teach a school for adults in the afternoon. The school for children occupies from nine till twelve o'clock. She has several classes that spell well in the book and out of it. She is also teaching writing and the elements of arithmetic, with encouraging success. She intersperses the Lord's Prayer, the Ten Commandments, catechetical exercises, singing, etc. It is certainly a model school, considering the circumstances."

In one of Mr. Lockwood's letters, he reports a portion of a coloured brother's prayer, though he says it is impossible for him to give its force and beauty, as follows :—

"O Lord! if you please, look down upon us this evening, I pray, and give us a closing blessing. We thank and praise Thee for all that we have heard from the lips of our Northern brethren, who have come over the briny waters to preach to us the pure gospel. We confess that we are like the children of Israel, ever ready to murmur and complain. But for murmurings, O Lord! you have given us blessings, and this makes us come for more. O Lord! we believe that you have come to deliver your people. Oh! trample the Secessionists under foot, bless the Union cause, and right every wrong. Bless the President, the Congress Hall, and the Senate. Help them to make laws that shall be for the good of the Union, and the freedom of thy oppressed people, O Lord! I pray. Bless the army and the officers. Make them wise as a serpent, and bold and persevering as a lion, till thy people are delivered. Look this evening upon our dear brethren and sisters and children far away in the home of bondage, especially those who have been carried away by the Secessionists. Comfort their minds and interpose for their deliverance, and if they are not in Christ, bring them in, O Lord! I pray. Remember our dear brother who has been with us and is about to leave; preserve him on the mighty waters, and reward him for his labours of love. And remember our brother who has come back to us. Strengthen him in the inner and outer man, and give him grace and strength for suffering time, that he may go in and out before us and do us good. And when you have remembered all, remember me, and after you have done and suffered your holy will with me, please to receive me to yourself, O Lord! I pray, through Jesus Christ our Lord. Amen."

The following extracts from Rev. Mr. Lockwood's letters, of different dates, will give some idea of the spirit and power manifested by some of the freedmen in religious meetings. In a letter dated November 27th, he says :—

" The eleven o'clock service at Wood's Mill, near Hampton, was very interesting. A ' contraband,' who is rapidly learning to read, made some sensible, Scriptural, and even eloquent impromptu remarks on the text, ' Restore unto me the joy of thy salvation,' etc., adapted to make a good and deep impression upon both saints and sinners. He said :—

" The joy of salvation! You, Christian, know what it is. When first converted, it was to you a joy unspeakable and full of glory. Then you could tell to sinners around what a dear Saviour you had found. Jesus all the day long was your joy and your song. When the Christian is cold in religion, he has no joy, no freedom, no heart to praise, no tongue to speak what God has done for his soul. But when God has restored to him the joy of his salvation, and once more upholds him with his free Spirit, his heart overflows, and his tongue is loosed. Then a man will speak with power. The words will catch fire and go from heart to heart. I see sinners out of Christ going to hell. This is a hard word, but true. They have no joy of salvation, no free spirit, they are in Satan's chains. Can I help warning them? If I saw a child near the fire, the flames darting out to seize its clothes, would I not run and pull it away? And so I would pull a soul out of the fire. O sinner! it will double my joy to save your soul from death.

z

Oh! let me point you to the Lamb of God who taketh away the sins of the world. Let me point you to his redeeming blood, and say, behold the way to God. Then may you have this joy of salvation and this free spirit."

Another of the refugees said :—

"We have been in the furnace of affliction, and are still, but God only means to separate the dross, and get us so that like the pure metal we may reflect the image of our Purifier, who is sitting by to watch the process. I am assured that what God begins, He will bring to an end. We have need of faith, patience, and perseverance, to realize the desired result. There must be no looking back to Egypt. Israel passed forty years in the wilderness, because of their unbelief. What if we cannot see right off the green fields of Canaan; Moses could not. He could not even see how to cross the Red Sea. If we would have greater freedom of body, we must first free ourselves from the shackles of sin, and especially the sin of unbelief. We must snap the chain of Satan, and educate ourselves and our children, so that they may be worthy, and compel all to confess that they are deserving of liberty."

At another time Mr. Lockwood says :—

"In the afternoon George Green (a coloured brother) made a thrilling exhortation, comforting saints and warning sinners with great power. The effect was truly terrific, as he spoke in his terse, crowded, and electrifying language, and with fitting manner, of God's melting the skies, burning up the seas, dissolving the solid ground, and flinging his wrath abroad—pouring his unbottled vengeance upon the sinner's head in one eternal storm. Oh! said he, a star called worm-wood shall be cast into the sea, and make it boil like a pot; and the frightened sinner shall cry to the sea, 'Swallow me up;' but the sea shall say : 'I have a God to obey!' He shall then cry to the mountains, 'O mountains! cover me, and hide me from the face of Him that sitteth upon the throne, and from the wrath of the Lamb!' But the mountains shall say : 'We have a God to obey!'"

Miss Green wrote, July 24th :—

"The people are happy; rising very early in the morning, and do all in their power for my comfort, as I do for them. My school numbers one hundred and sixty-three. Our quarters are very close and primitive. When I look around on my dark-browed boys and girls, and think that they have immortal souls; when they turn to me for aid and sympathy; when they bring me fruit and flowers, and in various other ways express their love, I am stimulated to work on, in spite of inconveniences. Human nature is the same here as elsewhere; and here, as elsewhere, I find a great variety of capacity for mental improvement. . . . . What some people mean by saying these people are neither affectionate nor grateful, is more than I can tell; they are so, here; they are industrious, persevering, and patient, and many of them bright examples of what a Christian should be. I have visited many of their homes, thinking I might, perhaps, say something to cheer and strengthen their faith in God, but most invariably have I come away, mentally exclaiming, *you* are the sweet example, I will learn of you! A dear friend of mine sent me, yesterday, a rich gift of fruit and cake. She is, I fear, not long for this world; her health is ruined by the treatment which she received from her master's family."

From Mr. J. McCrea, Beaufort, South Carolina:—

"We have in our church and school the elements of noble manhood and womanhood. The principles of Christianity implanted in the heart, nourished and strengthened by education, will develop all the latent energies of the mind, and from among the poor down trodden ones will arise many who will exert a powerful influence over the minds of their fellow men; and better than this—more glorious thought—from these now freed from earthly fetters, shall be gathered many who shall swell the numbers of the blood washed multitude above, ascribing glory and honour to Him by whom and through whom they were released from the galling fetters of sin and Satan, and made to rejoice in the liberty wherewith Christ makes free."

CHURCH MEETING.

In September, 1861, Rev. Mr. Lockwood wrote:—

"Last Thursday I had an opportunity to observe the intellectual status of a considerable number of the brethren at a church meeting. I was surprised at their understanding and wisdom in regard to church order and propriety, and tone of discipline. As the church records had been burnt up in the church edifice at Hampton, I inquired how far any of them could recall their contents. One or two replied that they could almost repeat the church regulations from memory.

"In the discussion, high ground was taken in regard to the Sabbath, the temperance cause, and other matters of Christian morality. In discipline, stress was laid on the propriety and duty of private admonition, in its successive scriptural steps, before public censure. The duty of forgiving offenders, and undoing wrongs, was also insisted on. Several had been improperly excluded from church privileges through the influence of white power. It was therefore decided to-day that those who had the confidence of the church should be restored to church-fellowship unconditionally."

MARRYING THE FREEDMEN.

"Yesterday morning I commenced at the Fortress the new business of marrying those who had 'taken up with each other.' As I stated in my last letter, there is a large number of this class, including many church members. Such are the abominable results of slavery. . . . Five couples were married in the morning, and six in the evening. On both occasions I had with me Chaplain Fuller, of the Sixteenth Massachusetts Regiment, a beloved brother and co-labourer, who has from the first taken a deep interest in this matter, and in everything concerning the welfare of this downtrodden, but now uprising race. We both prayed that no human power might ever separate those God had joined together. Considerable time was occupied, and very profitably."

I wish to place before the reader the evidence of intellectual power and the promise of efficient progress in the poor people, so long debased and oppressed. The Missionary Society is called to labour in a field white for the harvest, and they have had labourers whose hearts have been wholly set to do good. Men that cannot co-operate in warlike or sectarian organizations and yet profess to be anti-slavery in sentiment, need not wrap their talent in a napkin or hide it in the earth. Here are objects of compassion and ways for relieving and improving the victims of a cruel oppression. The devoted men and women who have engaged themselves as teachers, missionaries, and superintendents, and the funds which are contributed from all parts of the Northern States, manifest the awakened sympathy which is now prompting those who have been charged with *prejudice* against colour. The ready attention given by the government authorities, by such men as Generals Mansfield, Mitchell, Hunter, Banks, Thomas, and Grant, as is attested by the reports of the Society, evince the pervading interest which exists among the the intelligent and humane classes of society. There are officers, no doubt, and private soldiers, who despise and even plunder the coloured refugees; and so there would be among the armies of all nations. There remain still, and have been manifested, contemptuous and contemptible ebullitions of hatred to the coloured people, as a class, in America; and so would there be in England, by its gentry, towards costermongers, coalheavers, and hodmen, if the lower class appeared to trench upon the prerogatives of the other in Belgravia, etc. But a better and wiser rule of intercourse begins to pervade English society; and so is it among American citizens, under Christian influences. The tale told by the accompanying extracts, opens a promising vista in the prospects of the negro and his friends :—

THANKSGIVING-DAY IN CAMP.

"August 6th, 1863, appointed by the President of the United States as a day of thanksgiving for the many victories of our army, was a day long to be remembered in Camp Fiske.

"The large church and schoolhouse was filled to overflowing with a sable crowd, and appropriate religious exercises were conducted by the camp missionary and the post superintendent, Chaplain Fiske. More than fifty boys, in all kinds of positions, occupied the beams above the audience—some sitting, some lying down, and some hanging around the beams ; while the little girls, in large numbers, gathered round the stand, on the platform just behind the speaker.

" After the exercises, forty couples presented themselves for marriage. Twenty-seven pairs were called out. This was all that could be formed in line at once, and Chaplain Fiske proceeded with the ceremony in the following brief and appropriate manner :—

" ' You, Africa Baily, you, Wilson Polk, you, Dennis Richardson, etc., here, in the presence of God and all these witnesses, do each take the woman whose right hand you hold, to be your *only*, your lawful wife. You promise to love and cherish her ; to maintain her honourably, by a manly industry and energy ; to nurse her in sickness ; to bear with her faults ; to be true to the thought of her in all the separations through which Providence may lead you, carefully avoiding improper intimacy with any other, till God shall separate you by death. Do you thus solemnly promise ?' (Response.)

" ' Then, turning to the women, he continued, ' And you, Emma Turner, you, Martha Woods, you, Julia Whitmore, etc., do, on your part, each take the man whose right hand you hold, to be your *only* and lawful husband. You promise to love and care for him ; to aid him, diligently, in gaining an honourable livelihood ; to be true to him in prosperity or adversity, in sickness or in health, whether you be together, or by Providence separated, avoiding all improper intimacy with any other, till God shall separate you by death. Do you thus solemnly promise ?' (Response.)

" ' Then by authority vested in me as a minister of the cross of Christ, a chaplain in the military service of my country, and in special charge of the coloured people at this post, I pronounce you, Africa Baily and Emma Turner, you, Wilson Polk and Martha Woods, you, Dennis Richardson and Julia Whitmore, etc., to be lawful husband and wife, and whom God has here and thus joined together, let not man put asunder.'

" Afterward the rest were married, and with solemn

injunctions to be faithful to each other, they proceeded to their cabins, where tables were spread, some very invitingly, and celebrated their marriage day, though many of them had considered themselves married for years.

"They begged the chaplain and others who went around to see their tables, to take some of the wedding-cake for themselves and friends.

"It was interesting to see the aged and the young coming up together for this purpose; also to see the varieties in their style of dress. Most of the women were adorned with bits of ribbons of various colours. As I said before, many of these had been living together; but it is a law of the camp that all such shall be legally married. They were furnished with marriage certificates, neatly printed, bearing a picture of the 'old flag.'

"Seventy-five couples were married the same day, by Chaplain Kingsbury, who has charge of the island camp at the same post. Thus, on the 6th of August, 1863, was laid the foundation of 115 homes. Could our friends of the North see, as we see, the evils arising from the state of things among them in regard to the social relation, they would look upon this circumstance as one worthy to crown a thanksgiving-day."

FROM REV. G. N. CARRUTHERS.

"CORINTH, *August* 24, 1863.

"The desire to learn, with all classes, amounts to enthusiasm; old and young pant for knowledge, as the thirsty beast for the brook. I have mothers in my school, whom I have to excuse, at intervals, to nurse their children. Our children, as soon as taught, become teachers at home; and it is within bounds to say one thousand have learned to read since the schools were established here last spring. We have just organized an interesting Sabbath school, in our new church and school building, numbering between three and four hundred scholars. Many more would come out, if they could *fix up*, so as to look as neat as 'other people's children.' I have laid their case before the Oberlin Sabbath school, and asked each one to send us a garment for our Sabbath school scholars. Their effort to look neat is very commendable, and we encourage it every way; and they need but the means and instruction to become as neat and tasty as any class of people.

"The girls and women need and desire instruction in needlework. Most of them know nothing but to hold the plough, drive the mule, and hoe and pick cotton. But I have wandered. I meant to give our method in our Sabbath school. We meet at nine o'clock, and sing until half-past nine; this brings them out, as they are very fond of our Sabbath school songs. Then Miss Warren reads to them a story from some Sabbath school paper, and accompanies it with such illustrations and applications as are proper. I then take up the Bible lesson, some assigned topic, such as the Creation, the Commandments, Birth of Christ, Children of Israel, etc., and have such as can read repeat in concert a certain number of verses appropriate to the topic. Rev. A. D. Olds follows, with remarks and applications, and we close with the Lord's prayer in concert. We have quite a number of distinguished visitors, who enjoy our exercises very much, and encourage us with their remarks and compliments."

"FORTRESS MONROE, *July* 27, 1863.

"The work of the mission, under the fostering care of God, seems to be finely prospering. I cannot say that there is more than ordinary interest in the meetings, yet it is quite manifest from the attendance. This people, who so long have sat under the preaching of those who had a zeal, not for God's glory and the triumph of a pure gospel, but for the triumphant success of slavery, are striving to improve, and enjoy the privileges which, after so many years of endurance, have fallen to them. Many times have I heard these expressions in prayer: 'O, Lord, I do thank you for dis glorious priv'lege!' 'I thank you that you have spared me to see dis time.' 'I thank you for de glorious gospel of your dear Son.'

"I find the most of the adults very anxious to learn to read. I have heard many express a desire to be able to read the 'Blessed Bible.' The earnestness manifested and the effort made by them to learn, give satisfying evidences of their becoming an educated people. It is an old but true saying, 'Where there is a will there is a way.' That they have a will to learn to read is beyond a doubt. It is not uncommon to find the labouring men with a book in their pocket, and when a leisure moment arrives, it is used in diligent study.

"My day school is somewhat larger than usual. The daily average is now about ninety. My school, like many others, has been very changeable ; but a small proportion have been with me from the beginning. I find that the same earnestness pervades the minds of both old and young. I must frankly say that their rapid progress has entirely robbed me of the vague idea of the inability of the coloured race to become an educated people. The question is often asked, do you find those who are partially white, more apt to learn ? This has been a difficult question to answer, as there are very few which might be called real Africans. I can say that some of the blackest are among those who make the most rapid progress. I have one girl and boy about sixteen years old, as much African as any in my school, who have, in about seven months learned their letters, read through the 'Picture Lesson Book' twice, and now are reading in Cobb's First Reader. These cases can by no means be called isolated ones, as I have heard other teachers speak of the same aptness in their pupils."

I was in New York, both at the beginning and at the close of the riots, in July, 1863. I had, the previous week, attended a meeting of coloured people in the Rev. H. H. Garnet's church. Six or seven hundred assembled, and seven or eight pastors—one Methodist Bishop among them. There had been, among one portion of the coloured people, special religious services in one of the New York suburbs, a greater number of their pastors were therefore probably present. I delivered an address, and read the letter from the Manchester Anti-Slavery Conference. The leading men present forthwith appointed secretary, chairman, and committee to prepare a response. But they made an urgent appeal to me to renew my visit and deliver a similar address, and they would assure me of a much larger meeting. I consented to attend, in the same church, on the evening of

Monday, the 13th July. That was eventually the first day
of the riots. I had engaged to dine with Dr. Asa D. Smith
and his family, and as I expected to leave New York for
Washington soon after, I was not in circumstances to be
conversant with events in other parts of the city. From
Dr. Smith I first heard definitely of acts of riot and violence
among the populace, and noticed his family listening to noises
on the street with nervous solicitude. After dinner, I prepared to fulfil my engagement with my coloured friends,
and Dr. Smith accompanied me down Broadway. We
could find no convenient omnibus, and therefore walked
toward the place. The population was in a universal fer-
ment—every person looking at his fellow passenger, as if
apprehensive of danger. We reached the church where the
meeting was to have been held, but there was no light
visible, or preparation—an instance of forethought which
greatly relieved us. We ultimately found the sexton, who
did not at first recognize us, and with great reluctance he
informed us where Mr. Garnet could be seen. We found
him and two male and two female coloured friends, waiting
in obscurity and with much perturbation the events of the
evening, dreading every falling footstep which seemed to
approach the door—one of the men had just escaped from
personal assault with his life.

The riots, which lasted nearly a whole week, were represented by some Journalists as having been excited by
the draft, which followed the conscription. The conscription was prescribed by an act of Congress, to render the
government strong enough to put down rebellion without
dependence on volunteers. It was the law of the land.
The draft was by ballot: no man was excluded from its
action by the Federal administration. The rioters attacked
men supposed to be supporters of the general government;
but the aldermen and Governor Seymour pretended to
appease the mob by promising to have the draft suspended.

The offices of the "Tribune" were attacked, because the editor was charged as an advocate of the abolition of slavery. Hundreds of coloured people were assailed, hunted as wild beasts, their humble dwellings gutted, and burned to ashes. Children, old men, feeble women, and sick and helpless negroes were killed, hung to lamp-posts, and cast into the river. Soldiers and their officers, policemen, and respectable private citizens were murdered in deadly strife; Colonel O'Brien was brutally beaten and guarded till he expired as the victim of mob outrage. The Coloured Orphan Asylum was sacked and burned, and the little inmates only escaped by the daring and skilful management of the matron and superintendent, who risked their lives in conveying them to the police station. Streets, avenues, stations, arsenals, stores, and printing offices, as also telegraphs, were ravaged, occupied, and fired, while the mob were armed with all kinds of missiles and fire-arms, and acted in concert as the agents of a conspiracy. The "New York Herald" stood by, and chuckled with glee. For several days the "World" and the "Express" found excuses and palliatives for the incendiary mob; holding up to ridicule men who, they alleged, had to hide themselves from the infuriated savages. The "Tribune" reported the acts of murder, as did the "New York Times" and the "Evening Post," and measures taken to suppress the riots, and charged the origin of the riots to conspirators who sympathized with the slaveholding rebels. Extracts from the "Tribune" and the "Times" leaders will disclose the opinion of many men whom I met. The "New York Times" is not professedly so *outré* in its advocacy of Abolition as it thinks the "Tribune" is, but it is earnest in upholding Mr. Lincoln's policy. The "Tribune" is Horace Greeley in his own paper, which is circulated in tens of thousands every day, and has an immense power in America. I give extracts from the "Times" first, and then from the "Tribune."

"THE RIOTS YESTERDAY."

("*Times*" *of New York.*)

"The outrages upon law and public order yesterday in this metropolis will revive the heart of every rebel, and of every hater of our institutions the world over. The assiduous fanning of every malignant passion by a portion of our public press, and by platform demagogues, has at last resulted in an open outbreak, and for hours a mob embracing thousands raged at its full bent through an extended section of our city, with arson and bloody violence. The absence of nearly our entire military force in their great patriotic work of aiding to beat back the invaders of Northern soil, gave these public enemies a rare opportunity for carrying things with a high hand. The law was not only defied, but was successfully resisted. For the first time within the memory of this generation, it could not command means for its protection. It stood paralyzed, helpless, humbled. It was a spectacle that may well crimson the cheek of every true American with shame. Yet, if that were all, there might be some resignation, for public humiliations have been no rarity in New York. But, unfortunately, there is danger in it, as well as disgrace. There is something portentous in this lawlessness at this juncture.

"It has been declared by the rebel journals, and also by the European journals in the interest of the rebels, that the Conscription act could not be enforced, and that this would compel a discontinuance of the war. The anti-war journals here in the North, while they in general have not ventured to recommend violent resistance to the Conscription, have yet studied to excite against it every unreasoning passion and prejudice. Malignants, too, of the Vallandigham type have for months been doing their best by artful harangues, to foment a spirit of resistance. These men understood their work thoroughly. Their business was to bring about violence, and at the same time keep themselves personally uncommitted to violence; and ANTONY himself never managed that business more skilfully. Every discerning man saw what it would end in—the mob in the street taking upon themselves all the risks, these gentry in their closets rejoicing in the fray in which they dared not mingle. The government could not blind itself to this flagitious course of action. It made some effort to defeat it ; but it was found that this only armed these public enemies with new power, for they turned it to their advantage by pretending that it was now a question of freedom of speech, and gained new influence by setting themselves up as its champions. Thus the dangerous element has been continually growing. It has spread more or less through every part of the North. It has reached all the baser portions of society everywhere, and made them restless, and ready for almost any violence. In most communities this spirit is effectually kept under by superior public opinion. But there are localities where this public sentiment has no such force. This has been shown in the rural districts by the outbreaks which have already occurred in Ohio and Indiana. It is now being shown amid a city population, where the passions of men are far more inflammable, and where the facilities for effective organization are far greater. What its real strength is no man can yet measure ; but yesterday's demonstrations sufficiently attest that it is quite strong enough to be formidable and dangerous.

"The practical question now is, how this spirit of resistance is to be met. Is it to be done by discussing the merits and the necessities of the Conscription act? Decidedly No! It will be a fatal mistake for the friends of the government to suspend their action on the turn of any such question. No man who is at heart for the war, by which alone the government can be sustained, has a serious doubt about either the constitutionality, or the justice, or the propriety, or the necessity of this resort for replenishing the national armies. Even were it otherwise, were the measure actually one that could be reasonably questioned, it would not affect present duties one tittle. The one sole fact that must determine the action of our public authorities against these demonstrations is, that the Conscription act stands on the National Statute Book *a law*. It was enacted by the two bodies in which, under the Constitution, ' *all* legislative powers ' are granted, and it was ' approved ' by the President. There has never been in this Republic a law of more absolute validity, or more perfect sanction. Until it is repealed, or pronounced by the highest court unconstitutional and null, it must stand, and its requirements must be satisfied. The administrators of law have no alternative but to enforce its provisions, without fear or favour. Come what may, they are shut up to that line of action. And it is the duty of every law abiding man to sustain them in it. The official or the citizen who falters is treacherous to every civil obligation.

"The issue is not between Conscription and non-Conscription, but between order and anarchy. The question is not whether this particular law shall stand, but whether law itself shall be trampled under foot. Is this city to be at the mercy of a mob? Have the statutes of the land to await the approval of all the Jack Cades of society before they can attain any binding force? Nobody ever imagined that this Conscription act would suit either rebels in the South, or rebel-sympathizers in the North. No valuable law is ever passed that has the favour of the evil-minded. Yield to them the ratification of our public legislation, and you will speedily be reduced to the condition of being without any law whatever. There is not a man's life in this city that is safe, nor a dollar's worth of property, if the spirit which dominated this city yesterday is to be left to its own working. It is as fatal to our whole civil and social organization as the plague is to the physical constitution of man. To give way before it is simply to invoke destruction. Our authorities, we perfectly understand, have been taken at a great disadvantage. These riots have been precipitated upon them at the very time when they were least able to meet them with promptitude. It has proved to have been a great mistake to suffer our city to be so completely stripped of its military defenders. But it is idle now to repine over this. There are yet available means enough, if seasonably and properly taken in hand, to crush, before another twenty-four hours, this twin hydra of the rebellion utterly, beyond all possibility of its ever writhing again. But it will require boldness, decision, nerve of no ordinary character. The responsibility is practically with Governor SEYMOUR and Mayor OPDYKE. Men in their positions never were confronted with more stupendous duties."

"THE NATIONALITY OF THE RIOTERS.

"The 'Tribune' of yesterday morning has the following :—'It is a curious fact that of all the arrests made, every one is Irish.' However this may be, it is a fact patent to every one who has seen anything of the mob that it is composed almost exclusively of Irishmen and boys. In view of this fact, the following appeal from the distinguished prelate whom the Irish particularly revere, and whom everybody respects, is timely and appropriate :—

"'AN APPEAL TO THE IRISH CATHOLICS FROM ARCHBISHOP HUGHES.

"'In the present disturbed condition of the city, I will appeal not only to them, but to all persons who love God and revere the holy Catholic religion which they profess, to respect also the laws of man and the peace of society ; to retire to their homes with as little delay as possible, and disconnect themselves from the seemingly deliberate intention to disturb the peace and social rights of the citizens of New York. If they are Catholics, or of such of them as are Catholics, I ask, for God's sake—for the sake of their holy religion—for my sake, if they have any respect for the Episcopal authority—to dissolve their associations with reckless men, who have little regard either for divine or human laws.   "'JOHN, ARCHBISHOP OF NEW YORK.'"

("*Tribune.*")

"'Kill the d——d nigger!' was the infuriated howl raised at the sight of any unfortunate black man, woman, or child that was seen on the street, in the cars, or an omnibus. Resistance to the draft was merely the occasion of the outbreak ; absolute disloyalty and hatred to the negro were the moving cause. It was not simply a riot, but the commencement of a revolution, organized by the sympathizers in the North with the Southern Rebellion. It was meant, undoubtedly, to break out on the 4th, but postponed by the defeat of Lee in Maryland. It was well known on Sunday that preparations were made for the outbreak on Monday, and the points of attack and for destruction were designated. Like incendiary fires, it broke out at different places at the same moment, and at the extreme ends of the city. While the first assault was made in the upper Wards, the mob appeared in front of our office; all through the day it appeased its wrath and hate on any stray negro that was so unfortunate as to be found, and attacked the dwellings here and there of those miserable people. Re-inforced at dark by ruffians from the upper part of the city, they made their assault upon this building, completely sacking its publication office. By the timely, energetic, and brave efforts of a company of policemen, under Captain Thorne, the whole structure was barely saved from destruction. But the chief devastation was up town, where private houses were sacked and burned, the Coloured Orphan Asylum destroyed, and at least one child burnt to death. To the efficiency of the police it is alone due that the city is not already given up to utter sack and pillage.

"Whatever others may have done, *we* have not been accustomed to underrate the strength of the Slaveholders' Rebellion in the Free States, and especially in this city. We were long ago convinced that every thief, every black-leg, with nearly every one else who makes a shameful living at the cost of public morals or the well-being of individuals, is an instinctive and vehement partizan of that rebellion. Everyone who lives luxuriously yet earns nothing and does no good, is the natural ally of those who steal their livelihood by conspiring to make others work for them without pay. Hence we have long regarded with more serious apprehension the plottings and manœuvres of Northern Copperheads than those of the open traitors with whom they intensely sympathize. We could always measure and calculate the force of the former; not so that of the latter. And in the dark hours now happily past, we felt that if the Union was destined in the mysterious providence of God to go down, it would owe its destruction far more to the covert stabs of its Northern betrayers than to the manlier assaults of its Southern enemies.

"The storm, long gathering, has finally burst, and its fury falls short of our expectations. The mob that has for two days ravaged, and burned, and slaughtered, almost at will, has been strong only in the weakness of the military and the complaisance of the civil authorities. A single battalion or light battery, earnestly commanded, might have quelled it at the outset, captured its leaders, and stopped its career. Impunity in the beginning, stimulated by the hail-fellow speeches of magistrates who have no right to be cheek by jowl with incendiaries, miscreants, robbers, and assassins, has given it all its disgraceful prestige

and license. Had the civil power alone confronted it with
stern denunciation, with scornful abhorrence, no military
demonstration would have been needed.   But with sympathizing harangues from aldermen, echoed by judges, and a
governor to address it as 'Friends,' and enforce its demands on the President, it would have been the weakest
and meekest of mobs if it had not presumed upon such
familiarity and gone ahead."

A strong force of regular soldiers was marched from
Washington, and the skilful and determined conduct of the
officers placed in command all co-operating with the Mayor,
Mr. Opdyke, and the mercantile and respectable classes,
finally subdued the rioters.   Order was restored, and philanthropy humanely sought out surviving victims among
the coloured people.   Probably never did political chicanery and fraud more effectually defeat their own ends than
did the schemers who originated or plotted this demonstration.   Nothing ever occurred which more served the cause
of the coloured people in the United States.   So soon as
order was restored, a committee of merchants was formed
for the relief of coloured sufferers who had lived through
the riots.   I had the benefit of personal services from the
Mayor on the first days of the outbreak, and I was, by the
favour of the treasurer of the fund now formed, permitted
to sit in the midst of the gentlemen dispensing the charity,
and the afflicted recipients of the money contributed.   I
was also supplied with copies of the report before they
were given to the public.   From this report I can only embody a few extracts, but they will inform and illustrate
better than any mere descriptions I might attempt :—

"Driven by the fear of death at the hands of the mob,
who the week previous had, as you remember, brutally
murdered by hanging on trees and lamp posts several of
their number, and cruelly beaten and robbed many others,
burning and sacking their houses and driving nearly all
from the streets, alleys, and docks upon which they had
previously obtained an honest though humble living—these

A A

people had been forced to take refuge on Blackwell's Island, at police stations, on the outskirts of the city, in the swamps and woods back of Bergen, New Jersey, at Weeksville, and in the barns and out-houses of the farmers of Long Island and Morrissania. At these places were scattered some 5000 homeless and helpless men, women, and children. The first great point to be gained was the restoring of the confidence of the coloured people in the community, from which they had been driven. To do this a central depôt was to be established to which they should be invited to come and receive aid with the fullest assurance that they should be protected. Temporary aid might be sent them to their residences, as was done through the hand of Rev. Mr. Dennison, and through the Society for improving the condition of the poor. This plan met your approval, and that evening, Tuesday, July 21st, I was instructed to look up an office and announce in the morning papers the contemplated purpose, and I did so. On Wednesday, the present office, No. 350, Fourth Street, was secured, vacated by its former occupants, cleansed and opened for business the following day, Thursday, July 23rd, when 38 applicants received aid. On Friday, July 24th, the wants of 318 were attended to, and on Saturday, July 25th, the streets in the neighbourhood were literally filled with applicants. The 'New York Express' thus describes the scene :—

"'At ten o'clock, Fourth Street, near Broadway, was filled with coloured people of both sexes, and all ages. They presented an aspect of abject poverty, and many of them bore evidence of the assaults made on them during the riots.

"' The building where relief was given to the applicants at No. 350, Fourth Street, was soon surrounded by nearly three thousand negroes. Some of them had come into the city from woods and fields in different parts of the state, where they took refuge. They appeared to be no strangers to hunger ; for when the good soldiers of the Twelfth Regiment who are quartered up-stairs in the building, 'brushed' out their rations to the throng, there was a pitiable scramble to obtain them, and the lucky blacks retired to eat them.'

"During the month ending August 21st there have

been 3942 women, and 2450 men, making a total of 6392 persons of mature age, relieved; full one-third being heads of families, whose children were included in the relief afforded by your committee, making a total of 12,782 persons relieved.

" From these persons 8121 visits were received and aid was given; to which add 4000 applicants whose calls were not responded to, as they had previously been aided sufficiently, and you have 12,121 applicants whose cases were considered and acted upon at the office during the month. Add to this the work of the members of the legal profession, Messrs. James S. Stearns, and Cephas Brainerd. who have been indefatigable in their labours, assisted by several other gentlemen, by whom 1000 notices of claims for damages against the city have been made out, copied, and duly presented to the comptroller, while our clerks have recorded on the books over 2000 claimants for a sum of over 145,000 dollars. together with a considerable distribution of clothing by two coloured clerks, and a fair idea of the work done in this office during the month may be obtained, and a reason for what might otherwise appear a large amount of expenditure.

" Of the 2450 men relieved, their occupations were as follows :—1267 labourers and longshoremen ; 177 white-washers ; 176 drivers for cartmen ; 250 waiters ; 124 porters ; 97 sailors and boatmen ; 72 coachmen ; 45 cooks ; 37 barbers ; 34 chimney sweepers ; 25 tradesmen ; 20 butchers ; 15 bootblacks ; 11 ministers or preachers ; 11 shoemakers ; 11 tobacconists ; 11 wood sawyers ; 8 carpenters ; 7 basket-makers ; 6 scavengers ; 5 carpet shakers ; 4 tailors ; 3 artists ; 3 music teachers ; 3 coopers ; 2 engravers ; 2 janitors ; 2 measurers ; 2 oystermen ; 2 undertakers ; 1 landlord ; 1 flour inspector ; 1 teacher : 1 copyist ; 1 farmer ; 1 botanist ; 1 physician ; 1 book-binder ; 1 tin smith ; 1 upholsterer ; 1 blacksmith.

" Of the 3942 women, were—2924 day's work-women ; 664 servants hired by month ; 163 seamstresses ; 106 cooks ; 19 worked in tobacco factory ; 13 nurses ; 13 hucksters ; 4 teachers ; 1 artist ; 1 boarding-house keeper ; 1 basket-maker ; 32 infirm.

" In the height of the crowd of applications it was found necessary to employ as many as ten clerks, and

several special policemen. These last, together with one
regular patrolman who is still with us, preserved excellent
order and were kindly furnished by Mr. Acton, of the Metropolitan Police, free of charge."

ABRAHAM FRANKLIN.

"This young man, who was murdered by the mob on
the corner of Twenty-seventh Street and Seventh Avenue,
was a quiet, inoffensive man, twenty-three years of age, of
unexceptionable character, and a member of Zion African
Church in this city. Although a cripple, he earned a
living for himself and his mother by serving a gentleman
in the capacity of coachman. A short time previous to the
assault upon his person he called upon his mother to see if
anything could be done by him for her safety. The old
lady, who is noted for her piety and her Christian deportment, said she considered herself perfectly safe; but if her
time to die had come, she was ready to die. Her son
then knelt down by her side, and implored the protection
of Heaven in behalf of his mother. The old lady was
affected to tears, and said to our informant that it seemed
to her that good angels were present in the room. Scarcely
had the supplicant risen from his knees when the mob
broke down the door, seized him, beat him over the head
and face with fists and clubs, and then hanged him in the
presence of his mother.

"While they were thus engaged, the military came and
drove them away, cutting down the body of Franklin, who
raised his arm once slightly, and gave a few signs of life.

"The military then moved on to quell other riots, when
the mob returned, and again suspended the now probably
lifeless body of Franklin, cutting out pieces of flesh, and
otherwise mutilating it."

BURNING OF THE COLOURED ORPHAN ASYLUM.

"Our attention was early called to this outrage by a
number of letters from the relatives and friends of the
children, anxiously inquiring as to the whereabouts of the
little ones. It is well known that, as soon as the 'Bull's
Head' Hotel had been attacked by the mob, their next destination was the Coloured Orphan Asylum, on Fifth
Avenue, near Forty-third Street. The crowd had swelled

to an immense number at this locality, and went professionally to work in order to destroy the building, and, at the same time, to make appropriation of anything of value by which they might aggrandize themselves. About four hundred entered the house at the time, and immediately proceeded to pitch out beds, chairs, tables, and every species of furniture, which were eagerly seized by the crowd below, and carried off. When all was taken, the house was then set on fire, and shared the fate of the others.

"While the rioters were clamouring for admittance at the front door, the Matron and Superintendent were quietly and rapidly conducting the children out of the back yard down to the police station. They remained there until Thursday (the burning of the Asylum occurred on Monday, July 13th), when they were all removed in safety to Blackwell's Island, where they still remain.

"There were 230 children between the ages of four and twelve years in the home at the time of the riot.

"The Asylum was located on the Fifth Avenue, between Forty-third and Forty-fourth Streets. The main building was nearly 200 feet in length, three stories and light basement in height, with an hospital 100 feet long, three stories high, connected with the main building by a covered way. Several workshops were attached, and the residence of the Superintendent, Mr. William Davis, was next door. The buildings were of brick, and were substantial and commodious structures. A number of fine shade trees and flowering shrubs adorned the ample play-grounds and front court-yard, and a well-built fence surrounded the whole. "The main buildings were burned. The trees girdled by cutting with axes; the shrubs uprooted, and the fence carried away. All was destroyed except the residence of Mr. Davis, which was sacked." [I have abridged the report of cases from lack of space.]

"By referring to the first twelve incidents it will be seen that among the killed are men, women, and children— white, coloured, and Indian—from the tender babe of three days old up to the venerable man of three-score years and three. The two young men, Abraham Franklin and William Henry Nichols, were members of Christ's body—

the Church; both were seized and murdered while striving
to comfort and protect their mothers. Joseph Reed was a
Sabbath-school boy, aged seven years. Augustus Stuart
was a Christian man, and *insane* at the time he was killed,
and, as if to show that it was not the timidity of the
blacks that encouraged the rioters, James Costello was
killed for having defended himself with a pistol. And all
were slain either while in the peaceful pursuit of their
honest, though humble vocations, providing for their
families, or while endeavouring to escape from the hands of
their destroyers.

"Furniture and clothing has been provided for all of
these families, and everything in our power done to make
them comfortable. That an unprovoked persecution, when
occurring in the midst of a justice loving and right-
minded community, always results to the final advantage of
the people abused, is remarkably illustrated in the fact
that, since the riots, the demand for coloured servants has
increased ten-fold. Families of the highest social position,
both in the city and country, have applied for servants in
vain.

"In looking over the list of occupations on page
355, it will be seen that of the women there are 3,122
who obtain their living by going out to day's-work, and
787 servants hired by the month, a proportion of nearly 6
to 1; while of the men there are 1,823 day labourers to 609
workers by the month, a difference of 3 to 1. The largely
increased demand for servants by the month may change
this, but the habits of a people cannot be thrown off in a
moment. It has been said by their enemies that the
coloured people of the North are idle and dissolute; some
few cases of the latter we did find, but with more than
ninety-five out of every 100 a prompt response to the
inquiry as to 'what was their occupation?' was always
given as above stated. As a rule they were evidently hard-
working, honest, humble people, though many, in both
education and respectability, compare favourably with any
of our citizens.

"The great good which the coloured people feel has
already been accomplished by the Committee in the opening
of this office and the bringing together of so many different
religious denominations, trades, occupations, stations in

life and nativities in friendly and harmonious action, has caused a number of their leading men to ask whether it might not be to the advantage and lasting benefit of the coloured people in New York city to have this mission continued permanently among them. They say that they have been made acquainted with the condition and wants of their people by observation of the doings here, and have seen what opportunities and means there are for improving their condition far beyond their previous conception. Understanding that the present committee, on the conclusion of its labours will be disbanded, the idea has suggested itself whether a committee could not be found who would place this friendly intercourse on a permanent foundation, and carry on the work as above suggested. Having had charge of nearly 10,000 refugee slaves in North Carolina within the past year, I cannot but remark the difference between them and the free coloured people, who have these last few weeks come under my notice. The free coloured people are very much the superiors of their Southern brethren in education, cultivated intelligence, refinement, and in a quick and independent way of maintaining and asserting their rights. While in kindness towards each other—patience under trial and affliction— cheerfulness, willingness to labour, and an entire absence of everything like revenge, or a cherishing of ill-will towards those who have injured them, both those of the North and the South are alike remarkable.

"In physical strength and vigour of body I think the Southern refugees are their superiors. Several applications for relief and claims for damages were made by those who had previously resided in Canada and the British West Indies, and I have observed with some interest that all such persons have had a more clear, straightforward, unembarrassed, yet equally respectful way of presenting their claims. Whether this comes from habits formed by living in a country where the black man is more respected than with us, I am unable to say.

"I cannot close without calling attention to the generous and kind way in which the New York press has aided in this noble work. Although we have had lengthy notices in the editorial columns of their widely-distributed newspapers, we have not had one unkind criticism and but few bills for all their valuable services rendered. Grateful to a kind heavenly Father for the privilege of having been permitted to assist in alleviating the sufferings of these much-abused, persecuted, and greatly misunderstood people, and for the harmony, good order, and success which has attended this mission, now brought to a close,

"I am, Gentlemen, ever faithfully yours,
"VINCENT COLLYER, *Secretary*."

I must find room for one extract from the coloured people's grateful acknowledgments :—"We cannot, in justice to our feelings, permit your benevolent labours to terminate, even partially, without offering some expression of our sincere gratitude to the universal Father for inspiring your hearts with that spirit of kindness of which we have been the recipients during the severe trials and persecutions through which we have passed. When in the pursuit of our peaceful and humble occupations we had fallen among thieves, who stripped us of our raiment and had wounded us, leaving many of us half dead, you had compassion on us. You bound up our wounds and poured in the oil and wine of Christian kindness, and took care of us. You hastened to express your sympathy for those whose fathers, husbands, sons, and brothers had been tortured and murdered. You also comforted the aching hearts of our widowed sisters, and soothed the sorrows of orphan children. We were hungry and you fed us. We were thirsty and you gave us drink. We were made as strangers in our own homes, and you kindly took us in. We were naked and you clothed us. We were sick and you visited us. We were in prison and you came unto us. Gentlemen, this generation of our people will not, cannot forget the dreadful scenes to which we allude, nor will they forget the noble and spontaneous exhibition of charity which they excited. The former will be referred to as one of the dark chapters of our history in the empire state, and the latter will be remembered as a bright and glorious page in the records of the past."

CHAPTER VIII.

THE executive of the United States has had difficulties and drawbacks in the administration of military affairs from the fact that there had not been a standing army, or an extensive corps of medical and hospital officers ; and as there is no national church, there was not a clerical supply of military chaplains. The army, too, constituted as so many state contingents, and coming from the several loyal states, could not be very promptly supplied with Federal officers in these branches of service. I am not sorry there was not a standing army, and I do not regret that an established church is not among the accessories of a military staff ; and yet I can perceive the lack of such service as experienced and efficient medical and clerical officers could have rendered. The American people have seen what was needed, but they have not been satisfied with unavailing regrets. Men of medical experience have rendered willing service ; ladies of all ranks, and women in humbler walks of life, have contributed hospital assistance in attendance, and in materials suited for the wounded and sick soldiers. Christian ministers and devout men of every sect have served in the field, and in the camp, with honour and acceptance. Perhaps in the history of this sanguinary conflict no more beautiful developments of character and patriotism will have been seen, than in the action of these two commissions. Mr. Everett has beautifully delineated woman's work :—

"One drop of balm alone, one drop of heavenly life-giving balm, mingles in this bitter cup of misery. Scarcely has the cannon ceased to roar when the brethren and sisters of Christian benevolence, ministers of compassion, angels of pity, hasten to the field and the hospitals to moisten the parched tongue, to bind the ghastly wounds, to soothe the parting agonies alike of friend and foe, and to catch the last whispered messages of love from dying lips. 'Carry this miniature back to my dear wife, but do not take it from my bosom till I am gone.' 'Tell my little sister not to grieve for me, I am willing to die for my country.' 'Oh, that my mother were here!' When, since Aaron stood between the living and the dead, was there ever a ministry like this? It has been said that it is characteristic of Americans to treat women with a deference not paid to them in any other country. I will not undertake to say whether this is so; but I will say that since this terrible war has been waged the women of the loyal states, if never before, have entitled themselves to our highest admiration and gratitude. Alike those who at home, often with fingers unused to the toil, often bowed beneath their own domestic cares, have performed an amount of daily labour not less than hers who works for her daily bread, and those who in the hospital and the tent of the Sanitary Commission, have rendered services which millions could not buy. Happily, the labour and the service are their own reward. Thousands of matrons and thousands of maidens have experienced a delight in these homely toils and services, compared with which the pleasures of the ball-room and the opera house are tame and unsatisfactory. This on earth is reward enough, but a richer is in store for them. Yes, brothers, sisters of charity, while you bind up the wounds of the poor sufferers—the humblest, perhaps, that have shed their blood for the country—forget not who it is that will hereafter say to you, 'Inasmuch as ye have done it unto one of the least of these my brethren, ye have done it unto me.'"

The Sanitary Commission of New York honours as its chairman one of the most patriotic clergymen in the city, the Rev. Dr. Bellows, who has been indefatigable in his services, and efficient in his duties. I speak thus from no

personal favours or intercourse ; since though he requested me to occupy his pulpit after a brief interview,
and from other engagements I could not comply, when I
called again to apologise he had started for the field of
Gettysburg the day after the fight, a journey out and
back of 500 miles, that he might promote the efficient discharge of his commission among the wounded and the
sorrowing. He only did as scores of other men did from
all parts of the country. The names of gentlemen acting
on this commission with Dr. H. W. Bellows were Professor A. D. Bache, LL.D.; Professor Jeffries Wyman ;
Professor Woolcott Gibbs, M.D.; W. H. Van Buren,
M.D.; Samuel G. Howe, M.D.; R. C. Wood, surgeon,
U. S. A.; George W. Cullum, U. S. A.; Alexander E.
Shiras, U. S. A., and others. I found as far as I journeyed
to St. Louis in the west, and Portland in the east, in Boston
and at Buffalo, in Ohio, and Illinois and Michigan, ladies' committees working and preparing materials for the wounded,
for the sick and convalescent, in lints and flannels, in
shirts and under-garments, as well as in cordials. There are
nineteen permanent hospitals for the reception of wounded
and sick soldiers, besides temporary and regimental hospitals,
and on every battle field remote from the permanent
centres of reception. In Washington 2532 packages were
distributed from May, 1862, to May, 1863, including
52,000 shirts, cotton, flannel, and woollen, and nearly
27,000 drawers of the same materials ; and 1133 boxes of
groceries, dried fruits, jellies, wine and syrups, and pickles ;
besides many other comforts, all the contribution of the
Woman's Central Association of New York. This will
serve to show what may come from other sources.
Perhaps from this city more may have been received than
from others ; yet Philadelphia, Boston, Cincinnati, and St.
Louis, have in proportion forwarded their quota. The
claims of the sick and suffering, who are far from home

and friends, are felt to be urgent. The committee of the
ladies report, on the testimony of Dr. Bellows as president,
that probably half of the sick, numbering it may be 50,000,
are so situated.

The ladies say for themselves :—

" While we are fully sensible that the Commission de-
pends wholly upon the voluntary efforts of the women of
the land, we are also conscious that the burden has been
unequally sustained; and we are, therefore, desirous of
deepening the interest of those who have as yet made
small contributions, and of stimulating them to greater
exertions. This was one of the motives for adopting the
plan of extending our work, which was brought forward
in the Second Semi-Annual Report; and we have attempted to induce all the societies which have at any time
sent us donations to enter into a systematic plan of organization. To facilitate the movement we have selected a
number of ladies, who have consented to act as associate
managers. They will communicate with all the societies in
their respective districts, either by letter or by personal
visits, and give such information in regard to the demand
for articles, facilities for transportation, interesting items
from the hospitals, etc., as may be desirable. It is our
hope eventually to divide our whole field into these sections, with an associate manager for each. We feel much
encouraged by the cordial letters already received from
these ladies, and by the earnestness with which they have
entered upon their new labours.

" The Sanitary Commission has recently established, in
this office, a directory, in which the names of all the
patients in every government hospital in New Jersey, New
York, and the New England states are recorded, with the
number of their regiments, and all important particulars
in regard to their condition. The record is corrected by
comparison with the morning reports of the hospitals.
Similar directories are kept at Washington, Philadelphia,
and Louisville, and hundreds of applicants have thus been
relieved from anxiety, and aided in their search after missing relatives.

" To enable our auxiliaries to expend all the money
they may be able to collect for materials, the prices of

which have increased so much, our association will, for the present, pay all transportation charges on sanitary supplies delivered at No. 10, Cooper Union. We would, at the same time, remind our friends that the American Express Company brings all boxes sent by them free of charge. This has been their uniform practice, and has proved a most valuable donation in aid of the cause. The United States and the National Express Companies, as also the Harlem, New Haven, and Long Island Railroads have promised, through their presidents, 'to transport all packages free of charge from places along their lines for the United States Sanitary Commission.'

"We cannot close without making special mention of the Relief Association of Brooklyn, by which nearly half of the woollen clothing received this winter was prepared. With unexampled energy, they have awakened the interest of almost every one of the numerous congregations of their city. Our cordial thanks are due to the ladies who have continued to assist in assorting, marking, and packing our supplies, and whose faithful attention has made that a great pleasure which otherwise would have been a serious labour. Above all, we are indebted (speaking always on behalf of our soldiers) to the women who, with tireless devotion, have stitched together the four hundred thousand articles which we have received. Have they not proved themselves equal in patriotism to the men who, leaving their comfortable homes, have, without complaint, endured untold miseries that they may leave to others undisturbed the priceless treasure we have received from our fathers?"

The communications of correspondents would afford an idea of the duties and scenes to which the members of this commission are familiar. I had selected some truly interesting extracts, but space is limited, and I retain only one, concerning a long-expected " Chapel Tent " from a chaplain's journal.

"At last it came—three great bundles of canvas and two of tent poles, with ropes, pins, and everything complete—the ' chapel tent.'

"We had concluded not to wait to petition Congress for the article, but to apply directly to our friends at home ;

and they, as friends at home ought always to do in such circumstances, at once raised the necessary funds, and forwarded the tent.

"So the quartermaster sent over a team, and brought it to the camp. The colonel selected a fine place for it to stand. The major detailed the police to clear and terrace the ground. The waggon-master went down into the valley to a field where the summer crop of hay had been left standing by a runaway secessionist, and brought up a load of it to spread on the ground for a floor. The carpenters made a platform and desk, and fixed up temporary seats. A large sheet-iron stove was put in. Bayonets were fastened to the poles for candlesticks. And when retreat sounded at sunset on Saturday, the chapel tent was pitched and furnished, ready for service on the morrow.

"Probably no present from our friends at home could have been more useful and acceptable than this. Its want had been especially felt as the inclement season advanced. The temple of nature, which was every way sufficient in summer, had proved to be rather too breezy and chilly in December. Moreover it had become so leaky overhead and so wet under foot as to repel rather than invite worshippers. Almost the only meetings possible to us had been by twos and threes, in little tents; and most of the privileges which the regimental church is designed to afford had been, in a manner, temporarily lost Now they were restored. We had a church and divine service. We had our prayer-meetings, class-meetings, Bible-class, and musical gatherings. We even went further, and bought a melodeon; and, as the leader of our band was an accomplished organist, we had much enjoyment of music during the long winter evenings.

"Some idea of the uses to which the chapel tent was put may be obtained from the notices read at our first meeting in it on Sunday afternoon: Sunday evening, divine service; Tuesday evening, prayer and conference meeting; Wednesday evening, singing-school and glee club; Thursday evening, class-meeting: Friday evening, Bible-class lecture; Saturday evening, rehearsal of sacred music. In addition to these regular meetings, the chapel tent was at all times open and warmed, affording to such as cared to avail themselves of it an attractive place of resort from the crowded company tents.

"Thus the tent was used all the winter steadily, until on the 24th of February, in that terrible gale which blew the chimney off the hospital, and tipped over so many steeples in its progress over the country, it was torn a little at one end, and taken down for safety.

"After that our meetings were held for a time in the barracks inside the fort, where they continued to increase in interest, in the number that attended them, and, let us hope, in good and permanent results.

"The tent is now stored with other regimental property in Alexandria, awaiting the time when we shall be once more settled so that we can use it.

"While speaking of the chapel tent, I may as well allude to another gift of our kind friends at home, the value of which cannot be too highly estimated. I mean the regimental library.

"This consisted of between seven and eight hundred carefully selected volumes, of all departments of literature. The books were carefully numbered, and were given out according to strict regulations. Every evening, immediately after dress parade, the tent containing the library would be crowded. There was scarcely a volume but what was read with interest by different members of the regiment. Nor were stories and works of fiction the only ones in demand, but scientific and philosophical books. One man wants a treatise on astronomy—a fine place for star-gazing was Fort Richardson; another would like to review his algebra; another to pick up a little botany. Shakspeare, Schiller, and Tennyson are always out, except when presented according to the rules. Frederick Law Olmsted's books are special favourites. Prescott's Histories are greedily read.

"Think of the value of such institutions in the camp. Think of their restraining and correcting influences amid the temptations to vice on every hand. There is nothing that so quickly leads to vice as idleness. Indeed, idleness is itself a vice. 'Keep your men constantly employed,' is a first principle of military discipline. just as on board a ship, when there is nothing else to be done, the sailors are set to scouring the anchors. But on rainy days, and during the long cold evenings of winter, what is there to do in camp but to sit in the tent and talk, play cards, or in some way dissipate the time ? Then it is that habits of impure conversation are formed, swearing and gambling are acquired, and the soul is made a prey to vices of all sorts. And then most of all do we feel the need of home with its gentle influences and restraints ; of Christian fellowship with its safeguards and right impulses ; of well-selected books to occupy and to refine the mind. All of these we could not have. Home cannot be found in camp. But Christian fellowship exists wherever Christians are ; and our chapel tent supplied all the external wants of a Christian church. Our library was constantly enjoyed. How many of us have to thank the influence of these two enterprises as the means of our security from the moral perils of the camp. How many others might have been saved from falling, had they availed themselves of the same. Let us hope that there may be in the future many more to profit by these influences."

Eight hundred and fifty towns are reported by name as having sent contributions to the ladies' branch, while receipts in money are acknowledged to the amount of 16,692 dollars. From one branch of these operations we may suppose what will be the work done by the general Sanitary Commission, and those who fancy that the Union is unpopular, or that the government lacks the sympathies of the people, may ponder this feature of the movement.

But we cannot mingle in American society without observing the direct intercourse which is maintained between the families of the citizens and the battle-field. So soon as an engagement has taken place, the telegraph is in motion inquiring for kindred, and, if satisfactory answers are not received, some one of the family hurries to the scene of action and suffering. "After a battle there are many thrilling scenes at our headquarters. Fathers, mothers, brothers, sisters, and friends gather to inquire for loved ones on the battle-field, the name of the soldier and his company are taken, entered in a book with the name and address of the inquirer. The message flashes across the wire—it goes

free to the delegate, and soon it may be an answer of joy
or sadness is sent to the anxious heart. A letter was received from a lady, the widow of a Presbyterian clergyman,
after the battle of Murfreesboro. Her only son was in the
battle. She wished to send to him what money—two
dollars and a half—she could spare. The order was sent
to the delegate requesting him to find this only son of a
widow, and give him these savings of his beloved mother."
Not since the days of the Egyptian Pharaohs has there
been in any land so many embalmed bodies to enable
relatives to convey the deceased to the resting-place of
their fathers. Every such death is a renewed consecration—a baptism for the dead—binding survivors to every
possible sacrifice that the foul crimes of slavery and rebellion may be wiped away from the nation. As many of
the seriously wounded as can safely be conveyed from the
scene of suffering to be the care of the family circle, and
to revive the watchful solicitudes of those who love them,
are removed. Several of the railway companies have prepared cars for the wounded.

The " Christian Commission " dates its first meeting of
delegates from November 16, 1861, and was originated by
a convention from the Young Men's Christian Associations, held in New York. The suggestion seems to have
originated with Mr. Vincent Collyer. This gentleman
began his visits to the Sixth Massachusetts Regiment of
Volunteers. He extended his personal intercourse for three
months to the camps in the vicinity of New York. But
the first battle at Bull's Run induced him to proceed to the
more extended field around Washington. The authorities
welcomed and facilitated his voluntary services. His sphere
of labour extended, and he appealed on the 1st of October
to the president of the New York Young Men's Christian
Associations for a more vigorous organization, and concluded by the following recommendation :

B B

" I need not say what a blessing such a work will prove to the New York Y. M. C. Associations themselves. It is well known that many of these societies are now languishing for the want of means to meet their current expenses; and it might reasonably be asked, seemingly, how can they, then, undertake a new and extensive work like this ? The answer is, they can readily collect money for this special army mission, when they cannot for anything else. The community is so sensitively alive to the wants of the soldiers—nearly every city, town, village, or family, having their own citizens and members in the army—that the subject takes immediate hold of their sympathies, and will command their ready aid and support. We have tried it, and found it so.

" Having had a personal interview with the President of your Committee, and learned his hearty readiness to co-operate in this work, I visited Boston, and there met with an equally cordial response. That Society will send an able delegate, and our New York Society will select a prominent citizen and member to represent it, and I doubt not, if the time would have admitted, other societies would have promised the same. I therefore leave the matter in your hands, and pray that a Convention of all the Young Men's Christian Associations of the loyal states may be called at an early day.

" With Christian esteem, fraternally yours,

" VINCENT COLYER,

" *Chairman Com. on Correspondence with Convention New York Y. M. C. A.*"

The numerous incidents of interest narrated by Mr. Colyer in his six months' experience served to stimulate a work which gives a peculiar character to the military operations in the United States. Mr. G. H. Stuart of Philadelphia, and Mr. W. E. Dodge, sen., of New York, have generously identified themselves with the organization. " The DESIGN of the Commission has been to arouse the Christian associations and the Christian men and women of the loyal states to such action toward the men in our army and navy, as would be pleasing to the Master; to obtain and direct volunteer labours, and to collect stores

and money with which to supply whatever was needed,
sending matter and articles necessary for health, not furnished by government or other agencies; and to give the
officers and men of our army and navy the best Christian
ministries for both body and soul possible in their circumstances." The Report, which I have carefully examined,
contains hundreds of instances and incidents of the deepest
interest, and fully warranting the general statements brought
together in the following lines :—

"We have now given a report of our special work as
we could; but no report can give a full idea of its interest
or importance.

"Our general work has been to supply religious services, aiding chaplains where there were any, and preaching
to multitudes of soldiers who had no chaplains or means of
religious instruction, except what we provided; supplying
reading matter for the armies and for hospitals, regimental
and general; distributing bodily comforts, and bringing
home influences to the camp. We have had delegates in
all our great armies, who have been welcomed by the chaplains and by the men. The generals and officers have given
them free access, and encouraged them in their work. They
have found everywhere great eagerness to obtain religious
reading, great desire to hear the preached Word, and great
willingness to converse on the subject of religion. Many,
many will rise up that last day to call them blessed.

"They have gone to the men, held under the stern discipline of war, and treated as parts of a great machine;
taken them by the hand as brethren, and revived the sympathies and affections of their souls; shown them that
many hearts cared for them at home, and, above all, that
there was One who could sympathize in all their trials.
We can testify that our whole army is prepared in an
unusual degree to receive the gospel. And what we have
done is only the beginning of a mighty work, to fully
accomplish which will call for all the resources of our
churches."

The Commission has employed in the battle-field 356
Christian labourers, and in home work 1033, who have

held 3945 meetings with soldiers and sailors, besides nearly
200 public meetings, and have awakened and sustained a
growing interest in the special work in all places of the
Union. Their abstract of the first annual Report as presented January 29, 1863, will speak for itself:

" The work of the Commission, together with that of the
various Young Men's Christian Associations and Army Committees co-operating with it, is, when summed up, as follows :

Cash disbursed for expenses, stores, and pub- lications	$40,160 29
Value of stores and publications distributed by the Commission	$142,150 00
Christian ministers and laymen commissioned to minister at the seat of war to men on battle-field, and in camps and hospitals .	356
Christians actively working with the army committees in the home work . .	1033
Meetings held with soldiers and sailors exclu- sive of those at the seat of war . .	3945
Public meetings held on behalf of the soldiers and sailors	188
Bibles and testaments distributed . .	102,560
Books (large and small) for soldiers and sailors, distributed.	115,757
Magazines and pamphlets, religious and secu- lar, distributed	34,653
Soldiers' and sailors' hymn and psalm books distributed	130,697
Papers distributed	384,781
Pages of tracts, etc., distributed . . .	10,953,706
Temperance documents distributed . .	300,000
Libraries supplied to hospitals, etc. . .	23
Boxes and barrels of stores and publications distributed	3691

" In addition to the above, there is much of which no
record has been kept worthy of especial mention. For
example, a large number of Christian men and women
have been associated as helpers with our delegates and
committees in their work in hospitals and camps, not included in the 1033 reported, and the meetings at the seat

of war with the soldiers, held by those sent by the commission, amounting to many thousands, and many more thousands of letters written for the soldiers to their friends, or to obtain discharges or descriptive lists."

Were the work an effort of a sect or only a development of the influence of Christian principle, I should hesitate to extend any further representations. But I wish to show the sympathy of the nation, and the most enlightened and benevolent portion of the community, not only with the army, but with the object for which the army exposes itself in the midst of warfare. The United States Government at present are sustained by the *people*, the Protestant Churches, the Christian families, and the wisest patriots in the country, with few and insignificant exceptions. " One of themselves" has said in beautiful earnestness :—

" If we, as women, can devise new duties for ourselves, if we can find new channels of help, new inspiration for good, new modes of evincing our love of country without public demonstration, let us not shrink but rejoice. And it may be that some among us who, seeing no present distress, have never yet fairly awakened to the full perception of the requirements and privileges of the hour, will, for the honour of the sisterhood, now come forward, and, being fresh in the work, press on beyond the foremost. We are all needed, and we must not hold back, supposing the work to grow less pressing. The spring budding around us, reminds us that the time of comparative inaction in our armies is over, and that our boys will soon be in want of everything we can do for them. Let us abridge our luxuries for their sakes ; let us give them of our leisure ; let us consecrate a large portion of our thoughts to them ; let us write them innumerable letters of hope, and love, and cheer, full of sweet home chat and bright visions of the future, when their toil shall be over and the victory won. Let us pledge ourselves to treat with a true disdain every insidious attempt at corrupting public feeling at the North ; every man who is engaged in fomenting these miserable party divisions, which form the last hope of our traitorous enemies."

CHAPTER IX.

THE army which fought under Washington in the revolutionary struggle was disbanded at the close of the War of Independence. The eighth section of the Constitution of 1787 empowered Congress to " raise and support armies," and in the second article of the section the President was constituted " Commander-in-Chief of the army, and navy, and of the militia, when called into the service of the United States." A war department was established in 1789. The present articles of war were enacted in 1806, and form the military code which governs all American troops when mustered for service. In 1791 the rank and file of the army were 2116; but in 1792 an act of Congress provided for a uniform militia throughout the United States. Few alterations have been since introduced into the system. In 1796, four regiments of infantry, eight companies each, two companies of light dragoons, and a corps of artillerists and engineers, constituted the body of the army; a brigadier and major-general, with a suitable staff, were the controlling authorities; but, in a short time, the major-general was dispensed with as an unnecessary extravagance. The excitement stimulated by the wars of the French Revolution induced Congress to authorize the President in 1798 to raise a provisional army of 10,000 men. The peace establishment was again adopted in 1802, but in 1807 the retaliatory French and English decrees on commerce prompted warlike apprehensions, and again the Congress authorized the President to accept 30,000 volunteers, and in 1808 the entire militia of the country was newly equipped. In January, 1812, an act directed that an additional force should be raised ; in February the force was increased, and on the 18th June of that year war was declared, and 35,000 were voted to carry on successfully what had been commenced with 10,000 men. At the close of this war, in 1815, the provisional army was disbanded. In 1821 a systematic organization was given to the new peace establishment, which remained with slight and only temporary enlargements till 1861. The several parts of the American *army of peace* were seven infantry and four artillery regiments, with the various staff corps and departments, which were the nucleus of the present war establishment. A regiment of dragoons took the place of irregular *mounted* rangers in 1833, and a second regiment of the same class was raised in 1836. The Florida war occasioned disturbance and apprehension from 1835 till 1839, but a treaty, which took full effect in 1842, gave promise of future peace. The scheming of Southern slaveholders involved the Union in prospective war with Mexico in 1845-6, which caused temporary additions to the army. In May, 1846, the aggregate of the line troops was 7,244. Regulars were enlisted during the war in total number 29,000, and 50,000 volunteers were employed for various terms of service. In 1848, at the treaty of peace, the volunteers and regulars were brought home and disbanded : the only addition left being a regiment of mounted riflemen. In 1855 two regiments of infantry and two of cavalry were added to the standing army to defend frontiers, etc., in an increased territory. General Winfield Scott was by brevet nominated Lieutenant-General, the only successor in that title to Washington.

When Fort Sumter was attacked, in April, 1861, the

United States army consisted of only 14,000 regular troops, scattered in small parties over the whole land by a preconcerted arrangement of the members of Mr. Buchanan's cabinet. The United States' navy numbered no more than 5000 seamen, stationed in all parts of the *world*, beyond the reach of speedy recal. Officers high in rank had resigned their positions in the service of the Union, and joined the conspirators, diminishing the force of the United States, and strengthening their foes. All the troops in rebel states were either turned out from their territories, or conquered as being few, or bribed to enter the service of the secessionists. Only one garrison remained flying the flag of the Union within the Southern states. Major Anderson had conveyed his small band from Fort Moultrie or another less secure, and had occupied Fort Sumter in Charleston Harbour. General Beauregard and his confederates laid seige to it, and surrounded it by forces which a small body of men, less than a hundred, could not hope to withstand. Vessels were sent with provisions and assistance to the beleaguered fortress, but could not reach it through the armed obstructions placed in the channel. Here, then, was the commencement of the war, under the generalship of the secessionist Beauregard, and in obedience to the commands of Mr. Jefferson Davis and the men who with him had conspired to break up the Union, and set up a rebellious confederacy in violation of their oaths and regardless of the bloodshed and ruin which might follow. It has been often urged that the United States began the war between the South and North, and that they are responsible for its continuance. Men who ought to know better and should have led in a wiser path have spoken rash and harsh things. The Confederate Secretary of War, Mr. Walker, Montgomery, Ala., threatened that before the 1st of May the Confederate flag should be waving over the capitol at Washington, and Faneuil Hall, Boston.

The army of the United States, throughout the present conflict, is not constituted as modern European armies have been. The Highland regiments of earlier times, when the chief of a clan and the cadets of his family drew together all who bore his name, or by collateral lineage had their sympathies, and dwelling in the glens and associations of their strath, or mountain range, were nearer, in comparison, to the Illinois, Michigan, Ohio, Pennsylvania, Rhode Island, Massachusetts, Connecticut, and even Kansas battalions, which have been marshalled in battle array. When President Lincoln first called on the loyal states to help him to meet the rebels, multitudes rallied fresh from the plough, the loom, the forge, the workshop, fresh from college seats, professors' chairs, the bar, the pulpit, and the counting-house. From every department of American industry the army of the Union was promptly convened to hasten into the field of war. They were enrolled as volunteers, many of them only for three months, and others for nine months ; they expected the struggle would be brief and their return to peaceful pursuits would be speedy. The men first in command were mostly as unskilled in military tactics as were the ploughmen who filled the ranks. Many men who marched rank and file, were, in their home circles, as high in position as were the officers who stood as leaders. But few of them had ever fired a musket, even on parade, until they had to stand the fire of an enemy. The Secessionists had been familiar with bowie-knife and revolver, and had, many of their chief men. contemplated the fate of war, and had been familiar with the necessity of self-defence among the slaves, whom they were wont to oppress and pursue. They had tasted blood and smelled powder ; while the mass in rank and file of the Southern army had the idle brute habits, which gloried in violence and plunder ; fit as *automata* to be wielded by those who promised rapine and murder as their guerdon. The first rebel bands were di-

vided into provisional and regular Confederate armies.
The provisionals were enlisted for the space of a year, and
were generally drawn from the state militia—their pay,
eleven dollars *per mensem*. Large numbers, as enrolled,
were placed at Montgomery, it was said, much to the annoy-
ance of the peaceful inhabitants. They visited taverns,
ordered what they wanted, but never paid—drinking and
carousing night and day, flourishing their revolvers in the
streets, swearing vengeance on all Northern men. The
regulars were enlisted for three years, composed of the
lowest class of white population, gathered from the *débris*
of society in New Orleans, Mobile, and other sea-ports;
they were enticed to enter the Southern army by large
bounties, etc., in paper money; their pay was only seven
dollars *per mensem;* their uniform, a red shirt, black hat,
and blue pants. They are described as the hardest looking white men that could be drawn together, after the
manner of filibusters, representing all nations. Another
class, however, had to be gathered as these were swept
away; conscription, of all above sixteen and under forty-
five, was the first measure enforced by the bayonet or revolver. . More recently, it is alleged, age is no defence;
whoever can carry a rifle or revolver must go forth to the
slaughter; and hence, when prisoners are taken they are
not anxious to be exchanged or paroled—many offer to
enter under the Northern banner, and others pass into
foreign lands.

The Secretary-at-War, on July 1, 1861, stated in his
report to the President, that " the conspirators against the
Constitution had left nothing undone to perpetuate their
infamy. Revenue steamers had been betrayed by their
commanders, or overpowered by rebel troops at the command of disloyal governors. The government arsenals at
Little Rock, Baton Rouge, Mount Vernon, Appalachicola,
Charleston, Fayetteville; and the government works and

ordnance depôt at San Antonio, and elsewhere in Texas,
containing immense stores of ammunition and arms, had
been surrendered by their commanders or seized by disloyal hands.   Forts Macon, Caswel, Johnson, Clinch,
Pulaski, Jackson, Marion, Barrancas, M'Kee, Morgan,
Gaines, Pike, Macomb, St. Phillip, Livingstone, Smith, and
three at Charleston; besides the barracks at New Orleans,
Barrancas, and Oglethorpe, Fort Jackson, on the Mississippi, the battery at Bienvue, Dupre, and Ship Island, had
been stolen or betrayed by their commanding officers;
custom-houses and branch mints at New Orleans, Mobile,
Savannah, Charleston, at Charlotte and Dahlonega, containing large amounts of government funds, had also been
illegally seized for rebellious purposes; and a brigadier,
General Twiggs, withdrew the forces which were placed
to defend the people on the frontiers of Texas from savage
Indians, and handed his troops and all the public property
under his control to the rebels.   A few, and only a few, of
the military servants of the Union, in active service, proved
faithful, though they were encouraged by others who had
been living in retirement.   Major Robert Anderson at
Fort Sumter, Lieutenant Slemmer at Fort Pickens, and
Lieutenant Roger at Harper's Ferry, are named as "faithful among the faithless found."   The old veteran General
Scott, and others, militia officers, venerable by years and
service, continued their devotion to the Union and its flag.

When it was ordered by the President's proclamation to
call out a portion of the states militia for three months, the
governors of Virginia, North Carolina, Tennessee, Arkansas,
Kentucky, and Missouri, directly refused, though in some
of these states loyal citizens united to raise forces for the
Federal government.   The President issued his proclamation on the 15th day of April, 1861, in conformity with an
act of Congress, February 28, 1795, requiring the several
loyal states to furnish the aggregate number of 75,000

militiamen for three months. They were to be embodied
in 98 regiments, and the several states were enjoined to
furnish each a proportion according to their population.
On the 4th of May following, the President again invited
volunteers to serve during the war; 208 regiments were
raised in answer to this appeal before July 1, and the united
force of the Union troops was thus raised to 225,000, while
50,000 more were provided for and ready to be embodied,
as the three months' men retired. In the month of December following, under General M'Clellan, were enrolled
as present, 185,327, besides 10,000 who were absent from
duty. The officers, who are numbered, were — *general*
officers, 48; general staff-officers, 270; field officers, 531;
regimental and battalion staff-officers, 881; and company
officers, 5119; absent officers were 1046—giving altogether
8304 officers to 186,479 rank and file, and providing a commissioned officer to every $22\frac{1}{2}$ men. If these gentlemen
had enjoyed a military education or experience, qualifying
them to lead their comrades into action, confidence might
have been warranted. But, without any disposition to
underrate their bravery and patriotism, it may be fearlessly
said that many among them needed themselves to learn
the first rudiments of military tactics. All regimental
officers of the volunteers, from colonels down to second
lieutenants, are appointed by governors of states. Other
regiments were ordered to be raised, containing, officers
and men, 22,068, infantry, artillery, and cavalry, as a permanent force. The desire to secure efficient officers led to
the appointment of half the new officers from civil life and
half from the existing army—many of the former had
attended "West Point Academy," and had served with
distinction in the field; the second lieutenants were selected
from meritorious sergeants of the regular service.

Distinctions of military rank in the Union army.—Rank
can readily be ascertained by observing the shoulder-straps
of officers. A major-general is distinguished by two *silver*

stars on his shoulder-straps; a brigadier has but one star;
a colonel has a silver embroidered eagle; a lieutenant-
colonel has a silver embroidered leaf; a captain is known
by two gold embroidered bars; a first lieutenant has but
one gold bar on the strap; a second lieutenant none at all.
The cloth of the strap is, for staff-officers, dark-blue; artillery, scarlet; infantry, light or sky-blue; riflemen,
medium or emerald green; cavalry, orange colour.

In December, 1861, the Secretary of War reported the
number of the army, 680,971, all of whom had volunteered;
but they were divided as volunteer militia, 640,637, and in
the regular army, 20,334. Congress passed an Act on the
22nd of July, authorizing the President to call out 500,000
volunteers; and on the 25th of the same month it
authorized him again to call out 500,000 more volunteers.
In all he thus received the power to employ one
million of men to suppress the rebellion. In virtue of
these powers Mr. Lincoln, ordered on the 4th of August,
1862, a draft of 300,000 men to serve for nine months, and
a further draft was ordered to complete the *quota* of the
previous call for 300,000 three years' volunteers; unless
the same should have been raised before August 15th, 1862.
These drafts were made in proportions on the states,
according to their population in the census of 1860. In
several states coloured regiments had been raised and sent
into the field, where their services, at first suspected, came
ultimately to be highly appreciated; and the President
and his Cabinet, adopting the plan of a large coloured
force, have determined to embody 200,000 such men, and
to place them in the field, with rights and immunities of
war, the same as those claimed for white troops. The
Congress passed an Act in their session 1862-3, enjoining a
conscription for draft by ballot among all the citizens, to
call out 300,000 more men, which came into operation in
July, 1863. The whole number may not have been raised

in all the states. It is alleged that in some districts there was a surplus of volunteers; it is now understood that another order is to be met by volunteering, to render unnecessary a second conscription. It is not unlikely that the coloured troops will remain embodied for a longer time than any of the other volunteer corps. Mr. Lincoln casually mentioned to me in July, 1863, that there were on the roll of the United States army probably *one million of men*. They occupy fortresses, and serve in the field, and guard freedmen's plantations in Louisiana, North Carolina, and Florida, in Texas and Tennessee, on the Potomac and the Mississippi, in New Orleans and in front of Charleston, and guarding rebel prisoners.

The time of service for which the several portions of the U.S. troops have been enrolled has not only interested a wide circle in the movements of the army, but has, doubtless, misled many cursory observers in their calculations, both as to the strength and vicissitudes of the entire force. The soldiers have returned in companies, as I have seen, and in regiments to their homes when they had finished the time for which they had volunteered. It is not unlikely habits were nurtured in the field which were not so congenial with the peaceful employments from which they had gone, and which they the less wished to resume, and not a few returned volunteers afterward enlisted for a longer time; nevertheless it is manifest that, from an army so composed, the mere mercenary character is alien. It is a great mistake to conclude that the United States' troops are largely drawn from Irish emigration,—it is a citizen army, as is manifested by those occasions when the vote is taken for candidates for election in Maine, Ohio, Massachusetts, and other states.

Much of the devotedness and bravery of the battalions may be thus accounted for; but many of the early disasters at Bull's Run, Manassas Gap, Ball's Bluff, Williamsburg,

and other of the subsequent mistakes may have arisen
from the defects in a new and unorganized army. Battles
were fought without reconnoitering the position, without
concert of action among the different corps and divisional
commanders, and almost without orders; one general
fancying that another gave his orders and answered telegraphs in ill temper, and another general feeling wounded
that he was not in the confidence of his immediate
superior. They had to learn war by defeat, and caution
and vigilance by disaster. From General M'Clellan to
Generals Stone, and Pope, and McDowell, and others, who
fell in their own brave blunders, the American officers have
had to learn, as English officers did in their Peninsular
campaigns under Sir John Moore and Sir Arthur Wellesley,
that the science and practice of war can only be mastered
by patience, prudence, and suffering. To meet an enemy
spurred by passion, flushed with victory, and confident of
continued success against the charge of his war horse,
whose neck is clothed with thunder, and his flying artillery
and batteries of rifled cannon, amidst the onset of trained
warriors led by skilful chiefs, requires combatants equally
prepared. Army can only be met by army, battery by
battery, squadron by squadron, and the shock of organized
thousands must be encountered by the firm breasts and
valiant arms of other thousands as well organized and as
skilfully led. The Duke of Wellington answered the cry
of the brave men in the square at Waterloo, "Lead us on,
general, lead us on." "No, my lads, you must stand;"
and they stood, while cannon balls were mowing them
down as grass before the scythe, and those who were left
still stood, and gained the day; while if they had moved
they would have been as the untrained bands were at
Bull's Run.

The moral character and social position of many soldiers
in the ranks of the Northern army may be collected from

the conduct of multitudes in the camps, from the value set upon ordinances of religion and the Word of God, and from the incidents on the field of battle. The copies of the sacred Scriptures distributed and gratefully received, tell a tale; but the fact that multitudes brought their Bible with them from home and carried it into the field to be there used in the hour of suffering and sorrow, speaks of earlier and hallowed influences with which they have been blessed. "Bring me my knapsack," said a young soldier, who lay sick in one of the hospitals at Washington, "Bring me my knapsack." "What do you want of your knapsack?" inquired the head lady of the band of nurses. "I want my knapsack," again said the dying young man. His knapsack was brought to him, and as he took it his eye gleamed with pleasure, and his face was covered all over with a smile, as he brought out from it his hidden treasures. "There," he said, "that is a Bible from my mother. And this, 'Washington's Farewell Address,' is the gift of my father. And this," his voice failed. The nurse looked down to see what it was, and there was the face of a beautiful maiden. "Now," said the dying soldier, "I want you to put all these under my pillow." She did as she was requested, and the poor young man laid him down on them to die, requesting that they should be sent to his parents when he was gone. Calm and joyful was he in dying. It was only going from night to endless day—from death to eternal glory. So the young soldier died.

Yet another illustration is recorded in the "Sergeant's Memorial": "John Hanson Thompson, born at New Haven, Sept. 3, 1842, was a lineal descendant of a New England settler, who arrived in America in 1635. Educated in the best seminaries in his native land, and by private teachers in England and France, he had established for himself, in the minds of parents and discerning friends, a reputation for noble qualities, unselfishness, courageousness, and deference to the opinion of others. When Mr. Lincoln's election was followed by rebellion, he wrote to his father informing him that he had been chosen among his class mates at Andover, Captain of the " Ellsworth," or Phillip's cadets, in which seventy academy boys had been enrolled; and having received his father's reply, that the time might come when he "must bid him go, and when he must be ready to take every risk;" he rejoined, "I am strong for war; it seems to me that the South needs a lesson, which cannot be taught by 'compromise' or 'starvation.' Do you want me to go, or do you only *not* object if it be necessary?" A New England governor, who had witnessed his Andover drills, offered to give him a commission in a regiment just starting for the South. But when war seemed pressing at the door of the Capitol, and General M'Clellan was retreating down the Shenandoah Valley, his father sent by telegraph his consent for the lad to lay down his books and take up his musket. In twenty-four hours he was enrolled as a private, in Company G, of the 22nd New York National Guards, and was on his way to join the regiment at Baltimore. After a few days his regiment was ordered to a post of danger; and he then wrote: "I am very glad indeed. We may be brought into active service; may not. I will not speculate where I know nothing. But whatever may come, I am ready—it is what I came for. I have been happy thus far, and shall not complain at any orders. We take one day's rations, and each man twenty rounds of ball cartridge, so we are ready for anything, and hurrying on. Much love to all, and as I know not what may come, good-bye to one and all."

At the close of the three months' campaign, for which he had promptly volunteered, he wrote to his father: "I have for a few days considered the whole subject carefully, and think I had better go again for three years or the war—that it is my duty to go." He was now offered a ser-

geancy in the 111th New York State volunteers, but was
finally appointed to the same rank in the 106th New York
State volunteers. He did his duty efficiently and faithfully, and was beloved by officers and men. He believed
it the duty of every man to fight for his country. " I
know we want education, but where is the good of education without your country? And where is your country
without your men to fight and make it?" In the opinion
thus expressed, the father found comfort, and Dr. Lieber
endorsed it for parental consolation. When assured of
promotion, he replied, he " had enlisted with a determination to do anything for his country, and he sometimes felt
that he could serve it better as he was, than in some higher
office with more temptations to consult his own ease."
While he discharged severe camp and picket duty, a storm
of snow fell, in the midst of which he passed the night,
and was attacked with *typhoid pneumonia*, and with difficulty
was he conveyed to his death-bed. When visited by the
doctor, he inquired if he thought he could stand it; and as
the reply gave no hope, he said, " Would it not be well to
telegraph to his father?" And when answered it was
already done, he replied he was glad of it, "father will be
sure to come to-morrow." Taking good-bye of one of his
watching comrades: " send my love," he added, " to my
dear father and mother, and brothers and sisters. I hope
to meet them in heaven." He prayed for himself, and
asked one that stood by to sing, " Asleep in Jesus, blessed
sleep," then requested some one to pray; and when all
were too overcome to comply, he himself prayed and died,
16th March, 1863.

The father of this brave lad has since surrendered a
second son to his country's service. An instance from a
wealthier family, accustomed to the refinements and luxuries
of cultivated society in America and Europe, is appropriately honoured by Mrs. Gaskell in the " Macmillan."

Colonel Robert Gould Shaw, as she testifies from intimate intercourse with his family, deliberately risked and cheerfully laid down a prosperous, happy, beloved, and loving life. Referring to her correspondence with his mother, she proceeds with a beautiful sympathy :—

"Presently I heard that Robert Gould Shaw, the only son, had entered the 7th New York Lancers, the crack regiment, into which all the young men of the 'upper ten thousand' entered, a dashing corps, splendidly horsed and arrayed. By and by, perhaps before the war had deepened to grim, terrible earnest, Mrs. Shaw sent me word how, unable almost to bear the long separation from her only boy, she and his sisters had gone to camp (I forget where), to see him. And then he had left the gay regiment of the 7th Lancers and had gone to live with, and train and teach, the poor forlorn coloured people, 'niggers,' who were going to fight for the freedom of their brothers in the South. The repugnance of the Northerners to personal contact with black or coloured people, has been repeatedly spoken of by all travellers in America. Probably Colonel Shaw had less of this feeling than a Northerner would have had who had been entirely brought up in America. But still it must have required that deep root of willingness to do God's will, out of which springs the truest moral courage, to have enabled him to march out of New York at the head of the 54th Massachusetts, all black or coloured men, amidst the jeers and scoffings of the 'roughs,' and the contemptuous pity of many who should have known better. Yet this did Colonel Shaw one day this last spring, with a brave trustful heart, leaving home, leaving mother, leaving new made wife, to go forth and live amongst his poor despised men, the first regiment of niggers called into the field ; and to share their hardships, and to teach them the deepest and most precious knowledge that he had himself. Two months afterwards he was with them before Fort Wagner, 'sitting on the ground and talking to his men,' says an eye-witness, 'very familiarly and kindly.' He told them how the eyes of thousands would look on the night's work on which they were about to enter, and he said, ' Now, boys, I want you to be men !' He would walk along the line, and speak words of cheer to his men. We could see that he was a man who had counted the cost of the undertaking before him, for his words were spoken so ominously' (remember, the Confederates had openly threatened to make an especial aim of every white officer leading coloured troops)—'his lips were compressed, and now and then there was visible a slight twitching of the corners of the mouth, like one bent on accomplishing or dying. One poor fellow, struck no doubt by the colonel's determined bearing, exclaimed as he was passing him, ' Colonel, I will stay with you till I die ;' and he kept his word, he has never been seen since.'

" The 54th coloured Massachusetts regiment held the right of the storming column that attacked Fort Wagner on the 18th of July last. It went into action 650 strong and came out with a loss of one-third of the men, and a still larger proportion of officers, but eight out of twenty-three coming out uninjured. The regiment was marched up in column by wings, the first being under the command of Colonel Shaw. When about 1000 yards from the fort the enemy opened upon them with shot, shell, and canister. They pressed through this storm, and cheered and shouted as they advanced. When within a hundred yards from the fort, the musketry from it opened with such terrible effect that the first battalion hesitated—only for an instant. Colonel Shaw sprang forward, and waving his sword cried, ' Forward, my brave boys ;' and with another cheer and shout they rushed through the ditch, gained the parapet on the right, and were soon hand to hand with the enemy. Colonel Shaw was one of the first to scale the walls. He stood erect to urge forward his men, and while shouting to them to press forward he was shot dead, and fell into the fort. His body was found with twenty of his men lying dead around him, two lying on his own body. In the morning, they were all buried together in the same pit."

She quotes from his mourning mother the breathings of patriotic devotion in her own words :—

" ' Yes, my darling, precious, only son has joined the host of young martyrs who have given their lives to the cause of right in the last two years. He and I had thought and talked of what might happen to him, and I thought I was ready for the blow when it should come, but when can a mother be ready to give up her child? It has been a terrible struggle, and no relief comes to me but from prayer. I do not mean that I would have had it otherwise, for it was a fitting end for his noble and most beautiful life. Ah! dear friend, when I think of the agony that has torn the hearts of mothers and wives in this country, North and South, I feel sure that God is performing a mighty work in the land; and, purified from our curse of slavery, our descendants will reap the reward of our suffering.'"

The Rev. R. Spencer Vinton, chaplain of McKim's Hospital, relates the following incident:

"Among other, Sylvester McKinley of Pennsylvania, was received into the hospital, immediately after the battle of Antietam. He was a noble-looking youth, of fine figure and intelligent face. He had lost his left arm and was much reduced; he was in great destitution, having neither coat, vest, or hat. All who saw him were interested in him, and the ladies of the Relief Association took charge of him, and rendered him comfortable. His condition being critical, I at once began to give him religious instruction. Having been a Sunday-school scholar, he easily understood my teachings, and listened with attention, desiring to know if I thought Jesus would be his friend and Saviour. He received my assurances of Christ's interest in him with joy, and was made happy in the belief that he should reach heaven. In my daily visits to him, I always found him with his Testament in his hand or near him. I prayed with him and found him trusting in God and confident in his hope of heaven. His nurse was faithful, and he was grateful for all kindness. Worn out by his sufferings and almost fainting, he asked his nurse to hand him his Testament. He opened it, read a brief passage: 'Now,' said he, in a feeble voice, 'place it under my head.' The nurse did as he wished. He calmly laid his head upon the treasured volume, and in a moment was asleep in Jesus."

The solitary and the dying soldier naturally recall the associations of home, and the sacred hours passed under the influence of domestic and parental religion. But it is possible, in the noisy throng and boisterous mirth of merry associates, to drown the whispers of conscience and banish thoughts of eternity for a season. The efforts of pious benevolence are, however, aided by latent and long sown principles of truth and wisdom, imparted by the teaching given around the family hearth in youthful days. "Train up a child in the way in which he should go, and when he is old he will not depart from it," is a promise often verified in these armies.

" Soldiers' Communion.

" After a revival, and as some regiments were about to leave Camp Douglass, it was determined to have a communion season before they went. The chaplains of the regiments were of different denominations, but the Christian Commission united all. The arrangements were made by Mr. Farwell, one of its members, in conference with the chaplains, and it was held in their chapel. The Sabbath came. Long before the hour the chapel was densely crowded; the ministers with difficulty reached the platform. Chaplain Hagerty, after singing and prayer, stated the object of the meeting and announced the order of exercises. Chaplain Stoughton then simply and appropriately warned any against eating and drinking irreverently, and invited those who truly believed in Jesus, and desired to live a holy life, to eat and drink in remembrance of Christ, and offered prayer somewhat after the Episcopal form. The bread and wine were served by Mr. Hoag, a venerable elder, whose son was present as Colonel of the 113th Illinois, about to leave.

" There sat the dusty and battle-worn veterans from the Potomac, who, for eighteen months had not been in the house of God, side by side with fresh recruits about to enter the combat; while the aged father served them all together, his own son among them, with the symbols of life to them, as they were memorials of the death of Jesus. Oh, it was a solemn scene. Sobs and sighs, that could not be repressed, broke the silence, and the scene will never be forgotten. Over two hundred communed. This done, Chaplain Brown offered thanksgiving, the venerable Chaplain McReynolds gave the exhortation to communicants,

Rev. Mr. Pratt spoke of preparation for death, a German brother, in broken English, from a full heart, talked of the love of Christ, and Rev. Robert Patterson concluded the communion service by an address to the unconverted,—all showing forth the Lord's death till He come. Eighteen presented themselves for prayer; and fervent prayer was offered for them, followed by praise. And thus ended the Soldiers' Communion."

CAMP DOUGLAS AGAIN.

Rev. Dr. Patterson writes under date November 1, 1862 :—" God is evidently at work in the army. Here our meetings are well attended and conversions taking place daily. To-day, in noon meeting, a man who ten days ago was so wicked that the men removed his tent out of hearing, stood up to give glory to God for his conversion.

"One night a dancing party was going on, and the leader felt disposed to curse the praying men for spoiling the sport. However, the fiddler consented to lead the music of the prayer-meeting, and thinking 'John Brown' a solemn thing, he soon had the camp singing 'Glory Hallelujah.' But when the religious nature of the meeting was explained, he played, 'Come, ye sinners, poor and needy,' and the men all chimed in and sang enthusiastically, the sentries around the camp calling out, when the line was read, 'Louder!' and joining in the singing. Thirty came forward for prayers at the close of the meeting. When the services closed, the person who was so angry because the amusements had been interrupted, got upon a box and made an address, of which this was the conclusion : 'Now, all you fellows that mean to give up this nonsense, just shy up your cards as I do,' and immediately a shower of cards went up into the air, and came down on the heads of the audience and were trodden into the mud."

Among the sanguinary engagements in which the Northern army has been exposed to the casualties of war since the attack upon Fort Sumter till the present time, it would be difficult to attempt an aggregate estimate of those who have been killed in the field and those who have died in hospitals of their wounds. From official returns an approach to accuracy may be made, and nothing more. From *data* which are presented in tabular returns from April 13, 1861, when Fort Sumter was taken without any loss of life, till the end of 1862, reckoning that the half of the wounded die, I find nearly 45,000 fatal cases. I can hardly conjecture how many cases of sickness, brought on by military services, may have terminated fatally, and in how many the seeds of disease have been sown to grow up in the home circle and mature in the premature decease of the victim; but perhaps altogether we should have 45,000 more. The Bull Run, Wilson's Creek, Ball's Bluff, Fort Donelson, Pea Ridge, Winchester, Newbern, Shiloh, Williamsburg, Fair Oaks, and Cross Keys, Gaines' Mills and other places for seven days; Cedar Mountain, Centreville, Richmond, Kentucky, South Mountain, Antietam, Shephard's Town, Corinth, Perryville, Prairie Grove, Murfreesboro, and Fredericksburg, all preceded great battles which have been fought in 1863; Vicksburg, Port Hudson, Helena, Gettysburg, Chattanooga, Chickamauga, Knoxville, and other sanguinary memorials of the Cumberland army have proved the resting-place of many brave and patriotic dead. I venture not to depict the conflict or recount the daring exploits of men flushed with victory, or obstinately resisting the assaults of mortal adversaries. Mr. Everett's funereal oration at Gettysburg, eloquently and pathetically consecrating a national mausoleum, warns me how presumptuous any description of mine would be. Moreover I seek not the living among the dead. The field of battle is an appalling spectacle. The old Duke of Wellington could speak from oft-repeated experience, and his testimony was, that, "next to a defeat, the saddest thing is a victory." The terrors of the battle-field after the contest is over—the sights and sounds of woe—no words can adequately depict.

A brief extract from Mr. Everett on Gettysburg will supply my deficiency here:

"From eleven till half-past one o'clock all was still; a solemn pause of preparation, as if both parties were nerving themselves for the supreme effort. At length the awful silence, more terrible than the wildest tumult of battle, was broken by the roar of 250 pieces of artillery from the opposite ridges joining in a cannonade of unsurpassed violence—the Rebel batteries along two-thirds of their line pouring their fire upon Cemetery Hill and the centre and left wing of our army. Having attempted in this way for two hours, but without success, to shake the steadiness of our lines, the enemy rallied his forces for a last grand assault. Their attack was principally directed against the position of our 2nd corps. Successive lines of Rebel infantry moved forward with equal spirit and steadiness, from their cover on the wooded crest of Seminary Ridge, crossing the intervening plain, supported right and left by their choicest brigades, and charged furiously up to our batteries. Our own brave troops of the 2nd corps, supported by Doubleday's division and Stannard's brigade of the 1st, received the shock with firmness, the ground on both sides was long and fiercely contested, and covered with the killed and wounded, till after 'a determined and gallant struggle,' as it is pronounced by General Lee, the Rebel advance, consisting of two-thirds of Hill's corps and the whole of Longstreet's, including Pickett's division, the *élite* of his corps, which had not yet been under fire, and was now depended upon to decide the fortunes of this last eventful day, was driven back with prodigious slaughter, discomfited, and broken. These were the expiring agonies of the three days' conflict, and with them the battle ceased. It was fought by the Union Army with courage and skill, from the first cavalry skirmish on Wednesday morning to the fearful rout of the enemy on Friday afternoon, by every arm and every rank of the service; by officers and men; by cavalry, artillery, and infantry. The two armies, after the first day, were numerically equal: if the Union force had the advantage of a strong position, the Confederates had that of choosing time and place, the *prestige* of former victories over the army of the Potomac, and of the success of the first day.

"Victory does not always fall to the lot of those who deserve it; but that so decisive a triumph, under circumstances like these, was gained by our troops, I am inclined to ascribe, under Providence, to the spirit of exalted patriotism that animated them, and a consciousness that they were fighting in a righteous cause. All hope of defeating our army and securing what General Lee calls 'the valuable results' of such an achievement having vanished, he thought only of rescuing from destruction the remains of his shattered forces. In killed, wounded, and missing, he had, as far as can be ascertained, suffered a loss of about 37,000 men, rather more than a third of the army which he is supposed to have brought with him into Pennsylvania. Such, most inadequately recounted, is the history of the ever memorable Three Days, and of the events immediately preceding and following. It has been pretended, in order to diminish the magnitude of this disaster to the Rebel cause, that it was merely the repulse of an attack on a strongly defended position. The tremendous losses on both sides are a sufficient answer to this misrepresentation, and attest the courage and obstinacy with which the three days' battle was waged. Few of the great conflicts of modern times have cost victors and vanquished so great a sacrifice. On the Union side there fell in the whole campaign, of generals killed, Reynolds, Weed, and Zook; and wounded generals, Barlow, Barnes, Butterfield, Doubleday, Gibbon, Graham, Hancock, Sickles, and Warren; while of officers below the rank of general, and men, there were 2834 killed, 13,709 wounded, and 6643 missing. On the Confederate side there were killed on the field or mortally wounded, General Armistead, Barksdale, Garnett, Pender, Pettigrew, and Semms, and wounded, Heth, Hood, Johnson, Kemper, and Trimble. Of officers below the grade of general, and men, there were taken prisoners, including the wounded, 13,621, an amount ascertained officially. Of the wounded in a condition to be removed, of the killed and the missing, the enemy has made no return. They are estimated from the best data which the nature of the case admits, at 23,000. General Meade also captured three cannons, and forty-one standards. I must leave to others, who can do it from personal observation, to describe the mournful spectacle presented by these hill-sides and plains at the close of the terrible conflict."

The Southern armies have achieved deeds of great daring, and have proved their courage in hard-fought battles and their frequent superiority in military strategy, in advancing and retreating, and on the field. But their wisdom has not excelled in the conduct of any protracted campaign. However adventurous and overwhelming have been their designs, they have always been counter-checked and foiled. They have protracted the war, but they have not conquered a foot of land, and have lost hundreds of thousands of square miles. They have exhausted their exchequer, slaughtered many, perhaps, hundreds of thousands of their poor dupes who had not a benefit for which to fight, and they have failed in the object of their conspiracy. No doubt men among them have fancied they could appeal to God and ask his blessing on their arms, and died trusting in his mercy. But looking to slavery as *their avowed origin of the war*, I cannot have any sympathy for them except where they have repented and obtained forgiveness. I borrow from the Rev. T. N. Haskell of East Boston a photograph of the man who has been the inspiration of the rebellion.

THE CAREER OF A LEADER IN THE REBEL WAR.

"On the 3rd of June, 1808, a revolutionary cavalier from Georgia received a son born to him at his country inn, which he then kept in Christian County, Kentucky. When two years old, the young child and his mother were taken down into Mississippi, where he spent his childhood in a half wild way at Woodville. The boy was then sent to a neighbouring academy, and afterwards to Transylvania College, in Kentucky, but after a few terms was transferred to West Point, and, at Government expense, disciplined in the scientific arts of war. At graduation, in

1828, he received a second lieutenancy in the regular army of the United States, which he held for some years, during which time he fought fiercely with the Indians in the Black-Hawk war. For this he was breveted first lieutenant of mounted dragoons, and sent to fight the Comanches and Pawnees, the most fierce and subtle of savage men. After proving his ability to cope with Indian cunning and ferocity to his own satisfaction, he retired to a cotton plantation in Mississippi, and won the fair daughter of General Zachary Taylor, afterwards President, for his wife. Through her he received all 'the old Chieftain's' communicable knowledge and force of will, as both his father and confiding friend. He was of the Electoral College in 1844, and cast the vote of his state for James K. Polk, to the Chief Magistracy of the nation, over whom he exerted great influence, especially in favour of the Mexican war, for the avowed reason that it was essential to slavery, of which he had become even fanatically fond. His niece and adopted daughter assured me that he was wont to meet the steamboats at their landings near his plantation, and, with cane in hand, notify any '*Northrons*' that they need not stop. He was elected a Representative to Congress in 1845, and Colonel of Mississippi Volunteers, to serve under General Taylor, in Mexico, in 1846. At Monterey and Buena Vista he fought with such valour as to be commended to the President in two despatches by his father-in-law, and was, in consequence, appointed by Mr. Polk a 'Brigadier General of Mississippi Militia.' This, from policy, he declined, as being only in the gift of the Governor of his own 'sovereign state.' (He has since changed his mind as to the *military* sovereignty of States and Governors). He was next appointed a United States Senator by his Governor, to fill a short vacancy, and was re-elected to the same seat by his State Legislature for the following term of eight years. In the meantime he was nominated for Governor of Mississippi, and was so sanguine of success that he resigned his chair as Senator, but saw his rival inaugurated Governor in his stead. He was largely responsible for his States' *repudiation* of her honest debts, and encouraging her citizens to do the same. He was made a member of the *Cabinet of Constitutional Advisers* of President Pearce, in the most important seat as Secretary of War, and was his confidential friend, having the credit of ruling the executive councils of the nation, and the party then in power as he willed. As Secretary of War, he introduced camels, at Government expense, to swell the triumphal processions of the cotton king. He ordered and superintended more military surveys than any other Secretary ever in his seat. He studied every military post from Maine to Mexico, stood in every noted stronghold of the North, and especially inspected the New England forts: declaring in Faneuil Hall, when on one such investigation tour, that if the peculiar institution of the South could not be nationalized in the whole Union, it should be at least in a part by a dissolution of that Union. He was again re-appointed to the Senate of the United States; and, the easier to dissolve the Union, he then devised the dissolution of the dominant party at its nominating convention, in Charleston, S. C. (*i. e.*, in case he were not the favourite candidate, placed on a platform of unmitigated pledges to nationalize slavery, by right of way at least, in all the North), and under shelter of a solemn oath to defend the Union, and obey the Constitution and the laws of the United States, he advised his Cabinet successor to send all the arms possible from New England and the North to the Carolinas, Georgia, Alabama, and other Southern states; and, as so advised, Secretary Floyd issued an order on the last day of 1859, to transfer thither 115,000 stands of rifles and other guns from Massachusetts and New York. Five days later this leading Senator laid before his Southern colleagues—all under as solemn oath as mortals ever took, to defend the *union* of the Republic—a series of long-meditated plans for the permanent severance of the Southern states. Nearly all present at that Saturday night meeting, January 5th, 1860, acknowledged themselves ready for any feasible scheme of dissolution, and approved his measures one by one, given in brief, as follows:—

"Assume as Senators, as far as possible, the political powers of your several states, devising immediate measures to forestall regular elections by the people. Inaugurate at once a Provisional Government by the following means:— Urge by mail and telegraph the several Cotton State Conventions, now and soon to be in session, to refer no acts for

ratification to their constituents, as contemplated on their
appointment, but pass, as near as possible, one and the
same act of Secession, and another calling a Joint Convention of all the states so seceding, ostensibly to devise
measures suited to their common welfare, but really to
assume the immediate functions of the Provisional Government. In defence of this scheme, urge the several
governors (or, if necessary, irresponsible men) to take
possession of all the forts and arsenals, mints and custom
houses, in the name of their respective states, till the Provisional Government may safely assume them to itself, and
even supervise the post and telegraph offices, allowing the
United States to carry still the expensive Southern mails:
Dragoon the Legislatures of Texas, Tennessee, Kentucky,
and Virginia into unanticipated acts or *quasi* resolutions of
secession, or, at least, to call Conventions which may so re-
solve: Make sure of the sympathy of army officers by such
personal influences as will best secure the end: Retain
seats in the United States' Senate unless positively recalled,
till at least the 15th day of April, in order to tie Mr.
Buchanan's hands, prevent enabling legislation, and keep
the North in doubt; and, if the way be clear and exigencies
demand, instigate and aid desperate men in Baltimore to
kidnap (kill?) the incoming President in transit of
Maryland."*

   "This daring and consummate plan was adopted without a dissenting voice, and its perjured author put at the
head of a committee to begin to carry it out. The idea of
a joint convention of cotton states took like lightning, and
that of a Provisional Government followed like the stealthy
thunder in its train, and their author was elected its chief
executive. He took his leave of the United States senate
with the emotions of a Cæsar. He knew the die was cast,

---

   * This programme was, in substance, published in the
"National Intelligencer" the following week, and confirmed by a letter of Senator Yulie, found by Federal
troops in Florida, and by other credible persons at the
time in the confidence of Davis. The foregoing sketch of
his life is from personal acquaintance and public documents,
and is authentic.

for he had already crossed the Rubicon. He assumed the functions of his new office with such evident pride, to be *a* President, that the press of his own State acknowledged that he had now his 'outstanding *wish*.' He gathered about him the best of bad men, and boasted, amidst huzzahs which rent the heavens, that they would give the free defenders of our country the 'smell of Southern powder,' and the touch 'of Southern steel.' He has already fulfilled his boast in the sacrifice of millions on millions of money, and thousands upon thousands of men—of our own flesh and bone; and, with one of the largest armies in the world is, lo! this third year, seeking to blot out the first word in our *dear country's* name with his and our own brother's blood! It is a great humiliation for our country to have begotten and nourished such a son. It is a severe chastisement from God that he is still allowed to use his diversified experience and tact in tearing down the pillars of our Republic, with men of genius, and may be, too, of grace, misguided enough to die in his defence; and, unless the Lord turn to nought his counsels, he will yet, with his little figure and dyspeptic, sycophantic face, and unsurpassed sagacity and stern purposes of ill, be the greatest scourge of this or any other land. To be afflicted with incarnate treason in such a son, and his arch accomplices, is enough to make the Government and all loyal men go weeping through Gethsemane like David before the unsheathed sword of Absalom, looking for God to 'turn to nought the counsels of Ahithophel'—to 'arise Himself that his enemies may be scattered.' Our patriotism cannot burst forth in too deep solicitude and sorrow over these insurgents and traitors whom the interpositions of God's providence are essential to overthrow."

General R. E. Lee has been a great hero in the estimation of some. I heard enough from the lips of those whom he ought to have let go as free men and women according to the will of his relative, but whom he forced back into bondage under the whip in his own hand, to prevent me from any admiration of whatever he does or says, except as a penitent. Major-General Thomas J. Jackson was reputedly the best and bravest commander in the rebel service. His sobriquet "Stonewall" is said to have been given him after the battle of Bull Run ; a battle in which history will in vain look for any glory to either party, in attacking or pursuing. During that affair General Lee asked Jackson if his brigade had not better retire under the heavy fire they were sustaining. "No, sir,': said General Jackson, "I will stand here like a *stone wall.*" He did not stand like a stone wall in the Shenandoah Valley. But he often dashed into the heart of a fight, and by the speed of horses came upon feeble forces at unawares.

He became the monumental hero of a few English champions of the South, headed by Mr. Hope Beresford, Mr. Gregory of Galway, and other such members of the aristocracy. They determined to have a colossal statue raised to his memory. Twelve or fifteen of these gentlemen suffered their names to appear under the dictation of some Southern sympathiser, and consented to ask others to help them in raising £1500 to pay the sculptor, and erect a basement for the figure in some part of Virginia. Perhaps, before this immense undertaking, of such a millionaire as Mr. Hope, is finished, it may be necessary to obtain leave from Congress and the President at Washington to choose a site in Virginia. One of his own countrymen has anticipated the event and otherwise immortalized the hero by describing—

"STONEWALL JACKSON'S WAY."

"Come, stack arms, men, pile on
  the rails,
  Stir up the camp fire bright,
No matter if the canteen
  fails,
   We'll make a roaring
   night.
Here Shenandoah brawls
  along,
There burly Blue Ridge echoes
  strong
To swell the brigade's rousing
  song
  Of 'Stonewall Jackson's way.'

"We see him now, the old
  slouched hat
Cocked o'er his eye askew ;
The shrewd, dry smile, the
  speech so pat,
  So calm, so blunt, so true.
The 'Blue Light Elder' knows
  'em well ;
Says he, 'That's Banks, he's
  fond of shell ;
Lord, save his soul, we'll give
  him—' Well,
  That's 'Stonewall Jackson's
  way.'

"Silence! Ground arms! Kneel
all, caps off!
 Old Blue Light's going to
 pray.
Strangle the fool that dares to
 scoff!
Attention! it's his way.
Appealing from his native sod,
In form: pauperis to God.
Lay bare thine arm, stretch
· forth thy rod!
Amen! That's 'Stonewall's
 way.'   *

" He's in the saddle now, 'Fall in!
Steady! the whole brigade!
Hill's at the ford—cut off—will
 win
His way out, ball and blade!
What matter if our shoes are
 worn?
What matter if our feet are
 torn?
Quick step! we're with him be-
 fore dawn!'
That's 'Stonewall Jackson's
 way.'

" The sun's bright lances rout the
 mists
Of morning, and, by George!
Here's Longstreet struggling
 in the lists,
Hemmed in an ugly gorge.
Pope and his Yankees whipped
 before,
'Bayonets and grape' near
 Stonewall roar;
'Charge, Stuart! pay off Ash-
 by's score!'
Is 'Stonewall Jackson's way.'

"Ah! maiden, wail, and watch
 and yearn,
For news of Stonewall's band.
Ah! widow, read with eyes that
 burn
That ring upon thy hand.
Ah! wife, sew on, pray on, hope
 on,
Thy life shall not be all forlorn,
The foe had better not been
 born
That gets in 'Stonewall's
 way.'"

Such is the record of glory put into song of one who
died from wounds inflicted upon him, as the champion of a
confederation founded on the slavery of the industrious
man of colour as its corner-stone, and cemented by the
tears and blood of every negro descendant for whom, if
found helping on the cause of his own liberation, was reserved the decree of extermination or the perpetual bondage
of his race.

A BATTLE HYMN.

"God, to Thee we humbly
bow,
With hand unarmed and naked
brow,
Musket, lance, and sheathed
sword
At thy feet we lay, O Lord!
Gone is all the soldier's boast
In the valour of the host:
Kneeling here, we do our
most.

"Of ourselves, we nothing know:
Thou, and Thou alone, canst
show,
By the favour of thy hand,
Who has drawn the guilty
brand.
If our foemen have the right,
Show thy judgment in our
sight
Through the fortunes of the
fight.

" If our cause be pure and just,
Nerve our courage with thy
trust :
Scatter, in thy bitter wrath,
All who cross the nation's path.
May the baffled traitors fly,
As the vapours from the sky
When thy raging winds are
high.

" God of mercy, some must fall
In thy holy cause. Not all
Hope to sing the victor's lay
When the sword is laid away.

Brief will be the prayers then
said ;
Falling at thy altar dead,
Take the sacrifice instead.

" Now, O God, once more we rise,
Marching on beneath thy eyes,
And we draw the sacred sword
In thy name and at thy word.
May our spirits clearly see
Thee through all that is to be,
In defeat or victory."

G. H. BOKER.

Among the million of men now under the United States'
banner, there are hundreds of thousands of citizens who
have seen with their own eyes and heard for themselves
the terrible and vitiating facts of slavery in Florida, Alabama, Mississippi, the Carolinas, Georgia, and Louisiana ;
countries which but for the war they would never have
visited. To them slavery is no longer a mere theory or a
tale of fiction, however truly coloured, but it is a hideous
and brutally cruel system, deforming and cursing every
owner and every victim, and dishonouring the land in
which it has been tolerated. It has no longer any secrets ;
but lies naked and exposed under all its various aspects, in
the cotton-field, whether in Sea Islands or the Uplands, in
the sugar-plantations of Louisiana, in the rice swamps of
Georgia and Carolina, and other scenes of gang and whip
labour. Northern cavalry have explored to the walls of
Richmond, and gun-boats have sailed upon the affluent
streams, on whose banks dark tragedies of the slave masters' and overseers' barbarity have been enacted. These
men now know what they have in God's providence been
called to contend for, and in the strains of an English
poet I would exhort them to constancy and fidelity.

SOUTHERN TREASON.

How sadly, through sons so de-
graded,
  Pigmies ill-sprung from great
men,
Even your glories look faded,
  Washington, Franklin, and
Penn.

Popular government slandered,
  'Mid the deep scorn of the
world ;
Liberty's star-crowded standard
  Fouled by black treason, and
furled !

Southerners ! shame on such
treason !
Woe for your folly and guilt,
Woe for this war of unreason,
  Woe for the brothers' blood
spilt !

Curse on such monsters unfilial,
  Tearing their mother to
shreds ;
Curse on those children of
Belial ;
Curse on their parricide heads !

"FREEDOM.

"No blots on the banner of light !
  No slaves in the land of the
free !
No wrong to be rampant where
all should be right,
  No sin that is shameful to
see !
America, show the wide world
in thy strength
  How sternly determined thou
art,
To cut from thy soil in its
breadth and its length
  The canker that gnaws at thy
heart.

" Uprouse thee ! and swear by thy
might
  This evil no longer shall be ;
For all men are brothers, the
black as the white,
  And sons of one Father are we.

America, now is the perilous
time,
  When safety is solely decreed
To ridding the heart of old
habits of crime,
  And simply repenting indeed.

" Away to the bats and the moles
  With the lash, and the goad,
and the chain !
Away with the buying and sell-
ing of souls,
  And slavery toiling in pain.
America, this is thy chance, now
at length,
  Of crushing, while crouching
to thee,
Those rebels and slaveholders,
slaves to thy strength,
  The curse and contempt of
the Free."

MARTIN FARQUHAR TUPPER.

CHAPTER X.

THE GOVERNMENT OF THE UNITED STATES—SENATE AND CONGRESS—THE END CONTEMPLATED, AND RESULTS OF THE WAR.

IT is not my purpose to attempt an elaborate essay on the subject-title of this chapter. But some of my readers may welcome the opportunity of perusing the Declaration of Independence, and the Constitution under which the United States have been governed since 1788. The first of these documents was the creation of brave and noble men who had resolved to be free, and the second was the result of ten years' experience under a confederation of independent and sovereign states, digested and prepared by thoughtful and patriotic men who loved their nation and wished to bequeath to their posterity the blessings of freedom and a wisely-ordered government. Their influence was great, their virtues were unquestionable, and their names are held in grateful remembrance :—

"DECLARATION OF INDEPENDENCE.

"When in the course of human events, it becomes necessary for one people to dissolve the political bands which have connected them with another, and to assume, among the powers of the earth, the separate and equal station to which the laws of nature and of nature's God entitle them, a decent respect to the opinions of mankind requires that they should declare the causes which impel them to the separation.

"We hold these truths to be self-evident—that all men are created equal; that they are endowed by their Creator with certain unalienable rights; that among these, are life, liberty, and the pursuit of happiness. That, to secure these rights, governments are instituted among men, deriving their just powers from the consent of the governed; that, whenever any form of government becomes destructive of these ends, it is the right of the people to alter or to abolish it, and to institute a new government, laying its foundation on such principles, and organizing its powers in such form, as to them shall seem most likely to effect their safety and happiness. Prudence, indeed, will dictate that governments long established should not be changed for light and transient causes, and accordingly, all experience hath shown that mankind are more disposed to suffer, while evils are sufferable, than to right themselves by abolishing the forms to which they are accustomed. But when a long train of abuses and usurpations, pursuing invariably the same object, evinces a design to reduce them under absolute despotism, it is their right, it is their duty, to throw off such government, and to provide new guards for their future security. Such has been the patient sufferance of these colonies; and such is now the necessity which constrains them to alter their former systems of government. The history of the present king of Great Britain is a history of repeated injuries and usurpations—all having, in direct object, the establishment of an absolute tyranny over these states. To prove this, let facts be submitted to a candid world.

" He has refused his assent to laws the most wholesome and necessary for the public good.

" He has forbidden his governors to pass laws of immediate and pressing importance, unless suspended in their operation till his assent should be obtained; and, when so suspended, he has utterly neglected to attend to them.

" He has refused to pass other laws for the accommodation of large districts of people, unless those people would relinquish the right of representation in the legislature—a right inestimable to them, and formidable to tyrants only.

" He has called together legislative bodies at places unusual, uncomfortable, and distant from the depository of their public records, for the sole purpose of fatiguing them into compliance with his measures.

" He has dissolved representative houses repeatedly, for

opposing with manly firmness his invasions on the rights of the people.

" He has refused, for a long time after such dissolutions, to cause others to be elected; whereby the legislative powers, incapable of annihilation, have returned to the people at large, for their exercise : the state remaining, in the mean time, exposed to all the danger of invasion from without, and convulsions within.

" He has endeavoured to prevent the population of these states; for that purpose obstructing the laws for naturalization of foreigners ; refusing to pass others to encourage their migration hither, and raising the conditions of new appropriations of lands.

" He has obstructed the administration of justice by refusing his assent to laws for establishing judiciary powers.

" He has made judges dependent on his will alone, for the tenure of their offices, and the amount and payment of their salaries.

" He has erected a multitude of new offices, and sent hither swarms of officers to harass our people, and eat out their substance.

" He has kept among us, in times of peace, standing armies, without the consent of our legislatures.

" He has affected to render the military independent of, and superior to, the civil power.

" He has combined with others, to subject us to a jurisdiction foreign to our constitution, and unacknowledged by our laws, giving his assent to their acts of pretended legislation ;

" For quartering large bodies of armed troops among us,

" For protecting them, by a mock trial, from punishment for any murders which they should commit on the inhabitants of these states,

" For cutting off our trade with all parts of the world,

" For imposing taxes on us without our consent,

" For depriving us, in many cases, of the benefits of trial by jury,

" For transporting us beyond seas to be tried for pretended offences,

" For abolishing the free system of English laws in a neighbouring province, establishing therein an arbitrary government, and enlarging its boundaries, so as to render it at once an example and fit instrument for introducing the same absolute rule into these colonies,

" For taking away our charters, abolishing our most valuable laws, and altering fundamentally the powers of our governments,

" For suspending our own legislatures, and declaring themselves invested with power to legislate for us in all cases whatsoever.

" He has abdicated government here, by declaring us out of his protection, and waging war against us,

" He has plundered our seas, ravaged our coasts, burnt our towns, and destroyed the lives of our people,

" He is, at this time, transporting large armies of foreign mercenaries to complete the works of death, desolation, and tyranny, already begun with circumstances of cruelty and perfidy scarcely paralleled in the most barbarous ages, and totally unworthy the head of a civilized nation.

" He has constrained our fellow-citizens, taken captive on the high seas, to bear arms against their country, to become the executioners of their friends and brethren, or to fall themselves by their hands.

" He has excited domestic insurrections amongst us, and has endeavoured to bring on the inhabitants of our frontiers, the merciless Indian savages, whose known rule of warfare is an undistinguished destruction of all ages, sexes, and conditions.

" In every stage of these oppressions we have petitioned for redress in the most humble terms; our repeated petitions have been answered only by repeated injury. A prince, whose character is thus marked by every act which may define a tyrant, is unfit to be the ruler of a free people.

" Nor have we been wanting in attention to our British brethren. We have warned them, from time to time, of attempts made by their legislature to extend an unwarrantable jurisdiction over us. We have reminded them of the circumstances of our emigration and settlement here. We have appealed to their native justice and magnanimity, and we have conjured them, by the ties of our common kindred, to disavow these usurpations, which would inevitably interrupt our connections and correspondence. They too have been deaf to the voice of justice and consanguinity.

We must, therefore, acquiesce in the necessity which denounces our separation, and hold them, as we hold the rest of mankind—enemies in war, in peace, friends.

"We, therefore, the representatives of the United States of America, in general Congress assembled, appealing to the Supreme Judge of the world for the rectitude of our intentions, do, in the name, and by the authority of the good people of these colonies, solemnly publish and declare, That these united colonies are, and of right ought to be FREE AND INDEPENDENT STATES; that they are absolved from all allegiance to the British crown, and that all political connection between them and the state of Great Britain, is, and ought to be, totally dissolved: and that as free and independent states, they have full power to levy war, conclude peace, contract alliances, establish commerce, and to do all other acts and things which independent states may of right do. And for the support of this declaration, with a firm reliance on the protection of Divine Providence, we mutually pledge to each other, our lives, our fortunes, and our sacred honour."

All the people in the early American colonies of Great Britain were subjects of her king, and owed allegiance to him; and from the head of the British empire all civil authority then exercised or existing was derived; all the colonists were fellow-subjects, and in many respects one people. They cherished to each other, though in separate colonies, the goodwill which had been engendered by uninterrupted peace and a free commercial intercourse secured by English legislation. Between the New England colonies, in 1643, a league, offensive and defensive, was formed, which existed for forty years. A congress of commissioners, in 1754, representing New England *and several central* colonies, resolved that a union was absolutely necessary for their preservation. And after the English legislature had passed the *Stamp Act*, in 1765, nine of the colonies sent delegates to a congress at New York to uphold their right of self-taxation and trial by jury, as inherent. In 1774 Massachusetts more formally sought, by a congress assembled at Philadelphia, from all the colonies, to effect a union. It was referred "to the good people of these colonies" to authorize an organization on fundamental rules, and a declaration of rights, by which they might secure what they held themselves entitled to enjoy—" the Common Law" of England and the benefit of such English statutes as they might deem applicable to their condition. The delegates adopted a petition of grievances to the crown, and urged redress. In the following year a second congress of colonial delegates met in May at Philadelphia, and adopted the resolution that the exercise of every kind of authority under the crown of England should be suppressed. On the 4th of July, 1776, the Declaration of Independence was adopted by an assembly which was appointed partly by conventions of the people, and partly as chosen by representative branches of colonial legislatures; but the former preponderated.

The Articles of Confederation were the result of deliberation among the duly organized representatives of the American nation, after its revolutionary independence had been established and recognized by the English nation. The record of their adoption is in these words, " Done at Philadelphia, in the state of Pennsylvania, the 9th day of July, in the year of our Lord 1778, and in the third year of the independence of America." They were not, however, finally ratified by all the states, which had been colonies, until March 1781. On the following day Congress assembled under the Confederation. After the vicissitudes of ten years under the Federated Union of States, Jefferson, Madison, and Washington saw it impossible for the presidential government to act as an organized Union with a head; though in the first article of Federation it was declared that " the style of this Confederacy shall be the United States of America;" the second article provided "that each state retains its sovereignty, freedom, and independence, and every power, jurisdiction, and right which is not by this Confederation expressly delegated to the United States in Congress assembled." By the counsel and influence of the founders of the Republic, a preliminary convention was held at Annapolis in 1786. Twelve representatives from four of the states attended, and Messrs. Randolphe, Hamilton, and Madison were among them. They agreed to report as resolutions, "that there are important defects in the system of the Federal government is acknowledged by the acts of all those states which have concurred in the present meeting; that the defects may be found greater and more numerous than even these acts imply, is at least so far probable from the embarrassments which characterize the present state of our national affairs, foreign and domestic, as may reasonably be supposed to merit a deliberate and candid discussion in some mode which will unite the sentiments and counsels of all the states." The Congress upon this report, recommended all the states separately to appoint delegates to a convention for revising the basis of Union. Twelve states accepted the recommendation, and in their appointment of delegates, gave instructions, some less precise, but others authorizing them " to devise and discuss all such alterations and further provisions as may be necessary to render the Federal Constitution fully adequate to the exigencies of the Union."

The convention duly assembled; George Washington its president, and some of the ablest men then living among its members. Four months' protracted debate brought them to the 17th September, 1787, when the representatives of the twelve states unanimously adopted the draft of improvements, and resolved that it should be "laid before the United States in Congress assembled," and recommended that it should afterwards " be submitted to a convention of delegates chosen *in* each state by the people thereof, under a recommendation of its legislature for their assent and ratification," the result to be reported to Congress; and in these terms Congress transmitted the Constitution to the states. General Washington desiderated a *supreme* " power to regulate and govern the general concerns of the Confederated Republic, without which the Union could not be of long duration." Madison sought a ground which may at once support a due supremacy of the national authority, and not exclude the local authorities wherein they can be *subordinately* useful. General Knox said, " I speak entirely of the Federal government, or which would be better, one government instead of an association of governments." Mr. Hamilton, without circumlocution, clearly expressed the great end of the revision when he said, " The government of the American Union must be a national representative system. It must, therefore, be made completely sovereign, and state power as a separate legislative authority must be annihilated, otherwise the states will be not only able, but will be constantly tempted to exert their own authority against the authority of the nation." The new constitution was submitted to the state conventions, and finally adopted by them all, and issued bearing the signature of George Washington, president. An extract from Mr. Edward Everett will serve as seasonably explanatory of certain modifications then adopted :—

" But to hide the deformity of the crime under the cloak of that sophistry which makes the worse appear the better reason, we are told by the leaders of the Rebellion, that in our complex system of government, the separate states are 'sovereign,' and that the central power is only an 'agency' established by these sovereigns to manage certain affairs, which they could not so conveniently administer themselves. It happens, unfortunately for this theory, that the Federal Constitution (which has been adopted by the people of every state of the Union, as much as their own State Constitutions have been adopted, and is declared to be paramount to them) nowhere recognizes the states as

'sovereigns,' in fact that by their names it does not recognize them at all; while the authority established by
that instrument is recognized, in its text, not as an
'agency,' but as 'the government of the United States.'
By that Constitution, moreover, which purports in its preamble, to be ordained and established by 'the people of the
United States,' it is expressly provided 'that the members
of the state legislatures, and all executive officers, shall be
bound by oath or affirmation to support the Constitution.'
Now it is a common thing, under all governments, for an
agent to be bound by oath to be faithful to his sovereign,
but I never heard before of sovereigns being bound by
oath to be faithful to their agency. Certainly I do not
deny that the separate states are clothed with sovereign
powers for the administration of local affairs. It is one of
the most beautiful features of our mixed system of government, but it is equally true that, in adopting the Federal
Constitution, the states abdicated by express renunciation
all the most important functions of national sovereignty,
and by one comprehensive self-denying clause gave up all
right to contravene the Constitution of the United States.
Specifically, and by enumeration, they renounced all the
most important prerogatives of independent states. for
peace and for war, the right to keep troops or ships of war
in time of peace, or to engage in war unless actually invaded; to enter into compact with another state or foreign
power; to lay any duty on tonnage, or any impost on exports or imports without the consent of Congress; to
enter into any treaty, alliance, or confederation; to grant
letters of marque and reprisal, and to emit bills of credit;
while all these powers and many others are expressly vested
in the general government. To ascribe to political communities, thus limited in their jurisdiction—who cannot
even establish a post-office on their own soil—the character
of independent sovereignty, and to reduce a national
organization, clothed with all the transcendent powers of
government, to the name and condition of an 'agency' of
the states, proves nothing but that the logic of Secession
is on a par with its loyalty and patriotism. Oh, but the
'reserved rights'! And what of the reserved rights? The
tenth amendment of the Constitution supposed to provide
for 'reserved rights' is constantly misquoted. By that

amendment, ' the *powers* not delegated to the United States nor prohibited by it to the states are reserved to the states respectively or to the people.' The ' powers ' reserved must of course be such as could have been but were not delegated to the states—could have been, but were not, prohibited to the states—but to speak of the *right* of an *individual* state to secede, as a *power* that could have been though it was not delegated to the *United States* is simple nonsense. But waiving this obvious absurdity, can it need a serious argument to prove that there can be no state right to enter into a new confederation reserved under a Constitution, which expressly prohibits a state ' to enter into any treaty, alliance, or confederation,' or any ' agreement or compact with another state or a foreign power '? To say that the state may, by enacting the preliminary farce of secession, acquire the right to do the prohibited things—to say, for instance, that though the states, in forming the Constitution, delegated to the United States and prohibited to themselves the power of declaring war, there was, by implication, reserved to each state the right of seceding and then declaring war; that though they expressly prohibited to the states, and delegated to the United States the entire treaty-making power, they reserved, by implication,—for an express reservation is not pretended,—to the individual states, to Florida, for instance, the right to secede and then to make a treaty with Spain, retroceding that Spanish colony, and thus surrendering to a foreign power the key to the Gulf of Mexico—to maintain propositions like these, with whatever affected seriousness it is done, appears to me egregious trifling."

Eleven of the states, to conventions of which the revised Constitution was submitted, expressed their assent immediately; and Congress resolved on the 17th September, 1788, that it should go into operation on Wednesday the 4th day of March, 1789. The citizens of Rhode Island, I believe, hesitated for some little time longer than those of any other state; but ultimately all the thirteen states became one nation ; so that they could heartily say, " We the people of the United States."

" CONSTITUTION OF THE UNITED STATES.

" We the people of the United States, in order to form

a more perfect union, establish justice, insure domestic tranquillity, provide for the common defence, promote the general welfare, and secure the blessings of liberty to ourselves and our posterity, do ordain and establish this Constitution for the United States of America.

"All Legislative Powers herein granted shall be vested in a Congress of the United States, which shall consist of a Senate and House of Representatives.

"The House of Representatives shall be composed of members chosen every second year by the people of the several states, and the electors in each state shall have the qualifications requisite for electors of the most numerous branch of the State Legislature. No person shall be a Representative who shall not have attained to the age of twenty-five years, and been seven years a citizen of the United States, and who shall not, when elected, be an inhabitant of that State in which he shall be chosen. Representatives and direct taxes shall be apportioned among the several States which may be included within this Union, according to their respective numbers, which shall be determined by adding to the whole number of free persons, including those bound to service for a term of years, and excluding Indians not taxed, three fifths of all other persons. The actual enumeration shall be made within three years after the first meeting of the Congress of the United States, and within every subsequent term of ten years, in such manner as they shall by law direct. The number of Representatives shall not exceed one for every thirty thousand, but each State shall have at least one Representative; and until such enumeration shall be made, the State of *New Hampshire* shall be entitled to choose three, *Massachusetts* eight, *Rhode Island* and *Providence Plantations* one, *Connecticut* five, *New York* six, *New Jersey* four, *Pennsylvania* eight, *Delaware* one, *Maryland* six, *Virginia* ten, *North Carolina* five, *South Carolina* five, and *Georgia* three. When vacancies happen in the representation from any State, the executive authority thereof shall issue writs of election to fill such vacancies. The House of Representatives shall choose their Speaker and other officers; and shall have the sole power of impeachment.

"The Senate of the United States shall be composed of two Senators from each State, chosen by the Legislature thereof, for six years ; and each Senator shall have one vote. Immediately after they shall be assembled in consequence of the first election, they shall be divided as equally as may be into three classes. The seats of the Senators of the first class shall be vacated at the expiration of the second year, of the second class at the expiration of the fourth year, and of the third class at the expiration of the sixth year, so that one-third may be chosen every second year ; and if vacancies happen by resignation, or otherwise, during the recess of the Legislature of any State, the executive thereof may make temporary appointments until the next meeting of the Legislature, which shall then fill such vacancies. No person shall be a Senator who shall not have attained to the age of thirty years, and been nine years a citizen of the United States, and who shall not, when elected, be an inhabitant of that State for which he shall be chosen. The Vice-President of the United States shall be President of the Senate, but shall have no vote unless they be equally divided. The Senate shall choose their other officers, and also a President, *pro tempore*, in the absence of the Vice-President, or when he shall exercise the office of President of the United States. The Senate shall have the sole power to try all impeachments. When sitting for that purpose, they shall be on oath or affirmation. When the President of the United States is tried, the Chief Justice shall preside ; and no person shall be convicted without the concurrence of two thirds of the members present. Judgment, in cases of impeachment, shall not extend further than to removal from office, and disqualification to hold and enjoy any office of honour, trust, or profit under the United States ; but the party convicted shall nevertheless be liable and subject to indictment, trial, judgment, and punishment according to law.

"The times, places, and manner of holding elections for Senators and Representatives, shall be prescribed in each State by the Legislature thereof ; but the Congress may at any time by law make or alter such regulations, except as to the places of choosing Senators. The Congress shall assemble at least once in every year, and such meeting shall be on the first Monday in December, unless they shall by law appoint a different day.

"Each House shall be the judge of the elections,

returns, and qualifications of its own members, and a majority of each shall constitute a quorum to do business; but a smaller number may adjourn from day to day, and may be authorized to compel the attendance of absent members, in such manner and under such penalties as each House may provide. Each House may determine the rules of its proceedings, punish its members for disorderly behaviour, and, with the concurrence of two thirds, expel a member. Each house shall keep a journal of its proceedings, and from time to time publish the same, excepting such parts as may in their judgment require secresy; and the yeas and nays of the members of either House on any question shall, at the desire of one fifth of those present, be entered on the journal. Neither House, during the session of Congress, shall, without the consent of the other, adjourn for more than three days, nor to any other place than that in which the two Houses shall be sitting.

"The Senators and Representatives shall receive a compensation for their services, to be ascertained by law, and paid out of the Treasury of the United States. They shall in all cases, except treason, felony, and breach of the peace, be privileged from arrest during their attendance at the session of their respective Houses, and in going to and returning from the same : and for any speech or debate in either House. they shall not be questioned in any other place. No Senator or Representative shall, during the time for which he was elected, be appointed to any civil office under the authority of the United States, which shall have been created, or the emoluments whereof shall have been increased during such time ; and no person holding any office under the United States, shall be a member of either House during his continuance in office.

"All bills for raising revenue shall originate in the House of Representatives ; but the Senate may propose, or concur with amendments, as on other bills. Every bill which shall have passed the House of Representatives and the Senate, shall, before it become a law, be presented to the President of the United States; if he approve he shall sign it ; but if not he shall return it, with his objections, to that House in which it shall have originated, who shall enter the objections at large on their journal, and proceed to reconsider it. If after such reconsideration two thirds of that House shall agree to pass the bill, it shall be sent, together with the objections, to the other House, by which it shall likewise be reconsidered, and if approved by two thirds of that House, it shall become a law. But in all such cases the votes of both Houses shall be determined by yeas and nays, and the names of the persons voting for and against the bill shall be entered on the journal of each House respectively. If any bill shall not be returned by the President within ten days [Sundays excepted] after it shall have been presented to him, the same shall be a law, in like manner as if he had signed it, unless the Congress by their adjournment prevent its return, in which case it shall not be a law. Every order, resolution, or vote to which the concurrence of the Senate and House of Representatives may be necessary (except on a question of adjournment) shall be presented to the President of the United States; and before the same shall take effect, shall be approved by him, or being disapproved by him, shall be repassed by two-thirds of the Senate and House of Representatives, according to the rules and limitations prescribed in the case of a bill.

"The Congress shall have power to lay and collect taxes, duties, imposts, and excises, to pay the debts and provide for the common defence and general welfare of the United States; but all duties, imposts, and excises shall be uniform throughout the United States; to borrow money on the credit of the United States; to regulate commerce with foreign nations, and among the several states, and with the Indian tribes; to establish a uniform rule of naturalization, and uniform laws on the subject of bankruptcies throughout the United States; to coin money, regulate the value thereof, and of foreign coin, and fix the standard of weights and measures; to provide for the punishment of counterfeiting the securities and current coin of the United States; to establish post-offices and post-roads; to promote the progress of science and useful arts, by securing for limited times to authors and inventors the exclusive right to their respective writings and discoveries; to constitute tribunals inferior to the Supreme Court; to define and punish piracies and felonies committed on the high seas, and offences against the law of nations; to declare war, grant letters of marque and re-

E E

prisal, and make rules concerning captures on land and
water; to raise and support armies, but no appropriation
of money to that use shall be for a longer term than two
years; to provide and maintain a navy; to make rules for
the government and regulation of the land and naval
forces; to provide for calling forth the militia to execute
the laws of the Union, suppress insurrections and repel invasions; to provide for organizing, arming, and disciplining
the militia, and for governing such part of them as may be employed in the service of the United States, reserving to the
states respectively, the appointment of the officers, and the
authority of training the militia according to the discipline
prescribed by Congress; to exercise exclusive legislation in
all cases whatsoever, over such district (not exceeding ten
miles square) as may, by cession of particular States, and the
acceptance of Congress, become the seat of the government of the United States, and to exercise like authority
over all places purchased by the consent of the Legislature
of the State in which the same shall be, for the erection of
forts, magazines, arsenals, dockyards, and other needful
buildings; and to make all laws which shall be necessary and
proper for carrying into execution the foregoing powers,
*and all other powers vested by this Constitution in the govern-
ment of the United States, or in any department or officer thereof.*

"The migration or importation of such persons as any of
the States now existing shall think proper to admit, shall
not be prohibited by the Congress prior to the year one
thousand eight hundred and eight, but a tax or duty may
be imposed on such importation, not exceeding ten dollars
for each person. The privilege of the writ of Habeas
Corpus shall not be suspended, unless when in cases of
rebellion or invasion the public safety may require it. No
bill of attainder or ex-post facto law shall be passed. No
capitation or other direct tax shall be laid, unless in proportion to the census or enumeration hereinbefore directed
to be taken. No tax or duty shall be laid on articles exported from any State. No preference shall be given by
any regulation of commerce or revenue to the ports of one
State over those of another: nor shall vessels bound to or
from one State be obliged to enter, clear, or pay duties in
another. No money shall be drawn from the Treasury, but
in consequence of appropriations made by law; and a

regular statement and account of the receipts and ex-
penditures of all public money shall be published from time
to time. No title of nobility shall be granted by the
United States; and no person holding any office of profit or
trust under them shall, without the consent of the Congress,
accept of any present, emolument, office, or title of any
kind whatever from any king, prince, or foreign state.

"No State shall enter into any treaty, alliance, or confederation; grant letters of marque and reprisal; coin
money; emit bills of credit; make anything but gold and
silver coin a tender in payment of debts; pass any bill of
attainder, ex-post facto law, or law impairing the obligation
of contracts, or grant any title of nobility. No State shall,
without the consent of the Congress, lay any imposts or
duties on imports or exports, except what may be absolutely necessary for executing its inspection laws; and the
nett produce of all duties and imposts laid by any State on
imports or exports shall be for the use of the Treasury of
the United States; and all such laws shall be subject to
the revision and control of the Congress. No State shall,
without the consent of Congress, lay any duty of tonnage,
keep troops or ships of war in time of peace, enter into any
agreement or compact with another State, or with a foreign
power, or engage in war unless actually invaded, or in such
imminent danger as will not admit of delay.

"The Executive power shall be vested in a President of
the United States of America. He shall hold his office
during the term of four years, and, together with the Vice-
President, chosen for the same term, be elected as follows:
Each State shall appoint, in such manner as the Legislature thereof may direct, a number of electors, equal to the
whole number of Senators and Representatives to which
the State may be entitled in the Congress: but no Senator
or Representative, or person holding an office of trust or
profit under the United States, shall be appointed an
elector. The electors shall meet in their respective States,
and vote by ballot for President and Vice-President, one of
whom, at least, shall not be an inhabitant of the same State
with themselves; they shall name in their ballots the
person voted for as President, and in distinct ballots the
person voted for as Vice-President, and they shall make
distinct lists of all persons voted for as President, and of all

persons voted for as Vice-President, and of the number of votes for each, which lists they shall sign and certify, and transmit sealed to the seat of the government of the United States, directed to the President of the Senate ; the President of the Senate shall, in the presence of the Senate and House of Representatives, open all the certificates, and the vote shall then be counted : the person having the greatest number of votes for President shall be the President, if such number be a majority of the whole number of electors appointed ; and if no person have such majority, then from the persons having the highest numbers, not exceeding three on the list of those voted for as President, the House of Representatives shall choose immediately, by ballot, the President. But in choosing the President, the votes shall be taken by States, the representation from each State having one vote ; a quorum for this purpose shall consist of a member or members from two-thirds of the States, and a majority of all the States shall be necessary to a choice. And if the House of Representatives shall not choose a President whenever the right of choice shall devolve upon them, before the fourth day of March next following, then the Vice-President shall act as President, as in case of the death or other constitutional disability of the President. The person having the greatest number of votes as Vice-President shall be the Vice-President, if such number be a majority of the whole number of electors appointed, and if no person have a majority, then from the two highest numbers on the list, the Senate shall choose the Vice-President ; a quorum for the purpose shall consist of two-thirds of the whole number of Senators, and a majority of the whole number shall be necessary to a choice. But no person constitutionally ineligible to the office of President shall be eligible to that of Vice-President of the United States. The Congress may determine the time of choosing the electors, and the day on which they shall give their votes ; which day shall be the same throughout the United States. No person except a natural born citizen, or a citizen of the United States at the time of the adoption of this Constitution, shall be eligible to the office of President, neither shall any person be eligible to that office who shall not have attained to the age of thirty-five years, and been fourteen years a resident within the United States. In case of the removal of the President from office, or of his death, resignation, or inability to discharge the powers and duties of the said office, the same shall devolve on the Vice-President, and the Congress may by law provide for the case of removal, death, resignation, or inability both of the President and Vice-President, declaring what officer shall then act as President, and such officer shall act accordingly, until the disability be removed, or a President shall be elected. The President shall, at stated times, receive for his services a compensation, which shall neither be increased nor diminished during the period for which he shall have been elected, and he shall not receive within that period any other emolument from the United States or any of them. Before he enter on the execution of his office, he shall take the following oath or affirmation :—' I do solemnly swear (or affirm) that I will faithfully execute the office of President of the United States, and will to the best of my ability preserve, protect, and defend the Constitution of the United States.'

The President shall be commander-in-chief of the army and navy of the United States, and of the militia of the several States, when called into the actual service of the United States ; he may require the opinion, in writing, of the principal officer in each of the executive departments, upon any subject relating to the duties of their respective offices, and he shall have power to grant reprieves and pardons for offences against the United States, except in cases of impeachment. He shall have power, by and with the advice and consent of the Senate, to make treaties, provided two-thirds of the Senators present concur ; and he shall nominate, and by and with the advice and consent of the Senate, shall appoint ambassadors, other public ministers and consuls, judges of the Supreme Court, and all other officers of the United States, whose appointments are not herein otherwise provided for, and which shall be established by law : but the Congress may by law vest the appointment of such inferior officers, as they think proper, in the President alone, in the courts of law, or in the heads of departments. The President shall have power to fill up all vacancies that may happen during the recess of the Senate, by granting commissions which shall expire at the end of their next session.

The President shall from time to time give to the Congress information of the state of the Union, and recommend to their consideration such measures as he shall judge necessary and expedient; he may, on extraordinary occasions, convene both Houses or either of them, and, in case of disagreement between them, with respect to the time of adjournment, he may adjourn them to such time as he shall think proper; he shall receive ambassadors and other public ministers; he shall take care that the laws be faithfully executed, and shall commission all the officers of the United States. The President, Vice-President, and all civil officers of the United States, shall be removed from office on impeachment for, and conviction of, treason, bribery, or other high crimes and misdemeanours.

"The judicial power of the United States shall be vested in one Supreme Court, and in such inferior courts as the Congress may from time to time ordain and abolish. The judges, both of the Supreme and inferior courts, shall hold their offices during good behaviour, and shall, at stated times, receive for their services a compensation, which shall not be diminished during their continuance in office.

"The judicial power shall extend to *all cases in law and equity, arising under this Constitution*, the laws of the United States, and treaties made, or which shall be made, under their authority; to all cases affecting ambassadors, and other public ministers, and consuls; to all cases of admiralty and maritime jurisdiction; to controversies to which the United States shall be a party; to controversies between two or more States, between a State and citizens of another State, *between citizens of different States*, between citizens of the same State claiming lands under grants of different States, and between a State, or the citizens thereof, and foreign States, citizens, or subjects. In all cases affecting ambassadors, other public ministers, and consuls, and those in which a State shall be party, the Supreme Court shall have original jurisdiction. In all the other cases before mentioned, the Supreme Court shall have appellate jurisdiction, both as to law and fact, with such exceptions, and under such regulations, as the Congress shall make. The trial of all crimes, except in cases of impeachment, shall be by jury; and such trial shall be held in the State where the said crime shall have been committed; but when not committed within any State, the trial shall be at such place or places as the Congress may by law have directed.

" Treason against the United States shall consist only in levying war against them, or in adhering to their enemies, giving them aid or comfort. No person shall be convicted of treason unless on the testimony of two witnesses to the same overt act, or on confession in open court. The Congress shall have power to declare the punishment of treason, but no attainder of treason shall work corruption of blood, or forfeiture, except during the life of the person attainted.

" Full faith and credit shall be given in each State to the public acts, records, and judicial proceedings of every other State. And the Congress may by general laws prescribe the manner in which such acts, records, and proceedings shall be proved, and the effect thereof.

" The citizens of each State shall be entitled to all privileges and immunities of citizens in the several States. A person charged in any State with treason, felony, or other crime, who shall flee from justice, and be found in another State, shall, on the demand of the executive authority of the State from which he fled, be delivered up to be removed to the State having jurisdiction of the crime. No person held to service or labour in one State, under the laws thereof, escaping into another, shall, in consequence of any law or regulation therein, be discharged from such service or labour, but shall be delivered up on claim of the party to whom such service or labour may be due.

" New States may be admitted by the Congress into this Union; but no new State shall be formed or erected within the jurisdiction of any other State; nor any State be formed by the junction of two or more States, or parts of States, without the consent of the legislatures of the States concerned as well as of the Congress. The Congress shall have power to dispose of and make all needful rules and regulations respecting the territory or other property belonging to the United States: and nothing in this Constitution shall be so construed as to prejudice any claims of the United States, or of any particular State.

" The United States shall guarantee to every State in this Union a Republican form of Government, and shall protect each of them against invasion, and on application of the Legislature, or of the executive (when the Legislature cannot be convened) against domestic violence.

"The Congress, whenever two-thirds of both Houses shall deem it necessary, shall propose amendments to this Constitution, or, on the application of the Legislatures of two-thirds of the several States, shall call a convention for proposing amendments, which, in either case, shall be valid to all intents and purposes, as part of this Constitution, when ratified by the Legislatures of three-fourths of the several States, or by conventions in three-fourths thereof, as the one or the other mode of ratification may be proposed by the Congress; provided that no amendment which may be made prior to the year one thousand eight hundred and eight shall in any manner affect the first and fourth clauses in the ninth section of the first article; and that no State, without its consent, shall be deprived of its equal suffrage in the Senate.

"All debts contracted and engagements entered into, before the adoption of this Constitution, shall be as valid against the United States under this Constitution, as under the Confederation.

"This Constitution, and the laws of the United States which shall be made in pursuance thereof; and all treaties made, or which shall be made, under the authority of the United States, shall be the supreme law of the land; and the judges in every State shall be bound thereby, anything in the Constitution or laws of any State to the contrary notwithstanding. The Senators and Representatives before mentioned, and the members of the several State Legislatures, and all executive and judicial officers, both of the United States and of the several States, shall be bound by oath or affirmation to support this Constitution; but no religious test shall ever be required as a qualification to any office or public trust under the United States.

"The ratification of the conventions of nine States, shall be sufficient for the establishment of this Constitution between the States so ratifying the same.

"Done in convention by the unanimous consent of the States present, the seventeenth day of September, in the year of our Lord one thousand seven hundred and eighty-seven, and of the independence of the United

States of America the twelfth. In witness whereof we have hereunto subscribed our names.

" GEORGE WASHINGTON,
" President and Deputy from Virginia.

"NEW HAMPSHIRE—John Langdon, Nicholas Gillman.
" MASSACHUSETTS—Nathaniel Gorham, Rufus King.
" CONNECTICUT—William Samuel Johnson, Roger Sherman.
"NEW YORK—Alexander Hamilton.
"NEW JERSEY—William Livingston, William Patterson, David Brearly, Jonathan Dayton.
" PENNSYLVANIA—Benjamin Franklin, Thomas Mifflin, Robert Morris, George Clymer, Thomas Fitzsimons, Jared Ingersoll, James Wilson, Governeur Morris.
" DELAWARE—George Read, Gunning Bedford, jun., John Dickinson, Richard Bassett, Jacob Broom.
" MARYLAND—James M'Henry, Daniel of St. Tho. Jenifer, Daniel Carroll.
" VIRGINIA—John Blair, James Madison, jun.
" NORTH CAROLINA—William Blount, Richard Dobbs Spaight, Hugh Williamson.
" SOUTH CAROLINA—John Rutledge, Charles Cotesworth Pinckney, Charles Pinckney, Pierce Butler.
" GEORGIA—William Few, Abraham Baldwin.
" Attest,   WILLIAM JACKSON, *Secretary*."

" AMENDMENTS.

" Articles in addition to, and amendment of the Constitution of the United States of America, proposed by Congress, and ratified by the Legislatures of the several States, pursuant to the Fifth Article of the original Constitution.

" Congress shall make no law respecting an establishment of religion, or prohibiting the free exercise thereof, or abridging the freedom of speech, or of the press ; or the right of the people peaceably to assemble, and to petition the government for a redress of grievances. A well-regulated militia, being necessary to the security of a free State, the right of the people to keep and bear arms shall not be infringed. No soldier shall, in time of peace, be quartered in any house, without the consent of the owner, nor in time of war, but in a manner to be prescribed by law. The right of the people to be secure in their persons, houses, papers, and effects, against unreasonable searches and seizures, shall not be violated, and no warrants shall issue but upon probable cause, supported by oath or affirmation, and particularly describing the place to be searched, and the person or things to be seized. No person shall be held to answer for a capital, or otherwise infamous crime, unless on a presentment or indictment of a grand jury, except in cases arising in the land or naval forces, or in the militia, when in actual service in time of war or public danger; nor shall any person be subject, for the same offence, to be twice put in jeopardy of life or limb; nor shall be compelled in any criminal case to be a witness against himself; nor be deprived of life, liberty, or property, without due process of law, nor shall private property be taken for public use without just compensation. In all criminal prosecutions, the accused shall enjoy the right to a speedy and public trial, by an impartial jury of the State and district wherein the crime shall have been committed, which district shall have been previously ascertained by law; and to be informed of the nature and cause of the accusation; to be confronted with the witnesses against him; to have compulsory process for obtaining witnesses in his favour; and to have the assistance of counsel for his defence. In suits at common law, where the value in controversy shall exceed twenty dollars, the right of trial by jury shall be preserved; and no fact tried by a jury shall be otherwise re-examined in any court of the United States, than according to the rules of the common law. Excessive bail shall not be required, nor excessive fines imposed, nor cruel and unusual punishments inflicted. The enumeration in the Constitution of certain rights, shall not be construed to deny or disparage others retained by the people. The powers not delegated to the United States by the Constitution, nor prohibited by it to the States, are reserved to the States respectively, or to the people. The judicial power of the United States shall not be construed to extend to any suit in law or equity commenced or prosecuted against one of the United States by citizens of another State, or by citizens or subjects of any foreign State."

The Cabinet offices of the United States Government, and the salaries attached to each office, in English money, may surprise some English readers :—

The President—Abraham Lincoln . . £5000	
His Private Secretary . . .	500
Secretary to Sign Patents . . .	300
Vice-President—Hannibal Hamlin .	1600
Secretary of State—William H. Seward .	1600
Secretary of the Treasury—Salmon P. Chase	1600
Secretary of War—Edwin M. Stanton .	1600
Secretary of the Navy—Gideon Welles .	1600
Secretary of the Interior—John P. Usher	1600
Post-Master General—Montgomery Blair.	1600
Attorney-General—Edward Bates . .	1600
The compensation of a Senator is, per an.	600

But the Senator has mileage, £1 12s. for every twenty miles he has to travel from his home to Congress, going and returning, for two sessions in each Congress. The Speaker of the House has, per annum, £1200. The representative or delegate has the same allowance as a senator. Congress assembles on the 1st December every year. The times, places, and manner of holding elections for these offices are prescribed in each state by its Legislature; Congress can, however, modify the regulations for time and manner of election by law. No senator or representative can, during the period for which he was elected, be appointed to any civil office under authority of the United States, which shall have been created, or the emoluments of which shall have been increased, during such time ; and no person holding *any* office under the United States shall be a member of either House during his continuance in office. A "Congress" in legislative language continues for two years, viz., from March 1861 to March 1863, and March

1863 till 1865, commencing and expiring always in the odd number. The first Congress was dated from 4th March 1789 till 1791, and the thirty-eighth Congress commencing 4th March in 1863, to terminate in 1865. But the session does not close on that day. According to the census taken in 1860, the members in the Representative Chamber for 1863 should have been two hundred and forty-one, besides seven delegates from the Territories; but in the unsettled condition of eleven states, fifty-seven members will have vacated their places, the filling of which will much depend on the success of an anti-slavery policy. The Senate should contain sixty-four members, but there are fourteen compromised in the rebellion. The parties remaining have been classified into—*unequivocal supporters* of the present administration, ninety-three; *supporters of the Union* from border states, fifteen; in *opposition to the policy* of the administration there are seventy-four. One border state representative adheres to the Democratic opposition. The Republicans may, therefore, be reckoned one hundred and eight, and the Democrats seventy-five; the whole members who have votes will therefore be one hundred and eighty-three in the House of Representatives.

Two objects must reasonably occupy the mind of the men in whose hands the destinies of America are placed. The regular government of the loyal states is only incidentally affected by proceedings in Congress, and the State Legislatures have such matters under their usual care. Yet it is requisite that the national rulers watch that the state take no damage from concurrent events. The restoration of the whole country to a peaceful state, and the subjugation of the rebellion in every part of the slave states, will continue the care of the executive. This will accumulate upon Congress and the administration much solicitude.

Mr. Edward Everett acknowledges that perhaps he was tempted *too long* to tread in the paths of hopeless compromise, in the fond endeavour to conciliate those who were predetermined not to be conciliated ; but now he affirms " that the war can have no other termination compatible with the permanent safety and welfare of the country but the complete destruction of the military power of the enemy. I have on other occasions attempted to show that to yield to his demands and acknowledge his independence, thus resolving the Union at once into two hostile governments, with a certainty of further disintegration, would annihilate the strength and the influence of the country as a member of the family of nations, afford to foreign powers the opportunity and the temptation for disastrous and humiliating interference in our affairs ; wrest from the Middle and Western States some of their great natural outlets to the sea, and of their most important lines of internal communication ; deprive the commerce and navigation of the country of two-thirds of our sea-coast and of the fortresses which protect it ; not only so, but would enable each individual state, some of them with a white population equal to a good-sized Northern county—or rather the dominant party in each state—to cede its territory, its harbours, its fortresses, the mouths of its rivers, to any foreign power. It cannot be that the people of the loyal states, that twenty-two millions of brave and prosperous freemen will, for the temptation of a brief truce in an eternal border war, consent to this hideous national suicide. Do not think that I exaggerate the consequences of yielding to the demands of the leaders of the rebellion. I understate them. They require of us not only all the sacrifices I have named, not only to cede to them, a foreign and hostile power, all the territory of the United States at present occupied by the rebel forces, but the abandonment to them of the vast regions we have rescued from their grasp—of Maryland, of a part of Eastern Virginia, and the whole of Western Virginia, the sea-coast of North and South Carolina ; Kentucky, Tennessee, and Missouri ; Arkansas, and the larger portion of Mississippi and Louisiana ; in most of which, with the exception of lawless guerillas, there is not a rebel in arms, in all of which the great majority of the people are loyal to the Union. We must give back, too, the helpless coloured population, thousands of whom are perilling their lives in the ranks

of our armies, to a bondage rendered tenfold more bitter
by the momentary enjoyment of freedom. Finally, we
must surrender every man in the Southern country, white
or black, who has moved a finger or spoken a word for the
restoration of the Union, to a reign of terror as remorse-
less as that of Robespierre, which has been the chief instrument by which the rebellion has been organized and
sustained, and has already filled the prisons of the South
with noble men, whose only crime is that they are not
traitors. The South is full of such men."

In answer to the argument that alienation, embittered
by the incidents of war, will for ever prevent harmony or
a restoration of mutual confidence, appeals are made to
historical parallels, the wars of the Roses and the Parliamentary wars in England, the "thirty years' war," and the
seven years' war in Germany, and to the intestinal hostilities between states and cities in Italy, to warrant the
hope that strife may be followed, between South and
North, by amity, and momentary exasperation may be
soothed into generous friendship. Mr. Everett proceeds :—

"It is of course impossible to prevent the lawless acts
of stragglers and deserters, or the occasional unwarrantable proceedings of subordinates on distant stations; but
I do not believe there is, in all history, the record of a
civil war of such gigantic dimensions, where so little has
been done in the spirit of vindictiveness, as in this war, by
the Government and commanders of the United States;
and this, notwithstanding the provocation given by the
rebel Government by assuming the responsibility of
wretches like Quantrell; refusing quarter to coloured troops;
and scourging and selling into slavery free coloured men
from the North who fall into their hands; covering the sea
with pirates; and starving prisoners of war to death. In
the next place, if there are any present who believe that,
in addition to the effect of the military operations of the
war, the confiscation acts, and emancipation proclamations
have embittered the rebels beyond the possibility of recon-
ciliation, I would request them to reflect, that the tone of
the rebel leaders and rebel press was just as bitter in the

first months of the war, nay, before a gun was fired, as it is now. There were speeches made in Congress in the very last session before the rebellion, so ferocious, as to show that their authors were under the influence of a real frenzy. At the present day, if there is any discrimination made by the Confederate press in the affected scorn, hatred and contumely with which every shade of opinion and sentiment in the loyal states is treated, the bitterest contempt is bestowed upon those at the North, who still speak the language of compromise, and who condemn those measures of the administration, which are alleged to have rendered the return of peace hopeless. No, my friends, that gracious Providence which overrules all things for the best, from seeming evil still educing good, has so constituted our natures, that the violent excitement of the passions in one direction is generally followed by a reaction in an opposite direction, and the sooner for the violence.

"While the defeated and dishonoured leaders of the rebellious war may properly be left to seek exile or obscurity, why should not kindred sympathies be revived between the several members of the American family? The removal of the one class of influences will give place to others, which will heal the breaches and open paths for wider and healthier intercourse and commerce between all parts of America. The people of loyal America will never take to their confidence, or admit again to a share in their government, the hard-hearted men, whose cruel lust of power has brought this desolating war upon the land; but there is no personal bitterness felt even against them. They may live, if they can bear to live after wantonly causing the death of so many thousand fellow-men; they may live in safe obscurity beneath the shelter of the Government they have sought to overthrow, or they may fly to the protection of the governments of Europe—some of them are already there, seeking, happily in vain, to obtain the aid of foreign powers in furtherance of their own treason. There let them stay. The humblest dead soldier, that lies cold and still in his grave before us, is an object of envy beneath the clods that cover him, in comparison with the living man who is willing to grovel at the foot of a foreign throne for assistance in compassing the ruin of his country. But the hour is coming, and now is, when the power of the

leaders of the rebellion to delude and inflame must cease.
There is no bitterness on the part of the masses. The
people of the South are not going to wage an eternal war,
for the wretched pretexts by which this rebellion is sought
to be justified. The bonds that unite us as one people, a
substantial community of origin, language, belief, and law
(the four great ties that hold the societies of men together),
common national and political interests ; a common history ;
a common pride in a glorious ancestry ; a common interest
in this great heritage of blessings ; the very geographical
features of the country ; the mighty rivers that cross the
lines of climate, and thus facilitate the interchange of natural
and industrial products ; while the wonder-working arm of
the engineer has levelled the mountain walls which separate
the East and West, compelling your own Alleghanies, my
Maryland and Pennsylvania friends, to open wide their
everlasting doors to the chariot-wheels of traffic and travel ;
these bonds of union are of perennial force and energy,
while the causes of alienation are imaginary, factitious, and
transient. The heart of the people, North and South, is for the
Union. Indications, too plain to be mistaken, announce the
fact, both in the east and the west of the states in rebellion.
In North Carolina and Arkansas the fatal charm at length
is broken. At Raleigh and Little Rock the lips of honest
and brave men are unsealed, and an independent press is
unlimbering its artillery. The weary masses of the people
are yearning to see the dear old flag floating again upon
the capitols, and they sigh for the return of the peace,
prosperity, and happiness, which they enjoyed under a
Government whose power was felt only in its blessings."

There are others not so dilatory in receiving lessons
from slavery as was Mr. Everett, and who have a keener
sense of what is due to the helpless coloured victims of the
task-master, and perhaps a wiser and deeper perception of
the accursed and degrading action of property in man on
every noble sentiment and virtue in the owner as well as
the oppressed sufferer. But Mr. Lincoln and his coadjutors must complete the work they have begun, not alone
for their own credit's sake, but to provide against the recur-
rence of such a conflict in after times. Happily, he and

his colleagues have accepted the mission. The proclamations are part of the work, and are preparing the way for a yet brighter day. Mr. Seward and Mr. Chase feel and acknowledge that slavery must be buried in the same grave with the rebellion. Everywhere in all the states, where the owners have forfeited their estates, and where the law confiscates their property, does the proclamation of January, 1863, come, giving liberty to the slave. Whatever is done with the states as subjugated republics the individual rebels are disqualified for government appointments within those territories, and for legislative functions in a recognized state. A new order of institutions must, therefore, be inaugurated in all slavedom. The border states cannot now *retain* their coloured fellow-men in slavery, and liberty and a free commerce will assert their sway. America must *all* become the land of the brave and the free.

The policy to be pursued hereafter is indicated in the Message of the President to Congress, December, 1863; and the following extract from it is alike consistent with the good faith and sound judgment of Mr. Lincoln and his cabinet. The reconstruction of the rebellious states is necessarily a question in prospect of the termination of the war, and the President says :—

" An attempt to guarantee and protect a revived state government constructed in whole, or in preponderating part, from the very element against whose hostility and violence it is to be protected, is simply absurd. There must be a test by which to separate the opposing elements so as to build only from the sound, and that test is a sufficiently liberal one which accepts as sound whoever will make a sworn recantation of his former movements. But if it be proper to require as a test of admission to the political body an oath of allegiance to the United States and to the Union under it, why not also to the laws and proclamations in regard to slavery? Those laws and procla-

F F

mations were put forth for the purpose of aiding in the suppression of the rebellion. To give them the fullest effect, there had to be a pledge for their maintenance. In my judgment they have aided, and will further aid, the cause for which they were intended. To now abandon them would be not only to relinquish a lever of power, but would also be a cruel and astounding breach of faith. I may add at this point, while I remain in my present position, I shall not attempt to retract or modify the emancipation proclamation ; nor shall I return to slavery any person who is free by the terms of that proclamation, or by any of the acts of Congress. For these and other reasons, it is thought best that support of these measures shall be included in the oath ; and it is believed that the executive may lawfully claim it in return for pardon and restoration of forfeited rights, which he has a clear constitutional power to withhold altogether, or grant upon the terms he shall deem wisest for the public interest."

In order to give greater definiteness and point to the contemplated arrangement, a proclamation is added, and to complete the outline, I subjoin the paragraphs which provide for a reconstruction :—

" Therefore I, Abraham Lincoln, President of the United States, do proclaim, declare, and make known to all persons who have directly or by implication participated in the existing rebellion, except as hereinafter excepted, that a full pardon is hereby granted to them and each of them, with restoration of all rights of property, except as to slaves ; and in property cases where the rights of third parties shall have intervened, and upon the condition that every such person shall take and subscribe an oath, and thenceforward keep and maintain said oath inviolate, and which oath shall be registered for permanent preservation, and shall be of the tenor and effect following, to wit :—

" ' I, ——, do solemnly swear in presence of Almighty God that I will henceforth faithfully support, protect, and defend the constitution of the United States and the Union of the states thereunder ; and that I will in like manner abide by and faithfully support all acts of Congress passed during the existing rebellion with reference to slaves, so long and so far as not repealed, modified, or held void by Congress, or by the decision of the Supreme Court; and that I will in like manner abide and faithfully support all proclamations of the President made during the existing rebellion having reference to slaves, so long and so far as not modified or declared void by decision of the Supreme Court. So help me God.'

"The persons excepted from the benefits of the foregoing provisions are, all who are or shall have been, civil or diplomatic officers or agents of the so-called Confederate Government; all who have left judicial stations, under the United States to aid the rebellion; all who are or shall have been military or naval officers of said so-called Confederate Government above the rank of colonel in the army, of lieutenant in the navy; all who left seats in the United States Congress to aid the rebellion.

"All who resigned commissions in the army or navy of the United States, and afterwards aided the rebellion, and all who have engaged in any way in treating coloured persons, or white persons in charge of such, otherwise than lawfully as prisoners of war, who have been found in the United States service as soldiers, seamen, or in any other capacity.

"And I do further proclaim, declare, and make known that whenever, in any of the states of Arkansas, Texas, Louisiana, Mississippi, Tennessee, Alabama, Georgia, Florida, South Carolina, and North Carolina, a number of persons, not less than one-tenth in number of the votes cast in such state, at the presidential election of the year of our Lord, 1860, each having taken the oath aforesaid, and not having since violated it, and being a qualified voter by the election law of the state existing immediately before the so-called Act of Secession, and excluding all others, shall re-establish a State Government which shall be Republican, and in nowise contravening said oath, such shall be recognized as the true Government of the state, and the state shall receive thereunder the benefit of the constitutional provision which declares that

"'The United States shall guarantee to every state in this Union a Republican form of government, and shall protect each of them against invasion, on application of the legislature, or of the executive, when the legislature cannot be convened, against domestic violence.'

"And I do further proclaim, declare, and make known that any provision which may be adopted by such state Government in reference to the freed people of such state which shall recognize and declare their permanent freedom, provide for their education, and which may yet be consistent, as a temporary arrangement, with their present condition as a labouring, landless, and houseless class, will not be objected to by the National Executive.

"And it is engaged as not improper that, in constructing a loyal state government in any state, the name of the state, the boundary, the subdivisions, the constitution, and the general code of laws as before the rebellion, be maintained, subject only to the modifications made necessary by the conditions hereinbefore stated, and such others, if any, not contravening said conditions, and which may be deemed expedient by those framing the new state government."

This proclamation leaves it as a point which may be litigated in the Supreme Court whether the Emancipation proclamation is according to law, or may be invalidated. This contingency is deprecated by some earnest friends of the coloured freedman. I cannot profess to correct their judgment. But my hope is, that an effective defence against any evil result from this quarter will be found in the prevalence of anti-slavery sentiment among the people, and abolition legislation in the Congress. The condition of the coloured man in the United States is under the guardianship of public opinion, which moves presidents, judges, senators, and all possessors of authority. The voice of truth and the power of liberty will triumph.

CHAPTER XI.

EVERY facility is given by postal authority in America for
the conveyance throughout the country of periodical publications. Except, however, in New York, perhaps too in
Boston, I found no letter carrying or delivery of letters or
papers by postal officials. Boxes at the offices, ranged in
alphabetical order, received all such communications for
resident inhabitants, which lay there till called for. Lists
of unclaimed letters were periodically printed. America
has not kept pace with England in this respect. But in
conveying newspapers from place to place she excels.
Weekly papers, within the county where published, go
free. Charges are so made for other publications that they
may be paid quarterly, either at the place of issue, or of
reception. The rates chargeable per quarter for a daily
paper do not reach half a dollar, going all over the United
States, when it is under three ounces; if under an ounce
and a half the charge is only half the amount. Recently
arrangements have been made by which packets may be
sent at much lower rates. This is shown in the following
note from the publisher of the "American Missionary:"—

"By the new law, to take effect July 1, 1863, the
postage on the 'American Missionary' paper or magazine,
will be one cent a number, or three cents a quarter; but
packages of not over four ounces (that is, five papers or
three magazines) can be sent to one address for the same

postage (one cent) and one cent for each additional four
ounces; but in the packages no names can be put on the
separate papers. Our friends in each town may, if they
please, so arrange as to receive their papers at the lowest
rates of postage."

In every town visited by me I found local journals,
secular and religious. Every denomination has its recognized organ for the state. In Pittsburg, for instance, I
found three Presbyterian bodies, and each had its journal
conducted with talent, energy, and liberality. In Boston
journalism has attained an extent and influence unequalled
in Europe: Theological, political, Puritanic, Congregational, Methodist, Episcopal, Presbyterian, Orthodox,
Heterodox, Evangelistic, Unitarian, Missionary, Latitudinarian, and controversial, which almost defy enumeration. In the year 1860, the State of Massachusetts had
published nearly two million dollars' worth of newspapers.
But in the State of New York the value of newspapers
published was little less than thirteen millions and a half of
dollars; and the total reported for all the states was
20,653,371 dollars invested in newspaper literature alone;
while the aggregate in books was 11,843,459 dollars for
the whole United States.

The stenographic or phonographic art is perhaps not
so universal as is the daily press in America: as I found
frequent applications for the "Notes" of the speaker, and
which I never could supply. But I am bound to testify
that even in the Western States, in Cincinnati, St. Louis,
and Pittsburg, I read reports of my addresses which were
verbatim, and did not make me ashamed of what I had
delivered. They were promptly produced and widely circulated. I was, however, amused on one occasion to read
in the "New York Herald," a mere paraphrase of what I
had spoken. From beginning to end hardly one word
which I had uttered, but in other words throughout a pretty

correct version of my thoughts; a free translation of the speech, and in strong contrast with the "New York Times," which reported my words as well as my sentiments. I was told by Dr. Tyng of a case which had recently occurred to himself. On the Thanksgiving day in August, he had been taken by surprise in his own lecture room by the attendance of a much larger assembly than he had anticipated, which rendered expedient an address as well as "prayers." He had not prepared, and therefore his address was extempore. Something like a free translation of what he uttered was *reported* in one of the New York papers—for which he was in no sense responsible, as he had not seen it before or after. His attention to it was however enforced by an elaborate critique on his discourse, as if it had been his publication, which he read to me from the London "Record." The words and phrases, which were not his, were held up to scorn, and he was severely and ungenerously slandered as a man who had departed from his duty, the principles of piety, and the character of a Christian minister. Writers who live in glass houses should not cast stones.

A few papers in the states, where slavery lingers, still serve as champions for the *soi-disant* patriarchal institution, and denounce all measures tending to its abolition; in Kentucky advertisements of sales and the running away of negroes still appear, and even Mr. Prentice in the "Louisville Journal" avows a belief that the negroes are normally suited only for forced labour and the slave's fare; these are *vestigia relicta* of departing times.

The two main political distinctions in the daily press are the Democratic and Republican creeds; the former again divided into Peace Democrats—sometimes called Copper-heads, as the copper-head snake ministers to the rattle-snake, when uncoiling the last folds of its skin: and as the banner of South Carolina bears the rattle-snake for its *insignium*. There are also War Democrats who say the Government should be supported till this rebellion is subdued; but they reserve something to be hereafter adjusted about the sovereign rights of separate states and the inter-communal immunities of their citizens. The Republican papers are also divided into Anti-slavery and Slave-tolerating parties more or less vehement. The "New York Herald" is *sui generis;* sometimes hot and sometimes cold, and sometimes hot and cold—sometimes it reports the truth, and contains well-written descriptive articles—at other times it reports what has more fiction than truth, or again, what has no truth at all, but with all the gravity of a truthful chronicler. If its correspondents do not send lies, there is some one at head-quarters who can *make* them to order in any number—chiefly of a sensational character. As to any principle of truth or virtue, I never could see it; one principle it holds as the devil has held murder from the beginning—malevolent, malicious hatred to the coloured race and all who would uphold his cause. When the South began this rebellion, this paper rallied under its banner, till the roughs on the right side threatened consequences which Mr. Bennet, with all his Scottish calculation, as a renegade did not covet, and therefore he hung out for a time the stripes and stars. He is believed to be as much with the South still; but he serves it by lies and deception, by the sewer garbage of New York partizanship and the brazen hypocrisy which every intelligent man in New York penetrates. The paper panders to the momentary passions of those who live by their wits, and hate honesty and the coloured man. Were the energy, enterprise, and management expended on this journal devoted to a benevolent and patriotic cause, multitudes would rejoice in its success. The "World," the "Sun," and the "Express," as also the "News," are also supposed to sympathize with opponents to the present administration. The first of these had a better character till it became the property of an agent of the Jew firm of Rothschild, who trades in stocks, exchanges, discounts, and loans.

This transatlantic broker has realized, as is reported, a large fortune by the trade in which he has engaged since the rebellion began. His special telegrams to London, as well as Reüter's, are thought to have been manipulated for influences on the stock and gold market more than to convey the truth in facts concerning the war.

Financially the "Express" was under the care of assignees while I was in New York, and I scarcely ever heard of the others. As a stranger I cannot speak of all the New York journals, many of which I never saw; but I refer to such as I found in reading-rooms, in clubs, and at private residences, or as were prominently announced for sale in cars, etc. The "Daily News" does not sympathize with Mr. Lincoln's administration; the "Journal of Commerce" urged every citizen to stand by the laws and the constituted authorities of the city, state, and nation, but regarded slavery and the slave system with an eye to commerce. The "Express," the "Sun," and other minor papers have not prospered as far as they adhered to the South. The "New York Evening Post," the "Tribune," and "Times" deserve a higher eulogium than I can write; the first, as a literary journal, sustains a reputation which the prolonged connection with it of a Bryant, Bigelow, and Godwin in editorial labours has been well qualified to insure. Calm and philosophical, chaste and refined, enriched with original and eloquent inspirations of the muse, and breathing always a lofty patriotism, it has served with efficiency the country, and drawn out men, as statesmen and scholars, who have done honour to their age. Its antagonism to the system of slavery has not been so uncompromising or energetic as to rank it among abolition or emancipation journals, but it has proved faithful as an advocate of the party who would

restrict the growth and finally root out the upas tree from
their fair land. The "Times" in New York is not merely
an establishment—it is more like an institution. The conspicuous and ornamental building, occupied as its publishing premises, prove not only the financial resources by
which it is sustained, and the reproducing revenue by
which the capitalists are rewarded, but also the position of
the journal in the esteem of the public. Its literature is
pertinent, the tone of its politics comparatively moderate,
its reporting is correct and extensive, and its correspondence varied and authentic, especially on war matters and
proceedings at Washington. In its staff are men of distinguished literary attainments personally unknown to me.
A few extracts from its columns during the Riots will indicate the position on the slave question which it occupied,
and its estimate of contemporaries.

"THE MOB AND THE PRESS.

" The mob last evening broke the windows and demo-
lished the furniture in the counting-room of the ' Tribune,'
and attempted to crown their infamous and fiendish ruf-
fianism by setting the building on fire. The prompt arrival
and vigorous action of a body of police interrupted their
proceedings, and deprived them of the pleasure of being as
brutal as they had hoped and expected to be.

" We have not always agreed with our neighbour on
political topics, and have not deemed it wise on grounds of
the public welfare to make slavery and the negro so prominent in these discussions as the ' Tribune' has done. But
that is a matter concerning which judgments and tastes
may differ. It is intolerable that a mob should undertake
by violence and destruction of property to dictate topics
for public discussion, or to control the sentiments and
utterances of the public press. When such an issue is
forced upon journalists, they must make it their common
cause.

" We regret that the ' Tribune' should have suffered in
such a shape even the trifling loss which last night's mob
inflicted upon them. They had the aid of some among our

employés in protecting their property, and shall have it again whenever the invidious favour of the mob shall again release us from the necessity of defending our own.

" It is too true, that there are public journals who try to dignify this mob by some respectable appellation. The ' Herald' characterizes it as the people, and the ' World' as the labouring men of the city. These are libels that ought to have paralyzed the fingers that penned them. It is ineffably infamous to attribute to the people, or to the labouring men of this metropolis, such hideous barbarism as this horde has been displaying. The people of New York and the labouring men of New York are not incendiaries, nor robbers, nor assassins. They do not hunt down men whose only offence is the colour God gave them—they do not chase, and insult, and beat women—they do not pillage an asylum for orphan children, and burn the very roof over those orphans' heads. They are civilized beings, valuing law, and respecting decency ; and they regard with unqualified abhorrence the doings of the tribe of savages that have sought to bear rule in their midst.

" The ' World,' with an eager ferocity which finds its proper counterpart in the ranks of the mob, seizes this opportunity to denounce those journals which support the government as responsible for the riot, and to point them out to the mob as proper objects of its vengeance. ' We charge it plainly,' says the ' World,' ' upon the radical journals of this city,' that, by their mode of discussing the political topics of the day, they have provoked this outburst of public passion. The ' World' knows better. It knows perfectly well that these causes have nothing whatever to do with the riot that is striking death-blows at the life and property of the very class that is made at once its tool and its victim. Grant all that the ' World' may claim as to the bad taste and injustice of the tone in which these journals have canvassed these topics, they do not touch the real cause of the outbreak.

" The ' World' permits itself to read a lecture to the ' radical journals' for not having heeded its warnings of the ' rude vengeance' of which it gave them notice, and, with an apparent consciousness of temporary power, it deals lavishly in threats of still further punishment at the hands of the mob. We do not know whether the ' Times' is among the 'radical journals' who are thus addressed or not. We have conducted the political discussions of the day without much reference to party or class relations, according to our own sense of justice and propriety. Without giving undue prominence to any of the secondary issues of the controversy, we have done everything in our power to sustain the government, and crush rebellion wherever it has appeared. We have done this because we deem it our duty, and we shall continue to do it without regard to the warnings of the 'World', or the menaces of the mob. We scorn to owe anything, still more to owe freedom of speech on questions of great public concern, to the forbearance or the favour of the gang of ruffians who are doing everything in their power to convert this metropolis into a hideous haunt of vagabonds and thieves. We would rather see every stone in the building which shelters us levelled with the ground, than feel that it stands only through our truckling to a mob which threatens every public interest and every private right with swift and remediless destruction. We have nothing to regret in our mode of treating these subjects hitherto. Most certainly, we have neither apology nor toleration for the mob that has ruled and disgraced New York. It finds no shadow of excuse in any act of the government, and the only palliation for the conduct of those who have taken part in its excesses, is found in the fact that they have been betrayed into them by men more cunning and more cowardly than themselves."

The "Tribune" was selected specially by the rioting mobs of July, and its editor personally and in his residence as well as his publishing office was threatened with violence. I was engaged with him repeatedly on the day of the outbreak, and witnessed his manner and the conduct of his assistants in a time of great excitement. In a cowardly manner, and in untruthful statements, the "Herald" and its political confederates held him forward in taunting language as timidly *shrinking* from the brutality of the rioters, and concealing his person while dictating directions to his workmen. Illustrative of his character, as well as the state of things in New York, I extract a para-

graph from his paper on the 18th of July, the sixth day
from the commencement of the disturbance :—

"The 'World' on Tuesday blazoned 'the lie with circumstance' that the editor of the 'Tribune' had not dared
to enter his own office on Monday, but had spent the day
at a restaurant and left it at last in disguise! There was
no truth in this; but it did not seem worth while to con-
tradict it. But on Wednesday the 'World' returned to the
charge, in an article specially intended to incite the mob
to murder Republican editors, saying—

"'It might have been supposed that the lowering approach of the rude vengeance they have courted would
have made these people feel at last how mad their course
has been. It might have been supposed that the editor of
the "Tribune," TREMBLING ALL DAY LONG IN THE SAFE UM-
BRAGE OF A FRIENDLY RESTAURANT, AND ESCAPING AT LAST
UNDER COVER OF THE DARKNESS TO HIS HOME, might have
been led by these hours of seclusion to fling away the
torch he had so long and so thoughtlessly brandished.'

"There must be a stop to this. Briefly, then the editor
of the 'TRIBUNE' came to his office on Monday morning at
nine o'clock, walking to it from a Harlem car in plain sight
of scores; remained at his work till dinner time; then
walked deliberately through the crowd to Windust's, ate
his dinner, and at once took a carriage thence to his lodging in broad daylight and with no sort of concealment or
disguise. He prevented the arming of the 'Tribune'
office until after the assault upon, sack, and attempt to burn
it that evening; then he thought the time had come for decisive measures; and the next morning (Tuesday) he devoted
mainly to aiding to put it in fighting trim; coming again
openly by car down town, walking from the car through the
crowd to his office, and remaining there from nine a.m. to
four p.m., when he walked away undisguised and unas-
sailed as before. Yesterday he was again at the office by
ten a.m., coming in a carriage because there were no public conveyances then in motion, and spending the day about
his business as usual. (N. B.—The fighting arrangements
did not require renewal.) He left at a proper dinner-hour
as before, and expects to be back at his post in good season
this morning. He may be murdered, as the 'World' threa-

tens, but he does not expect to be frightened. And if the
'World' will advise his friends not to devastate the dwellings
of inoffensive people who kindly watched over him in sickness two years ago, but with whom he has never 'boarded'
since, and who are nowise related to him, it will be all the
favour he asks from *that* quarter."

Horace Greeley is a man of inextinguishable ardour and
exhaustless mental resources. His whole soul is absorbed
in the success of the cause which he espouses. The phases
of his religious opinion are said to have repeatedly changed.
He has dipped into Spiritualism, I heard, but I suppose he
found table-rapping would not quell a riot, or convince a
nation. He has thought or written some things favourable
to Universalism, but whatever he postpones to the future
and invisible he has no salvation for the Rattle-snake, the
Copperhead, or the Demon of Slavery. A Republican and
friend of liberty, he welcomes co-operation from all, and
willingly lends his aid to all who would hunt to the deepest
recesses of its den the foul fiend of oppression. I found
him frank and accessible. He had heard my address the
night before, and was now ready to give his powerful aid
to my mission, and that day, at his office, was prepared a
brief outline of what had been already done, under my own
suggestions, including the New York response, which was
put to press that night and appeared next morning, among
the rioting of thousands of misguided and infuriated men.
Mr. Greeley does not confine his contributions to his own
daily paper; but in the "Independent" and other religious
or literary journals his writings appear as the welcome
contributions of a popular writer. He has access to the
occupant of the White House, and such influence as to
elicit responses on momentous questions with which he
may in some measure fashion the politics of the nation. Some
fear him as a dictator, and others hate him as a radical,
but I believe he is one of the present elements of American
society.

The "Independent," the "Evangelist," the "Congregationalist," the "Anti-Slavery Standard," the "Liberator," the "Principia," the "New York Observer," the "New York Chronicle," the "Scottish American," "Missionary Advocate," the "Christian Times," "The Eclectic," and "Covenanter," are weekly in their issue, and are of a mixed character, partly secular and partly special. I take them as representative rather than as the only journals of the class. The "Covenanter," as representing the Reformed Presbyterians, is thoroughly anti-slavery in action. The "Christian Times" is Episcopalian in its connection, but liberal, evangelical, and thoroughly practical in its piety. I have not seen it but accept the testimony of the contemporaneous press. I give an extract from the paper to show its spirit:—

"Evangelical Episcopalians are occasionally criticized for the alleged affinities for 'the denominations,' as they are styled. If the reference is to communions non-Episcopal, but thoroughly orthodox in their creed, we are not anxious to deny the allegation. But what is it? It is an affinity for their orthodoxy, their love of the truth, and their adherence to the doctrinal teaching of the Scriptures. These brethren receive the Bible as the pure Word of God, the only rule of faith, and so are in perfect accord with the articles of our Church. If, providentially, our Church had been equal to the work of leavening this whole land with the doctrine and spirit of Christ, we should have rejoiced in it; but seeing that we are but one among many to whom this great work has been committed, we are glad when we hear of, or see tokens of success in its performance of the part of 'the denominations.' Nor is this merely a speculative question, in regard to which Churchmen may hold any views without any danger of spiritual detriment. Who fails to see that it must make a great difference in our feelings toward others, according as we look upon their relation to the cause of Christianity, the kingdom of our Lord?"

The missionary journals are numerous, including the

" Home and Foreign Missionary Record," the " American
Missionary," the " Missionary Advocate." The second of
these three devotes its columns largely to missions among
the coloured men who have been *freed* in virtue of the President's proclamation, and the incidents of the rebellion.
I saw the " Scottish American" only rarely, and thought
there was more in it of the Scotchman than the loyal
American. The " New York Chronicle" is an organ of the
Baptists, and breathes fervently the loyalty of that sect
in the North, supporting President Lincoln most heartily.
Besides denominational matter, essays, and extracts on
practical Christianity and religious intelligence, it presents
in summary but briefly the political incidents of the week.
It is said the Baptists number one million of members. I
hope they are all as good as their " Chronicle." The
" Observer " has seen 2120 weeks, and is, therefore, in the
forty-first year of its age. I have remembered as long as
I have had any notice of American affairs the name and
reputation of Mr. S. Morse, sen., and his " Observer." I
think I met him once in England. I was sorry one day I
was dining at a restaurant in New York to find he and I
had dined at the same table without a personal recognition.
The paper had formerly more celebrity than it has now,
and I fancy I remember it was then more pro than anti-
slavery. I would hardly recal the sins of its youth had it
not now a more deserving position. The paper is the property of Sidney E. Morse, jun., and Co., and sustains its
character by original contributions on local, historical, critical subjects, natural history, and husbandry, in its secular
department. It has a youths' department, giving tales
and extracts. In the " religious department," miscellaneous matters, places of worship, expository essays on prophecy, Christian work, Walking worthy, the Heavenly
Baptism, National thanksgiving, and a page of political
articles, one part on the rebel intentions, and another on

the persecution of negroes, in which the editor expresses himself as follows :—

"Nothing in the late riots in this city is more disgraceful to the guilty parties than the wanton, cruel, and deadly assaults made upon the negro population. Innocent of all blame in the matter, far more peaceful and orderly than their persecutors, the coloured people were marked for vengeance by the mob, hunted down in the streets, some of them put to death, and their houses sacked and destroyed. Such deeds of shame are enough to bring a blush upon the cheek of the most hardened offenders, yet there are thousands of men among us who have participated in these outrages. Measures have been taken to raise funds to supply the immediate wants of hundreds of these poor people who have been made homeless and destitute, and their situation presents the strongest appeal for our compassionate aid."

The intelligence of an ecclesiastical character, embraces colleges : Congregational, Presbyterian, Episcopal, Baptist, Lutheran, Reformed Dutch, and Missionary. The contents would fill an ordinary volume, each paper at the charge of twopence farthing. "The Principia" claims the editorship of Dr. Cheever and the Rev. W. Goodall, and J. W. Alden as publisher. These three gentlemen appear the agents of five trustees of the Principia Association, a company of shareholders who announce interest at the rate of seven per cent. The paper is published at two dollars per annum. It seeks to develope *first principles* in religion, morals, government, and the economy of life. Perronet Thompson, Major-General, sends his racy and pungent morsels of literature from Blackheath to the "Principia." One lies before me, under the title, "Space for Repentance to Americans, also for the Working-classes in England." Mr. Goodall divides the page on "The Players and the Puritans;" and Mr. Jocelyn narrates "A Visit to the Freedmen of East Virginia, Washington, and vicinity." The whole

G G

of the next two pages are occupied with anti-slavery discussions from Dr. Cheever's stand-point in the conflict.
There is an earnest persistency and self-abnegation in the
argumentation of the editors which give an idiosyncracy to
their paper, by which it is made to occupy an isolated
position.

The "Liberator" bears as a woodcut a symbolic frontis-
piece, representing the negro auction mart on the left side,
and a scene of negro life under emancipation on the right side
of a central emblem, round which is the gracious proclamation, "I come to break the bonds of the oppressor ;" which
seems an answer to the prayer of a chained negro, from
whom a tyrant white man is made to flee. The paper is
wholly devoted to the interests of the coloured millions of
America ; narration, argumentation, poetry, and all the
solicitudes of an unflinching and self-denying advocate,
are employed to promote the emancipation of the enslaved
race. The editor and his party had long excluded themselves from political action with any of the candidates for
office, being unable to identify themselves with any programme within the limits of the Constitution. They feel
themselves relieved by the rebellion of the slaveholders,
and are now able and eagerly solicitous to strengthen the
administration of Mr. Lincoln, and the enrolment of
coloured troops as an armed force of the United States.
The "Liberator" zealously promotes this organization.
The "Anti-slavery Standard" knows only one object and
renders all its influence and action subservient to its
attainment—the abolition of slavery, in all places, at the
earliest practicable time : "without concealment, without
compromise," is its watchword and talisman. With a
vigilance that never slumbers and a zeal that continueth
ever, in this course, it goes straight onward. Turning the
curse of man's wrath into a blessing, and the venom of
man's malignity into a medicine, it culls the worst passages

of pro-slavery dialectics and the most furious invectives of slave-holding passion, and giving them a prominence which in their native sphere they could never reach; it points the finger of scorn upon the system, and casts down the dagon of its idolatry as a headless and limbless trunk, to be trod upon by the lovers of truth and liberty. I have not always concurred in the style or course of some parts of the internal or inter-denominational warfare of my friends; but I thank them for their service to the slave, and I testify to their vigorous maintenance of the anti-slavery parts of Mr. Lincoln's administration.

The "Congregationalist," as does the "Liberator," emanates from Boston, and is the property of Galen James, C. A. Richardson and William L. Green. It is nearly sixteen years old. It is well printed, well arranged, and well written as a journal. The men who write for the paper are generally designated by initials, or other incidents by which they are known in the denomination as worthy of regard. The duties of the editorial department are fulfilled more in selection and arrangement than by the production of ela-borate essays or authoritative impositions; though I have seen learned disquisitions which were ascribed to the edi-tors on "the relation of female members to the public services of the church," and "strictures on the proceedings of church councils," which seemed intended to prove that Congregationalists required yet to learn how doubtful a policy in their churches is anything approaching to clerical authority and synodical action. The sufferings of Jonathan Edwards will not probably foreshadow the trials of Mr. Charles Beecher. Dr. Bacon, Dr. J. P. Thompson, and other authorities, beyond the state of Massachusetts, contribute to the vitality and attractions of the "Congregationalist," which moves almost wholly in its denominational orbit, in discus-sion, and in the records of collegiate institutions. The principal exception to this course is the earnest mainte-

nance of the cause of the slave, and the cordial support
rendered to Mr. Lincoln's policy against the rebellion.
The " Evangelist " was the property of Dr. Bidwell, but
has lately passed under the editorship of Henry M. Field
and J. G. Craighead. It is largely occupied with paragraphs of religious news, and incidental illustrations of the
progress of spiritual or revived religion. Essays and reviews
and sometimes a sermon, find a place. I do not know that
it connects itself with any denomination; but it is as much
identified with the Presbyterians as with any other body.
It gives its entire support to Mr. Lincoln, and urges the
wisdom of emancipation, and the hopelessness of any future
peace unless slavery be abolished in the subjugated states.

I do not name the " Independent " as if it needed my
imprimatur or that I should introduce it to my English
readers. Henry Ward Beecher knows how to array by his
side, and in the columns of an Independent journal, men of
kindred spirit and congenial talent. Dr. Tyng, an Episcopalian; Theo. Cuyler, a Presbyterian; Dr. Storrs, a Congregationalist; Horace Greeley, a " Corporation sole," and
many other men contribute to his pages and charm his
readers, while his own inimitable sermons and platform
orations diversify the communications and enrich the literature of America. I need not tell how all is made to
subserve good government and the liberty of the negro or
the coloured slave. The hatred of the South which hunted
and yelled its curses on the head of Beecher in his European
tour, manifest the dread with which men-stealers and
traders in human flesh abhor him and his services. The
demoniac hatred with which he was pursued in his public
appearances in Britain were a far stronger attestation to
his work, his virtue, and the influence of the "Independent,"
than all the eulogies of his friends, their complimentary
resolutions or festive demonstrations. In vain was the
effort to lessen his triumph.

There are journals, especially the organs of Episcopal Methodists, but their name is Legion; and in all parts of the states have they a powerful influence in support of Mr. Lincoln's Government. I borrow a paragraph from the " Congregationalist," referring to one gentleman whom it was my pleasure to meet and admire in his manner and opinions. Dr. Haven is worthy of the affectionate esteem of all who know him :

"We find in' this week's issue of 'Zion's Herald' the valedictory of the Rev. E. O. Haven, D.D., for seven years editor of that paper, he having been elected President of the University of Michigan. Under his management the 'Herald' has been ably edited, and has uniformly shown an excellent spirit. He has also filled many important public positions, has been a member of the Massachusetts Senate for two sessions, a member of the State Board of Education, an active leader in the temperance cause, and has secured the high esteem of the community by his uniform courtesy, and his consistent and earnest course in defence of the right and true, wherever found. We regret his departure from this vicinity, and wish him abundant success and usefulness in his new field of labour. He is to be succeeded as editor of the 'Herald' by the Rev. N. E. Cobleigh, D.D., now President of McKendree College, Illinois."

" METHODIST LITERATURE.—The Central Ohio Conference of the Methodist Episcopal Church at its late meeting appointed a committee to report on the periodicals of the denomination. Their report adopted by the Conference, mentions with gratitude the fact of the uniform loyalty to the government of their religious periodicals in the North; recommends all the members of their churches 'to pray that God by his Spirit would bless our editors and writers;' pledges the ministers connected with the Conference to exert themselves to obtain subscribers for their papers and reviews; and finally lays down the law of Methodism in this wise: 'That all of our membership be expected to take and read our periodicals, and that it is expected of them to stand by the doctrines of the Church, and aid in forming a moral sentiment derived from the teachings of

the Bible, instead of the teachings of partisan newspapers.'"

The Southern cause has vigorous exponents of its interests and principles in the editorial staffs of Richmond
journals, and others in Memphis and Mobile, Charleston
and Savannah; there is often exhibited much vigorous
writing and unscrupulous assertion. Baron Munchausen
serves instead of a reporter occasionally. But slavery is
the grand idol before which their daily publications are
presented as incensed offerings. Harmoniously they shout
with trumpet-tongues, " Great is Diana of the Confederacy."
They denounce Northern Democrats who would recommend
restoration to the Union, and European commissioners or
agents who would temporize at the expense of the *patriarchal institution*. They repudiate Mr. James Spence, because he says he is against slavery, though they know
better. They shrink not from the broad and continued
avowal that the conflict is waged for maintaining and
extending their domestic institution. Mr. Mitchell, who
would have rebelled in Ireland, with W. Smith O'Brien,
but that the battle was fought in a cabbage-garden, and
the victory achieved by complying with the poetic prescrip-
tion—

> " He who fights and runs away,
> May live to fight another day."

It may be guessed how he would have sought the liberty
and welfare of the WORKING Irishman by the system he
now advocates, which, in his own words, is "liberty to
wallop the nigger." When he went down South he proclaimed his preference for the plantation and the slave,
and his hatred to all Yankee industry. He is no shuffling,
mawkish hypocrite, now at least; and his writings have
all the odour of an unveiled, slaveholding Democrat.

Besides the extracts which may be gathered, thick as
leaves in Vallombrosa, from the Southern press, and their

disguised sympathizers in the North, the English press has
an exhaustless and ever fresh supply from its "special"
sources.   Dr. Mackay and the Hon. Mr. L. have con-
genially laboured, the latter in Richmond, and the former
at New York; the latter an *ex* private secretary and dealer
in funds; and the former an *ex* politico-poetic advocate of
the working poor 'and their seamstresses.   For a time, at
least he was succeeded in his "Special" Commission, by a
man who is said to have been an avowed apologist of
assassination in political economy.   A kindred spirit with
these is a "Special," *Manhattan*, whose antecedents may
not have been less honourable, but whose slashing style
and pretensions are thought adequate to the demands of
Anglican conservatism.   There are other "specials," or
"occasionals," who supply the press with what they hear
or what they fancy.   I have read a description of one of
the most hotly contested battles of the war, at Chancellors-
ville, and where the carnage was great; the divisions of
the armies occupying heights and valleys, on right and left
of streams, where an angel wing would have been required to have a full view of the appalling and distracting
scene.   But the "special" correspondent not only saw all,
but could describe what one man did and another said,
and could detail the hand-to-hand fights, and single out
the gallant actions of his favourites, in the most thrilling
and graphic terms.   I heard men who had risen from
perusing the recital in ecstacies of admiration for the
writer, and pronouncing their verdict on the cowardly and
spiritless Yankee soldiers.

The Democratic peace policy has been satirically exposed
in the pages of a small publication bearing the title "The
New Gospel of Peace according to St. Benjamin;" and
thus the ridicule of the American public has been
poured on the sympathizers with the Confederacy.   To
their underhand devices and gross perversions of public

sentiment General Robert Lee's temporary successes were
ascribed. He is said to have taken " an army of phiretahs
(fire eaters), and marched into two of the provinces of the
land of Uncul Psalm (Uncle Sam), proclaiming the New
Gospel of Peace at the point of the sword. And he laid
parts of those provinces waste with fire, and he destroyed
the bridges that were over the rivers, and carried off their
horses, and their corn, and their cattle; and put all them
that resisted the New Gospel of Peace to the sword.
So the people began to understand the mystery of the
New Gospel, and they glorified; and they said, yet a
little while and the niggah (negro) shall be restored to his
bondage, and the Shivalry and the Phiretahs shall be our
masters, and peace shall rule the land with a rod of iron,
and we shall compromise ourselves for ever. And there
was great rejoicing." Such is said to have been the prophecy of a modern Balaam whom the Democrats consulted.

The friends of the Union, determined that such adversaries shall not have it all their own way, have organized
a " Loyal Publication Society," whose objects are expressed
in the following resolution :—

" That the object of this organization is, and shall be
confined to the distribution of journals and documents of
unquestionable and unconditional loyalty throughout the
United States, and particularly in the armies now engaged
in the suppression of the rebellion, and to counteract, as
far as practicable, the efforts now being made by the
enemies of the Government and the advocates of a disgraceful peace, to circulate journals and documents of a
disloyal character."

"In fulfilment of their purpose, they have issued,
among other works, twenty tracts with titles such as :—
'Future of the North West,' by Robert Dale Owen.
'Echo from the Army.' 'Union Mass Meeting, Speeches
of Brady, Van Buren,' etc. 'Three Voices; the Soldier,
Farmer, and Poet.' 'Voices from the Army.' 'Northern
True Men.' 'Speech of Major-General Butler.' 'Sepa-

ration; War without End.' Ed. Laboulaye. 'The Venom and the Antidote.' 'A few words in behalf of the Loyal Women of the United States,' by One of Themselves. 'No Failure for the North.' Atlantic Monthly. 'Address to King Cotton.' Eugene Pelletan. 'How a Free People conduct a long War.' Stillé. 'The Preservation of the Union, a National Economic Necessity.' 'Elements of Discord in Secessia,' etc., etc. 'No Party now, all for Our Country.' Dr. Francis Lieber. "The Cause of the War.' Col. Charles Anderson. 'Opinions of the Early Presidents, and of the Fathers of the Republic upon Slavery, and upon Negroes as Men and Soldiers.' 'Military Despotism! Suspension of the Habeas Corpus! Curses coming home to roost!'

There is a publication, periodical in its issue, but so authentic in its contents that the statements it contains are accepted in evidence in courts of law: it is entitled "The Rebellion Records, a Diary of American Events," etc. Six volumes are now published, five of which lie before me, in royal 8vo, and each contains about 700 pages, with numerous engravings, etc. Southern documents and records are given, as well as those from authority in the loyal states. It is intended to serve the cause of truth. Mr. Frank Moore is the Editor, and G. P. Putnam of Broadway, New York, is its publisher. The sixth volume brings down the diary and documents of events till June 1863. I cannot take farewell of these volumes till I transcribe from them three or four verses, which I believe will be verified in the struggle as it closes on American soil.

> " Another laurel wreaths to-day
>   Our country's honoured fame;
> The seal is set which wipes away
>   A long recorded shame.
> Thank God! the rulers of the land
>   For Freedom have decreed,
> And Justice lifts her sacred hand
>   To bless the righteous deed.

" Her battles fought, her victories won,
    No field of bloody strife
Sends forth its cloud to blot the sun
    Or drink the nation's life.
But peace and all her shining bands
    Their tuneful voices raise,
And sing throughout the happy land
    Their songs of joy and praise.

" From sea to sea, from gulf to lakes,
    And o'er the watery world ;
The wind of heaven our banner takes,
    Against the sky unfurled ;
The dear old flag, its stars all there,
    And where it proudly streams
No guilt of treason taints the air,
    No slave of Freedom dreams.

" O nation, fairest born of time !
    O people blessed of fate !
'Tis yours to make the world sublime,
    By being nobly great !
To rise from out this trial hour,
    If true to man and God,
To heights of fame and fields of power,
    And glory all untrod."

APPENDIX.

UNION AND EMANCIPATION SOCIETY.

PRESIDENT—THOMAS BAYLEY POTTER, ESQ.

VICE-PRESIDENTS.

Thomas Bazley, Esq., M.P.
E. A. Leatham, Esq., M.P.
P. A. Taylor, Esq., M.P.
James Kershaw, Esq., M.P.
W. Coningham, Esq., M.P.
Guildford J. H. Ouslow, Esq., M.P.
  Winchester
Charles Sturge, Esq., Birmingham
G. L. Ashworth, Esq., Rochdale
Lieut.-General T. Perronet Thompson
Professor J. E. Cairnes, A.M., Dublin
Professor Jno. Nichol, Glasgow
Professor Goldwin Smith, Oxford
Professor F. W. Newman, London
Professor Beesly, London
Hon. and Rev. Baptist W. Noel,
  London
Rev. Thomas Guthrie, D.D., Edinburgh
Rev. Newman Hall, LL.B., London
Rev. James W. Massie, D.D., LL.D.,
  London
John Stuart Mill, Esq., London
Thomas Hughes, Esq., barrister-at-law
F. G. Haviland, Esq., Cambridge
W. E. Adams, Esq., Newcastle-on-Tyne
W. P. Paton, Esq., Glasgow
George Wilson, Esq., Manchester
Dr. John Watts, Manchester
Mr. Edward Hooson, Manchester
Alderman Abel Heywood, Manchester
Alderman Robert Kell, Bradford
Alderman Henry Brown, Bradford
Alderman William Harvey, J.P., Salford
Alderman Thomas Livsey, Rochdale
Councillor Murray, Manchester
Councillor T. Warburton, Manchester

Councillor Geo. Booth, Manchester
Councillor Clegg, Manchester
Councillor Williams, Salford
Councillor Butterworth, Manchester
Councillor Ogden, Manchester
Councillor Ryder, Manchester
Max Kyllman, Esq., Manchester
S. P. Robinson, Esq., Manchester
H. M. Steinthal, Esq., Manchester
Francis Taylor, Esq., Manchester
Thomas Thomasson, Esq., Bolton
Joseph Leese, Esq., Bowdon
John Epps, Esq., M.D., London
J. A. Langford, Esq., Birmingham
Rev. Hy. W. Crosskey, Glasgow
J. J. Colman, Esq., Norwich
James M. Clelland, Esq., Glasgow
William Brown, Esq., Glasgow
Edward Alexander, jun., Esq., Glasgow
Councillor John Burt, Glasgow
Professor Henry Fawcett, Cambridge
Henry Lightbown, Esq., Pendleton
Abraham Howarth, Esq., Manchester
James M. Paton, Esq., Montrose
Thos. R. Arnott, Esq., Liverpool
E. K. Muspratt, Esq., Liverpool
J. B. Whitehead, Esq., Rawtenstall
Isaac B. Cooke, Esq., Liverpool
Thomas Crosfield, Esq., Liverpool
R. Gladstone, Esq., Liverpool
John Patterson, Esq., Liverpool
Councillor J. R. Jeffrey, Liverpool
C. E. Rawlins, jun., Esq., Liverpool
Charles Robertson, Esq., Liverpool
Robert Trimble, Esq., Liverpool
Charles Wilson, Esq., Liverpool
William Shaen, Esq., London

Duncan M'Laren, Esq., Edinburgh
Handel Cossham, Esq., Bristol
S. C. Kell, Esq., Bradford
Richard C. Rawlings, Esq., Ruabon
J. S. Barratt, Esq., Southport
Thomas C. Ryley, Esq., Wigan
R. S. Ashton, Esq., Darwen
Eccles Shorrock, Esq., Darwen
John Crosfield, Esq., Warrington
Jacob Bright, Esq., Rochdale
John Petrie, Esq., Rochdale
Oliver Ormerod, Esq., Rochdale
J. C. Dyer, Esq., Burnage
George Crosfield, Esq., Lymm
F. Pennington, Esq., Alderley
J. B. Foster, Esq., Manchester
James Galloway, Esq., Manchester
Charles Cheetham, Esq., Heywood
Joseph Cowan, jun., Esq., Newcastle-upon-Tyne
Rev. Samuel Davidson, LL.D., London
Rev. Francis Bishop, Chesterfield
Rev. J. Parker, D.D., Manchester
Rev. J. Robberds, B.A., Liverpool
Rev. Marmaduke Miller, Darlington
Rev. T. G. Lee, Salford
S. Pope, Esq., Barrister-at-law
E. Jones, Esq., Barrister-at-law
Dr. Louis Borchardt, Manchester
Charles H. Bracebridge, Esq., Atherstone Hall
Rev. Goodwyn Barmby, Wakefield
William Jeffery Etches, Esq., Derby
Rev. C. M. Birrell, Liverpool
Professor J. E. Thorold Rogers, Oxford Row
Mr. Serjeant Parry, London
William Biggs, Esq., Leicester
Rev. Leslie Stephen, Fellow of Trinity Hall, Cambridge

Rev. Robert B. Drummond, B.A., Edinburgh
Andrew Leighton, Esq., Liverpool
Edward Dicey, Esq., London
Rev. N. M. Michael, D.D., Dunfermline
James Ross, Esq., Carlisle
Robert Ferguson, Esq., Carlisle
Robert Johnson, Esq., Manchester
Joseph Spencer, Esq., Manchester
Rev. Geo. D. MacGregor, Farnworth
Thos. Spence, Esq., Barrister-at-law
Rev. G. T. Fox, Durham
Arthur Trevelyan, Esq. J.P., Teinholme
James M'Culloch, Esq., M.D., Dumfries
Peter Redford Scott, Esq., Edinburgh
W. E. Hodgkinson, Esq., Manchester
Sir John Hesketh Lethbridge, Bart., Taunton
J. Mackenzie, Esq., M.D., J.P., Inverness
Thomas Nelson, Esq., Edinburgh
John Ashworth, Esq., J.P., Turton, near Bolton
Thomas Emmett, Esq., Oldham
Rev. John Guttridge, President M. F. Church
William C. Leng, Esq., Dundee
Robert Service, Esq., Culcreuch, Glasgow
E. W. Thomas, Esq., Mayor of Oswestry
James Aytoun, Esq., London
Hon. George Brown, Toronto
Professor Rogers, Glasgow
Rev. W. L. Alexander, D.D., Edinburgh
R. Peek, Esq., J.P., Hazlewood
Col. Henry Salwey, Runnymede Park, Egham
James Taylor, jun., Esq., Birmingham
Rev. Henry Bachelor, Glasgow

TREASURER—Samuel Watts, jun., Esq., Manchester.
BANKERS—Manchester and Salford Bank.

JOHN C. EDWARDS,
EDWARD OWEN GREENING, } *Hon. Secs.*

RESPONSE

FROM THE CHURCH OF THE PURITANS, NEW YORK.

(Note to page 113.)

RESPECTED AND BELOVED,—We respond with delight to your fraternal and sympathizing mission and appeal. We thank you for your Christian and manly utterances against "the slave-trade and slavery," and against "the Confederacy" seeking a new nationality on the basis of the perpetuity and extension of these crimes. We thank you for your "manifestations of sympathy for the coloured race, so long oppressed and debased by Christian nations." Particularly do we thank our British brethren for distinctly saying: "It is the duty of American statesmen and Christian ministers to guard against any reaction in the policy of Emancipation, when arrangements consequent on the termination of the war may come under discussion." Precisely at this point it is, at the present crisis, that your friendly cautions were needed. Since the arrival of the British delegation, our victories in Pennsylvania and at Vicksburg have been made the occasion for reviving the previous clamours of the pro-slavery party for a repeal of the President's edict of Emancipation.

In connection with this, we are compelled to advert to the recent military instructions, Article 32, declaring that although the commanders of our armies have authority, under martial law, to suspend or abolish the relations of "service" from one person to another in rebel states conquered by our armies, yet the permanence of such change, or its temporary nature, must be determined by the treaty of peace. You have well said, in your address to us, that "A retrograde course would assuredly give a triumph to the adversaries of freedom, and put to shame all who have sympathized with the cause of the slave." And just here, honoured and beloved brethren of France and Great Britain, you will allow us, with the frankness of brotherly confidence and affection, to disclose our deepest perplexities and most anxious apprehensions, that you may know at what points we most need your assistance, your sympathies, and your prayers.

We are grieved and alarmed to notice that while the Divine judgments are so heavily resting upon our nation and government for our great national sin, while slaveholders themselves, through their wicked rebellion, are the scourges, in God's hand, by which He is chastising us for our disobedience to Him, in permitting their oppressions, instead of executing justice for the relief of their victims, we witness little or nothing like repentance for the sin, or even a nominal recognition of its sinfulness. In nothing that has been done or attempted by our Government, in nothing that has been proposed in our national councils, in none of the proclamations for national fasts, has our great national sin of tolerating slavery been recognized. Emancipation has not been proclaimed as an act of obedience to God, or of humanity to the slave, or as a protection for the essential rights of human nature, or as a performance of the essential duties of human government in general, or as the necessary workings of free institutions in particular, nor as a requirement of international and general Common Law, the product of Christianity and natural justice, essential to a true civilization. All this has not merely been ignored, but laboriously disclaimed.

The consequence has been that emancipation is resorted to, only as a military necessity, and, in the last extremity, when no other mode of relief seems possible. Emancipation is proclaimed in one region of the country and withheld from another. In States professedly and nominally loyal, though kept such by the presence of national troops, the pretended right of slavery is secured by government, and fugitive slaves are remanded back into slavery, their servitude, in many instances, being enforced by Union soldiers. It is only in rebel states, or in rebel sections of states that emancipation is proclaimed. Thus the slave system, in the hands of our national government, becomes a boon offered to the slave states, to bribe them into loyalty. Emancipation, on the other hand, is the threatened punishment of disloyalty. While the rebel states retain possession and power over their own territory, the President's Proclamation fails to secure its objects, because our government cannot enforce it. In the border slave states, in possession of national troops, and where emancipation could be easily enforced, slavery is protected by the national government, because the state is accounted loyal, so that in either case, as a general rule, slavery is sustained, either by the nation or the rebel states. Only the comparatively few who come within our military lines, are protected as "freedmen," and there is no security for the permanence of their freedom.

Whether, on the return of peace, the Emancipation Proclamation would be enforced in the now rebel states, after their submission, is a mooted question among lawyers as well as politicians. The repeal or the inherent nullity, or both, of the liberating proclamation are urged on the ground that, by the Constitution, under which the Union is to be restored, the states will have a "sovereign right" to re-establish slavery, and that the national government cannot interfere. By others it is conceded that although the freedmen under the proclamation may not be legally re-enslaved, yet the returning and restored states may, in the exercise of their "sovereign state rights," enslave whomsoever else they please. You see, then, honoured and dear brethren, that the military conquest of the rebellion is in great hazard of being succeeded by a diplomatic surrender of that very liberty against which the rebellion was itself organized. To prevent this result, more than human wisdom and energy will be required. You perceive the nature of the suicidal concession, that while our national government is fighting to subdue seceding states and charging them with rebellion, those states are, nevertheless, so sovereign that, while loyal, they have the "state right" to enslave any of the citizens of the United States, within their jurisdiction. You perceive the libel against our "free institutions" for which we have challenged the admiration of mankind, that, unlike all other institutions of civil governments on earth, the state governments possess the tremendous prerogative of enslaving any or all of our native citizens, while our national government has no authority to protect from such enslavement a single one of them. You see the consequences of such false teachings in the doctrine involved and promulgated, that our war against the slaveholders' rebellion is not, and must not be made a war against that slavery for the extension and perpetuity of which the rebellion was inaugurated and is maintained ; but a war merely for the political subjugation of the rebels and tyrants, and not for the deliverance of their victims ; a war which, when finished, shall leave the slavery question precisely where it was before.

In view of all this, honoured brethren, and in reference to the language of your admirable address which we have quoted, we cannot complete our Response, in harmony with your truly Christian exhortations, without solemnly protesting to you, and through you, so far as possible, to the whole Christian world, as we now earnestly do, against any continued complicity with slavery, or sanction, or toleration of it, either on our part as recounted, or on the part of your own government or people, or of any other government or people in Europe, or especially on the part of any denomination or society of Christian churches or ministers on earth. We invoke, in the name of God and justice, the union of all governments and powers of Christianity and civilization to put an end to this enormity, and for this purpose, to seize the opportunity for the utter annihilation of slavery afforded by the judgments of the Almighty in this gigantic rebellion. It is a rebellion, invasion, and war against the United States by the Rebel Confederacy, for the establishment of their supremacy through the perpetuity of the slavery of the coloured race ; a race, though coloured, yet native American, as truly as the race of Anglo-Saxons, and entitled before God and the government, to the same privileges of freedom and rights of justice, without respect of persons. If Anglo-Saxons born on our soil are citizens without need of any law designating them as such, so are Anglo-Africans ; if Anglo-Africans are not, neither are Anglo-Saxons. No opinion of any Attorney-General, and no decision of any court is requisite to establish the citizenship of Anglo-Saxons born in this country ; neither is there of Anglo-Africans. The former are citizens by birth ; so are the latter. What would be thought of the assertion that an Act of Parliament, or a patent from Queen Victoria, was necessary in your country, in order to constitute a coloured person born in England a citizen and subject of your government ? But such an act is no more necessary in this country than in yours.

And we earnestly implore your attention to the facts in the case, and to our principles and rights in this conflict. The document of our Government, held as sacred with us, and as obligatory as your Magna Charta, declares that all are created equal, with inalienable rights to life, liberty, and the pursuit of happiness, for the security of which governments are instituted among men ; and our Constitution carries out that declaration in detail in the article that NO PERSON shall be deprived of life, LIBERTY, or property, but by due process of law. All children under the Constitution born on our soil are persons born in the right of liberty, and by the letter of this Constitution that liberty can never be taken from them. The guarantee of their freedom is even more perfect in our Constitution than in yours; for the grand article in your Magna Charta merely reads that "no free man shall be taken, or imprisoned, or be disseized of his freehold or liberties, or free customs, or be outlawed or exiled, or any otherwise destroyed; nor will we pass upon him, nor condemn him but by lawful judgment of his peers, or by the law of the land;" whereas our Constitution, after, and in addition to the article in the Declaration of Independence, affirming that all are born equal with the inalienable right to liberty, also provides that NO PERSON shall be deprived of that LIBERTY but by due process of law. No process of law can deprive any person not a criminal, and then only on trial by jury; and if any person or persons are so deprived, or attempted to be deprived by the Constitution or laws of any State, the Constitution of the United States, framed by the people, not by the States, declares that justice and liberty for ourselves and our posterity are the object of its establishment, and ordains that "this Constitution and the laws made in pursuance thereof shall be the SUPREME LAW OF THE LAND, *anything in the Constitution and laws of any State to the contrary notwithstanding.*"

Besides all this, our Constitution forbids the passing of any bill of attainder by any of the States, thus guarding against the possibility of the condition of slavery ever descending from parent to child, and making every statute null and void that decrees or attempts to establish any such attaint. There is no possibility, therefore, under our Constitution of depriving any innocent person of liberty, or permitting any such person to be so deprived. We advert to these facts on this occasion first, to show the greatness of the crime and guilt of slavery committed or tolerated by such a people under such a Constitution, and our conviction that no just nation on earth can sympathize with ours, unless we put an end to this iniquity. After the industrious circulation in Europe of the false impression that our own Constitution guaranteed slavery as a right of State Sovereignty, and that we meant to abide by it, and that we could not and would not make justice and the rights of the enslaved our object in this war, but that, on the contrary, we had resolved at the outset that the pretended slaveholding rights of the States and the condition of the slaves should be the same after the war as before, we need not have been surprised, if such representations were believed, that the sympathy of the world was withheld from us. We ourselves could not sympathize with ourselves, nor with our own Government in this struggle, if it were a struggle only for our own supremacy, disregarding the rights of the enslaved.

How profoundly, then, have we been astonished that any degree of sympathy could have been found on the part of any Christian nation in the world with the Rebel Confederacy, basing their empire avowedly on the right of human slavery. The laws of God and of international justice require that every State founding itself on this impiety and inhumanity should be excommunicated from the family of nations, and that all other States should combine to restrain and forbid this atrocity, as so many of them have combined to abolish the slave trade, which is a claim and a crime, by no means so dreadful as the attempt to found an empire on the right of slavery as perpetual and supreme. If the United States should maintain that right as a right of Government, they also, as well as the Rebel Confederacy, should be excluded from the family of nations.

We state these things, in the second place, that we may make our own principles and purposes, both as Christian and as Constitutional Abolitionists in this struggle, plain to all the respected friends of freedom in the world. These principles are founded, first, upon the claims of God, and the nature of the ordinance of government by Him, as supreme, for freedom and justice. Second, upon the claims, under God and the government, of the enslaved, whose rights have been entirely sacrificed and denied heretofore, and still are, to a great degree, ignored and trampled upon, even in the present struggle. We demand for them, for every one of them, in the name of God and our own Constitution, nothing less than the same freedom that we ourselves enjoy. The inalienable right to life, liberty, and the pursuit of happiness, affirmed in our Declaration of Independence as belonging to mankind, are theirs, exactly as they are ours. We are bound to maintain and administer the Government for them, as well as for ourselves, and for their interests as much as for our own. No continuance of any wrong against them from generation to generation can change it into a right, or make it, as has been pretended, an heir-loom in the national family, which religious as well as political conservatism requires us to venerate and avoid breaking up. We remember the ground taken by Wilberforce and Buxton, when the latter laid down the principle that, in this conflict the slaves are our clients, and that nothing is to be yielded to the Government but for their sakes.

Our principles are founded, third, upon the perfect accordance of our own Constitution, and of our Government if only administered according to it, with these claims. We, therefore, proclaim it to be the duty of the Government in a time of peace, as well as war, to do justice to all, and to execute the Constitution in behalf of freedom and justice *for* all. We freely admit that a Government which could do justly only on occasion of the necessity of putting down a rebellion by war, would not be worthy to stand, any more than a Government that bases its right to independence on the right of human slavery. A Government that denies the right to interfere for the protection of its own subjects against slavery in a time of peace has no claims on God or man for support in a time of war. But such a Government was never contemplated by our Constitution, nor could be made consistent with it, any more than a religion, and church, and ministry are contemplated in the Word of God, that would sanction infidelity or refuse to plead in God's name in behalf of the oppressed. The exasperations of our iniquity in so long tolerating this crime when it was our right and duty to abolish it are not only our violation of the Word of God, but our falsifying of our own charter of freedom, and the sanction and concentration of injustice into a State right and claim by that falsehood; the rearing of irregular villany into organized crime; the teaching that this is a right superior to natural right, and to God's law; the terrible example thus set before the world; the pretence that we could not interfere against slavery in the States where it was, but only in the territories where it was not; the pretence of slavery being a domestic institution, and as such, wholly under the dominion of State Sovereignty, and not to be disturbed; the public attainder of the children of four millions of innocent beings, and the consecration of them and their posterity to perpetual slavery; the enthronement of the slave codes for this purpose as supreme; the setting up of this crime as a right of loyalty to our own Government: the refusal to abolish slavery even in a time of war in States under martial law, and where every slave still continued in slavery is kept such by authority and action of the Government itself; the neglect to repeal the infamous Fugitive Slave Bill, the continued execution of that iniquity, even in the district of Columbia, notwithstanding the proclaimed abolition of slavery there; the neglect to abolish the internal slave traffic, notwithstanding that it is as completely within the jurisdiction of the General Government to do this, as it is to forbid the Foreign Slave Trade.

All the nations of the earth have reason to thank God, that the Almighty has arisen in judgment against these vast crimes. It was in the power of the church, under God, to have procured the abolition of them had the church proved faithful to Him; but the church has not done it, though Christianity required it at her hands. God himself has arisen in vengeance, and is breaking in pieces the oppressor, and saving the children of the needy. We are still in the midst of the conflict. Let no more opportunity be given to the world to allege that the fetters of human bondage were broken, not by our Christianity, but in spite of it. The Christianity of the gospel is not ours if we tolerate slavery. But we throw ourselves on God and his Word, on the freedom and justice of the Constitution requiring us in peace or war, to put an end to slavery and to forbid it for ever. We reaffirm that the Constitution of the United States, so far from recognizing any state right to enslave, imperatively forbids it by forbidding the cardinal features of the slave code, such as its perpetual attainder, its *ex post facto law*, its laws impairing the obligation of contracts, its deprivation of liberty without due process of law, its infringements of religious freedom and freedom of speech and of the press, features so essential to its existence. We affirm that the declared objects of the Constitution, the establishment of justice, the securing of the blessings of liberty to the people of the United States and their posterity, together with the guarantee of a Republican government to every state in the Union, bind the Federal government to abolish slavery in the states. We affirm the constitutional duty of that national abolition, and that the culpable and criminal neglect of that duty in a time of peace was the cause of the rebellion; and that the calamities we are now suffering are righteous divine retributions for that negligence.

We agree with Jefferson that the slaves are citizens. We affirm that as citizens the slaves of this country stand on a legal and constitutional equality with all other American citizens, the Constitution making no distinction of race, colour, or condition. We affirm that not one of the clauses of the Constitution claimed as guarantees or recognitions of slavery can be thus construed without a gross violation of all the just rules of legal interpretation laid down by our courts, and by those of all civilized nations; nor without flatly denying that the Constitution is an honest document, that it means what it says, and says what it means. We affirm that not only its strict letter, but that its living spirit, with its historical antecedents and concomitants, justify and require the foregoing assertions. The founders of our republic, in framing that Constitution, appealed to the Supreme Judge of the world for the rectitude of their intentions to establish a national government for the security of the inalienable rights of life, liberty, and the pursuit of happiness for all. By that solemn pledge, the nation is still bound. We call on you, honoured and dear Christian brethren, and through you we call upon all the friends of the slave, the friends of free institutions, liberty of conscience, and Christianity in all lands, to join with us in pressing, in the name of God and humanity, this righteous demand of universal freedom. "The French law," says M. Cochin, "more logical and more just than the English, declared that it would no longer recognize a Frenchman in a slaveholder." May the time soon come in which Great Britain, the United States, and all other civilized and Christian nations shall, in this particular, follow the example of France. May that kingdom of Christ now come in which the oppressor shall be broken in pieces, and the children of the needy be delivered and saved; when men shall sit, every family under their own vine and fig-tree, with none to make them afraid; when nation shall not lift up sword against nation, neither learn war any more, the effect of righteousness being peace and assurance for ever. For such peace, on the plan of the Prince of Peace, we shall unitedly labour and pray; but we never can assent to any pretended peace that, by slavery, wages war against the millions of our oppressed fellow-citizens. We commend you, dear brethren, and the cause for which you plead, to the defence and keeping of the Almighty.

(Signed by)   GEO. B. CHEEVER.
                WILLIAM GOODELL.
                S. S. JOCELYN.

DR. MASSIE'S VISIT AND ADDRESS.

(Note to page 284.)

REV. DR. MASSIE, of London, visited Pittsburg on the 16th instant, according to the notice last week published. In the evening he presented the addresses of four thousand English ministers and seven hundred and fifty Protestant French ministers, which he bore to the ministers and Christian people of this country. Dr. Massie introduced the reading of his paper with some most interesting remarks. He is a real Englishman. He was for some years of his earlier life a missionary in India. Since his return to his native land he has been labouring for the cause of Evangelism in the Dissenting churches. He is a good speaker—not attractive by the graces of his oratory, but impressive by his real earnestness.

A gentleman who was present, makes the following report of Dr. Massie's remarks :—

"He did not know when he left England that there was so much need for the interchange of sympathies and confidential communication between the people of England and America. He did not know how deeply had entered into the heart of the people of this land the feeling of sorrow and disappointment which he now found to prevail, because of misapprehension and misrepresentation concerning England in America, and concerning America in England. The first object of his mission was to seek to strengthen the hands of those who were striving to destroy the source of the present war, the spring of the rebellion, and the power of those who are acting as rebels against the Government by which they themselves had previously enjoyed the highest rights that man can enjoy. It was from an anti-slavery conference that he received his commission, but it was as the friend of the Union and emancipation that he appeared before them that evening. His mission was nominally to the ministry of all Christian churches throughout the States of America, and it was that he might convey to them the judgment of Christian men in England that he had come. And not to them alone had he been called to speak, but to those who sympathize with the ministry; so that the pulpit has held something like a correspondence with the pew, and the minister's study has been invaded by the earnest and solicitous of those who are his loving people.

"We were induced to move in the matter, in England," he said, "because we saw that there were many who misrepresented the state of things in England. We had a feeling of interest in reference to the people of America. We believed them to be possessed of the best political Constitution that was ever possessed by any nation under heaven—that they had the best portion of liberty, and were subjected to the least exaction by the Government as regards taxation, or in reference to authority. We believed that America, if she continued to prosper, would prove a blessing at least to the transatlantic world, and that gradually her institutions, her liberties, and her religion would spread over the other parts of the continent of America, and we wished her God speed in such prevalence—prevalence by reason, by righteousness, by justice, by law, and by an equitable Government. We look to the people of America as a kindred people, that had sprung from our own ancestors.

"There are men in America who were born in my own country—men from England, Scotland, and Ireland—men of my kindred, who have grown to be Americans in every sense of the word—men whose blood has flowed as freely in the field of battle in behalf of your liberty as that of your own countrymen. Can it be a matter of wonder, then, that men are looking from those countries across the Atlantic to the vales of New England, and the vast prairies of the West, to see what their kindred are doing; feeling with them when they are wounded, and having a common interest with them, and with your existence, and your liberty and prosperity? Therefore it was that we were concerned when we were misrepresented here, and when you were misrepresented to us. There are two vast organs professedly that represent public opinion; the 'New York Herald' on the western side of the Atlantic, and the 'Times' newspaper on the eastern side of the Atlantic; both of them mouthing great words, and having the world to wonder after them, because they are such mighty powers. But they are not the organs of truth. They are not the agencies of liberty. They are not the instruments sustained by virtue and international integrity. They are the spawn of selfish enterprise; the enterprise of men who trade in politics, and who hate truth when it cannot be made to subserve *their purposes*. If you do not accept the 'New York Herald' and the political representations of those who are of the class of the 'New York Herald' as the representation of the feeling of the American nation, let the 'Times' go for the same value. In the first place we have no Government organ in England, any more than you have in America. There is no newspaper that speaks under the control of the Cabinet of Great Britain. Whatever may be known concerning the opinions of this or that statesman, there is not and there cannot be in England any constitutional representation through the press of our Government. In the second place the 'Times' is not the organ of the masses of the people. It is the organ of an enterprising commercial company, who have founded their branches of correspondence and operations in divers parts of the world, for the sake of gain; and who take care to have correct and primary information on commercial subjects, and who, for the sake of gain will write up a Confederate loan when that is to be written up, and will write down liberty and a government, when bringing it down will add to their prosperity. The 'Times' newspaper has never in all its existence been anything else than the 'Times' of to-day; its sole object being to serve the purposes of its managers. The 'Times' is, in no instance, the recognized organ of the liberal party of England. It never has consistently advocated liberty. It was the opponent of Wilberforce and others. So long as gain could be gotten from the West Indies, and not until the Government had taken up measures for the emancipation of our West India negroes, did a sentence in favour of liberty find a place in its columns. The 'Times' has been the fitting organ of those that were the political and absolute monopolists of every age. It not only opposed Wilberforce, Cobden, John Bright, and other champions of liberty, but it opposed them throughout with a resistance and persistence which showed that it felt the interests of its party were at stake, until it was constrained to see and acknowledge the league as a great fact. Then they turned as if they would eat their own words, but they never yet explained why they made the changes they saw fit to make."

The speaker then referred to the taking of the census for the purpose of ascertaining the strength of the Established Church and of the Nonconformists, showing that although the Nonconformists were in the ascendancy, yet in the 'Times' no recognition of them has ever been made, and although many conventions and meetings have been held, no report has ever yet appeared in the columns of the 'Times.' "Do you then wonder at it," he asked, "that they do not know you, especially as your institutions and principles recognized in the administration of your Government go directly in the teeth of all monopoly? Especially as you extend to every citizen the right of suffrage? That you give security as far as you can to him who exercises the right of suffrage; and that the rail-splitting labourer may occupy the highest seat in your Republic, where enterprise and generous ambition fire the soul of him that is their possessor. These are things which our 'Times' hates, because it is the sycophant of those who are called the aristocracy of England. You must not therefore go to that paper, or to papers of like kindred, in order to know what are England's thoughts concerning you."

He then touched on the great contest now going on in this country, and said that he looked upon the American struggle as a struggle between the magistrate and the rebel, and that God would not favour a rebellion for the sake of oppression. He then referred to the Union Emancipation Society of Manchester, formed for the purpose of proclaiming the excellence and defending the rights of the Union and of the United States; it was formed in the midst of five hundred thousand people who were receiving their sustenance from the hand of charity, and who had been impoverished by reason of what was called the "cotton famine," which was produced by the policy of your rebellion, the leaders of which desired, by bringing King Cotton to bear on the artisans of England, to constrain her to recognize them as an independent power. Cotton was kept back, and then was seen such a time of misery as we seldom meet with. These poor labouring people of the manufacturing districts were deprived of their employment, and therefore their bread. In their distress they sold their furniture to the brokers, and parted with their very clothing to supply the necessaries of life. The little shopkeepers, who used to supply the working-classes around them had run up such scores that their capital was sunk, and the general ruin fell on them also. In the midst of all this, the Confederate conspirators interposed and said: "Come up and help us, and recognize us as an independent government, and you shall have a return for your recognition, not in mere bales of cotton, but in actual gold." These working men and these impoverished, honest labouring men, who lived by their toil and paid by their labour for their bread, held up their sinewy arms and skeleton hands in indignant protest against the claims of the South, and said: "No!" They saw that this was a contest about the rights of the labourer. The South hate to give wages. They want work performed without reward, except it be such a stingy supply of food as may support the labourer; and they would have us to recognize them and join hands with them, then we, too, shall be slaves. They saw this was the great object the conspirators had in view, when they inaugurated the great rebellion of the slave States.

In continuing his remarks, the speaker alluded to the mass meeting which had been held last winter in Exeter Hall, which was thronged to its utmost capacity by the labouring and middle classes of London—a hall which was capable of containing an audience of four thousand people, and yet such was the interest which the people of England felt in the cause of freedom in America that an hour before the time of meeting it was impossible to gain admission even in the lobby and entrance of the capacious building. There the assembly unanimously endorsed an address which had been prepared, and was afterwards forwarded to the President of the United States, expressive of the cordial sympathy of the people of England with him, and with the people of the United States, in the great struggle in which they were engaged. At one of these meetings, held in Manchester, among the artisans and working classes of that city, some sympathizer with the South raised a question against the North, but the sturdy voice of an honest labourer in the audience demanded, "Who began the war?" The answer was unanimous that

it was the South who had been the aggressor; and thus was the single
dissentient voice silenced. We have seen from this that the lower and the
middle classes are entirely with the loyal States, and as it is with you,
so it is with us. The Government derives its power from the labouring
classes. On them rests the main burden of taxation, and from them
must the real policy of the Government emanate. The great body of
the people are with the North, and no Government would receive the
support of the people if they opposed the North in this great struggle.

"Now there is another point to which we arrive, and that is the case of
the pirates "Alabama" and "Florida." I say that this is a disgrace
to England, as slavery is a disgrace to America. As those that run the
blockade sailing out from the port of New York are a disgrace to that
port. I say that if the "Alabama" should be seized upon the high seas,
and every man of her crew should be hung at the yard-arm, it would be
nothing but strict justice. I say that this will make more mischief between this country and England than it will make profit to the men
who are engaged in it. But let me assure you that with the exception
of the officials at Liverpool and the Custom Houses, who are certainly
chargeable with neglect of duty, our Government from that day to this
has done all that it could do in order to prevent the sailing of such
ships. It has done all that the law empowered it to do—yes, and more
than the law empowered it to do. But you ask, 'Why do you not
change the law, if it is so imperfect, as we changed the law in this country?' I answer that we can't do it there—that there are too many interested in the matter to enable us to do it." The Speaker then enlarged
on the proceedings of the London Emancipation Society, and the
Union and Emancipation Society of Manchester, recounting at length
the history of each, and referring to the address issued by the Emancipation Society to the ministers and pastors of the United States. This
address, he said, had been delivered to the President, Abraham Lincoln.
When he was in Washington he called on the President and asked him
if he had read the letter. The President replied that he had, but would
read it again before him, which he did, reading it aloud. It is not my
duty, the speaker said, to tell you what passed between us, but " I will tell
you what is my impression concerning him. He is the enemy of slavery
and wishes its abolition. He is the friend of the slave and wishes him
liberty. He has issued his proclamation of liberty, and will not retract
one syllable of it. He is as pure a patriot as probably ever sat in the
Presidential chair. He is a true Christian and a man to be trusted as
honest, and worthy of all praise."

The speaker next specified his two principal objects in accepting the
mission in which he was now employed. He desired to strengthen the
Anti-slavery cause in the United States, and uphold the hands of those
who sought to profit from the present crisis, for the speedy accomplish-
ment of the freedom of every slave within the Republic. He had
been deputed by the committee of an Anti-slavery Conference in Manchester. His second object was to diffuse in America an assurance of
a cordial and friendly sympathy among the mass of English people—
the middle and working classes, who are the back-bone and sinews of
England. He trusted no momentary irritation or hasty language by
one or other, would be suffered to create a warlike or belligerent tone

in the intercourse of the two nations, who were, in fact, but *one* people. Dark and fearful would be the day which witnessed the first out-break of strife between England and America. Neither of them could gain anything except the gratification of a vindictive feeling. England could not conquer America, and the Americans could not anticipate the conquest of England. They might, indeed, destroy each other's commerce, and spoil the goods of each other at sea, and thus individuals of both people would suffer and become the prey of war. But what misery would follow the rending of family relations, the destruction of brothers and sons in the opposing ranks! What dishonours would be brought on their common religion, and on the name of Him whom they loved! How would the despots of Europe triumph! It would indulge the hatred of Napoleon and the bitter animosity of the priests of superstition, and mar the religious and harmonious action of their missionary and philanthropic institutions. It would make hell rejoice and angels mourn. He implored all to use their power to promote a peaceful and forbearing intercourse, a conciliatory and liberal policy. Englishmen deplore the action of the "Alabamas" and "Floridas," and feel that they bring disgrace on the English name and the reputation of British enterprise. But they are only the proceedings of individual speculators, who sacrifice everything for sordid gain.

THE END.

HADRILD, PRINTER, LONDON.